A Mosaic of Life

Memoirs of a Russian Childhood

VALENTIN KATAYEV

A Mosaic of Life

or The Magic Horn of Oberon

Memoirs of a Russian Childhood

Translated by
MOIRA BUDBERG
and
GORDON LATTA

J. PHILIP O'HARA, INC.
CHICAGO

English text © 1976 by J. Philip O'Hara, Inc.

J. Philip O'Hara, Inc. 20 East Huron, Chicago, 60611.
Published simultaneously in Canada by Van Nostrand
Reinhold Ltd., Scarborough, Ontario

LC Number: 75–10698
ISBN: 0–87955–312–9

First Printing B

CONTENTS ✍

CONTENTS

Half-Asleep ✍

MAMMA TOOK ME to Ekaterinoslav to display me to her parents. I
think I was three or four years old at the time. It turned out that I
had a grandmother in Ekaterinoslav and this surprised me because
I already had one—Papa's mother, the widow of a Viatsk priest—a
small, old woman who lived with us. It was then I learned that everyone had two grandmothers: one, their papa's mother, and the other,
their mamma's mother.

After spending some time in Ekaterinoslav, where several of my
mamma's sisters—my aunts—lived too, we decided to go back to
Odessa by a train which left, according to the time-table, at 10:10 in
the evening. How well I remember those two tens, frightening in
their very precision and conceivably even blacker than the night I
was destined to spend in the train.

I had never yet seen the night.

By seven o'clock in the evening, I would begin to feel irresistibly
sleepy, and at eight my eyelids would be drawn down as if by magnets and, often without having heard the whirring and chiming of the
dining-room clock, I would fall into the still undiscovered and incomprehensible domain of night. But, at almost the same moment,
so it seemed, I would surface again from the depths of my sleep, open
my eyes and see the bright, southern dawn of a new day, as the sun

penetrated the cracks of the painted wooden shutters, which were attached to the inside of the windows instead of the outside, like all the shutters in our town.

And now, in the dining-room of Grandmother's and Grandfather's apartment in Ekaterinoslav, I kept on falling asleep and had the greatest difficulty in remaining erect in the uncomfortable high chair with a carved back decorated with two knobs, which seemed to me to be the height of luxury and wealth. In front of me stretched the big dining-room table of fumed oak; a square table, without a table-cloth, of a sinister colour, so dark that the lamp with a white lamp-shade, suspended from the ceiling on brass chains, very dismal too, could not light it up properly.

Everything was dismal in that large Ekaterinoslav room and every-thing frightened me, despite the presence of my kind, fat grand-mother, beautiful as an old queen, who loved me dearly, spoiled me, played polkas for me on the piano, and, lifting me up under the arms, dumped me down on her fat knees, where I pressed myself into her silk dress and seemed to sink into its rustle.

Mamma's sisters, my aunts—and there were a lot of them; seven in all, I believe—also spoiled me, loved me, pulled me about, gave me sweets, admired me for being such a clever little boy, and said how remarkable it was that I should have two whirly circles of hair, like crowns, on top of my head, a portent of good luck and happiness throughout my life.

The aunts were very different in character but looked much alike. There was young Aunt Margarita and Aunt Natasha, who worked for the Local Council, and Aunt Klionia—"Cleopatra"—who worked in the government Control Office, and Aunt Nina, a beauty and the pride and hope of the family, and various other aunts, among whom I lived an animated, sybaritic life.

Despite this, there was something in that apartment that troubled and frightened me, something for which I even felt a certain re-pulsion. At the time, I did not understand what it was, but now I do: what was frightening me was Grandfather—Mamma's papa; Grandmother's husband—a retired major-general with side-whiskers and the bony, sloping forehead of the liberator-tsar, who wore a long, tight-fitting tunic adorned by two rows of smooth brass buttons.

I liked Grandfather but, at the same time, was afraid of him, afraid of his bony knuckles, which he was able to crack, afraid of the rocking-chair in which he rocked with an effort, finding it difficult to bend his stiff knees, afraid of whatever lay beneath Grandmother's alarming, whispered words to my mother: "A second stroke."

Limonchik and Kudlatka ✍

IT WAS ALREADY well past eight o'clock in the evening—in my imagination, the middle of the night—and I was fidgeting the whole time, unable to go to sleep. Nobody slept; nobody showed any signs of setting out for the station, though our rugs in their leather straps, hat-boxes, and baskets lay ready in the dark hall and the cabs had been summoned. Everybody in the ill-lit dining-room seemed to be waiting for something.

On the verge of tears, I asked, "What are we waiting for?"

"Don't worry, you'll soon find out," said my gay Aunt Margarita, with a mysterious twinkle in her eye.

"But what is it?"

"A surprise."

At this moment, the door-bell rang and another of my aunts, Liuda, came in, followed by the yardsman carrying a large parcel wrapped in brown paper. Then the mystery was solved. Apparently, Grandfather had given Aunt Liuda ten gold roubles and told her to buy me the best present she could find in a toy-shop.

I tore at the wrapping-paper with my small, acquisitive hands, still sticky from Grandmother's famous strawberry jam, and saw a glass eye and part of a horse's wooden head with a mane and bright-red nostrils. My heart leaped with joy. The parcel contained a large toy horse on wooden wheels; a black horse dappled with yellow spots.

"What lovely little lemons!" I exclaimed delightedly, and the horse was immediately christened "Limonchik."

Without wasting a second, I started playing with him, dragging him by his oilskin reins through all the rooms in the apartment. But the time had now come for us to leave. Limonchik was put on the table and Aunt Klionia set about sewing him up in a piece of sacking with a large curved needle, as railway rules would not allow him to travel in the compartment with us and this was the only way he would be accepted in the luggage-van.

Seeing my wonderful, beloved Limonchik becoming transformed into a common, or garden, piece of baggage, I ran to and fro between Mamma and Grandmother, tugging at their skirts.

"Mamma! Grandmother! How will I be able to feed him his oats and hay and give him his drinking-water? Don't sew him up altogether! At least leave his head free!"

I could not pronounce all my words correctly yet and instead of "free" I said "flea," which made everybody laugh. But I was sobbing so broken-heartedly that Aunt Klionia had to cut a hole and leave the horses's head, with its wooden teeth and coarse mane, unencumbered.

Later, after receiving a rouble tip from Mamma, the sleeping-car attendant, in a round, astrakhan hat and wide trousers falling over short boots, which made him look like the emperor Alexander III, allowed Limonchik to travel in our second-class compartment, though it was already cluttered up with all our hand-luggage, and I was able to proffer oats and water to the head protruding from the sacking: as I lacked a pail, I had to carry the water in one of my new shoes, fastened by a metal clasp and ornamented with a pompon. While I was engaged in these activities, Mamma, in her grey coat with large mother-of-pearl buttons and her feathered hat, sat on the striped banquette and wept, taking her handkerchief out of her moiré handbag, raising her thick black veil and dabbing her red-rimmed eyes.

I do not know whether it was then or later that I realized, with vague anxiety, that the clean little linen handkerchief and Mamma's damp eyelashes and tanned cheeks and the dark veil were somehow connected with Grandfather, whom we were seeing for the last time.

When Mamma and I had our coats on, ready to leave the apartment and go downstairs, he stood in the doorway of the dining-room, holding on to the curtain with a trembling hand and unable to tear his glassy eyes away from us. Then, when I was down in the street, I glimpsed him through the window. He was continually making the sign of the cross with his bony fingers as we got into the cab and I carefully arranged Limonchik at my feet.

After an exhausting, slow journey lasting from dawn to sunset across the Novorossijski steppes, with the sunlight seeming to move with the same persistent leisureliness as the various well-sprung carriages, peering through the woollen curtains of the windows or shining obliquely down the corridor, sometimes raspberry-red, sometimes amber-yellow, sometimes with the dazzling light of high noon, but always impregnated with the special, fine, gelaming train-dust, night came, and with it a thick wax candle casting a flickering, purple glow from the shady lantern, and the clicking of the guard's ticket-punch as he passed by on his rounds; finally, early on a lovely morning, the train drew into the platform of our station, along which a familiar figure in a coat and soft hat, with a small beard and pince-nez, was running lithely and impetuously. It was Papa and, a moment later, I was squeezed in a tight embrace between him and my mother before the three of us drove off in a cab, weighed down by our luggage, along the dry, resounding roadway. Mamma and Papa sat on the back-seat and I on the folding bench, while Limonchik stood between us with his head peeping out of the sacking. Papa laughed, slightly embarrassed, because it turned out that he had made a fatal blunder: as a surprise for me, he had bought me another horse, which was already waiting impatiently for me at home. It was quite unlike Grandpa's Limonchik, being much smaller, with a fair mane, a wavy tail, and rockers instead of wheels. Its name was Kudlatka. Though they were of different colours and in no way a pair, I harnessed them to an upturned chair, transforming myself into a coachman and, singing racy songs, drove them at full gallop along the frozen Mother Volga on the amber-red painted floor, brightly lit by a southern sun that shone warmly through the window.

Two Horses! 🖋

I HAD NEVER even dreamed of such happiness. After rocking on Kudlatka and riding on tall Limonchik, I put my steeds back in their horse-boxes, heads to the wall, fed them oats and gave them fresh water to drink, then scrambled under Mamma's dressing-table, which was elegantly draped in bright chintz, with an elaborate looking-glass and many other interesting things standing on it, including a long lemon-wood box where Mamma kept her long gloves, small folding opera-glasses in a case, hat-pins with little black heads, and various veils and scarves.

Sitting under this dressing-table, screened from the rest of the world by a piece of material, through which the sun gleamed, I saw the wrong side of the wood: the coarsely hewn pine beams and legs glued together with almost black joiner's paste, which oozed out of narrow grooves emitting a nauseating smell of carrion. It was a smell that could have driven one mad, had it not been for the purifying drops of pine resin that glistened on the planed surface of the boards forming the ceiling of this secret shelter. I was a little frightened but also happy in my seclusion as I examined all the knots and flaws in the wood surrounding me. The whole world at such moments was limited to the small space in which I was voluntarily incarcerated.

Suddenly I heard Mamma cry out: "The postman!"

I crawled out from under the dressing-table and saw Mamma standing by the window staring with horror at the curiously immobile street, which might have been a drawing, with the one- or two-storied houses, roofed in either brick or iron, the cobbled roadway with acacias and the sturdy postman, without his usual large bag but with a small black wallet for telegrams attached to his belt.

"It's for us!" Mamma cried, and grew pale. "I know it. I feel it. I saw it last night in a dream."

There was still a hope that the postman would not stop at our front door. But, like a wound-up toy in his uniform hat and small black moustache, he suddenly turned sharply to his left, entered our building, and came up the stairs.

"God protect us!" Mamma muttered silently through clenched lips.

Now the only remaining hope was that the postman would ring the bell of the opposite flat, but it swiftly vanished as our wire whirred and the bell rang. Mamma rushed into the hall, the swirl of her skirt producing a breeze. Then she came back into the room with a white telegram in her hand and sat down; her head drooped and I saw the tears coursing down her pale cheeks.

I realised immediately that Grandfather had died in Ekaterinoslav.

The Pince-Nez 🖋

I THINK THAT the cause of this incident was Papa's pince-nez, with their steel frame, cork pads that clamped them to the bridge of his nose, and black cord looped to the top button of his waistcoat. Such pince-nez are now called old-fashioned or even Chekhovian, and you only see them on the stage, when the wearer is supposed to represent a pre-revolutionary member of the intelligentsia. I can see Papa putting on and taking off his pince-nez, or discarding them with a light twitch of his fingers, so that the shining oval lenses swung for a moment like a pendulum at the end of the cord and the coral marks on the bridge of Papa's nose became visible, somehow making his bearded face particularly dear and disarmingly helpless.

Mamma also wore pince-nez on a cord, but hers were in a black frame. I didn't like it when she put them on, for in my eyes she immediately became a stern lady and not my mamma at all. Papa in his pince-nez and a black felt hat with a wide brim, Mamma in her pince-nez and a jacket with narrow sleeves, a veil, and a hat with an eagle's feather tossed about by a fresh, rather angry sea-breeze, sat on the deck on a slatted bench; behind them, with a vertiginous uniformity, dark waves with crests of foam and lacy white horses rolled back after gushing out from beneath the wooden paddle-wheels of the steamship. Smoke poured in thick clouds from the two black funnels and soot flew obliquely across the deck, disappearing into the dark green water, now almost black from the approaching storm.

Papa and Mamma, shivering quite cheerfully, thrust their cold hands into their sleeves. Sitting between them, I tried to do the same, but discovered that I had grown out of my sailor coat with its golden buttons and could no longer insert my arms into the sleeves, which had become too short and narrow.

The sea continued to flow past us, angry and heaving, stretching out to the farthest horizon as a whirling column emerged from the low-flying clouds and another, farther ahead, rose to meet it: finally the two merged and a lead-blue tornado coursed along the horizon. I got up and began pacing up and down the deck in my large circular sailor's hat with floating ribbons, examining the life-belts, bearing the name "Turgenev," and the tarpaulin-covered life-boats. In the course of my promenade, I suddenly found myself among a bunch of students of both sexes, who were travelling third-class from Akkerman to Odessa. I had already seen the girl students, who wore small cloth caps, burnouses, and goatskin boots, glance at us with curiosity from afar, concentrating their attention mainly on Papa, towards whom they directed shy, mysterious smiles. They began fondling me and pulling me about, and one bearded male student in an old jacket and crumpled cap with a discoloured blue band even attempted to tickle me under the arms, which I particularly disliked; to make matters worse, he squatted down in front of me in an idiotic way, scratching my face with his bristly beard and frightening me with the magnifying lenses in his steel-rimmed spectacles. I began to howl and kick out at him, and the girls finally rescued me, thrusting a dried-up orange and a piece of chocolate with a coloured picture on its wrapper into my hands; the chocolate was quite soft and had no doubt reposed in one of their pockets for a long time.

"What's your name, little boy?" one of the girls asked, pressing me to her heart.

"Valia," I replied.

"How sweet!"

"And what's your surname?" another asked.

"Katayev."

"How strange! Is that your papa?"

"Yes. Why do you ask?"

"Your real father?"

I could not understand what she was getting at, and kept silent.

"You can't be telling the truth. Either you don't understand or you're just pretending."

"I'm not pretending. . . ."

"Well, then, Valia dear, what is your father's name? It's Anton Pavlovich, isn't it?"

"Nothing like it."

"Well, what is it?"

"Peter Vassilievich."

"How odd! Is he a writer?"

"No, he isn't, he's a teacher," I said angrily.

"It really is very odd," repeated the girl, the one who had given me the dry orange and the soft chocolate.

"There's nothing strange about it: he's just a teacher in the archdiocese school and in the cadet one, too."

"So he isn't Chekhov!" the girl said, disappointed. "What a pity! But, anyway, the likeness is remarkable: the beard, the sparkling eyes, the pince-nez on a cord and the gentle smile. . . . Hm . . . Well, why are you standing there, little boy? Go back to your parents: they're probably afraid you've fallen overboard."

At that moment I remained alone, like Chatsky at the ball.* Papa and Mamma, who had heard every word, were sitting huddled together shoulder to shoulder with their hands hidden in their sleeves against the background of the surging sea, and laughing helplessly as Mamma kept repeating, wrinkling her nose under the veil: "I always told you, Pierre, that with those pince-nez of yours, you're the spitting image of Chekhov."

It seemed to me that Papa was slightly embarrassed.

"Mamma," I asked, "what is Chekhov?"

"When you begin to read, you'll see what it is," said Mamma.

Nevertheless, I was left with a bad taste in my mouth because Papa was not Chekhov.

A Letter to a Granddaughter 🖋

MY DEAREST: When I was in hospital recently and reading Tolstoy's diaries of the later years, when he was about my age—or, rather, I am now the same age as he was then—I found a great number of remarkable ideas, and among them this one: "Memory destroys time."

How true that is, though one could equally well say that time destroys memory. But, on reflection, this is not quite so—something remains. Nonetheless, both are very largely true.

Here is something else I read in Tolstoy's diaries:

". . . if you have enough time and strength in the evening, note down what you remember, just as it comes, without bothering about chronological order . . . I've started remembering so vividly."

These are reminiscences of 1904. You will certainly read them one day. I very much recommend them to you. And this, from the diaries

* Main character in Griboyedov's famous comedy *Grief from Intelligence*, 1848. *Translator's note.*

of 1893, is even more astounding and fearless:

"Art, they say, cannot stand mediocrity. It also cannot stand self-consciousness." This entirely accords with my present ideas, so I will try to concentrate on my memories in exactly the way that Tolstoy advised: in no particular order, just as they come, as I remember them, never forgetting, however, that art does not tolerate self-consciousness.

From now on, may I be inspired by imagination and feeling.

So, my dear granddaughter, I will tell you, if you like, quite spontaneously, as things come back to me, about a small boy with a round face and narrow eyes, who is dressed like a girl in a little dress with wide, well-ironed, pleated ruffles.

I must explain that it was the fashion then to dress little boys as girls. When a boy was dressed for the first time in short trousers, he was very proud and kept begging his mother to lift him up to a mirror so that he could see the new trousers and his legs in long woollen stockings, with elastic garters attached to his waistcoat. Later, when this boy started going to school, he would wear long cloth trousers, and so on.

What is so extraordinary is that that boy was no-one else than myself, your aging, ancient grandfather with his dry hands, covered in brown, so-called "buckwheat," spots. . . .

This is about all I wanted to say to you, my dearest, beloved granddaughter. Now I'll make another effort to continue my reminiscences, "in no particular order, just as they come."

The Gilded Nut ✍

THERE WERE ALSO silver nuts, it's true, but I liked the golden ones better. There was something that made one think of death in the silver ones, whereas the golden ones shone on the Christmas tree like so many little suns, gladdening the heart.

Why is it that we have no more golden nuts on our Christmas trees?

I remember we used to colour them ourselves when we were children. Actually, it wasn't all that easy.

"What rubbish, how could it be difficult?" you're bound to say.

"Well, believe me, it was *not* easy. Not easy at all."

"But what is there to it? You take gold paint, dab it over the nut with a brush—and the thing's done!"

With the result that you get an ugly nut, golden maybe, but with a bronze shade of gold and not shiny, but muddy and obviously painted. *Our* nuts resembled reflected gold, and they shone like church cupolas, reflecting the sun and the sky. And this was because we didn't paint them with so-called "gold paint" but covered them with gold leaf, which used to be sold in small booklets, containing twenty flimsy leaves of real gold with cigarette-paper between them. Each leaf of gold was so thin and almost weightless that, compared with it, the cigarette-paper seemed thick and coarse.

In order to detach a gold leaf, you had first to blow gently on it. Then it rose with a light rustle and you could take it out of the book with your two fingers and hold it up, listening to the rustling sound that was almost inaudible but at the same time, strange as it may seem, metallic.

If that noise could have been increased, magnified, say, several thousand times, it would doubtless have sounded like the rumble of a sheet of corrugated iron. Such a sheet, bluish in colour, used to be suspended out of sight in the wings of a theatre at that time to imitate thunder. Hiding in the wings of the Temperance Theatre Society, I myself saw how a stage-hand shook a sheet of corrugated iron, hanging from the shafts of a cart, and struck it from time to time with a drum-stick, while the hushed audience listened to the rolls of thunder and saw flashes of lightning through the windows of the set, as the duke, with his false beard, shaking the raindrops from an artificial shower off his cloak, strode across the boards in oil-cloth jackboots and multi-coloured puffs resembling Japanese rice-paper lanterns on his sleeves, and sang for all he was worth to deafen the storm of the drums and rise above the orchestra as it played *Rigoletto*.

And the whole thing—the thunder and lightning and music and the matinee combined with the golden nut—was all in a curious way a part of Christmas.

In order to paint the golden nut, you needed the following things: a saucer of milk, a hammer, upholstering nails, and a small piece of multi-coloured worsted. You had to blow on the booklet to stir the golden leaves and then detach one carefully with clean, dry fingers. Heaven preserve you from dirty or even moist fingers, for they immediately left some golden traces like the pollen off a butterfly's wings and the gold-leaf was irreparably damaged and perforated.

If you succeeded in extracting a golden leaf from the booklet without damaging it and placed it with the utmost care on a clean, dry table, there was another operation to be performed; not such a delicate one, but still one that required cleanliness and concentration. You took a walnut, as beautiful a one as you could find, ripe from that year's harvest, with a clean, hard shell, and rolled it evenly in the milk in the saucer; after which, having waited for the surplus milk to trickle away, you laid it on the golden leaf and turned it over smoothly until the whole nut was covered in gold. Then the slightly moist nut, gilded in this manner and already shining beautifully, was deposited on a clean window-sill, where it quickly dried and became even more beautiful.

Yet the nut was not yet ready: to a small upholstery nail, of a kind that no longer exists, you had to attach a coloured worsted loop, so that the nut could be hung on a branch of the tree. The difficulty at this stage consisted in not damaging the gold and also in preventing the nail from breaking the shell, which often happened, because the nail had to be driven through the very crown, which was liable to split and divide into two, revealing inside, under the shell, what might be described as the grey-matter of the kernel. Therefore, you had to be extremely perspicacious in choosing the right place to insert the point of the nail and even more careful in hammering it in gently but firmly so that the worsted loop—green, crimson, yellow, or snow-white like the Russian winter itself—would remain attached and not get torn off.

Only then could the strong, beautiful, golden nut, wearing an upholsterer's nail as a hat on its head and adorned by a worsted loop —only then could the nut be considered ready.

All that remained was to hang it on the tree, thrusting one's hand into the prickly, misty thicket, with its intoxicatingly sharp smell of frosty pine.

In it the golden nut shone even when the candles were out and their paraffin vapour dispelled, leaving multi-coloured drops of wax on the needles; the room was dark, but it went on shining, reflected in the hoar-covered window behind which, in all its beauty, was a moonlit, wintry night, transparent as a lemon-drop.

Wrestling ✍

BEFORE THE LAST ACT of the performance, a thick carpet appeared as of its own accord and spread itself without a wrinkle across the sawdust, forming a magic square in the circular arena, surrounded by barriers draped in red velvet: two chains hung down on either side of the small, tightly drawn curtain through which the wrestlers were to come.

By now the circus was completely packed, from the gallery and the iron cupola down to the front rows, which had previously been empty: these latter presented an elegant spectacle of the town's beauties, wearing large hats trimmed with ostrich feathers and boas round their necks, and men in bowler hats, silk top-hats, or officers' caps with coloured bands, stiffly upright in the Prussian manner. Among them, too, were fur coats, gaiters, narrow, sharp-toed patent-leather shoes, students' narrow trousers strapped to their soles, gold-tipped canes, and opera-glasses reflecting in their projecting lenses a miniature picture of the circus arena with the carpet in the centre, lit by hissing arc-lights.

This hissing increased the tension as all eyes were glued to the entrance, to the white-boarded corridor running between the expensive boxes, occupied by the most important members of the audience, with the orchestra suspended between them, down which "they" were going to appear any minute.

The tension rose so high that even the smartest students, arriving at full gallop in his lacquered carriage drawn by pedigreed horses, jumped out before it had stopped and, clasping his beaver-collared "Nicholas"* coat round him, tiptoed in with bated breath and anxiously sought his front-row seat through golden pince-nez.

Finally, when the expectant silence had reached its peak, the famous "Uncle Vanya" strode in with professional aplomb in a dark-

* Cloak worn in the times of Nicholas I. *Translator's note.*

blue jacket, high boots, and a rather commonplace cap, his whiskers carefully curled, and, holding a whistle in his hand like a policeman, announced in a sonorous voice accustomed to circus acoustics that the world wrestling championships were about to take place; then, increasing the solemnity of his voice and causing the trapeze ropes hanging from the ceiling to begin to swing, he turned towards the curtain and shouted in a tone that was both authoritative and velvety: "Parade—*allez!*"

Almost simultaneously, the curtain was magically drawn asunder and, to the rousing music of the orchestra, the wrestlers made their entrance, thrusting out their chests and flexing their muscular arms. After parading round the arena once, they came to a halt, forming an impressive circle.

"The following wrestlers have arrived for the world championships," declared Uncle Vanya, glancing cursorily at the packed house, then, like a salesman enumerating his best wares, proceeded to read out their names.

As each man heard himself announced, he responded to the audience in his own particular way. One, for instance, would remain where he was with expanded chest and confine himself to a brief nod of his close-shaven soldierly head, adorned with thick cauliflower ears. Another would take a step forward and raise his arms to display his monstrously bulging Hercules-like biceps. Another would run nimbly on short, squat legs almost to the centre of the carpet, and press his hands to his heart and bow right and left before returning equally swiftly to his place. Another would stand completely immobile, like a classical statue, without giving even the semblance of a nod, then turn his handsome head, topped by blond hair in a hedgehog cut, very slightly from side to side, deeming the sight of his Grecian profile all the greeting that the audience could require. Whatever the method employed, it excited the crowd and aroused its admiration.

Though at first sight the wrestlers tended to look as much alike as soldiers on parade, each of them, in fact, possessed some distinguishing characteristic: black whiskers curled neatly upwards, or special elastic knee-caps, or high, artistically laced boots, or a scarlet ribbon covered with gold and silver medals, worn diagonally across his chest, or a "coxcomb" standing erect on his shaven head, so tightly grown together that a strip of metal could be bent against it. This

last had greatly added to the reputation of the famous Jewish wrestler Greenhouse, a world champion with the face of a dervish, who
was the idol of the Arnaut Street, where most of the small Jewish
tradesmen lived.

I can see today, as though it were yesterday, Greenhouse's unnaturally pale face with its black, uneven brows, grey cheeks which
seemed to be sprouting dark-blue, inky crow's feathers, and desperate, vacuous eyes beneath the bone-like comb on his bald head
streaked here and there with iodine.

Uncle Vanya uttered names which excite me even now and evoke
in my imagination figures that lay somewhere between magnificently
built Russian youths and Roman gladiators.

There was a multitude of them, all with their individual differences, and it was hard to decide who was the best. Those ladies who
made a habit of attending wrestling bouts completely lost their
heads over them and unashamedly acclaimed them loud enough for
the whole circus to hear, throwing at their feet lace handkerchiefs
scented with l'Origan de Coty, gloves, and even handbags, from
which small mirrors and powder-boxes scattered about the arena.

As Uncle Vanya called out the names, he added a number of
magniloquent details and comments:

"World Champion Ivan Zaikin, hero of the Volga, who threw the
unbeatable champion of the Polish tsardom, Pitliasinsky, who, shattered by his defeat, gave up wrestling and opened a private gymnasium in Odessa for the benefit of under-developed youth.

"Lurich the Second, the Estonian, handsomest of middle-weights
and a brilliant technician, with the strength of Hercules and the
body of Apollo of Belvedere."

And I could almost swoon as I gazed at the broad shoulders of
the Estonian demi-god under the arc-lights, at his narrow hips and
lumpy muscles protruding from the arms clenched behind his back,
his whole body dusted with powder that gave his skin the tint of
Carrara marble.

The audience broke into frantic applause which resounded for
a long time in the deep space between the cupola and the gallery,
reminding one of the cries of disturbed jackdaws: "Caw, caw, caw."

"And what has happened to Lurich the First?" someone would
shout, leaning over the metal bars of the gallery.

"Lurich the First?" Uncle Vanya would repeat solemnly, pacing up and down the carpet. "Lurich the First, the world champion who never suffered a defeat and received a Grand Prix for the beauty of his legs at the Paris World Exhibition, died five years ago in his home town from an excessive consumption of hot drinks and an absence of cold food!"

He was a great wit, that Uncle Vanya, whose surname was Lebedev, as he readily answered any question flung at him from the audience, as, for instance: "Uncle Vanya, why isn't Salvator Bambola taking part in the championship?

"The champion of Equatorial Africa, the middle-weight wrestler Salvator Bambola, is at the moment ill with measles and at the Zhmerinka Clinic under the observation of an experienced pediatrician."

Before the matches began, there was the formal warning about forbidden holds, which Uncle Vanya ran through expertly with the assistance of two mediocre wrestlers, who dexterously demonstrated such holds as were likely to cause severe physical injury or worse: *collier de gorge*," where one wrestler encircled his opponent's throat from behind and twisted it; the so-called "pincer grip" on the wrist, which was liable to crack the bone; and finally, of course, hitting below the belt or any of the jiu-jitsu tactics which had no place in correct wrestling practice.

The demonstration of the barred holds, performed in detail with artistic perfection, took some little time, but the audience appreciated it despite their impatience to see the matches get under way. It was the established ritual and the artificial delay only served to increase the general excitement and add a peculiar spice to the performance.

Once the demonstration was over, Uncle Vanya issued a curt command to the wrestlers. They turned their backs on each other and, to the accompaniment of a march from the orchestra, disappeared down the narrow corridor behind the curtain.

"Van Kil, Holland," my lips uttered soundlessly, and my heart turned to ice from ecstasy and happiness. Murzuk, Abyssinia; Homer de Bouillon, France; Muller, Germany; the Moscow hero, Ivan Shemiakin; the unbeaten world champion, Ivan Poddubni; Sarakixi and Okitano Ono, Japan; Jan Spuhl, Riga; the Petersburg student, an amateur who wished to conceal his name under the initials "A. Sh."; Uncle Pood, the heaviest wrestler of them all and the fattest man in the world, weighing 246 pounds, Russia; the giant from Viatka, Grigori Kashcheev, who was the nightmare of my childhood, standing two inches higher than Peter the Great, with monkey's arms that hung lower than his knees, a microcephalic head and a gaunt face that looked as though a horse had kicked it with both hooves simultaneously, leaving two arches above the brows between which the tiny nose with flaring nostrils was barely visible; the Negro, Salvator Bambola, with an agile, oily body and woolly hair, whom it would take the author of *Salammbô* to describe; Zbishko-Tsiganevich, Poland; and many others, all of them champions, with their own distinctive traits and famous names that make my heart beat faster even today.

The arena gradually emptied, and at the same time a small table appeared at one end of the carpet for the benefit of the jury, composed of local experts and sportsmen: a journalist, a student, and a member of the lower classes—a stevedore, railway-guard, or someone like that—who gave the jury a distinguished and widely representative appearance and guaranteed its complete impartiality. The judges sat down at the table already covered with large circus programmes and, to add to their importance, proceeded to spread out other papers containing further details and information, and note-pads for jotting down their opinions. The jury had, of course, been chosen by Uncle Vanya himself from among his friends and drinking-companions. After impressively seeking their advice in a whisper, while the audience sat in dead silence with bated breath, he announced the names of the first pair and summoned them into the arena with the slow, deliberate ceremoniousness characteristic of him, and only the faintest hint of amusement in his powerful baritone voice. They stepped onto the carpet, leaving their footprints in the sawdust, turned to face each other, exchanged a curt handshake, and backed away; then, in response to Uncle Vanya's whistle, they began circling each other warily, waiting eagerly for their opponent's slightest mistake to impose some particularly effective hold such as "*tour de tête*," "*bras roulés*," "double nelson," or "scissors."

Even now I sometimes repeat to myself those magic words of my adolescence and experience the same excitement and delight.

With his horn whistle, Uncle Vanya somewhat resembled a gluttonous policeman, but he was in fact a man of considerable intelligence and even edited a paper called *Russian Sport*.

While the wrestlers shuffled about, getting each other's measure, Uncle Vanya watched them like a hawk, on the lookout for any breach of the rules. When they finally came to grips and the match really got going, with the men on their knees or lying on the carpet, he, too, would kneel and peer underneath to ascertain whether both shoulder-blades or only one was touching the carpet. This was, of course, of the utmost importance, since the man underneath would only be considered beaten if both shoulders touched the carpet at the same time, though it might be only for a second. When this happened, Uncle Vanya would declare, with a cursory glance at the audience: "In the fourth minute Ivan Zaikin defeated Spool employing the *'bras roulés.'* "

After the ovation had died down, the second pair would be summoned.

How can I attempt to describe this beautiful contest between the two demi-gods on the carpet, their plastic movements, their straining bull-necks, their knee-caps, the bandages round the wrists of their athletic arms, their heavy breathing under the stress of their exertions, their grunts, the resounding slaps on the shoulders and nape of the neck, which always aroused the ecstasy of the gallery from which, infallibly, a sobbing, hysterical voice would shout: "Foul!" To which Uncle Vanya promptly replied in the deepest tones of which he was capable: "No foul! Carry on!"

How can I evoke the image of two struggling wrestlers, suddenly still for a moment, and then the upward flash of smartly sheathed white legs in a *"tour de tête"*; the unnatural entwining of two bodies gleaming with sweat, which conjure up visions of a single writhing being with two short-cropped heads, one pair of bloodshot eyes, turned upwards, the other downwards; and, finally, the loud applause from the stalls, the frantic roar of admiration from the gallery.

The ritual of the championships was strictly observed. One of the wrestling couples, in the heat of the contest, would invariably trip and fall over the jury's table, the jury would scatter in apparent terror, one of its members would sprawl headlong, provoking Homeric laughter from the audience, a student's cap would bowl across the stage, the ink-bottle and bell would go flying onto the sawdust, and sheets of paper scatter in every direction. It was, in fact, a well-rehearsed little drama which the innocent audience would long remember and consider themselves lucky to have witnessed.

In addition, the audience was always promised a sensational surprise before the last pair of wrestlers appeared. A printer's devil would come racing in straight from the press in the traditional blue blouse, with a starched collar and tie peeping from under it, and deposit a freshly printed, still damp programme of the next evening's matches on the jurymen's table. Uncle Vanya would put on a small pince-nez, which did not well accord with his plebeian face and bulbous nose, pick up the programme and read it aloud. From this it would emerge that it would actually be on the morrow that the most outstanding wrestlers would appear, whereas only yesterday the audience had been led to believe that nothing could exceed in interest what they had just seen that evening. This artificial build-up for the championships was very cunningly prepared, and Uncle Vanya, an expert on the psychology of circus audiences, displayed considerable talent in concocting programmes that suggested that every forthcoming performance would be far superior to the one that had gone before.

"Oh, hell!" the wrestling fans in the gallery would mutter despairingly to themselves, after having spent their last half-rouble on that evening's performance in the expectation of seeing the best contestants. "Oh, hell, it now turns out that it's tomorrow that the match between two unbeaten world champions takes place: the great Ivan Poddubni himself and the Volga champion Ivan Zaikin, the finest exponent of wrestling this country has ever seen." And there's no question of the match ending in an unsatisfactory draw. The audience is promised a fight to the finish, the chance to see with their own eyes which idol's shoulder-blades finally touch the floor. It's not a spectacle anyone can afford to miss! Hence the despair! And the poor occupants of the gallery would proceed to procure by hook or by crook the half-rouble they did not possess, even going so far as to pawn part of their shabby clothing or the best shawls of their long-suffering wives.

Wrestling had much the same effect as a drinking-bout: it diverted interest from politics and momentarily atoned for the drabness of everyday life.

How many times did I have to beg Papa or my aunt for half a rouble or even forty kopecks when I heard what remarkable wrestling there would be on the morrow! Neither my father nor my aunt shared my passion for wrestling, which they considered a debasing performance for an intelligent human being to witness, a vulgar show quite unworthy of his attention.

When interest in the wrestlers dropped and the demand for tickets diminished, Uncle Vanya fell back on a well-tried expedient. He would announce that a new wrestler had arrived in our town, wearing a black mask. He was prepared to challenge every competitor in the championships but would only take off his mask if he was defeated.

Black Mask did not take part in the parade but appeared suddenly, like thunder from a clear sky, down the narrow passage. From that moment the town was seized with something like an epidemic of insanity: everyone began to make wild guesses and betting on their hunches. The most incredible suggestions were put forward and almost every world champion's name was mentioned.

Perhaps it was the legendary Siberian, Sviatogor, perhaps even Lurich I himself, whose death had been falsely announced. Again, it might be the unbeaten Caucasian, Masuradze, or the mysterious middle-weight Czech wrestler, Pospeshil, who had never yet appeared in our town and was only known to us from picture postcards. Perhaps, after all, it was the sturdy, elusive Slutsky from Kiev, for whom French experts had foretold a brilliant future.

The Black Mask disappeared as suddenly as it had appeared. It was not an ordinary velvet mask as worn at balls: the wrestler's entire head, down to his muscular neck, was covered in a black hood, pierced with two round holes from which peered unknown eyes, sinister as an executioner's.

We racked our brains in our efforts to determine whence he had come and whither he had gone.

In my imagination I pictured a town at night, bathed in the eerie moonlight of crime stories, the snake-like glitter of granite pavements and a racing carriage on rubber tyres, in which the Black Mask is sitting, his face covered by his cloak. He is dashing from the circus, where he has just defeated his last opponent, to his hotel, hoping to cover his traces. The hotel, of course, is one of the smartest —the London, on Nikolaev Avenue between Pushkin and the Duke of Richelieu, or the Bristol, on Pushkin Street behind the Stock Exchange, built in the style of the Venetian palaces of the Doges. In my fantasies, Black Mask would be wearing a glossy top-hat like

Max Linder's and carrying a valuable gold-topped, rosewood cane. His wealth was enormous and, like all great champions, he was world-famous.

At that time, as we strolled about the town in our school-coats, made to last for years, attempting to find the mysterious Black Mask, my closest friend Boria and I never suspected that the champion wrestlers, those demi-gods with powerful necks and dyed moustaches, sporting their ribbons and medals, the champions of countries and even the world, were not living in the best hotels and racing along behind the best horses; that they were, in fact, not rich at all, just simple town-dwellers living with their families in cheap furnished rooms not far from the circus; and that their wives washed the babies' nappies, their own blouses, and their husbands' woollens in troughs, cooked cutlets with vermicelli, *golubzi*, and *vareiki* on a paraffin stove and looked after the children born during their wanderings with the multi-national crowd of wrestlers through the various towns of tsarist Russia.

The champions themselves, with the dye fading from their moustaches, would sit round a long table in Jaeger pullovers with short sleeves or cotton shirts, their braces slipped off their shoulders, playing dominoes, draughts, or simple card-games with frayed cards, greasy and thickened from constant use, staking mere kopecks and keeping their winnings in tin sweet-boxes from George Borman.

Their surnames were mostly simple commonplace ones and it was Uncle Vanya who substituted the exotic pseudonyms that caused our childish, vulnerable hearts to beat wildly and monopolised the minds of a whole town for several months while the championships lasted.

Work in the schools deteriorated, students threw their books on Roman law under their beds, officers neglected their duties and women lost their heads, dreaming of the wrestlers' marble torsos, their strong necks, and shaven arm-pits, powdered with swan's-down puffs.

Surrendering to this mass insanity, Boria and I bought post-cards with the champions' portraits on them with our last kopecks and spent our time trying to trace the Black Mask, waiting long hours in the shadow of the circus's stage-door for the moment when the foaming horse would draw up and Black Mask would spring lightly from the carriage. With terror in our hearts we roamed the narrow streets at night, or lingered near the entrance to the London Hotel, where laurels grew in green tubs on either side of the doors. Sometimes we even sat dismally at the station in the third-class waiting-room—we were not allowed into the first-class one—staring hypnotically at the door leading to the platform, through which the passengers emerged. Alas, our efforts were fruitless. The Black Mask eluded us. Now I know that he was almost certainly sitting all this time in the circus bar—naturally without his mask, in an ordinary black cap, drinking tea in the company of his fellow-champions and roundly cursing that miser of an Uncle Vanya who had not paid out for the last two months; or else he may have been playing lotto in some furnished room for small stakes, covering the winning numbers with small shells collected in Langeron.

On very exceptional occasions, a Red Mask made its appearance in addition to the Black Mask and whipped up still greater interest in the championships. Then the same old insanity overwhelmed the town, reaching its peak when Black Mask and Red Mask met in a fight to the finish. The circus was packed despite the prices being doubled or trebled. Finally, the audience discovered the identity of both masked wrestlers, since the sweating winner would tear the mask off his shaven head. Usually it was some well-known champion whom the audience for some reason had temporarily forgotten.

Eventually, of course, the championships came to an end. The wrestlers left with their wives, children, pots and pans for some other Russian town, or possibly abroad—to Constantinople, for instance, on a passenger-carrying ship of the Austrian Lloyd where, for a special price, they enjoyed the privilege of travelling in the hold. Down in the depths, by the green light of the waves rushing past the port-holes, they continued playing dominoes in their Jaeger pullovers for stakes of one kopeck, one centime, or one piastre with pieces resembling long lizards with white spots sliding about the rocking table.

And we stayed in town, filling in time until the next championships, by wrestling among ourselves with strict adherence to all the rules, on the beach or in a deserted forest glade, clearing the place of weeds, spreading sand on it for a carpet and surrounding it with shells the colour of apricot jam.

From our parents' point of view it was a calamity. Cupboards and suitcases were plundered of any woollen articles of clothing to pro-

vide costumes for the wrestlers. Stockings were particularly in demand for masks, and we ruthlessly cut circles out of them as eye-
holes.

Small girls sat round the "arena" and applauded as we, in striped
bathing costumes or shorts with ribbons across our shoulders, provided the grand parade, appearing one after the other from the
bushes before demonstrating the forbidden holds. I would emerge
in a mask made from one of my aunt's flimsy stockings and, in an en-
deavour to astound the audience with muscles and general athletic
build, similar to my hero Van Rils, would bend and flex my weak,
still-childish arms, turn in profile and full-face, and show off my
black shoes, painstakingly whitened with tooth-paste, as fat, grey
moths fluttered silently above the dusty autumn zinnias in the villa's
front garden and the moon shone faintly through the clouds over
the sea.

Bibabo and Bilboquet ✑

I RECENTLY READ in Maupassant's *Bel-Ami* about Forestier standing
by the fireplace and smoking a cigarette as he played with a bilboquet. He displayed great expertise, bringing the yellow plastic
ball back time after time on to the small wooden peg. When he
missed on the thirty-seventh throw, he opened a cupboard and
Durois saw some twenty remarkable bilboquets, numbered and carefully arranged in order, like some exotic objects from a collection.

This reminded me that, in my childhood, and my youth, we, too,
had bilboquets, though these, of course, were all of a coarser, more
commonplace kind; red-lacquered, wooden toys, in the shape of a
small pillar, with a cup at one end and a sharp point at the other.
A little red wooden ball with a round hole in it was attached to the
pillar on a long silk cord. With a deft movement of the hand, this
ball could be tossed into the air and caught in the cup with a pleasant
click or impaled on the sharpened end.

Naturally, it was much easier to catch the ball in the cup than
to get the hole to land on top of the spike, but some of us school-
children became extremely expert. Almost all the boys and girls

carried bilboquets in their satchels or pockets and produced them whenever they had a free moment, so that there was a constant clicking sound as balls struck the side of the pillar or fell dexterously into the cup; those impaled on the sharp end landed silently.

Later, this toy grew old-fashioned, but when I remember the word "bilboquet," it evokes a pleasant memory of the melodious click of wood against wood and the dark-red lacquered surface of the pillar, as much a part of our lives as the windmills, humming-tops, and spillikins.

I remember another toy, a new one that put a definite end to bilboquet.

A school-girl looked at me maliciously from under the brim of her little uniform beaver cap with its salad-green ribbon, from under her brown fringe, then turned her back on me mysteriously, rummaged in her satchel, made a brisk movement, and finally turned back to face me, stretching out her arm, the end of which had suddenly become a strange, funny, nice little being, with a narrow celluloid head, round cheeks, and big striped eyes. This being, dressed in a bright flannel gown, had two flannel hands, which moved ridiculously while the head shook like a Chinese doll's and seemed to be pulling faces at me.

I guessed immediately the simple operation of this toy; you slipped a glove rather like a bath glove with three fingers on to your hand; the empty celluloid head with puffy cheeks going over the middle finger and the two other fingers acting as hands.

The girl looked at me with her foxy little eyes, transparent as lemon-drops, and laughed.

"Like it?" she asked, making the empty little head nod to me in greeting. "It's the latest novelty in toys. It's called a bibabo. I was given it for my name-day."

The bibabo gave me a farewell flick with its flannel hands and the little girl uttered one of those quick, tongue-twisting sentences: "Three little Chinese boys: Jak, Jak-Zidrak, Jak-Zidrak-Zidroni. Three little Chinese girls: Zippi, Zippi-Dippi, Zippi-Dippi-Lampomponi. Jak married Zippi; Jak-Zidrak, Zippi-Dippi; Jak-Zidrak-Zidroni, Zippi-Dippi-Lampomponi."

Then she rushed away, her pencil-box clattering in her satchel, casting a glance at me from afar that was very like the one of the bibabo's.

Skating-Rink ✍

ONE BRIGHT DAY, roller-skates appeared in our town—a foreign novelty of which we had never heard. What a marvellous toy!

I first saw them when a boy I did not know, who went to another school, rushed noisily along the asphalt pavement outside our gate and seemed much taller than he really was. Then I noticed he was wearing steel roller-skates, attached tightly to his shoes by shiny straps. Each skate had four wheels, two in front and two behind, and these wheels tore along the pavement without leaving any trace but emitting a strange, loud metallic sort of rustle, their colour blending in with that of the asphalt.

What a divine discovery it was that enabled óne to skate in summer!

As if by magic, roller-skates suddenly appeared in every toy-shop, making a splendid addition to all the other summer toys: the green gauze butterfly-nets; oval tin botany-boxes; croquet-sets; bamboo fishing-rods with cigar-like, purple floats; hammocks made from strong coconut rope, and, inevitably, fireworks.

The roller-skates could be bought at various prices; from the expensive nickel ones down to the comparatively cheap ones with brown wheels made of compressed cardboard.

Wherever there were asphalt pavements, you would see boys and girls racing along with a rattling swish, enraptured by being able to skate in the town in summer, where smouldering cauldrons of tar on every corner brought to the stuffy atmosphere a strong suggestion of hell.

It was thus that the epoch of roller-skates arrived.

But it proved to be more than merely a childish pursuit: at almost the same time it caught the children's fancy, it was adopted by grown-up ladies and gentlemen, who turned the sport into an evening, even a night, entertainment, a substitute for a night-club. The new, fashionable word was "skating-rink," which sounded to us, boys and girls, not quite decent, almost obscene.

A skating-rink was an asphalt arena in an enclosed building, the entrance illuminated by heliotrope electric lights that shone in the evening, and from which alluring sounds of *matchiches* would reverberate through the hot street, striking us as faintly evil, too.

Rich young men and women drove up in smart carriages or arrived on foot, carrying their skates in their hands, and we, boys, were vaguely aware that roller-skates were not the main attraction there.

I, of course, had never been in a skating-rink and had no personal knowledge of what went on there, but, according to rumour, men and women danced waltzes on skates, pressed tightly against one another, and later, towards midnight, broke into *matchiches* and "cake-walks." Around the asphalt circle, we gathered, behind wooden, velvet-topped barriers; there were tables covered with starched cloths and, beside them, in special containers, shining silver pails with ice inside them and the golden tops of Roederer champagne bottles peeping over the top of them.

I can still see a dark little street running into the Greek square and, inside a gate, lit by a street-lamp, the figure of a woman, with roller-skates in her hand. Her face is partly shaded by her hat, partly green in the gaslight. She makes a hesitating gesture and whispers, as if it were an aside: "Young man, wouldn't you like to come and skate with me?"

Skating

DURING THE NIGHT, puddles had begun to be covered with thin layers of ice, which broke underfoot like window-panes in the morning, but we were already hurrying to the shoemaker's to get our shoes ready for the attachment of skates.

Winter began with these visits to the shoemaker and the arrival of glaziers to repair the school-windows, fit double panes and putty them in. The school-corridor became full of putty and glass. The old putty lay on the floor, dry and brittle, while the new lay on the window-sills like large oval blocks with fingerprints on them, giving out a strong smell of olives. There was a white variety and a yellow one. The white was used on the windows in the hall and in the director's office, the yellow in the classrooms, the corridors, and the teachers' room, where the frames were not white but a sort of yellowish-brown. One could feel winter in the sharp, thin sound of the commercial diamonds with which the glaziers drew straight lines on the glass with the aid of rulers. The long, narrow strips of glass they broke off vaguely reminded one of thermometers. These strips broke easily and held little interest for us, unlike the fresh putty, which we tore off the blocks and rolled between the palms of our hands like dough, transforming them into long, soft sausages with the lines of our hands imprinted on them. We also used it to model elongated, fanciful figures. The cement tickled our hands as we tore it off and left them pleasantly moist with linseed oil. The splinters of the old cement crackled under our feet, covering the floor with dust, and the thin strips of glass broke into tiny fragments under our heels. Perhaps this is why, even now, the first ice on the puddles makes me think of window-panes, the autumn smells of yellow cement and the beginning of winter—the white one.

But, as I have said, the beginning of winter also involved the preparation of shoes for skating.

Those iron—or perhaps they were steel—rhombuses with a hole in the middle, which were tightly screwed into the soles of our boots by the shoemaker, announced the opening of the skating season.

Our heels would clatter on the marble and iron stairs, on the flagstones of the corridors, and scratched the parquet floors of the classrooms.

Winter settled in slowly, reluctantly: the yellow leaves took their time in falling. The naked trees, not yet covered by snow, stood stiff and cold and dark, their colour differing little from that of the autumnal earth.

At long last the news spread that the ice was thick enough for skating. Whenever I hear that word, I immediately picture the key that screwed the skates to our boots and see the tight strap fitted round the back for additional safety. Then, conscious of how much taller I had grown, I walked clumsily out of a hot dressing-room, down the wooden slope creaking from the frost, on to the dangerously glistening, still immaculate mirror-like ice. Stumbling from lack of practice and clutching at the pine-wood banisters, white with rime, I embarked on the icy surface that reflected the electric lamps which hung over the avenues but left deserted corners, where it was darker than elsewhere, and a vaguely romantic atmosphere prevailed.

At first the place was empty, but it very soon grew crowded. There was a band and, as the rhythm of their marches echoed back from the large houses in the centre of the town, my heart would begin to beat faster.

Soon, a number of expert skaters, leaning forward with their hands clasped behind their backs, would be circling round and round, cutting into the ice when they changed direction with the sharp edges of their long "Norwegians" that whistled like knives. (And the famous stunt-skater, a student in a Canadian sweater and woollen cap pulled down over his red ears, was writing his name on the ice.)

It was here, one day, that a sturdy, red-haired man, with a straight parting in his hair and without a hat, tore impetuously down the slope on his elegant skates, flew out into the centre of the pond, and, without a pause, signed his name, Sergei Utochkin, on the ice with a number of dashing frills and the precision of a diamond; a feat which aroused universal admiration and was not soon forgotten . . . my heart went on beating wildly and finally I saw her.

Timidly moving her feet in a child's buttoned boots, she slid over the ice on her new skates with upturned points, breathing very fast and stopping every minute. She held on to the back of a chair shaped like a sleigh with one hand, and balanced with the other hidden in a muff. When she saw me, she moved the little muff in the air. We greeted each other and, tearing herself away with some reluctance from the security of the chair, she held out her hands and entrusted herself to me. As we linked our arms cross-wise, one of my hands crept into the warm nest of her muff and lightly pressed her moist, warm fingers, freed from her glove. Then I squeezed her whole wrist, which seemed to me as touching and helpless as an unfledged little bird. With our arms linked together, we skated rhythmically in a circle, trying to keep in step, and when we found ourselves under the naked electric lamp, our shadows disappeared for a moment, to reappear again on the opposite side, splitting into two, three, and eventually turning into a shadowy star.

The band played a magical, sad waltz, and the rhythm beaten out on a quivering Turkish drum flew beyond the area of the skating circle and rattled brilliantly lit window-panes in the street. Something was wringing my heart so painfully that I wanted to cry with happiness and, as I took her home, I smelled the aroma of her woollen coat with its beaver collar, slightly scented with some familiar eau de Cologne, fresh as a spring garden, and we squeezed damp hands and entwined our fingers inside the muff. I carried her skates as well as mine on a strap, and they clinked against each other while the metal plates on our boots clattered on the pavement, scratching the flagstones. And, close beside me, I saw her little face, rosy as a Crimean apple, and a pretty little ear, peeping from under curls, lightly touched with hoar-frost.

As the poet Fet once wrote: "The bold curl took the punishment and became grey at sixteen."

But she, I think, was no older than fifteen; perhaps even fourteen. I cannot remember her name any more. Was it Zina ... Zinochka ... ?

On my way home alone through Alexandrovsky Park, deserted at that late hour, I was aware of the dead silence of the wintry sea and the black stumps of naked trees, above the icy branches of which shone the seven brilliant stars of the Great Bear.

Frozen Sea

THE FAMILIAR BEACH was crowded with flat, quite thick blocks of ice that shone with the green-blue sheen of the Black Sea water. They were white as sugar on top, and one could walk on them easily enough without slipping, but it was more difficult to move from one to the other: sometimes one had to sit down on a higher block before dropping on to a lower one, or one could leap across, resting one hand on the jagged edge, apparently fragile but actually strong as granite. One had to move slowly over this shapeless mass before one stepped on to the even surface of the sea, covered with ice, as far as the horizon. But one had to walk warily along this seemingly unbroken ice-field, for there were frequently narrow crevices, where small, rippling waves had suddenly been caught by the frost and turned into floes.

Stretching into the far distance under a bright, cold sun, shining like the mercury in Captain Hatteras's bullet, glistened the unmarred whiteness of the salty, hoar-frosted ice, and only on the very edge of the horizon could be seen the blue-black line of the open sea and the outline of a trapped foreign collier.

The ice creaked under my feet, reminding me that below me was a sonorous, dangerous area of very deep water and that I was, as it were, treading on the echoing vault of a cellar, of which I could sense the dismal darkness. I can remember the accumulation of white air-bubbles, encrusted in the ice, which reminded me of lilies-of-the-valley. To the right and left, one could see the white towers of the lighthouses, illuminated by the January sun, one belonging to the port, the other standing by the big fountain, and, far away, the smoke of a small ice-breaker near the entrance to the serviceable harbour, reminding one of Frith of Nansen's famous *Fran*, buried to the very masts in the arctic ice under the Northern lights. Beneath the bright blue sky, in the deep, unnatural silence, the coast of the Dofinovka was bathed in a beautiful, pink, wintry light, and clearly visible through the crystal, corrosive air, which almost prevented one from breathing. Hoar-frost began to form along the edges of my camel's-hair scarf tied round my head over my school-cap, and a temperature of fourteen degrees Réaumur seemed more than any human being could stand.

Nevertheless, it was not so, for there were human figures moving about the ice-field towards the horizon, townsfolk taking their Sunday walk and curious to inspect the foreign ship at close quarters. A blue shadow accompanied every figure, and my own shadow appeared to me to be particularly large and dazzling, as it slid along in front of me over the uneven ice and leaped across the crevices.

At length, I reached the ice-floes, beyond which, in almost black, smoky water, lay the huge dark-red hull of the Italian collier, with a white monogram on her dirty black funnel, a monogram composed of Latin letters, which gave the ship a special sort of magic attraction.

An Italian sailor was standing on the upper deck, wearing a thick sweater, with a water-proof cloth pail in his hand, and smoking a cheap, Italian cigar with a straw mouthpiece. From a sluice as high up as the roof of a three-storied house, water was pouring uninterruptedly like a waterfall, and water dripping from the engine-room had left impressive icicles on the old iron plates. The Italian sailor was waving his hand to someone, and I saw two small figures, moving off towards the shore, who stopped now and then and turned round to wave back at him. The runners of the sleigh they were dragging behind them left two azure tracks on the ice. After strolling along close to the edge of the ice-floes and completing my admiring inspection of the collier, I started to walk back again. The sun was already sinking towards the west, behind the town, behind the chimneys on the white roofs, behind the blue cupola of the local theatre, behind the monument to the duke. The frost was growing sharper every minute. I walked automatically between the double tracks of the sleigh and suddenly saw, on the flat surface of a block of ice quite close to the bank, a large-lettered inscription deeply incised by some sharp instrument, possibly the pointed end of an iron bar which workmen from the factory often used as a stick when they went on their Sunday strolls. Or, possibly, the instrument had been specially designed for the purpose.

In any case, it was here on a block of ice that I read for the first time in my life a combination of words that at that age was incomprehensible to me:

"Proletarians of the world, unite."

But there was something menacing, full of secret meaning in that azure-blue, shining sentence, which later spread so widely and powerfully throughout the world.

What could be the meaning of this invocation that, in the space of a moment, seemed to bring me so close to the people of all countries? I wondered, with an odd pang of anxiety in my heart. Jumping from the last block of ice on to the frosty stones of the bank, I saw three frontier-soldiers in caps and *cashliks* (woollen hoods) with green edges who were climbing along the sharp hummocks on their way to the Italian ship.

The pink sun was reflected off their four-faceted bayonets of burnished steel with a hollow for the blood to flow down: they looked like men who had come too late.

What did all this mean and what connection did it have with the word "Iskra,"* cut into the last ice-block of all, probably with the same instrument as the longer sentence, by one of the pair who were carrying something wrapped in matting on their sleigh?

Treatment of a Tooth 🖋

ON HEARING THE WORD "Flemmer," I immediately envisage the immaculately white, starched and ironed overall, the bearing of a great

* Lenin said, "Out of the spark ('Iskra') comes the flame." *Translator's Note.*

scientist, and the noble head, if not of a Beethoven, at least of an Ibsen; not to mention the presence in the air of a static, excessively hygienic smell of creosote and clove-oil, which always filled me with resigned despair and a sense of inferiority.

Even my father, who in my opinion was morally superior to any other human being, suddenly became, in the presence of Dr. Flemmer, unsure of himself, a timid man, with a commonplace appearance and a hesitating manner.

I readily understood the reason for his uneasiness: he did not know what the fee for the visit would be and feared that it would set him back three roubles, though, to be fair, he never grudged spending any money on my behalf. As though reading his thoughts, Dr. Flemmer, wiping his hands on a towel, announced with a strong German accent that the first visit would cost two roubles and the subsequent ones one rouble each, not counting the tip to the maid and any necessary materials.

Then, numb with terror, I climbed into the torture-chair, and leaned back with my head against two small leather cushions as Flemmer began to work a pedal with one well-polished boot and I ascended jerkily upwards, slightly surprised to see that the glass containing disinfectant water of a pale-lilac hue and a special, scientific red spittoon with a bit of damp, hygroscopic cotton wool, no doubt left by the previous patient, adhering to it were doing the same.

In the comatose silence of the room the clock ticked mercilessly.

I sensed the starched overall drawing closer and opened my mouth as wide as I could, whereupon Dr. Flemmer's second finger was inserted into it, a slightly hairy finger but impeccably washed with carbolic soap. Protruding blue eyes in golden spectacles peered into my mouth with a certain distaste and, a moment later, I heard a fastidious voice informing my papa that my mouth was not a mouth but a refuse-pit. Then I heard the terrifying words uttered with even more disgust: "a cavity."

After a short lecture on the duty of every person of culture to take care of his teeth, Dr. Flemmer, with a significant frown on his splendid forehead, having meditated in silence on the new situation and carefully weighed all the pros and cons, declared that he would not pull the wretched tooth, but would do his best to save it by removing the decay, treating it medicinally, and finally filling it with a platinum filling.

At the mention of platinum, Papa gave a start, but Flemmer reassured him by saying that the filling and all the work connected with it would only come to eight gold roubles, which was much less than the cost of a silver one.

I can still see Papa's kind eyes beneath flushed eyelids and hear his prompt consent to the eight roubles, in which one could detect a sacrificial determination not to spare any money—even if necessary to apply for state aid—to save his son's tooth. I noticed that Papa's large-pored neck had sweated under his hard, detachable collar, and he pulled at it uneasily as though he were trying to free himself from an invisible yoke.

After this, Dr. Flemmer forced me to open my mouth even wider and gently touched the exposed nerve with something shiny. It produced such a pain that one can only describe it graphically in the following way: . . . a wavering, red-hot line, beginning at the spot of the exposed nerve, surrounding the jaw, rising along the temple-bone and exploding somewhere in the depth of the hearing area . . .

I screamed, but Flemmer paid no attention. In his eyes, I was not a human being. Rummaging in a jar on the glass shelf near the spittoon, he picked up a piece of cotton wool, immersed in a sharp essence of cloves, with a pair of pincers, pressed it into the cavity, and my mouth was instantly filled with hot saliva. Flemmer told me to rinse my mouth with the disinfectant and I reverently pulled a full glass of water out of the tight-fitting holder, took a gulp, and spat into the spittoon, admiring the stream of water and salvia as it ran down the red sides into the dark blue hole at the bottom.

Thus ended the first visit. Having paid Flemmer two silver roubles, which he immediately entered in a special, fat, very neat account-book, Papa, with trembling hands, helped me out of the chair, which had now been lowered again.

As the chair came down, the trees behind the window rose slowly upwards and the street's foreshortening altered.

We went in an electric tramway down a street, drowned in blooming white acacia. I felt as I did after taking Communion, and was deeply sorry for Papa, who had paid two roubles to Flemmer, fifty kopecks to the maid, and had guaranteed to pay a far higher sum later.

As Flemmer had predicted, my tooth went on hurting for two hours. I kept carefully touching it with my tongue and spitting out the hot saliva until the pain finally receded.

After that, I paid daily visits to Flemmer for the treatment of the tooth, which he carried out according to the highest standards of dental practice. I will not go into details, since they have no essential significance, beyond the fact that they formed a part of my life, of my existence at that moment.

I will only add that the smart street where Flemmer practised, his huge waiting-room expensively and solidly furnished, which always seemed to be empty, and the maid, in a lace cap, starched shirt, and a sort of mantle that made her look rather like a nun, remained for a long time in my memory.

The treatment of the tooth had its good points.

When I went alone to see Flemmer, without Papa, I did not spend the money for my tramway fares or the kopecks given me in case I wanted to buy a drink of water or kvass in the street. By the end of my treatment, I had collected a tidy little sum of about forty kopecks and meditated from morning till night on how to spend it.

I will not recall the machine that drilled my tooth: the noise alone penetrated into the depths of all my joints, to the very marrow of my bones, and made my whole body shudder. I will especially try to forget the moment when the needle-sharp drill touched my ex-posed nerve, when I was already going through hellish pain, and I felt as though every part of me were being pierced again and again by a red-hot wire. . . . After which, I gradually became aware of Flemmer, grimacing with disgust, lifting the drill, with a piece of stinking nerve adhering to it, up to his nose.

Everything went smoothly after that, though the machine with its drill, which had a small ball on the end whirring round as it cleaned up the cavity, continued to terrify me. However, this is an experience suffered by everyone and hardly worth mentioning.

As a contrast, how beautiful were the hot Odessa days and the green-blue lace of the acacias blooming all over the town; their sweet, I will even say voluptuous, smell; the feeling of lightness in one's still almost childish body; the lack of toothache; and the pleas-ant, warm sweat under my winter school-uniform, which I always put on whenever I went for the treatment, since it was considered impolite to visit such a celebrity as Flemmer in a shabby cotton summer uniform. The inside of the peak of my winter cap was soaked in sweat, too, and it streamed, hot as boiling water, down my temples. In spite of this, I felt unusually free, unearthly and unfettered. When the cavity was at last transformed into a smooth little nest for the filling, Flemmer prepared to perform the most important part of the treatment.

For a time, the majestic dentist was transferred into a German craftsman, exercising some delicate art—a jeweller or a sculptor or a colourman. Sitting in the chair, lifted almost to the ceiling, along which fluttered a pretty summer butterfly, with a starched napkin under my chin, I stealthily watched Flemmer pounding something in a small porcelain mortar, then grinding a silver powder on a glass slab, adding some drops to it and turning the powder into a dark, metallic paste. Then, with a small spatula, he began to fill the cavity in my tooth with the warm paste, which had an after-taste of cement. He worked slowly, now raising me, now lowering me like a bee, introducing nectar into its cell drop by drop, mixing it with flower-dust, and finally covering it with warm wax. When the cavity was filled, he cut away the surplus paste with a virtuoso flash of his instrument, pressed in the not yet hardened filling with his fat finger, forbade me to eat anything before evening, and told me to come back in two days' time to complete the treatment.

On the last day, I went to Flemmer with Papa and he polished the filling with the drilling-machine, to which this time a cardboard or, more likely, an emery circle had been attached. It whirled wildly, polishing the hot metal of the filling and sprinkling my tongue with dry, fine dust. At long last, the polish was considered perfect, and while Papa, flushed with excitement, lay the money, which had grown to twelve roubles something for the work, the material, and the tip for the maid in her nun's mantle, on Flemmer's table, Flemmer proudly wiped his hands on a towel and didactically informed me that the filling would last an eternity, that I would live with it to a great age and, ending the speech with a joke, that it might even survive me.

I walked out into the street beside Papa, who was smiling wryly.
The filling fell out exactly a month later.

The Saltpetre Cord ✍

IN ORDER to see this, one had to arrive at church before the beginning of the evening service, when the church was still empty and dark, except for the small oil-lamps in front of the icons, their flickering flames faintly reflected in the gold. The church-warden would be roaming silently round and the fur-coated village elder would be opening the lid of his desk with a grating key to disclose neatly stacked piles of wax candles, thick and thin, long and short. The church would still be cold and smelling of the previous day's incense.

In the centre of the church, under the dark cupola, a lustre is suspended on a long chain, the wicks of all its virgin candles linked together by a thin cord impregnated with saltpetre; the end of the chord hangs high up, just below the lustre, ready at any moment to ignite the two circles of candles, one inside the other. The church-warden stands underneath, grasping a pole with a small lit candle fixed into the top. As soon as the flame from this candle touches the end of the impregnated cord, a long flame flares up and races upwards; devouring the cord, it runs magically round both circles of candles like lightning, setting all their wicks alight almost simultaneously, and the church is suddenly filled with a warm, solemn light that brings into view various objects previously concealed in the dark corners of the building:

An ancient silver font, in which the sacrament of christening is celebrated (similar, no doubt, to the one in which my little brother Zhenia and I were christened); a bier covered with a moth-eaten black cloth; a painted image of the Crucifixion, with a scarlet wound in the pierced side, on a wooden support painted to resemble a little stone Golgotha, with a sinister skull of Adam embedded in its crude ornamentation; and a few well-known icons, vivid now that they are released from the darkness, looking like the gaily coloured illustrations in a children's Bible, among them.

Christ, sitting sideways on the donkey on his way to Jerusalem and the populace, in brightly coloured clothes, throwing palm branches under the hooves of his humble grey mount. All this was illuminated by the lustre and the myriad of twinkling candles which parishioners had lit in front of the icons. And the brighter and more colourful it became in the church, drowned in the lilac waves of incense, the more mysterious and caressing was the blue of a spring evening in March behind the narrow windows of the church.

Music ✍

MAMMA WAS HOLDING my fat little hand as we walked together to the corner nearest to our house, where there was a post-office. I had never walked so far before. In my small dark-blue coat, with golden anchor buttons, I did not reach up to the edge of Mamma's jacket, trimmed with braid, so I found little of interest in the post-office while she was registering her letter, apart from a painted iron trunk with two hanging padlocks and a strong smell of smoky, flaring sealing-wax somewhere beyond Mamma and the reflection of its seething, scarlet flame. On the same corner there was a kiosk, at which Mamma stopped and, lifting her veil from her chin to above her nose, drank a glass of soda-water, while I held on to her cloth skirt and, raising myself on my toes, tried to see what was going on inside the kiosk, but discovered nothing more exciting than two glass cylinders. In one there was some red syrup, in the other a yellow one. I promptly asked to be given some to taste, but Mamma laughed and did not allow it.

While she was taking a small purse out of her black moiré bag, edged with bugles, I stared down the street, which descended in a gentle slope into the limitless space of a town of stone, composed of a conglomeration of houses, streets, and churches with blue cupolas, that somehow eluded my mental grasp. I was not aware of any movement there, any manifestations of town-life; I only vaguely sensed them as existing.

I remember becoming interested in a new wall near the small one-storied building in which the post-office was situated. The wall was constructed of rough blocks of stone with frequent gaps between them, so that to my eyes it presented a series of rectangular vacuums alternating with grey slabs, in which here and there glistening sea-shells were encrusted.

It was a low wall, easy to clamber over, and I was on the point of doing so, having escaped from Mamma—I had already raised one foot in its shoe—when faint but persistent musical sounds suddenly reached my ears. They came from far away, from somewhere in the centre of that stony town.

I stopped, entranced by this strange musical interruption, straining my ears to catch the distant melody.

"Music!" I said to Mamma, pulling at her skirt.

She looked down at me in astonishment through her thick veil and pince-nez.

"Music, music," I repeated. "Can't you hear it?"

"What music? What are you talking about?" she asked.

"Over there!" I replied, stretching my hand out towards the street. "In the town."

"But we are in the town." Mamma laughed.

"No, over there in the real town. There's music!"

"I can't hear any music. There isn't a sound."

"There is music! There is!" I repeated stubbornly.

"What an imagination you have!" she said and dragged me back home along our Market Street, even though, despite the clatter of my new shoes on the pavement constructed of slabs of lava like many pavements in our town, I continued to hear strange music behind me, unlike anything I had ever heard before—now retreating, now coming back in waves, now silent, now louder than before. What could it have been?

For a long time I could not understand, then, one day, the explanation suddenly came to me: it had been a combination of the faint creak of cabs, the trampling of hooves, people's footsteps, the clatter of trams, church songs, military bands, the swish of bicycles, the rattle of window-panes, the hoot of trains and steamers, the whistles of pointsmen, the flapping of pigeons' wings, the clanging of goods-train couplings, the rustle of acacia trees, the crunching of gravel underfoot in Alexandrovsky Park, the gurgling of water spurting from the gardeners' hoses as they watered the roses, the bustle of the market, the songs of blind beggars, the high notes of Italian accordions, the roar of the waves.

Wafted along by the sea-breeze, all these sounds composed the music of our town, inaudible to grown-ups, but easily perceptible to small children.

Painting 🖎

MAMMA BOUGHT ME a sort of album which opened up like a harmonica in zigzags, and on its very thick cardboard pages were printed in colour innumerable pictures of household articles in no particular order: a lamp, an umbrella, a hold-all, a suitcase, a bed, a ball, a doll, a pram, and so forth. Nothing was written underneath them.

The idea was that you showed a child one or another of these articles and he identified it in a foreign language.

Mamma chose French.

She pointed to the articles one by one with her finger and called them by their appropriate names: *la lampe, le parapluie, le porteplaid*, and so on.

I remembered the French words rather easily and repeated them carefully, parrot-fashion: thereafter the ordinary coloured articles acquired a special meaning, for an ordinary window was transformed into *"la fenêtre"* and became in my imagination quite a different window—a window from a coloured world of small, pretty articles that surprised me by the precision and authenticity of their design and a certain conventionality of colour.

We subscribed to a magazine called *The Toy*, in which I liked to look at the coloured dogs, cats, and frogs, these last jumping into a pond in an attempt to catch the moon. According to the story, the frogs mistook the moon's reflection for some particularly succulent kind of goldfish. As I gazed at the frogs in the picture, soaring over the black, wind-swept reeds, their legs reminded me of an open pair of scissors, which, as I had already learned, were known in French as *"les ciseaux."*

There was also a picture of a sad, long-eared dog, sitting beside a sleeping child, and Mamma would read me the verses written underneath in a loud, clear voice but with a hidden smile:

> " 'A baby sleeping in its cot
> Caro the dog is on the watch
> He'd like to sing a lullaby
> But what if his bark made baby cry?' "

There were no pictures on the walls of our house. I did not even know that oil-paintings existed in the world. I was only acquainted with water-colour tablets, which had lost their pure virginal colours and become smeared because I used a dirty brush. I did not have the patience to wash it properly in the glass of water, already almost black, the sight of which would suddenly overcome me with boredom, and I would push the paint-box away as far as I could and crumple up the bits of paper with stripes and curves and a dirty semblances of human faces, painted with a rough brush which expanded when dipped in the glass and shrank again immediately it was taken out, its sharp point dripping grey drops of water, like tears, onto the paper.

My surprise, therefore, was considerable when one day in the storeroom I found two dirty canvases, covered with a thick layer of oil-paint. I began to examine them, and suddenly the coarse multicoloured smudges acquired the shape of a blue enamel bowl and some half-peeled potatoes. The peel descended in a spiral from an article which turned out to be a kitchen-knife, a knife held by a human hand, and above them was a woman's face with protruding lowered eyelids, a nose, lips, and chin the colour of flesh, painted with coarse daubs, on the hardened surface of which remained the traces of a thick brush. I realised that it was the portrait of a woman, peeling potatoes over a blue enamel bowl, which startled me by its resemblance, its natural character, its authenticity: one could even see the reflection of sun-lit windows in the blue enamel.

On the other canvas, I discovered a beach, a rock, and the sea.

I recognised them at once. It was our Langeron, equally coarsely and roughly daubed with a broad, hard brush made of pig's bristles; one of the bristles had stuck so firmly to the stripes of the deep-blue sea that I could not tear it off. The beach was of a creamy, light flesh-tint, every stone cast a short, thick shadow and the rock a longer, lilac one, so that I sensed from it all a seashore sweltering in the heat of midday. I could almost feel the red-hot pebbles and sand scalding the soles of bare feet, smell the dry foam and see that silent sea shimmering in the dazzling light.

Thus, for the first time, I was introduced to the miracle of painting.

I gather now that these two pictures, without frames, came to us as a surprise present. I seem to remember Mamma taking me to Langeron, where two students from a painting school were trying their hand; we got to know them and later they gave us their finished works as a graceful gesture.

I vaguely remember, too, their grey flannel shirts and their long brown hair parted in the centre: they looked very simple people. I was surprised by their boxes full of crumpled tubes of oil-paints, their palettes covered with multi-coloured daubs, the zinc tins containing lacquer and seed-oil, the small folding easels, and particularly by the huge linen umbrellas, across which swept the blue shadows of sea-gulls.

Of course, I understand now that they were just immature works, probably quite worthless. But, if so, why cannot I forget the dark blue enamel bowl, with the coarse brush-marks of a hard, cheap brush on it, the reflection of the window, and the grey spiral of potato-peel; why cannot I forget that July midday on the Langeron beach, Mamma in her tussor blouse, the red-hot pebbles scalding my bare feet, and the blue shadows of the sea-gulls?

The Theatre

I HAD a honeymoon period with the theatre, not the real theatre but a toy one, which I got as a Christmas or birthday present, in a beautiful box, its lid decorated with coloured pictures of the scenes contained inside. There was a cardboard stage with a pretty curtain, wings, scenery, and figures of the various protagonists that one could move about like chessmen.

The plays were usually an opera, or a patriotic-historical drama of the defence of Sebastopol, or exciting episodes in the life of the great Russian general Suvorov. In this last, the future marshal was first seen as a young soldier standing guard at the palace, where a thrilling scene with the empress took place. The empress, coming out on the balcony, takes a fancy to the brave, elegant sentry in a white wig, with a plait showing under his brass helmet, and a white uniform, his gun held at the ready. She tries to hand him a silver rouble as reward for his loyal service, but he refuses to accept it since he is on duty. Appreciating this attitude, the empress, a severe, buxom figure with a double chin, wearing a white wig and a

farthingale, with the ribbon of the Order of St. Andrew draped across
her chest and a diamond star pinned above one breast, praises the
young soldier for his strict adherence to the regulations and kindly
drops the silver rouble at his feet, from where he may retrieve it when
the guard is changed.

"I will do so, Your Imperial Majesty, and thank you kindly for
your imperial kindness," he says, a speech duly recorded in the explanatory booklet accompanying the set.

The scenery displays the pillars of the palace, the striped sentry-
box, the brightly coloured Tsarskoe Sielo trees, jutting out from
the wings one behind the other, and, in the background, the Tsarskoe Sielo ponds with snow-white swans floating on the surface.

Having set the scene, according to the plan included in the booklet, and lit the Christmas candles backstage, I would raise the card-
board curtain, beautifully decorated with brocade folds. Then, I
would remain enchanted by the sight of the theatre and fascinated
most of all, perhaps, by the small shell of the prompter's box.

It was, in fact, nothing more than a mute, still picture, lacking
human voices, movement, and music, but, despite the immobility
and the silence, the slanting warm lighting somehow gave it the
character and perspective of an exciting performance, seen from the
distance of an upper gallery.

Having had one's fill of that scene, one had to bring down the
elegant curtain, with its brocade folds, tassels, and a yellow lyre in
the centre, and begin to set the following scenes, the most beautiful
and moving of which was Suvorov's crossing of the Black Bridge
with his miraculous heroes—snow-covered Alpine peaks, a precipice
with a blue fog hovering in its depths, a heavy gun falling from a
rock, and Suvorov himself, a little old man on horseback, with a grey
tuft of hair above his narrow, bony forehead, waving his naked
sabre and shouting: "Forward, my miraculous heroes!" These words,
too, appeared in the booklet.

Primarily, it was the technique of the performance, the scene-
setting, the machinery of the rising curtain, the décor, the cardboard
characters, the artificial lighting, and the narrowing of the perspective that attracted me.

But I delighted, too, in the spectacular side of the performance:
the convoluted ceilings of the boyars' ornate banquet-halls, the
roasted swans on silver trays on the oak tables, the head-dresses and

costumes of the old-Russian beauties, the boyars in their tall sable hats and brocade tunics, the military heroes in steel armour and helmets, the white-bearded sorcerers and psaltery players, the monks and the brigands with bludgeons in their hands, lying in wait in dark, craftily cut-out cardboard forests.

I was moved to tears by the snow that descended in a thick net upon the brave old Ivan Sussanin, sitting on a tree-trunk, surrounded by Polish hussars, with grey moustaches, brandishing their sabres.

I was elated by the sight of the huge head in *Russlan and Ludmilla,* its distended nostrils from which flocks of owls emerged and— of course!—by the dwarf Chernomoz, flying through the air, his long beard waving, holding in his arms the indescribably beautiful Ludmilla in her Russian tunic and head-dress, similar to those worn by wet-nurses, her face white as death and her eyes closed.

Later on, I saw the same scene in a real performance, when we were taken to a matinée in the local theatre, where, in addition to the magic of the décor and the hidden lights, there was also the magic of the orchestra, the music and the singing; the magic of real actors, in rich costumes and made-up beyond recognition, moving about in the limelight on a huge stage, whence a cold wind blew into the over-heated auditorium, in accordance with what seemed to me to be a pre-arranged time-table as precise as a railway one.

At home I tried, on a self-made toy stage with my own resources, to reproduce the performances I saw at matinées with red fires and blue, moonlit nights (as in *Aïda*), which always reminded me of moonlit nights in Langeron, where the Black Sea shone from one end to the other as though it were covered with silver paper—as like as two peas to the Nile, except for the black silhouettes of pyramids and palm-trees.

I remember how difficult it was to depict moonlight artificially.

For this, you had to buy a piece of chocolate for two kopecks, remove its transparent, blue gelatine wrapping and let the light from a candle shine through it on to my self-made scenery, which, to my eyes at least, was beautiful. Then everything on the stage would appear to be bathed in blue moonlight. For the fire, you required red gelatine paper, and I had to run back to the grocer's for another sweet in the appropriate wrapper; the scene would then acquire an ominous purple glow. A sweltering day in the African desert was reproduced by means of a yellow paper. The shopkeeper was amazed by my voracity for sweets, unaware that I threw them into the dust-bin, so as to waste no time in putting the magic paper, needed for my scenic effects, to use.

Even now, when I walk through Peredelkino* on a bright moonlit night in winter and admire the snowy fields and the glitter of the golden onions on the church built in the time of Ivan the Terrible, it seems to me that I am gazing at the indescribably beautiful blue landscape through a piece of gelatine paper.

Then came the time of family performances.

The greatest difficulty was presented by the curtain. You cannot have a theatre without a curtain: it seems to me to be its most basic requirement. Stealthily, I snatched brand-new sheets, made of the best quality Dutch linen, with her initials embroidered on them, out of my aunt's chest of drawers and, lacking the patience to sew rings on them, mercilessly cut out round holes with scissors, and attached them to rings running on a wire stretched out between the two walls, into which, equally mercilessly, I had driven curved iron spikes.

My make-up was improvised in the same casual way: I gummed on a beard and whiskers, made of God knows what, rouged my cheeks with water-colour and, having donned Papa's new frock-coat with silk lapels, rushed onto the stage to deliver in a horrible singsong Chatsky's monologue. As my aunt wept over the irreparably damaged sheets, tried to withdraw the firmly seated spikes from the damaged walls, and blew out the oil-lamps I had placed on the floor to represent footlights, I screamed:

> " 'Elsewhere I'll go to search
> a shelter from outraged emotion
> My carriage, please!' "

I repeated the last words an infinite number of times, before dissolving into angry tears.

The family rows, which usually followed amateur performances, were also an integral part of the theatre, of dramatic art.

But only once in my life did I fully experience the formidable impact of the real theatre. This happened when Papa took me to see *The Girl without a Dowry,* by Gogol, the leading role being played

---

* A kind of writer's colony near Moscow. *Translator's note.*

by the great actress Komisarjevskaya, who was on tour. It is the tragic story of a poor, virtuous, proud young girl, abandoned by the man she loves, who turns out to be a scoundrel, slowly becoming transformed into a "thing," into little more than an inanimate object. I watched spellbound as Komisarjevskaya, in a white lace dress, emaciated and exhausted, with a guitar in her almost lifeless hands, sang despairingly in a cracked voice:

" 'No, he never loved me
No, he never did.' "

She possessed my whole soul and, being a school-boy of thirteen, I was incapable of following my father out in the interval, but remained motionless in my seat, clutching its velvet arms with both hands. I think my lips must have been ashen and dark circles must have appeared under my insane eyes: my fingers were like icicles. . . . And when, in the last act, the half-crazy Karandishev—pathetic and at the same time frightening with his starched false shirt-front protruding from his hollow chest, his stooping figure and uniform cap —suddenly rushed from the wings and shot Komisarjevskaya between the shoulder-blades, she did not fall, as might have been expected, but slowly moved upstage with only the slightest hint that she was mortally wounded, then suddenly grasped the back of an iron garden-chair and, leaning on a round, iron garden-table, so that she faced the audience, died against the background of a ravishing Volga landscape with sad, motionless clouds and misty, lilac distances. And, as she was dying, for some unknown reason, she took off her poor little straw hat with pink ribbons with one trembling hand, and with the other, a very white, lace-frilled hand, already growing cold, sent kisses in the direction of the auditorium, especially upwards towards the gallery, where the impoverished students, male and female, sobbed and raved and stormed, as she, Larissa, continued to send weakening farewell kisses to all sides, kisses of all-forgiveness, kisses of love, kisses which seemed to me to soar like a flock of white doves and whirl round and round under the theatre's lustre. And Komisarjevskaya leaned farther and farther away, almost lying now with her wounded back on the restaurant-table, from which the table-cloth slipped lower and lower, no longer able to see anything, through her closing eyes, except for the transparent doves, flying around the theatre. Tears coursed down my cheeks and I was powerless to stop them. . . .

Oh, how deep was my sorrow for her, how deep my love!

And as we drove home that night in a cab, crushed and over-whelmed, Papa was unable to fit my dead mother's small theatre-glasses back into their case, and I stared in terror at the gas street-lamps as they appeared at regular intervals with such chaos in my heart, such despair, and such a definite, unconquerable fear of death as I had never felt before. The fear of death, the terror of its in-evitability was—I do not know why—connected with the lazy clatter of hooves along the granite paving of our town, lit by the green, sin-ister gaslight; connected with the shadow of our cab and its wretched, bony horse, which became more and more elongated as we retreated from a lamp-post or began to shrink, disappeared for a moment somewhere underneath us and the wheels, then came to life again like a new moon on the other side, as we approached the next lantern, and stretched out mysteriously as before, attached to the slumped figure of our driver and two other shadows—father's and mine—as though emerging from another world.

The sharp shadows of the horse's legs, moving as though on hinges, of the turning wheels and of ourselves—three people travel-ling in the silence of the sleeping town—seemed to be death itself.

Fireworks

THEY WERE SOLD not only in toy-shops but also in small sweet-and-tobacco shops. The fascinating names of the various varieties were inscribed on the tops of the boxes: rockets, Roman candles, golden rain, fire-crackers, suns, gimlets, Bengal lights, the telephone and . . . all their younger sisters, the *balles mitrailleuses*.

They were cardboard cylinders of different sizes and calibres, filled with a mysterious grey powder: a small length of fuse, black as a dried tea-leaf, emerged from one end. They did not, however, all have the same shape. For instance, the fire-crackers consisted of a long, thin, macaroni-like tube, folded several times and bound tightly together in the middle with a cord, the fuse protruding from the circular wad that sealed in the powder. The sun represented the symbol of eternal movement and was something like a garden-sprayer: four cylinders were attached by the same kind of thin, very strong cord to a cardboard square, with a hole in the middle for the nail which fixed it to a pole or a tree. When the fuse was lit, the fireworks started by emitting a modest spray of yellow sparks, then suddenly began revolving wildly and was transformed from a motionless cardboard square into a dazzling, sunny disc, enveloped by the curving splendour of golden whirlwinds. Fire-crackers, when lit, jumped on the ground like smouldering frogs, zigzagging along the street, shooting out gunpowder at every turn and frightening dogs, horses, pedestrains, and cyclists. The gimlets' fat cylinders were buried deep in the ground, and from them, as from a mortar, fiery projectiles thundered out. The Roman candles, slightly longer and thinner, were also buried in the soil, but not so deep; they threw out burning balls at regular intervals and resembled the stem of a hollyhock covered with yellow and raspberry-coloured buds. We boys were particularly enchanted by the telephone—a cardboard cylinder, which ran horizontally along a tightly strung wire, spraying a tail of golden sand behind it until it hit the trunk of a tree, came to a halt, black and smouldering and, its combustible fuel exhausted, suddenly became inanimate. The Bengal lights were beautiful as they soared up from different sections of the seaside garden, illuminating various details in unnatural, sharp colours: from the blue night emerged plaster statues of Greek goddesses, a fountain constructed of porous limestone, a trellised summer-house at the top of the slope, the figures of a man and a woman in each other's arms on a marble bench. The golden rain, ejected from a number of modest cylinders, lived up to its name and descended in a gentle, glittering shower.

But it was the rockets, attached to long, thin fir-tree sticks, that fired my imagination the most. The fireworks were brought from town to our country residence in large parcels, wrapped in the best paper like parcels of linen from the laundry, and fastened in the same way with a number of small pins. The rockets came in tissue-paper like bunches of gladioli, the ends of their sticks protruding like stalks: we were always terrified lest they should break in the crush of the train journey. The summer-residents and their guests brought their fireworks to the country-houses in different ways. Some arrived by the tramway, which, with its squeaking cast-iron brakes, ran at that time straight to Arcadia, where, amidst clay slopes and shell quarries, the horses were unharnessed and watered before being harnessed again for the return journey. Some arrived in open carriages with brilliant leather wings, cracked by the heat, gentlefolk these in tussor costumes and Panama hats adorned with silken striped ribbon, or straw American hats which—so rumour had it—cost one hundred roubles! Others travelled in the little, summer, narrow-gauged trains, drawn by what looked like a toy engine with a tall funnel and a lead whistle that emitted a thin but piercing daredevil sound as it sped between the gardens, towards the cliffs and the sea, where, far out towards the horizon, there was always the rising black smoke of steamships and the elegant white sails of yachts.

In the evenings, by the sea, in the dusty green of the villa gardens, one could hear the near-by festive crackling of fireworks; see the glowing colours of the Bengal lights and the descending golden rain.

Still later, as night drew on and myriads and myriads of milky stars appeared in the grey July sky, the rockets began to soar and one's heart sank when the "bouquet" foretold the end of the entertainment and the imminent approach of bed-time. The bouquet consisted of several rockets set off simultaneously heading through the dark night towards the stars: they dispersed like ears of rye from an untied sheaf. Having reached their highest point, they burst, the noise of the explosion reaching the earth some time after the sight of their fiery disintegration.

Later, I read in a poem by Bunin: "It was late and suddenly, into the darkness, high up above the sleeping earth, cutting through the night with an orange-coloured trail, a rocket soared like a wild serpent. It soared in a burst of joy. But it was only a moment before the large diamond tears were pouring down into oblivion and their fall was long and silent."

The fireworks were manufactured in small factories outside the town. I remember one of those factories well. It was behind a solitary stone wall in a narrow street by the sea, which led to the Malofontain road. The wall was whitewashed and letters the height of a man, running down its whole length, proclaimed: FORTUNA PYROTECHNICAL INSTITUTE.

Above the wall, one could see the building's iron roof and the upper parts of mysterious windows. By adding a few broken slabs of stone to the wall and climbing on top of them, one could peer through the windows of the workroom, where there were a number of wooden contraptions, vaguely resembling lathes, for wrapping and tying the filled boxes. There was something medieval about those lathes—they might have been painted by Dürer—but the men working at them in no way differed from any of the other skilled workmen in the town: they wore the same black waistcoats with many-coloured glass buttons over cotton shirts worn outside their trousers, had the same beards and whiskers and, like shoemakers, held their hair back with narrow bands to prevent it from falling into their eyes. In other departments of the Fortuna Pyrotechnical Institute, they rolled out the cardboard cylinders, pounded brimstone, salt-petre, powdered charcoal, and potassium chlorate in mortars, crammed this explosive material into the cylinders, and inserted the fuses. The stacks of finished fireworks dried against the shell-en-crusted walls, the rockets standing in line, like soldiers and ranging from the bigger, more expensive ones down to the smaller five-kopeck ones on puny legs, which street urchins sometimes bought by pool-ing their resources. I once bought one of the latter, precariously at-tached to a thin fir-tree rod. To discharge them, one had to prop them up against something vertical and light the fuse. Then, with a loud hissing noise, spraying the ground with golden sparks, they would soar into the air, leaving a fiery trail behind them, a trail that pursued a meandering course due to the imperfect balance between the rocket-head and the length of its stem.

I did not have sufficient patience to wait till evening. Surrounded by my friends, the so-called "hungry ones," I quickly leaned the rocket up against the curb of the pavement and lit the fuse with the end of a burning cigarette, provided by a passing school-boy. A stream of golden sparks erupted from the bottom of the rocket. Re-acting to the force of the explosion, it leaped up on its pathetic, thin foot, which promptly broke, and it lost its balance, sprawling on the pavement like a legless cripple who has lost his crutch; then, as though half-conscious, it crawled forward helplessly in an uneven line, dragging its broken leg behind it, until it finally came up against the trunk of an acacia tree and collapsed forever, emitting a small cloud of musty smoke, as though surrendering its soul. . . . We stood aghast and almost in tears as if it had been a live, thinking being that had been destroyed, taking with it all our hopes, not to mention my five kopecks. From time to time the Pyrotechnical Institute caught fire, and then crowds would assemble as on some national holiday. It would present a multi-coloured, flaming, smoky spectacle, a whirling, noisy, elemental disaster; there was something medieval about it or even something more ancient than that—a Chinese feast-day, when the sons of the Celestial Empire moved in procession through the streets of Shanghai, Pekin, or Canton, amid the jumping, spluttering fire-crackers, carrying long, crinkled paper dragons on poles. Pieces of charcoal would fly up out of the fire and fall on the smoking stumps and weeds in the surrounding wasteland.

Sometimes I pictured the siege of Sebastopol, with the French and English frigates discharging flaming rockets from their decks onto the tiled roofs of the smouldering Russian town.

But no-one, no power on earth, can save him now, and he perishes in a cloud of fiery smoke, amid the fluttering Stars and Stripes, the whirring of cine-cameras and tense voices announcing the news. The cloud of smoke flies upwards into the impassive Atlantic sky, like a soul set free forever from the prison of the flesh.

The *mitrailleuses* had nothing in common with the famous *mitrailleuses* of the Paris Commune. They were fat little cardboard cylinders, covered with thin coloured paper, with a small piece of string protruding from the middle: when one pulled this string, there was a muted, unalarming bang and a whiff of gunpowder smoke as the firework discharged its contents of paper confetti. I can see them now, floating down onto the head of a pretty, neat young school-girl, and the well-waxed parquet floor of a beautiful ballroom across which a little shoe twirls and slides: and, out of the past, there seems to come the faint melody of a waltz.

My Illness ✒

DURING THE WINTER epidemics of scarlet fever and diphtheria, my aunt always attached a small bag containing garlic to the crosses we wore round our necks; this was considered to be an amulet, protecting the wearer against infection.

Alas, neither the Kiev-blue, enamel cross nor the amulet sufficed to protect me.

It required an imemnse effort to get home and I was sick in the hall as I tore off my heavy satchel and my still-heavier, almost leaden, overcoat. While I was being undressed and put to bed, I lost consciousness several times. My throat was very swollen and painful and I was running a high temperature.

On the whole, I enjoyed being ill when it was only a minor indisposition. I enjoyed the glass of raspberry juice on a chair by my bedside, the green lamp on Papa's table, half-covered with a book to prevent the light disturbing me, the pleasant silence, and the release from home-work and any obligation to get up early next morning. One could just day-dream and be a little capricious.

"Give me this . . . bring me the other . . . tell Zhenka not to make such a clatter with his bricks . . . I'd like a ham sandwich . . . couldn't you read me some Jules Verne?"

It was a real bed of roses!

But this was quite different, a depressing, grim silence, sickness, a heavy sleep—half dream, half reality, and the alarming shine of the thermometer as the quicksilver rose to the very top: "Forty-one and two-tenths." Papa's voice trembled as he took my temperature, the cool hand he had pressed carefully to my forehead was snatched away as from a red-hot stove, thunderclaps seemed to come from his starched cuffs: every noise was magnified a hundredfold. I moaned without any pretence.

"He's on fire!" Papa murmured in despair.

Whenever I heard Papa pronounce this sentence, which he did frequently, I experienced such a tug at my heart-strings, such a feeling of helplessness, that I was even more frightened than before.

After this everything proceeded as it always did when an illness was at all serious: the tedious wait for the doctor, the series of short, loud, urgent rings from the bell in the hall, the doctor's sinister-looking frock-coat, the even more sinister-looking leather bag, gold spectacles, gold watch, gold chain, and gold cuff-links; the silver spoon handed to him on a clean towel, taken out of the chest of drawers, and its cold handle pressed mercilessly down onto my extended tongue, thickly coated with white; the probing of the swollen glands under my ears, the insertion of some instrument into the depths of my inflamed throat, the examination of my chest and back, and, finally, the few horrid words that penetrated my clouded consciousness: "A typical scarlet-fever rash."

I almost fainted.

"Disinfection, complete isolation."

I presented a danger to all who surrounded me. My aunt, hurriedly packing a few necessities into a hold-all, left at once in a cab with my brother Zhenia to stay with friends. Papa and the cook remained behind to look after me.

Need I describe my scarlet fever, the doctor's daily visits, the pills, the lotions, the powders in their neat, white envelopes, the strong, very expensive salty meat broth, introduced into my throat through a tube, and the nightmarish nights, with the flickering flame of an icon-lamp, casting its light on Papa's motionless figure sitting by my bed?

There was, too, the painful sensation of heaviness in my wrists, as though they were continually growing bigger and bigger, becoming the size of pillows; heavy as lead and at the same time light as air, huge as the universe, then as small as a pin's head, even smaller still, diminishing the whole time, turning into nothing.

This dual sensation, of a micro and macro world, a universe and a pin's head, my wrist at one and the same time incredibly heavy and even more incredibly light, as weightless as an astral body, turned my slumber into a long torture. My fevered imagination transformed the folds of my counterpane and the crumpled sheet into precipices and crests of the Carpathian Mountains, along which rode a man with a dead child on the saddle behind him, and a dead woman lay in front of me in her open coffin, stretching her lily-white hands out to me lovingly; dead, with her eyes closed, yet alive at the same time, with a strange smile on her face that drove me crazy. And my soul seemed to come to life in the guise of a transparent cloud, rising above a blue flame, and a sorcerer tortured it, separating it from my body with his serpent-like glance and refusing to let it return, while the glass with the raspberry juice flamed beside me on the Viennese chair, like Patagonia, and everything around was flooded by the red glow of an erupting volcano, down the slopes of which flowed streams of glittering lava, but these streams were also icebergs from Yucatán or possibly the North Pole, and one iceberg suddenly flared up in the centre, bathing everything in an unimaginable polar light, and the figure of death in a white shroud slowly appeared through the dense blue ice, with a scythe in its bony hand.

It stared straight into my soul through its empty eye-holes, and I ran away from it, swimming across ice-fields, climbing among the ice-covered shrouds of an unmanned ship, battling against ice-floes, sinking beneath the huge blocks of ice that clicked and gurgled in the rubber ice-bag that lay on my forehead, drowning helplessly on a hot, crushed pillow; and all I wanted was to turn that pillow over onto the cool side, to find some way at last of protecting myself from the shivering that was overcoming me, while Papa, in his underclothes, knelt before the lamp-lit icon of the Saviour, making the sign of the cross, and bending forward to touch the shabby carpet with his dishevelled head, as he begged God for my life.

This was the crisis.

An objective observer might have though that I was dying or already dead. But I was aware that I was alive and had much longer to live: in my innermost consciousness, I sensed that my recovery had begun.

Oh, how long that recovery took, how long before my temperature fell; then, suddenly one morning, without rhyme or reason, it fell not only to normal but well below, and I dropped off to sleep in a cool sweat. From then on, the mysterious visions of my illness were dispelled and everything around me become commonplace as before. I could see the familiar, everyday objects, smell the familiar smells (grilled cutlets), and breathe the familiar air, while, outside the window, the protracted winter continued, the same winter in which my illness had struck me down.

The doctor's visits became more strung out. During the final one, he had prescribed for me a daily glass of good, foreign port, or, as he had said in his low, fruity bass voice, half closing his eyes with pleasure: "Oporto."

Papa, a convinced teetotaler, intolerant of all kinds of alcohol, even including Bavarian beer; Papa, aghast at the idea of wine entering our house, grew pale and his lips trembled at the mention of the word "Oporto." But the doctor, with a gentle smile, convinced him that a small glass of good port would assist my recovery and restore my strength, sapped by the onslaught of scarlet fever. So Papa finally agreed to the Oporto, though his consent sounded like an involuntary concession, dragged out of him under duress.

"Very well," he said. "Although I am against alcoholic drinks in principle, if it is vital for my boy's recovery—let it be so."

And he sighed heavily, sending a sidelong glance towards the Saviour's icon, as if calling on Him to witness that his submission had been from necessity.

I ate boiled rice, with butter and biscuits, chicken cutlets and cranberry juice, shaking out the crumbs that collected between the folds of my sheets under my emaciated, limp, clumsy body with a taxing physical effort. From where I lay, I was aware of the apartment, so empty that the silence seemed to ring in my ears, and could see the farewell rays of the wintry sun, before the advent of spring, first striking diagonally through the crack in the door, then penetrating the whole room, where the slow, delectable process of my recovery was taking place, and suddenly bathing the glass of Oporto in an amber light; the Oporto bought by Papa in the Krapinin wine-shop for two roubles, fifty kopecks, in a bottle with a foreign label and a green metallic top to the long Portuguese cork wrapped in thin, pale-pink paper.

Papa poured the Oporto into my glass with much the same expression as he would have had if he had been pouring poison, but the smell of the liquid mingled divinely with that of my medicine as it spread through the room. Oh, how deliciously my weak head swam from my first hesitant gulp of the strong, sweet wine, which seemed to evaporate off the tongue, restoring my strength and speeding my recovery!

Stars through the Ventilator

ACTUALLY, I had already completely recovered: the peeling period was over. But I continued to remain in bed, permitted now and then to go to the bathroom in my underclothes with an overcoat over my shoulders and my shoes unlaced, or to stand for a few minutes in front of the frosted window.

I awaited the evening with impatience and languished as before a lover's meeting. That, in fact, was what it was. A school-girl, whom I did not even know very well, having heard of my illness, suddenly began to write letters to me, sentimental letters in her still unformed, almost childish handwriting, with each individual letter carefully drawn and without faults in grammar. She would enclose a ribbon or a picture with the letter or spray scent on the note-paper, which made it smell as though she had crushed violets into the envelope and caused some of the writing to run as if from her tears.

And I would reply.

Finally, we fell in love, and the postman's short, sharp ring at four o'clock caused me to tremble with anticipation.

"A letter for you," Papa would say with a smile and toss on my counterpane an icy envelope that spread the fresh aroma of apple-glue through the room.

She confirmed the time for our meeting, which involved the two of us looking up at the stars through the round ventilator in our respective windows on the dot of eight and thinking tenderly of each other. Next day, we exchanged letters in which we described our feelings on gazing simultaneously at the same stars, it being understood that we should both concentrate our attention on the constellation Cassiopea, which looks like a W. Having read the letter over several times and smelled it carefully, I put it under my pillow: then began the tedious wait for eight o'clock to come round, the four intervening hours presenting a vacuum that nothing could fill.

The sun sank very slowly towards the horizon and I followed its yellow rays in our empty, silent apartment, in which the drops of water, dripping regularly and monotonously from the kitchen-tap into the sink, seemed to make the already almost imperceptible passage of time even longer. Twilight was nearing and I could hear Papa's light steps as he approached the piano and opened the lid, the rustle of pages as he leafed through the score, and the screech from the piano-stool as he adjusted its height. Carefully scanning the notes, Papa slowly began to play Tchaikovsky's "Four Seasons," Mamma's favourite piece. I sensed that, as he played it, Papa was thinking about her, about his love for her, and that his myopic eyes, concentrating on the score or the keys, were reddening and becoming filled with tears. Listening to the music, I could clearly see the Russian winter and hear the bells of a speeding troika. I conjured up pictures of the beach and the long waves, delicate as lace, almost touching my feet. I walked along a damp garden-path, swept by the wind, and yellow leaves, torn from the black branches, whirled

above me and fell on the wet benches. All this moved me unspeak-
ably—even the words "By the Fireplace"—and filled my heart with
such love, such tenderness, and such despair that I hid my face in my
pillow and wept, feeling the coolness of the pillow-slip under my
tear-stained cheek.

I liked "White Nights" the best. Papa played it poetically with
heartfelt emotion, and I could see the suburbs of a St. Petersburg,
which I had never really seen, and for some unknown reason the
still waters of the Obvodni canal, in which, amidst untrimmed
hedges and factory chimneys, the dawn, immeasurable in time and
space, flames but is never consumed, is reflected but is never done
justice; and I could sense the frightening loneliness and the icy
breath from the Ladoga and a presentiment of great events, which
I would one day be destined to witness, and the silence and freshness of the May, sung by the poet Fet, preceding those events, which
might lead to bloodshed, and the purity of the May eventually coming to us—from somewhere, from "the realm of storms and snow"
perhaps.

> "Oh what a night! Its softness all pervading
> My thanks to you, my native, hallowed land
> The realm of storms and snow,
> But swiftly they are fading
> And May is here, I touch it with my hand."

Our apartment gradually darkens and, as night begins to fall, a
slight frost settles on the window-panes and a mysterious, white
pattern of fern and palm-trees reappears; a new electric lamp under
a green lamp-shade lights up on Papa's desk, with the malachite
writing-set, the carved edges and the reams and reams of pupils'
exercises; and, in the dining-room, the clock on the wall begins to
croak, there is a sudden click, and finally we hear the musical spring
strike.

Eight!

By the fourth stroke, I am already standing, wrapped in my eider-
down, on the window-sill, and my heart is pounding as I open the
ventilator. I am afraid, terribly afraid, that the sky will be covered
in clouds. But, no, it is not. What happiness! The night is frosty
and clear and, above the roof opposite ours, the five stars of Cas-

siopea shine in the dark sky. I gaze at the familiar constellation with an unnatural tenseness in my heart and at the same time try to evoke "her" to myself; see her taking off her shoes, climbing in grey woollen stockings onto the cold window-sill, passionately dilating the nostrils of her short, pretty nose, as she breathes in the frosty air as deeply as she can, and opening wide her large, blue, languishing eyes. She looks at "our" stars, hanging in a slant over the roof of the diocesan college opposite their house. She has a round, tender face, half-open, full, slightly cracked, pink lips, tight sleeves, and a firm, still-childish but already developed bust, nicely outlined beneath her everyday dark-green woollen uniform, without the apron. I can clearly see the two press-buttons behind her high collar, edged with a thin line of lace.

Their clock is also striking eight, and she, too, gazing at the stars, must be trying hard to see me as I am; but I cannot imagine in what form she conjures me up. Is it possible that she can envisage me with my hair grown long down my neck, wrapped in an eider-down, with unlaced shoes on my bare feet, and a pale, gaunt face, wearing a very silly, passionate smile?

The clock stops striking eight and, with immense satisfaction, as though I have carried out a very important, very pleasant, loving duty, I close the ventilator, in the dark glass of which, as it resolves, flies past the frosty, slightly lurching reflection of Cassiopea, "our" constellation.

Fishing

I WOULD BE INCLINED to call this time of year in our town the season of bamboo fishing-rods. The town is sweltering under a summer sun. Fishermen in straw hats and tussor jackets carry their bamboo rods to the sea. There is not sufficient room for the rods inside the tram-cars: they are transported on the outside platforms, protruding from them in dozens, their slender, but remarkably solid, flexible tops brushing against the transparent green of fading acacia-trees.

The rods are equipped with all the necessary accessories; the half-blue, half-red narrow cork floats, the lead plummets, and steel hooks;

various thicknesses of line in coils are attached to the butts, now red-hot from the sun.

A good bamboo rod costs a lot of money: to own a real bamboo rod, canary-coloured, strong, light, and long, presents much the same unrealisable dream as the possession of roller-skates, a monte-cristo gun, or a second-hand bicycle. There cannot, of course, be any question of buying a new one.

Ah, how I envied the lucky owners of big, medium-sized, or even small bamboo rods that bend resiliently over the green sea-waves from the rocks, the bathing bridges, the piles, the break-waters, and the cement coffer-dams, scattered about the shore in Langeron, or are dangled from scows, riding at "anchor," the anchor consisting of a stone, which has broken off one of the chalky rocks, attached to the end of a rope.

How excited I was watching the blue-red floats, topped by goose-feathers, bobbing about gently and alluringly on the crest of the steel-grey waves!

But, most of all, I envied the very rich fishermen, who could afford the cost of an "eccentric" and catch mackerel from a scow, scudding under sail across our bay.

An "eccentric" was a sort of artificial, metal fish, with hooks, dec-orated with feathers, inserted in its sides. A skillful fisherman was able to manoeuvre it at the end of his strong rod with great dexterity, sometimes drawing the line in, with the bamboo bending into an arc, sometimes letting it out again, so that the bait leaped and plunged among the frothy waves behind the boat. The mackerel, avidly pursuing it, would rise almost out of the water to snap at it with its narrow mouth and would suddenly, silvery-blue in the dazzling sunlight, find itself impaled on one of the hooks.

With a moderate wind in the right quarter, the whole sea between Dofinovka and the harbour lighthouse was filled with the half-dark, half-white billowing sails of the "eccentrics'" scows, while their flat bottoms, tarred to a uniform black, slapped down on the choppy waves and threw up sparkling sprays.

On these days the market was full of mackerel: they were being grilled in all the houses and even beside them in the garden on kerosene stoves, placed on benches in the shade of acacia-trees. The smoke of mackerel, grilled in olive oil, drifted down the whole street.

I had neither a bamboo rod nor pretty floats, no plummets bought in a shop, and certainly no scow with a half-dark sail, filled by the morning breeze. I had to catch bullheads amateurishly, without a rod, by dropping a transparent fishing-line, with a self-made plummet and a cheap hook, into deep water off a rock. Below the slimy water, in a jungle of brown and dark-green reeds, with an occasional sandy clearing between them, the bullheads drifted warily, ready to dart to safety between the cracks of submerged stones at the slightest noise.

Before trying to catch one, one had to collect shrimps to serve as bait. Tearing off my trousers and pulling my shirt up above my navel, I walked into the warm sea-water, searching for them. They were hard to find and trap, being almost transparent and exceedingly timid. How did one set about it? It was difficult to do it alone, but one could always find a helper. All one had to do was to summon a little bather, his brown, close-cropped hair bleached by the sun, his body tanned from head to foot, leaving only the soles of his feet pink and his tummy tied round tightly with a rag. (In some families, this treatment of the stomach was considered economical, since the appetite decreased, less was eaten, and the stomach did not expand.)

We walked together side by side, holding my handkerchief by the edges and trying to bring it stealthily under a shoal of shrimps. Hardly daring to breathe, and avoiding any brusque movement, even when our feet trod on a slippery stone, a splinter or a piece of bottle-glass, polished by the restless movement of the surf, we went searching for our nervous prey. When, at last, we caught some, we climbed up the rock, porous, prickly, and red-hot from the sun.

The shrimps fidgeted in the handkerchief, which was dripping with water that evaporated almost instantly on the scorching stone. There was something galvanic in the convulsive movements of those poor prisoners confined in the knotted handkerchief—they crackled as though they were made of steel, and their feelers pierced the material. But we were merciless. We tore off their necks and stuck them on the hook of the self-made fishing-line.

The plummet was carefully dropped into the water, the thin line slipping through one's fingers till the plummet touched bottom, with the baited hook suspended a short way above it. Now we had to wait, with our eyes glued to the submerged realm, the dark, slimy, fairy-tale jungle, where reeds grew in profusion, shells glinted with a mother-of-pearl sheen, and sudden small sand-storms arose as a crab moved sideways to its bed, like the hand of a pianist running up the keys. As the sand-storms subsided, all was silent again, and the underwater kingdom dropped off into light, uneasy slumber. Then, out of a crack, overgrown with slippery, velvety grass, there emerged a big, large-headed bullhead with a rapacious snout, bared teeth, and greedy, protruding merchant's eyes.

Oh, how wonderful he was with his feathers spread out like a fan, the top crest swaying from side to side, the tail revealed in all its beauty and the gills gulping in oxygen avidly. Its shadow moved jerkily along the uneven bottom of the sea, on which the silvery wavering ripple on the surface is reflected by the sun.

The bullhead sees the shrimp's neck, which exhales a delicious, alluring smell. It does not snap at it at once, but circles round it, examining it from all sides. It probably suspects some treachery, senses danger, but it cannot overcome its coarse greed. It approaches the shrimp's neck very gingerly at first and touches it almost imperceptibly with its muzzle, which does in fact resemble that of a bull. This movement travels up the line, as though it were a telegraph-wire, to my fingers, and I experience a slight impulse through my whole body, a sensation of suddenly being linked with another living entity quivering somewhere deep, below, in the green twilight of the submarine world. It requires a considerable exercise of willpower on my part to prevent myself from pulling up the string right away. The telegraph link between me and the large-headed fish continues up the line: it has now become something like a transmission in Morse:

Dot . . . dash . . . dot . . . dash . . . dash . . . dot.

The bullhead is suspicious, still sensing some mysterious, indefinable danger: it receives no answer from above to his telegraphic questions. . . . At last, my silence lulls its vigilance to sleep, it is reassured, convinced that I do not exist at all, that I am the figment of his momentarily religious imagination—there is no danger—there is no God, it can seize the delicious piece in its rapacious mouth, with its protruding jaw. My fingers feel the strong, persistent pressure on the line. . . . Ah, now he is mine!

With a sharp pull, I hook the bullhead and drag it upwards, feeling its speckled body, so beautifully feathered, jerk and wriggle in the mysterious depth. I picture the hook—that perfidiously curved, three-dimensional weapon—embedded in its jaw, its mother-of-pearl cheek, and the valves in its gills convulsively opening and shutting. Then it appears above the surface. It is hanging from the hook, unable to release itself from the jutting prong.

I drag it out onto the rock. Wriggling a little, it hangs helplessly in the air, in surroundings that are hostile, unfamiliar, and incomprehensible. Water drips from it as from a painter's brush. Where have they gone; what has happened to the beautiful feathers, like those of the Samurai's, and his fan-like tail? All that remains is the huge head with convulsively breathing gills, the thin gristle of the lower jaw, the protruding eyes, and a pathetic little brush for a tail.

I clasp in my fist its slippery body, in the centre of which the little heart is still beating desperately, spasmodically. Mercilessly, I pull the hook out of the mother-of-pearl cheek and, piercing both bleeding gills with a stick, add the bullhead to the string on which a few other bullheads are already hanging, as though asleep, with the brushes of their tails stuck together.

At that hot, pre-sunset hour, fishermen congregated and walked about the town on their return from the sea, with their rods and pails and long bamboo poles with bunches of bullheads suspended from them. The bullheads are sandy-coloured, with dark spots.

I, too, carried my small bamboo with only some five or six little bullheads, covered with sand and white, flour-like dust from the road, hanging from it. I was sorry for them, particularly for their drooping, shrunken tails, from which the water had stopped dripping.

"Dear God!" I thought then (or is it, perhaps, now?). "Is it possible that somebody holds me, too, in his huge hand, like a small, worthless bullhead, clutching me so tight in his invisible fist, that my heart flutters, shrinks, and dies through every moment?"

Real fishing was something quite different.

The huge sandy spit lay between the estuary and the sea, beyond Akkerman, beyond Shabo, beyond the village Budaki, close to the frontier-line. There was a small barracks with a flag-pole for the frontier-guards, who would suddenly emerge, their rifles slung across their shoulders, and march in twos along the edge of the high, precipitous cliffs through an aromatic field of immortelles, as the day slowly drew to a close and, in the background, the first half-circle of a full moon appeared above the misty line of the horizon, as yet only a rosy pink but soon to burst into a fiery crimson and cast long shadows of the field-grass on to the dusty path.

On the sandy spit one could see the fishermen's bamboo huts and large, black, tarred boats, lying on their sides, their raised bows and sterns making them look like Indian pirogues. They had nothing in common with the light Odessan flat-bottomed craft; they were the real, serious fishermen's vessels from the Danube delta, or, as we called it, the "Danube throat." Perhaps my ancestors, the Zaporozhzi, had crossed the Black Sea to make raids on the Turkish coast and even reached Constantinople in such vessels?

It required a considerable effort for the fishermen to launch their heavy boats, dragging them over the sand, the shells, and the dried froth that lay on the edge of the surf.

The long, black boat drew the sweep-net, piled up on the shore, far out to sea, and sparkles from the moon flashed under the oars, as though towards the horizon fire was being struck from a flint, and then threw the contents of the sweep-net into the water. The net sank slowly to the bottom, its mouth attached to a tarred barrel, bobbing about on top of the waves. After the fishing-boat was dragged laboriously up onto the beach, the slow, exciting process of bringing in the catch began. As the moon grew smaller and a more vivid blue, the fishermen, standing on each side of the net in Indian file, hauled it into shallow water and then onto the shore. Below a thin layer of slime appeared a few starfish and needle-fish and a sea-horse, to be followed by crabs and the more lucrative part of the catch. These steadily increased in number, still jerking feebly in the mud. Here and there, an occasional fish glinted silver on the surface. The edges of the net drew together, enclosed in a tight ring. It emerged from under the water, crammed with fish, and was brought back to the shore, seething with its quivering, flapping catch. The moon, paling as it reached its zenith, bathed the cold, sandy spit, the estuary, whence came the putrid smell of filth mingling with the tang of salt-water, the cliffs overgrown with wormwood, the wild olive-trees, and it seemed to me that I was seeing in the moonlight the Badzhak steppe, the towers of an ancient Turkish fortress, gypsy bonfires and carts, a young curly-headed Rushkin, Zamphira's* eyes reflecting the silvery moonbeams, and Aleko with a glinting knife in his hand, and it evoked tormenting dreams of living somewhere quite close "in ragged tents" where "fatal passions powerless to turn

* In Pushkin's poem "Aleko." *Translator's note.*

the course of destiny abounded"—all this under a tiny moon, no larger than a sixpence, which peered down over the hedges and vineyards of Badzhak, through a light, summery cloud, like a fish's eye.

Late at night, I returned to our attic, transformed into a room for summer residents which we hired for the whole summer from a German colonist. Through the windows cut in the mansard roof, one could see the dark shapes of fruit-trees and a distant field, quite white in the moonlight. Zhenka was sleeping on his camp-bed. Papa was reading Leskov by the light of a candle under a ball-glass. It was a hot night and Papa had unbuttoned the collar of his embroidered Russian shirt. I pervaded the whole attic with the smell of salt and fresh fish. On my bare feet glistened silvery fish-scales. I went up to the wooden table where some sour milk had been left for me. Papa was a follower of Mechnikov and made us eat sour milk at night. A large dish of it stood there, covered by an old, yellowing sheet of paper. I took off the paper and sprinkled on some sugar, which first went yellow and then began to dissolve and sink into the sour milk. I ate the delicious cold food with relish from a big silver spoon with Mother's initials on it. The silver spoon and the sour milk and the distant steppe beyond the window and a part of Papa's linen shirt were all bathed in the beautiful bright but soft moonlight which illuminated the world and made the sea, invisible from our attic, shine dazzlingly.

Rough Version of a Poem ✒

My freckled English girl
(Your knees all bruises, barley-like your brows)
I still remember you, your sailor-suit and all
Your red hair coiled like fancy loaves around your ears.
You were eleven, with no nurse to guard you,
A brigand in a skirt, a cossack Robinson.
Do you recall a goat, that, tethered to a tree,
Grazed in a field all day, and those rough boys
Who threw a football at her just to tease her?

In prickly bushes there were myriad of berries
Like coral drops, concealed among the green.
You seized the ball, both light and hard it was
You held it in your hands, like Salome the head.
You also held a melon—both tail and gristle,
And laughed just like a princess of old days.
I was then strong and tanned—a shaggy-haired Jakanahan
And kept a diary, faithful as Pechorin*
This was your childhood's first deep-felt romance.
So many days have past, sad, crippled days,
Propped on the crutches of our casual trysts
In whirlwinds of fresh snow or by the lilac boughs
But overhead the same symbol: sword
And in the night the eyeless Negro waited
A comet in his hand, to strike the stage
And lift our love—in comical disguise, in curled wig.
Both wine and blood—a cursed heritage
The truth that destiny has left us is no more
Than a goat's tragedy to you—the dregs of filthy wine to me . . .
So, dance for me again, this time for me alone . . .
But oh, the childhood's ball, bounced on the stage,
Sounds empty, hollow as it strikes the boards . . .

The Dolphin 🐟

AFTER A VIOLENT STORM, during which huge hillocks and mountains
of dark brown waves, smelling of iodine and brimstone as though
torn from the bottom-most depths of the sea, hurled themselves
against the cliffs at the speed of an express train, with a thunder-like
gunfire that eched through the misty air for miles around—there was
suddenly a dead calm. A hot sun came out on the now calm, still
surface of the sea, as though nothing had happened, and we saw the
body of a dead dolphin lying on the smooth, unmarked sand.

He belonged to no-one.

* A hero of the poet Lermontov. *Translator's note.*

We saw him first and so, according to all laws, he became our property. We walked round him, admiring the strong, seemingly moulded, heavy body, covered with a black, glistening skin, the triangular flipper on the back, the beautifully shaped tail, the long mouth, more like a beak or a jaw, with strong, sharp, dog's teeth, and the passive, prominent eyes, which now reflected nothing.

He looked quite well and healthy, only he was motionless: something was missing. What was it? Life? Yes, of course, it was life that was missing. But what was life? That we did not know.

At first we decided, since he was a joint discovery, to divide him fairly, exactly, in half. But then we changed our minds. We were friends, so let the dolphin be considered as our joint property. But what would we do with him?

We were at that age when boys collect butterflies and beetles and herbaria, keeping them in formalin in tins together with sea-horses, sea-needles, small sterlets, crabs, jelly-fish, and scolopendra, as if seeking to defy death itself and its destructive power, and give eternity, protected from decay, to the beauty of the animal and vegetable world, spread before us in such abundance and variety of shape and colour.

But alas! Even when drugged with ether, butterflies soon began to disintegrate, filling our room in the attic with a heavy stink. It was hard to believe that such a smell could be exuded by the lovely, almost weightless bodies and the elegant, spread-out wings of red admirals and cabbage whites. The smell of formalin, mixed with that of the dried plants of the herbarium which left yellow stains on the paper beneath them, resembled the mouldy smell of old, leather-bound books, nibbled by rats.

Everywhere, death triumphed over life.

Nevertheless, we could not surrender such a big, beautiful, valuable thing as a dolphin into the hands of death. None of our friends had ever possessed such a treasure! It occurred to us to stuff our dolphin: it seemed a very simple task. All we had to do was pull off the skin, fill it with straw or, better still, with cotton wool, saturated in formalin, and we would have a beautiful stuffed animal, which could be sold, or if the worst came to the worst, donated to a museum. We could already visualise a metal plaque, inscribed with our names as the donors.

We ran back to the house to fetch some knives and got to work.

But the dolphin's skin turned out to be so thick, so impenetrable, so firmly glued to the body, that our poor table-knives scarcely left as much as a scratch on the surface. We ran back again to fetch other knives, sharp, kitchen ones, but these, too, proved incapable of dealing with the dolphin's skin. We tried to turn him on his back and open up his stomach, but the animal proved to be as heavy as a concrete block, and we were unable even to shift him an inch. After making a few more attempts and breaking one of the knives, we decided to abandon the idea of stuffing him and simply cut off his beautiful blue-black tail, which reminded one of a huge fan; or, *in extremis*, cut off his black flipper and put it in a jam-jar filled with spirits. Alas, it was as impossible to cut off the flipper as it would have been if it had been made of burnished steel, and the tail was just as bad.

Sweating from our efforts, we took a quiet bathe, lay for a while on the sand, and decided to limit our ambitions to a collar of the dolphin's teeth: it would be pretty, original, and require much less skill. We went up to the house once more to fetch pliers, but, try as we might, the dolphin's teeth would not yield to them. We got hold of some blacksmith's tongs, but they were of no use, either: we did not succeed in shaking a single tooth. The dolphin lay in front of us, still unblemished, his sharp, glassy eyes reflecting nothing but the white star of the midnight sun.

Perhaps we must just cut out the dolphin's eyes and preserve them in a jar with formalin? One eye for Zhenka, one for me. We embarked on the gruesome operation, using every possible instrument. Nothing came of it! We did not even pierce the eye when a sharp knife accidentally slipped from the dolphin's skin and landed in his pupil. The dolphin's eye proved to be as hard as a precious stone—a topaz, a beryl, or an agate.

Then, our patience at an end, we began to hit the dolphin with hammers, tried in some way or other to shred his skin with knives, hit his head, hard as rubber, with smooth sea-pebbles. . . . Useless! On the dolphin's skin there remained only a few, hardly distinguishable scratches.

Then Zhenka and I bathed again and, quite exhausted, rested once more on the sand—not my little brother, Zhenka, but my friend, the son of the German visitor, whose attic we hired for the summer: from it, there was a splendid view onto the vineyards, the maize-fields, and the black-blue clouds that brought sudden storms with hail and lightning. (They usually swept in from the sea over the steppe.) Zhenka had kind, weak, bright eyes that were always red as though he had trachoma; he was an excellent friend and I could not have found a better companion for the dolphin. But what could we do if the dolphin proved to be so unco-operative? We fussed around him till the moon came up and achieved nothing.

Next morning, when we came down to have a look at our dolphin, we saw clouds of metallic-green flies crawling on his skin and eyes and swarming round him with a nasty buzzing.

We left him hurriedly.

And, the morning after that, the dolphin was no longer there. He had probably been swept away by a wave, because a new bout of storms had begun coming to us from the Anatoli coast of Turkey, perhaps even from Trapesund.

A Storm at Sea 🖋

HE DISAPPEARED for twenty-four hours, and when he turned up again late at night, without cap or belt, his hair matted and his school-uniform very crumpled, he had obviously had a soaking and was not yet dry.

He stubbornly refused to answer any questions and there was a timid but at the same time proud smile on his bluish lips, while his brown eyes held the expression of bewildered, numb fear that is seen in the eyes of men who have faced death. It was only years after that he told me what had happened to him.

There were three of them, all young school friends, who managed to amass one rouble, fifty kopecks and hired an old fisherman's boat with a sail, a keel made of planks, and a stone attached to the end of a rope instead of an anchor.

At first they had merely intended to take a little cruise but, finding themselves well out to sea, suddenly decided, with the impulsiveness of twelve-year-olds, to make the voyage to Ochakov and back, actually only a few hundred versts, but, to them, a prodigious feat, and if the ambition to achieve an adventure of this kind is

A MOSAIC OF LIFE

liable to turn a grown man crazy, how much more so a young boy.

Suddenly, as often occurs in the Black Sea, somewhere off Dofinovka, they ran into one of these terrible tornadoes that come down from the north-east and transform the sea into a boiling cauldron, in which huge waves, constantly changing direction, collide with each other and fill the air with a hellish din and flying wisps of grey foam. I had never been fated to witness such a phenomenon in the open sea. I am telling this story as I heard it from my brother, not so much in his own words as from the impression I derived from the look in his eyes, which had undergone a change since the experience, maturing him and giving him an air of knowing something he alone would ever know, as though his whole future destiny had been decided during the squall.

The boat's rudder was broken and the sail rent in two. There were no oars. They were driven wherever the storm willed, now plunging down between two watery hills, now soaring up again and nearly overturning: they shipped water over the bows, stern, and sides till the old tub, with its creaking boards, was within an ace of foundering. The bailer and the flask of fresh water floated elusively about in the bilge.

It was pouring with rain and the wind tore at their soaking clothes: nothing could be seen through the surrounding grey. Night was already falling, but before darkness entirely enveloped them, a pink reflection suddenly appeared in the milky sky, high above the racing herd of waves: somewhere behind the clouds the sun was setting.

The boys believed that the hurricane had come to an end, but they were mistaken: the pink sunset was quickly extinguished by black clouds and night finally descended, even more frightening than the stormy day. The boys had swallowed a lot of salt-water and were sick. The boat appeared to be on the point of sinking at any moment. They were exhausted by bailing out the water with the black, wooden scoop, a pail riddled with holes, their school-caps, and even with their hands. Almost unconscious from seasickness and the violent tossing, they yelled and screamed as loud as they could into the darkness of the night, with no hope of anyone hearing their desperate cries for help.

In despair they began to pray to God, but apparently God had no wish or was unable to help them. During the night, for a short time, the clouds were split apart and through them flickered a misty, dying moon. Its face, pale as that of a corpse, gave a slight, silvery glimmer to the waves, but then the night enveloped them again, seemingly endless and more awe-inspiring than before.

Suddenly, they saw light: not far away, a small passenger-ship from Nikolaev was pitching and tossing in the tempestuous waves. The boys began to scream: "Ship ahoy! Save us! We're in trouble!"

Their voices were so hoarse their screams emerged as whispers.

The ship passed them by, without noticing them.

Then one of the boys remembered that he had brought with him a small lady's revolver. Clinging to the shroud, half-suspended over the surging depths, he began senselessly firing into the air until his ammunition was exhausted. With the storm at its height, the shots were almost inaudible: only minute tongues of flame flew out of the muzzle.

The ship's bright lights faded away into the darkness.

A squall broke the mast and it now dragged behind the stern, attached by the few remaining shrouds. There was no more hope: the night seemed to go on and on forever. But at dawn they were saved. I no longer remember by whom or how: it was probably by Dofinovka fishermen.

I cannot forget my brother Zhenka's agate-brown eyes, lilac lips, and drooping shoulders of a doomed man as he told me this story.

From that day, he was condemned to failure and was pursued by bad luck. Death followed in his footsteps. He swallowed too much sulphurated hydrogen in the school laboratory and was only just resuscitated in the fresh air on the lawn of the school garden, under a black pine-tree. In Milan, near the famous cathedral, he was knocked down by a cyclist and almost fell under an oncoming car. During the Finnish war, a missile fell on the corner of the house where he was spending the night. Near Moscow, he came under fire from the German rockets. At that time, too, on the Volokolamsk road, he crushed his fingers in the door of the leading, white-camouflaged MK when they were attacked by German planes and had to run from the car and take cover in a ditch.

Finally, the plane in which he flew from besieged Sebastopol crashed in the boundless Don steppe, while trying to evade Messerschmitts, and he remained there forever, lying to this day in a barren land to which he was a stranger.

The Toy Yacht ✍

HE MUST HAVE BEEN the son of rich parents, because only rich boys could possess such a wonderful toy yacht, the exact model of an English one, such as could be seen in our Black Sea and Ekaterinoslav yacht clubs and bore names such as *Nellie, Snow Drop* or *Mayana.*

He was carrying it on his half-bent arm and it was impossible not to stare at the perfect shape and proportions of the small ship, at the tall, slender mast, the light wooden hull, resounding like a musical instrument, the bowsprit, mainsail, and gracefully slanting triangular jibs, and, finally, the deep keep with its leaden cigar of a counterpoise. Down to the red water-line, the yacht's hull was painted a glossy snow-white: the lower part, including the keel, a delicate salad-green, which gave it, overall, an extremely elegant appearance.

The boy, in a new sailor-suit, walked proudly along the shady streets of the town, and the lacy shadows of the acacia-trees slid up and down the yacht's immaculate sails and the slightly freckled, hooked nose of her owner.

Before the boy had reached Otrada from the town centre, there was already a queue of street urchins behind him, gazing at the boat with envy and admiration and eagerly awaiting the moment of her launch. I joined the procession at its head, walking beside the rich boy and muttering appealingly from time to time: "Let me hold it! Don't be a dog in the manger!"

To which the rich boy replied: "Just look at him! What'll he want next?"

Passing through Otrada, its streets ever shadier and more blossom-filled than the others in our town, we accompanied the rich boy down the steep cliffs to the shore, where two carpenters in faded pink shirts and sackcloth trousers were building a fishing-boat. It was almost finished, and they were now nailing beautiful strips of pine-wood round the edge of the frame. Nearby, on a smouldering wood-pile, there were two smoking open cauldrons, one holding tar, the other red lead. The roughly constructed, portable joiners' bench was covered in golden shavings, which smelled of turpentine.

As we reached the water's edge, we made way for the rich boy, who reverently pushed his yacht out onto the long, crystal-clear waves. Her fresh, cool colours were reflected in the water as she scudded before the wind, her slender mast, balanced by the keel, rocking like a metronome. Compared with the stern, rocky cliffs, the yacht seemed a small, fragile, vulnerable little vessel.

But how beautiful she was!

The Hydrogen Explosion 🖋

It BECAME KNOWN that if you put a small piece of ordinary zinc into a glass vessel and poured some equally ordinary nitric acid over it, a chemical reaction set in and bubbles of hydrogen would begin to appear. If you collected that gas in a jar with a glass tube stuck through the cork, the hydrogen, being lighter than air, would rise; then, if you applied a match to it, it would burn with a long, placid flame, as was illustrated in Krajevich's thick text-book on chemistry.

The dream of producing at home by my own unaided efforts a harmless inflammable gas so captured my imagination that I could think of nothing else. I was already picturing a small dirigible, which I would build with my own hands, fill with hydrogen of my own making, and launch into the air to the astonishment of the whole street. There would be an animal—a cat or, possibly, a quiet dog— in the nacelle to give my experiment an added scientific aspect and arouse general admiration as well as surprise. How was it possible, people would ask, for such an unsatisfactory school-boy as I, who might be said to have nothing but bad marks, to perform such a brilliant scientific experiment? After this, it would clearly be a mistake to judge a pupil by his marks!

This and similar ambitious thoughts brought my impatience to boiling-point, and I decided to get down to work without any further delay.

However, the process of producing hydrogen, which, at first sight, had appeared so simple, suddenly proved to be rather more complicated, since it required materials and laboratory equipment which I was in no financial position to acquire.

Of course, the special vessel in which the nitric acid was to be poured on the zinc could be obtained easily enough by taking a tea-glass out of the cupboard, but this would scarcely be professional and would give the experiment a distressingly makeshift appearance. Only a special jar of very thin glass with a cork and a glass funnel, through which the gas would emerge, would suffice to lend my experiment the truly brilliant, scientific, academic character I was aiming at. The zinc presented no problem, as the exterior window-sills and water-pipes on nearly all the houses in our town were either made of zinc or iron covered with zinc, so that I could pick up as many fragments of it as I wanted at any building site. And this I proceeded to do. But, alas, people in the know warned me that this was not pure zinc and would be of no use at all for my experiment. What was needed was chemically pure zinc, free from any extraneous substances. Such zinc, in the shape of large grains, could be got at a chemist's, but not in every one, and more likely from an engraver; and it turned out that pure zinc cost about twenty kopecks a small packet. And I had no money at all! To make matters worse, I would also have to buy the glass jar and funnel, an India-rubber tube to pass the gas through water, and—the other basic essential—the acid. This last could only be obtained on prescription and then only by adults: children could not get hold of any however solvent they might be.

How bitterly, at that moment, I regretted that I was not yet an adult!

The fragments of zinc-covered iron, lying under my bed, provoked scornful smiles from my aunt, which affected me much more than a stern reprimand or even more serious measures.

Subduing my pride, I went to her and in an insinuating voice asked her to give me fifty kopecks.

It was a huge sum.

But my aunt showed no surprise, she merely asked suspiciously: "What for?"

"I need it very, very badly, dear Aunt," I replied, in a voice oozing bogus tenderness. "It's a secret at the moment. But later on, you'll be bound to find out. My word of honour."

"No, I won't give you a single kopeck before I know what it's for. It's no good your pestering me."

"But Aunt, dear Aunt," I whispered, falling back on my last persuasive resource. To tell you the truth, my aunt was really a kind, warm-hearted woman. But on this occasion she was implacable.

"What for?" she asked again in an icy voice.

"For a large glass jar and . . . and . . . some nitric acid," I managed to stammer.

"Nitric acid!" my aunt exclaimed in horror. "You must have gone crazy!"

"But Aunt, dear," I implored. "I have to have it. And it's very useful, too."

"Useful?" my aunt repeated scornfully.

"Yes, from a scientific point of view. For a chemical experiment." My aunt paled.

"That's all we need in this flat—experiments with nitric acid!" she exclaimed. "Certainly not! In no circumstances whatever! I refuse categorically. You understand? Categorically!" And she swept out of the room, rustling her skirt.

Well, tell me, what was there left for me to do? Only one thing! All my hopes were now centered on Petri's geographical maps. It was an excellent, thick collection of geographical maps, embracing all the countries, seas, and oceans of the world, in a hard calico binding, with metallic edges, which cost two roubles fifty to buy in a shop— an astronomic sum! Not all parents are in a position to acquire such a volume for their children: in fact, it was really beyond my father's means, but Papa had always dreamed of making an educated man of me, no matter what the cost. So he had made the effort, economized on some of his own expenses and bought me the atlas, begging me to take care of it, as if it were the apple of my eye, so that, later, it could be passed on to Zhenka, from Zhenka to his future children, and even on to their children, whereby we might all grow up into educated, intelligent adults.

And now this map provided my sole hope. At any moment, I could easily sell it to a second-hand book-shop for a rouble fifty, or, at the very worst, a rouble thirty.

I knew I was doing something despicable and mean, but I was obsessed and my conscience remained stilled by the picture of the great chemical experiment I was about to perform.

In fact, I was urged on by the desire to conquer my lack of faith in science, which I felt deep down inside of me, because, truth to tell, the transformation of zinc into hydrogen seemed to me quite incredible. I found it impossible to believe that one fine day I should apply a burning match to a glass and immediately a peaceful, harmless little tongue of pure flame would appear, so to speak, from nowhere. Yet, I did have confidence in the power of science when set out in such a convincing way as in Krajevich's text-book, with a picture of the container and the glass tube, with a long flame emerging from it, on the opposite page.

I was involved in a tormenting struggle between faith and disbelief, and the sooner I found a solution the better. I was consumed by impatience, or not so much consumed as driven mad by it, my subdued insanity, unnoticed by others, only being revealed by my staring eyes, which I caught sight of whenever I passed the mirror in the hall.

The man who was less aware than anyone of my fixed stare and bitten lips was the Jewish book-seller, who, after quickly leafing through the pages of the atlas—no doubt to make sure no maps were missing—thrust it carelessly behind the counter and brought out some silver change, amongst which two fifty-kopeck pieces with their profile of the emperor sparkled alluringly. I now had one rouble thirty in my pocket and rushed off to do my shopping. It was my lucky day. The assistant at the chemist's agreed at once to sell me nitric acid when he learned that I needed it for scientific purposes—the production of hydrogen, which, in those times, was considered quite harmless. He was also able to provide me with a packet of zinc. When he handed over these chemical ingredients, he did, however, warn me that if the hydrogen—God preserve me!—became mixed with oxygen, which was tantamount to saying the ordinary air in a room, the result was a gas which would easily explode if lit. To avoid this, he advised me to collect the hydrogen in an upturned glass funnel and wait patiently for it to expel all the air from it before lighting it. He also said that a twin-necked retort could be used in place of the funnel.

After thanking the chemist's assistant, I hurried on to the shop that sold laboratory equipment, where I was overwhelmed by the quantity of flasks, test-tubes, tripods, clamps, spirit-lamps, double-necked jars, and corks of all sizes and descriptions. I was particularly excited by the sight of retorts, like glass-stomached bubbles with mysteriously curved necks, in which, no doubt, extremely complicated products, even perhaps the elixir of life, could be distilled.

There was something medieval about these retorts, which had

been handed down to us from the workshops of alchemists in velvet caps and long, flowing robes bitten into by the various acids, with the assistance of which they produced philosopher's stones and transformed dust into pure gold.

I wanted very much to buy a retort, but it was beyond my means, and I had to be satisfied with acquiring a number of comparatively cheap test-tubes and flasks, and one cheap tripod, which I did not need at all, but which had such a scientific appearance that I was unable to resist it.

Panting with impatience like a dog, I carried all this paraphernalia home, crept up to my room like a thief by the back-door, and hid it under the bed, with a white, porcelain chamber-pot on top for additional security.

Next day, taking French leave after the second lesson, I ran home like greased lightning, relying on my family being out at that hour. The cook glanced suspiciously at my excited face when she opened the door and made some unfavourable comments, but I managed to persuade her that I had probably caught mumps. The good, credulous soul advised me to go straight to bed and drink raspberry juice.

With the cunning of a dangerous madman, I then succeeded in convincing her that it would all pass off very quickly if no-one came into my room and I was allowed to rest in peace.

First of all, I set about investing my experiment with a suitably impressive appearance. I did everything possible to make the room where all three of us—Papa, Zhenka, and I—slept on iron bedsteads look like the study of some great scientist such as Mechnikov, with his sinister face and lion's mane.

From the sitting-room, I fetched a little table covered with a much-valued, hundred-year-old, plush cloth, considered for some reason to be our apartment's finest possession, on which usually lay the family album with two spring-clasps and photographs of all our family and friends inside, inserted into oval and rectangular slots.

Tossing the album into a corner, I set the small table in the middle of the room and placed several volumes of the encyclopaedia from Papa's book-case on top of it, thereby making it conform to my image of a great scientist's writing-desk. By rights, there should have been a multitude of manuscripts as well, but as there were no manuscripts to be found in our house and my school exercise-books would have merely looked stupid as substitutes, I rolled up my class isotherm-tables, which had a reasonable resemblance to a scientist's written notes, and scattered them about beside the books. By the time I had added my laboratory equipment and an old magic lantern, the table, in my opinion, had a distinctly scientific aura about it: all it lacked now, for the picture to be perfect, was a goose-quill pen in the ink-stand. Alas, there were no goose-quills to be found in the house, either, and I even considered delaying the experiment for a short time while I climbed over Professor Starozhenko's hedge and tore a feather or two from the tail of the beautiful gander kept by his wife. But my impatience gained the upper hand and I resigned myself, not without a pang, to the absence of any goose-quills in the ink-stand, alongside the manuscripts.

I spent a few minutes admiring my writing-desk, with its row of test tubes and other laboratory equipment, then got to work.

I put a big, twin-necked jar on the plush table-cloth, in the middle of the table, and inserted the cone with the glass tube through it into one neck and tipped a few grains from my packet of zinc down the other: then, with immense care, I poured the nitric acid through the funnel. Up to the very last moment, I did not believe that hydrogen would emerge from the zinc. You can, therefore, imagine my delight and pride when I saw bubbles of gas begin to rise swiftly from the grains of zinc, soaring upwards like little beads on a chain. Then I inserted the other cork, and watched the reaction spellbound, as the magic, hissing sound from the jar reached my ears.

The miracle had happened!

The hydrogen was emerging regularly and abundantly as the nitric acid seethed and gave off a slightly putrid smell. I licked my finger, carefully placed it just above the top of the tube and felt the bubble of air expelled by the hydrogen. The experiment had succeeded beyond all my expectations. . . . Now I only had to wait about ten or fifteen minutes till all the air had been expelled and it would be pure hydrogen that came out of the tube.

I trembled with impatience to apply a lighted match to it and finally see with my own eyes the gentle, tranquil flame come into being.

The jar was rather large, and I had no definite idea of the time required for all the air to be driven out so that the hydrogen could be safely set alight.

I seemed already to have been waiting for several hours, when it was only a matter of two minutes, if that, but the real problem was that it was impossible to determine, just by looking at the jar, whether all the air had been driven out or not.

I wet my finger and pressed it to the tube several times, and, each time, a bubble came up, but I did not know whether it was hydrogen or air.

The violent reaction continued to take place in the jar, as the grains of zinc jumped about, dissolved, and exuded bubbles.

My impatience almost reduced me to a state of unconsciousness. I could wait no longer. And what exactly was I waiting for? Waiting for the hydrogen to expel the air? But how was I to distinguish them when both were colourless?

Finally, like some evil genius, impatience whispered in my ear: "Just have a try. Wet the tube and put a match to the bubble. Even if it is the explosive mixture, the explosion can only be a gentle one (the bubble is so small, after all), and if it is already pure hydrogen, there's no risk in either case. Surely you can see that?"

"No, that's not true," my instinct for self-preservation whispered back more prudently, in an effort to combat the insidious voice of impatience, but the temptation was so great that I closed my ears to the voice of reason.

Prancing with excitement, I put some saliva round the end of the tube, held my finger above it, and, when a bubble came up, struck a match and slowly brought it close to the bubble with a trembling hand. The bubble immediately exploded with a slight plop, but, alas, that was not the end. The small, almost toy-like explosion was followed by a sort of sniff and then a sinister sucking sound: I saw the flame from the match drawn like lightning through the tube into the jar, still filled with detonating gas, and there was such a violent explosion straight in front of my face that I lost consciousness, but came to almost at once to the tinkle of falling glass and the sight of poisonously yellow choking mushroom of smoke rising in what seemed to be a flaming room.

The black-and-green volumes of the encyclopaedia had been tossed about in the chaos of shattered test-tubes, charred pieces of isothermic cards, and the shapeless globe, which I had placed on the table at the last moment beside the magic lantern.

Everything around was splashed with nitric acid. I alone was safe amidst this Hiroshima, which once more confirmed my phenomenal luck, characteristic of all boys born with two cauls on their heads.

Rushing into the room with a wet rag in her hand, the cook some-how managed with rough determination to subdue the elemental, chemical storm, but when she tried to pull the famous plush cloth, wet from the stinking liquid, off the table, it proved to be burned through and through by the devilish acid. As a table-cloth, it had ceased to exist: it disintegrated in front of our eyes. As soon as the cook touched it with her coarse, resolute fingers, it fell apart into strange filaments, and these, in turn, became even stranger smoulder-ing flakes. The disappearance in front of me of such an expensive and beloved article of home luxury pierced my soul with such a belated sense of guilt and such horror that the sudden appearance of my aunt in the doorway, armed with her umbrella, copy-books under her arm and a dramatic expression in the blue eyes staring out of her pale face, was nothing in comparison.

"I knew it!" she muttered, wringing her gloved hands and letting the copy-books fall on the floor, from which a corrosive mist of nitro-gen was rising and bringing tears to our eyes.

Another Explosion 🖎

A LITTLE BOY brought a small bottle of naphtha to school. I had never seen naphtha, though I had heard a lot about it. That golden-black, chocolate-coloured liquid, from which, I knew, one could produce a variety of substances—kerosene, benzine, anilin—aroused my inter-est intensely and I was determined to get hold of it.

The boy was kind and gave me the bottle; actually, it cost him nothing, as his father was the chief engineer on a naphtha-carrying vessel. Anyway, I became the owner of a liquid that, in my eyes, was rare and very valuable. I wanted to learn all about its characteristics and obtain from it, if not benzine and kerosene, at least a little glyc-erine or *mazout*, though I was not quite certain exactly what *mazout* was.

When I got home, without even taking off my school-coat, I poured the naphtha into a test-tube, firmly rammed a cork into it to prevent anything untoward happening, and began to heat it on my laboratory spirit-lamp, which spread an exciting smell of methylated spirits about the room.

I could not stop admiring my spirit-lamp, with its cotton-wool wick, soaked in a lilac liquid, the colour of a jelly-fish, and its hinged top which enabled one instantly to put out the yellow-lilac flame that was scarcely visible by daylight.

It was all wonderful and scientific!

In my admiration for the glowing lamp, I forgot all about the naphtha, and suddenly there was the explosive sound of a popping cork, as loud as a shot from a gun, which shook the whole village of Otrada. The boiling naphtha had driven the cork out of the test-tube, and a greasy, golden-brown stream splashed on to the wall, ran down the wall-paper and, in a second, covered the three snow-white cotton, so-called "Marseilles" coverlets, which lay on top of our beds, with dark, smelly, uneradicable stains of naphtha, that substance that looked like liquid but for some reason was called a mineral, as I learned later, after the destruction of the Marseilles bed-covers.

Dippers

ONE DAY, A CADET, Zhorka Surin, joined us boys as we were playing in the street and announced, as though it were something quite ordinary, that on the floating bridges in Nikolaev one could buy a flat-bottomed river-boat, called a dipper, very cheaply from the fishermen: not a new one, of course, he explained, but an old one that had seen "better days," coarsely constructed of planks, blackened by time, and selling for the unbelievably low price of two or even one and a half roubles.

I can see that same Zhorka Surin as if it were yesterday, a small, erect figure in his uniform-trousers, well-polished boots which, however, did not bear inspection higher up, much-washed cadet shirt, held in by a leather belt with a brass plaque, cadet cap, and blue shoulder-straps: these last bore the letters "O.K.," which stood for Odessa Korpa, the academy where Zhorka studied during the winter, returning to his birth-place, Nikolaev, for the summer months.

As a rule, cadets were our primordial enemies: we hated them, and when one showed up in our street, we shouted insulting words behind his back: "Cadet, why are you so fat?"

To which the cadet always replied: "What about you and your schools, you miserable fools?"

Zhorka Surin was an exception. We liked him. He always carried a small, solid, India-rubber ball, which bounced very high, and he kept throwing it on the ground or against a wall, catching it again on the rebound in his small monkey's paw of a hand with extraordinary dexterity. When he became fed up with this game, he would drop the ball into the depths of his uniform-trousers.

I did not believe his story of being able to buy a dipper in Nikolaev for one rouble fifty at first, but he took off his cap, disclosing a white head covered with a sort of plushy down, made the sign of the cross in the direction of the Botanical Church's blue cupola, and swore that it was the truth, the holy truth: "May I be killed by lightning if I'm lying."

After that, I knew no peace. From morning till night, I thought about the boat, which only cost one rouble fifty. A plan to go to Nikolaev, buy the boat, make a mast, get hold of a sail by one means or another, proceed down the Bug to the Black Sea, and then return to Odessa under sail, to the delight and surprise of the inhabitants of Langeron, Otrada, and Small Fountain, quickly materialised. And all that for a rouble and a half!

The possibility of an old river tub being unable to stand a sea journey did not worry me at all, because one could wait for fine weather, leave the Bug estuary for the open sea when there was only the lightest of breezes, as often occurred during July, and then carefully hug the coast. The strangest thing of all was that I found nothing fantastic in the idea of embarking on such an expedition—under sail!—in an old river vessel, solely intended for transport between floating bridges; on the contrary, I was supremely confident of achieving my dream and could already visualise my triumph, in advance, though, of course, deep down in my consciousness there stirred a very small but unpleasant worm of doubt. But, as always, enthusiasm conquered reason.

It was exactly the right time for it. Papa and Zhenka had gone to the Crimea to enjoy the fascinating pleasures of a walking-tour, while I, faced with two examinations in the autumn, had to remain in town all the summer and, under my aunt's supervision, prepare myself for distressingly unpleasant ordeals in Latin and algebra. According to Papa's calculations, I should be obliged to work no less than five to six hours a day if I were to catch up on what I had failed to do in winter. I swore I would work untiringly and, of course, believed sincerely in my oath.

... A hot, southern July was approaching, the season of calm seas and gentle breezes. There was no time to lose. After a period of mental confusion, I suddenly found myself in Nikolaev, where I had arrived as a stowaway on a small steamer, accompanied by another boy, Yurka, who had dogged my footsteps, begging me to take him with me, and promising to pay a share of the costs up to one rouble. He had actually produced the silver rouble from the lining of his school-jacket and had sworn, with tears in his lying eyes, to recognize me as "the boss" and loyally obey me.

He had looked at me so pathetically, given me his word of honour so passionately, and sniffed so persuasively that I had finally agreed. In a way, I was flattered: I would at last have my own minion, as so many other older boys did—loyal, obedient, and devoted as a slave.

I believe that he adored me, regarded me as an idol, and was ready to do anything to prove his devotion. He certainly started well by readily handing over his rouble, probably acquired in some doubtful way, about which I thought it better not to question him. To this, I added my own eighty kopecks, the acquisition of which I preferred not to dwell on, either, and we then had sufficient capital to purchase the boat and all it required.

After walking through the empty southern town in the flimsy shade of young, white acacia-trees, we found Zhorka Surin in one of the little houses, whitened with bluish chalk like village huts. Barefooted, in a cotton shirt, he took us along dusty streets to his friends the Kiriakovs, who lived, as he explained, on a floating bridge.

The head of that family was an excise-man. He was sitting, dressed in a Ukrainian shirt, rolling cigarettes, which he placed in an old cigar-box, and paid no attention to us; then his son Genadi appeared, worn out by the midday heat, wearing a sailor-suit. He was a gaunt boy of my age and, as soon as he learned why we had come, offered at once to take us to the "floating bridge proper," where he could show us a fisherman's boat that the owner wanted to sell.

The fisherman was not there, but we saw the boat, lying in thick reeds. It looked like a long, black, open box, a third full of heavy, marshy water, in which a short-handled bailer was floating.

We bailed it out and Genadi began punting us with a long grey pole through the stretches of still water, between dark-green, very tall, dense walls of not yet ripened bamboo with light-green brushes on the top, where blue-eyed dragon-flies perched.

The twilight sky with pink, tender clouds was reflected in the un-rippled corridors between the floating bridges and water-spiders raced on their long thin feet across the motionless water, leaving behind them light concentric circles, which remained on the surface for a long time. Forgetting why I had come there, I sank into this unknown world of floating bridges as our boat glided on, separating from time to time the bamboo stems, sharp as swords, and rocking the floating oval petals of white water-lilies, which were already closing for the night and bobbed like little snow-white balls, with an egg-yellow stamen still showing here and there. And all this, to-gether with the falling darkness, which seemed to bring the impen-etrable banks of reeds still closer, the silence, the sweet, marshy smell of river-water, and the especially sharp aroma of cane or perhaps some nocturnal swamp-flowers, emitting a gentle, lethal poison, cast a spell on me.

Having swum to our heart's content alongside the bridges, we pushed the boat back into the reeds and returned to the Kiriakovs, without having seen the vessel's owner. We had to wait till the next day, but he did not appear even then and nobody knew where he lived. And so we remained with the Kiriakovs for several days, which now, sixty years later, I think of as a bewitching, feverish dream filled at one and the same time with languor, passion, and poetic fantasies, springing from God knows where, coupled with a loss of sense of time, so that it all seemed condensed into one endless July day—sweltering, intoxicating, and suddenly infiltrated by the clear reflections of the floating bridges. A sleepy stupor enveloped my mind, deprived me of all my will-power. I forgot everything under the sun and enjoyed the simple, meaningless happiness of my exis-tence on this earth, in much the same way, no doubt, as the gorgeous red admirals or the blue-eyed, four-winged dragon-flies, hanging on the stem of a reed and bending their tails, flexible as a string of turquoise beads, or the river-snakes, disturbed by some other crea-ture in the murky depths, gliding tortuously through the still, warm water, unaccountably enjoyed their own short lives.

Is was rather like a long, pleasant sunstroke, which deprived me of all understanding of who I was, why I was, and where I was.

The Kiriakov family accepted the presence of two strange boys in their house with patient good manners, and Mme Kiriakova only asked once, casually, in a tired voice: "Do your parents know where you are?"

Yurka, without batting an eyelid, declared that our parents had not been opposed to our making the journey to Nikolaev, had, in fact, been glad that we should broaden our horizons by visiting a town renowned for its shipyards and other attractions. It was not without a certain embarrassment that we sat down with the whole Kiriakov family to lunch, dinner, and supper; at first, we refused, swearing by all that was holy that we were not hungry, but this did not prevent us, at dinner, from gobbling up the excellent borsch and stuffed cabbage with sour cream, which Mme Kiriakova prepared so admirably with the help of her daughter. The daughter was a dull little girl, with colourless hair like flax rolled up and held by a round, celluloid comb, in the way that all the girls from the eparchial schools and orphanages wore it. Though she was far from ugly, she was so shy, silent, inconspicuous, and, above all, boring, that I hardly paid any attention to her, and in my memory she just remains a girl without a name in a cotton dress, with a habit of scratching one dusty bare foot with the equally dusty other one.

I vaguely recall her as I do those dusty-blue marsh-flowers growing in profusion among the reeds, the name of which I never knew, either, but called in my own mind "blue-eyed marshy," as they added their modest embellishment to the sweltering midday.

We slept on the terrace, where, through the wild grapevine-leaves, we could see the pale, starry sky, exhausted by the fierce heat that did not abate even at night and only softened slightly towards dawn, when, suddenly rustling the reeds, a breeze sprang up from the direction of the floating bridges; then the sky, still starry, 'twixt night and day, seemed to take on a new, mysterious, strangely unfamiliar aspect.

One of the windows of the house looked out on the terrace, the one belonging to the room in which the Kiriakov family bred silkworms. We heard them stirring indefatigably among the mulberry leaves, on which they fed in their meshed enclosures. The cocoons, when fully spun, were scalded with boiling water and kept in the bare, whitewashed room until sold to one of the silk-mills. This provided a small addition to the Kiriakovs' earnings, as did the cigarettes rolled by the head of the family, a non-smoker himself, in his spare time, and disposed of to a tobacconist. The family also kept hens, turkeys, and pigs in the yard, stained by the squashed blood-red mulberries; there were two cows as well. In short, they were exceptionally hard-working and Yurka and I felt like idlers and spongers.

However, this did not prevent us from enjoying the bewitching July days in this remote corner of the immense Russian empire, a corner that did not resemble any other. It was as though we had landed in an entirely unfamiliar country, into the delta of a fairy-tale river; a country with storks on the roofs and white lilies, completely covering the still waters by the bridges, where, in the dark, at the very roots of the reeds, grew horned water-nuts, looking like fat little devils; and the oval petals of the lilies, rocking gently above them, looked like floating palettes on which thick stars of white and chrome yellow had been squeezed out and become faintly dis-coloured by the rising, hot evaporation of the swampy waters. . . . It was long after this that I saw Claude Monet's *Nymphéas* for the first time in London.

We bathed from morning till night among the reeds, so tall that the sky above the corridors between the bridges was glimpsed only as a narrow strip of pale-blue with rare wisks of snow-white July clouds. Tearing off our clothes and naked, we swam round our black tub, in warm, almost hot water, picked lilies and dived to the bottom where the disturbed silt rose in smoky clouds and we were sur-rounded by the mysterious life of this swampy world.

The water-tigers filled us with disgust. They had only two paws, and looked as if the others had been torn off, leaving them crippled. They used these two paws as oars, were of an unpleasant, black colour and, at the slightest touch, emitted a white, stinking liquid which stuck to our fingers: try as we might, it was difficult to wash it off and rid ourselves of the nauseating smell.

There were, too, quick, sinuous water-snakes, fat tadpoles in which one could already envisage the frog—was it the eye, the jowl?—strange shells that seemed to open and shut, long sluggish worms. . . .

Punting ourselves away from the silt, we made our way to corners, surrounded on all sides by the impenetrable walls of cane, and so deserted that we felt uneasy, and this fear, this horror of isolation, this separation from everything human, gave me a sense of the bitter beatitude of an unrequited love or, at any rate, a foreboding of it. I wanted to write poems about floating bridges, reeds, white lilies, and "that dream of happiness, passionately savouring the moments, fleeting as the spellbinding fiery day," and other such nonsense.

Suddenly, the owner of the boat appeared, an ancient, barefooted man with white side-whiskers, wearing an old, brimless naval hat. He was, I learned afterwards, a hero of Sebastopol, where, as a sailor in a warship, he had seen with his own eyes the legendary Nakhimov and the famous Koshka; perhaps, too, the young artillery officer Leo Tolstoy. . . . He was led up to us by Zhorka.

"These boys want to buy your boat."

The old man looked at us with turquoise eyes from under his bushy eyebrows and asked: "How much do you offer?"

"With the pole and bailer, one rouble forty kopecks," I stammered with an effort, afraid the old man might feel hurt and want to fight.

But the Sebastopol hero agreed readily.

We gave him Yurka's rouble and two of my twenty-kopeck coins, and he hid them away in a small cloth bag, hanging beside a brass cross on a strip of rag underneath his shirt. Then he gave us both a formal, firm handshake, with a hand as hard as teak, and took himself off, puffing away at his small sailor's-pipe, blackened from smoke and bound with a copper ring.

What happened after that happened so quickly and simply that there is really nothing to tell. . . .

. . . We made a mast out of the punt-pole, stole a still-damp table-cloth that had been hung out to dry on the washing-line in the Kiriakov's yard, tied it to the mast, and, using our hands as oars, manoeuvered our tub with considerable effort out of the reeds into the pure waters of the river Bug at about the spot, I think, where it joins the river Ingool. We were still far away from the sea, which was not even in sight, but immediately we emerged from the shelter of the reeds, a gentle, warm whiff of wind overturned our craft and we were left standing up to our necks in water, watching it submerge and be swept away by the current, along with the pole and bailer.

We returned drenched from head to foot, with clusters of lilies clinging to our bodies as if we had been drowned: our legs were cut and bleeding. Yurka plodded along behind me, coughing up water, snivelling and cursing me under his breath. He grumbled the whole way back, insisting monotonously that I ought to give him back his rouble, or at least half of it. Finally, I struck him a blow on the neck, which effectively stopped his muttering but caused him to bear me a lasting grudge. The Kiriakov family came to meet us in its full complement, stern, silent, and upset by the loss of the table-cloth. That evening, Kiriakov himself put on his uniform cap and personally conducted us to the harbour, bought us deck-tickets, gave us a pound of good smoked sausage and two loaves of bread so that we should not starve, handed our tickets to the third mate, and watched us walk up the gangway. There were still twenty minutes before the ship sailed, during which Kiriakov remained, a stiff, uniformed figure on the quay-side, to make certain we did not slip ashore again. At last, the ship cast off and started on its way, but long after that we could still see Kiriakov standing motionless against the background of the pale-green evening sky, with its one lonely star and the faint, twinkling glimmer from the harbour-lights.

We waved good-bye to him with the sausage, but he did not respond. I feel certain that he did not set out for home until reassured by the sight of the ship entering the open sea.

It took me a long time to fall asleep, in my state of despondency that another dream should have fizzled into nothing, but at last I succeeded, tucked away near the engine-room, whence came a pleasant stream of hot air, impregnated with the smell of steel and oil.

. . . The swell started at dawn.

I felt that I was going to be sick, and made my way to the empty main-deck and lay down on a cold, latticed bench. Although the sea seemed almost motionless, the light-green waves, glistening in the dawn, gently rocked the frail, small ship from side to side, and my bench seemed to be transformed into a swing that slipped away from underneath me, then lifted me up again as the cold sunrise lit up a desert of water the colour of a glass bottle. For a moment or two, I would fall into a short, tormenting, listless sleep that oppressed my suddenly matured body. I fingered my nipples and found one of them swollen and painful to the touch: beside it, a thick, black, resilient, shiny hair had grown on my tanned skin. I felt a bout of nausea, not from the rolling, which I usually stood rather well, but from a sensation of having drunk warm, marshy water that smelled of water-tigers and their sticky, white secretions.

The sun rose from the horizon, and the sea changed colour, becoming more and more vivid, as though it were no longer water but melted aquamarine. . . .

. . . I saw the amphitheatre of our town. Our little steamer, leaving a lazy trail astern, was racing at full speed towards this amphitheatre. A cold twilight wind whistled in the masts. I was shivering and my teeth were chattering. It needed a great effort to descend the gangway to the landing-stage after giving my companion a farewell kick as though he had been responsible for the whole disaster: then I dragged myself home through the empty, still-unawakened town and found Papa and Zhenka awaiting me there, having returned the day before from the Crimea.

It turned out that I had typhoid fever.

Escape to Akkerman

WE EACH PAID ten kopecks and crossed the Dniester estuary to the town of Akkerman in a small steam launch, the *Friend*. The trip in the *Friend* across the estuary, which at this point was some ten versts wide, was so beautiful that it atoned fully for all the discomforts and tiredness experienced during our journey on foot from Odessa to Ovidiopol, which was more like a village, clumsily scattered about the long descent to the estuary, than a district town.

We had settled down on a semi-circular bench at the stern of the launch, so deep in the water that the surface of the estuary almost seemed to be above our heads, and it was only by climbing up on the bench and peering overboard that we were able to admire the moving mass of river-water, cloudy from the clay and rippling with small, chalky waves.

A strong wind was blowing along the estuary and I had gooseflesh all over my body. But one had only to go below-deck to be enveloped by the pleasant warmth of the panting steam-engine, with its smells of boiling water, lubricating-oil, polished steel, and oil-paint.

All this entranced us. The copper whistle hissed slightly from the steam-pressure, and we waited impatiently for the moment when the launch's captain, who was also the engineer, would pull the wire to hoot at the other launch, the *Arrow*, which was coming in the opposite direction.

The meeting of these two vessels in the middle of the estuary was one of the greatest attractions of the journey. Both captains, by way of greeting, lowered the flags on their comically small, short masts simultaneously, then pulled the whistles' wires, and, in a spurt of steam, there emerged deep-bass, hoarse sounds that might almost have come from a steamer's siren. Finally, the launches passed, dangerously close, at full speed, splashing each other with grey river-foam.

It was worth while running away from home just for that!

Meanwhile, in the distance, there appeared more and more clearly, like a transfer, the outline of the ancient Turkish fortress, with its round towers, which seemed to be suspended over grey cliffs on the other, distant shore.

Arriving at Akkerman shortly before sunset, we got off the launch and walked along the shore, composed of damp silt and a thick layer of flattened reeds, elastically resilient to one's legs, stiff from the uncomfortable seats on the launch.

Our plan was as follows: to spend the night in the fortress and, shortly before dawn, slip secretly aboard one of the ships tied up to the cargo pier; then hide in the hold and only emerge when the boat, which was waiting for the morning breeze, was already in the open sea on its way to Odessa and if luck would have it—to Constantinople.

Surely the navigating officer would not throw us into the sea, or put in to land just to get rid of us? The worst he could do would be to box our ears. Besides, we knew that the Black Sea merchant seamen, despite their sullen appearance, were kind at heart. Thus we looked forward to an exciting voyage in a ship under sail, seeing new people, and being seen ourselves, which for a long time had been our fondest dream.

As we strolled round the lading-wharfs, we decided, from various signs, that the ship *St. Nicholas*, with tall masts and a very small wheel near the chart-room, would be ready to sail with the morning breeze. She was standing alongside the wooden pier and her gangplank was not down. But even if it were not lowered later that night, we should still be able to get aboard by climbing up the mooring-ropes.

It was still light when we got to the fortress and walked through its inner yards, overgrown with white aromatic wormwood. We descended ruined stairs into cellars where in times immemorial the Turks kept their weapons. With a certain amount of difficulty, we clambered the dilapidated steps to the well-preserved towers and peered through the narrow loopholes in the immensely thick walls.

At close quarters, the fortress seemed even more enormous than when we had gazed at it from a distance. It was a complete town, composed of empty courtyards, narrow passages, subterranean cells with rusty rings and fragments of chains inserted into the walls, one-storied barracks for the garrison and other offices. Here and there among the weeds lay the cast-iron barrels of ancient guns and a number of cannon-balls, small to look at but so heavy that we could hardly lift them with both arms. In a particularly dismal, deserted courtyard, we saw a rotting wooden gibbet with a ring fixed in its blackened, projecting beam.

Presently, night fell and a white summer moon shone in the sky.

We were frightened. Some kind of black, noctural birds uttered strange cries as they flew across the background of the silver sky, and the bushes all seemed silvered, too: there was a strong smell of yellow camomile and the battlemented towers cast shadows like black calico across the silvery wormwood. There was a moat, now smothered in weeds, all round the fortress, from the depths of which the rustle of night-creatures, possibly serpents, emerged from time to time, while up above, from the tops of the towers, there came the occasional hoot of an owl.

Yurka stood just behind me, snivelling and repeating over and over again that we had far better go and spend the night in Akkerman on a bench in the public gardens, opposite the Hassert Hotel, than remain here, and that it would have been better still if we had never started on the journey at all.

I was petrified with fear, too, and would not have minded indulging in a little snivelling myself, but the desire to keep Yurka under control and demonstrate my iron will forced me to mutter through my teeth: "You wretched coward! Why did I ever let you come with me? If you like, you can go into the town and spend the night wherever you wish—perhaps the police-station would suit you?—but I'm staying here. And don't imagine I'll give you back your thirty kopecks from our joint funds. You can starve to death for all I care!"

This was my first expedition with Yurka, some three years before the famous journey to Nikolaev.

Yurka swore with a terrible oath that he would never travel with me again, and I swore I'd never take him with me again and—as you will have read—neither of us kept his word.

Finally, Yurka grew calmer, apologised, and we settled down to sleep in the bushes under the gillet—a location on which I insisted in order to build up our characters. The night was a disturbed one. We hardly slept at all owing to cold and fear as we listened to the sinister sounds around us in the bright moonlight mottled with dark shadows. Dew came up with the dawn, drenching us to the skin. The stars had not yet disappeared from the paling sky when we decided to go aboard the St. Nicholas. We were lucky: the landing-stage was empty and the gangplank down. With bated breath, we walked up the narrow board, made our way stealthily to the stern, and crawled under a tarpaulin, huddling close to each other to get some warmth.

The sky was growing light when we heard a smothered cough— judging by the sound of it, it came through a thick beard—and an elderly man in underpants and a linen shirt appeared on the damp deck. Yawning, he walked over to the side of the ship and we heard the sound of water falling in an arch across the rails into the estuary. Having relieved himself, he yawned again, made the sign of the cross, groaned a little, and looked towards the spot on the horizon where the sun was beginning to rise. He felt the direction of the wind with his finger, showed his displeasure, and cursed softly in a quivering voice.

Yurka could not control himself but had the good sense to clap his hand to his mouth before giving way to his giggles. I nudged him violently and told him in a whisper to shut up, but it was all in vain. The old man had heard us and raised the edge of the tarpaulin.

"Now, what sort of rascals have got aboard my boat?" he asked crossly.

"Uncle, dear . . ." Yurka snivelled pathetically.

"I'll give you Uncle! I'll Uncle you into the police-station," he retorted. "What do you think you're doing, sneaking aboard other people's boats? What are you after?"

He took a closer look at us in the dawn light and was surprised to find we were ten-year-old school-boys.

"School-boys, too," he said reproachfully. "So they teach you to do this sort of thing in those schools of yours?"

"Uncle, dear," said Yurka, "we wanted you to take us in your boat to Odessa. Our parents are waiting for us there and they'll be very anxious and we've no money for a steamer."

"Take us with you, Uncle, dear," I pleaded ingratiatingly.

"I'd willingly take you," the ship's owner said after a moment's reflection. "After all, why not? But we're not going to Odessa today, we're going to the Naked Pier to take on water-melons. From there —if God helps with the wind—we'll be passing by Odessa, but you can't count on it."

He looked down at us benevolently, small and trembling little kids as we were, still soaking from the dew.

"Well, boys, don't stay here, freezing under the tarpaulin. Come into my cabin, it'll be warmer there."

We followed the old man into a tiny cabin, with various little pictures, old calendars, strips of wall-paper, newspapers, and ladies' fashions from the *Niva** stuck on the walls, as soldiers do in the lids of their trunks. In the corner, above a wooden bed, covered with a patchwork counterpane, with a small green chest behind it, hung a big, dark icon of St. Nicholas, the patron saint of sailors, a figure with a grey beard, a brown, bald head, and stern eyes. A small blue lamp burned in front of it.

"Sit down," the old man said, rushing two ordinary kitchen chairs towards us and sitting down himself on the bed with another groan. "So there isn't much point in your coming with me all the way to the Naked Pier. You'd much better go and see the mate of the *Vassiliev*: he might take you free as far as Odessa. But steer clear of the *Turgenev*'s mate: he's well-known to be the biggest rogue on the Black Sea. But I've got a favour to ask of you young gentlemen. You're educated and all that and probably know the right people in Odessa. Couldn't you ask someone in the Marine Trade Office to give me a pilot's certificate so that I can take the ship into ports myself? Otherwise I don't see how I can carry on. I have to take a pilot on board everywhere I go and I need him about as much as a cart needs a fifth wheel: that's the very truth! I've applied God knows how many times, passed the examinations, and been at sea for over forty years, but they won't give me the certificate. Now, I ask you—you're educated boys—do you call that just? Is there any justice in our empire at all?

* Russian popular periodical of the time. *Translator's note.*

"Did you pass your examinations well?" I asked severely, adopting a superior tone.

"I always got 'excellent,'" the man replied, wiping a tear from his eye.

"Then it's outrageous!" I exclaimed indignantly.

"It is," the old man agreed. "So that's why I'm appealing to you, young men: I'm sure you've friends in the Marine Trade Office or your parents will know someone with influence. If you do me this favour, I'll pray every day to St. Nicholas for your happiness."

He went to the chest and brought out a letter. "This is my sixth application," he said, chewing his moustache. "See that it gets to the right people or I'll put an end to myself, I swear it!"

I remembered that the port superintendent's son went to our school and told the man that I was sure I could help him.

"God will reward you," he said with tears in his eyes and gave me the letter. "My name is Bondarchuk; every rat in the port knows me. Please do help me!"

We reassured him again as we said good-bye.

"If you really do it, I promise I won't grudge you three roubles," he told me slyly.

"You should be ashamed of yourself!" I replied angrily. "We'll do it because you've been unjustly treated. We don't want your three roubles."

"You idiot!" Yurka muttered behind my back. I gave him a good punch and he bit his tongue.

A hot sun had already risen. The crew of the *St. Nicholas*, three men who slept on different parts of the deck, had woken up and, yawning, were getting the ship ready to leave the Dniester estuary and put to sea: the morning breeze had sprung up. After we had taken leave of Bondarchuk, we spent a delightful morning in Akkerman. We bought a few rolls, two sea-roaches, and an aromatic melon in the market and descended into a wine-cellar, still empty and cool at that very hour. Sitting down at a table covered with oil-cloth, we spent our last six kopecks on a slightly sour Bessarabian wine, diluted it with water, and had an excellent lunch. What remained of the wine we poured into our travelling flask.

We dawdled about all day in the uninteresting, dusty town and in its public garden, where, on the lawns burnt brown by the sun, little gnomes in red caps, surrounded by bushes of night-glory, had been scattered here and there for decoration.

Having nothing else to do, I quarrelled with Yurka continuously, reinforcing my insults with rude gestures. I swore once again I would have nothing more to do with him, would never take him with me on any of my future expeditions. Keeping well away from each other, we finally went back to the harbour, where the *Vassiliev* had steam up, ready to leave for Odessa. The third warning from the siren had already sounded, consisting of one very long blast, followed by three short, sharp ones. We walked up the gangway and stood, with our heads hanging miserably down, in front of the mate, who was selling tickets near the hold.

"And you, you little idlers, pay up or go ashore."

"Uncle, dear," Yurka said, wiping his tears away, "we've lost our money and our old, sick parents are anxiously waiting for us at our homes in Odessa. Let us come with you and we'll pay later."

The mate examined us from head to toe—two small boys with short-cut hair and troubled eyes—and demanded to see our school-cards. We had to produce them and the officer read aloud the first sentence of our rules: "A school-boy must cherish the honour of his school as he cherishes his own." Then the whole thing began to bore him and he said: "Very well, you can travel on the lower deck, but no visiting the engine-room, no spitting on the floor, and behave your-selves as decent boys should. And remember—I'm not taking you for nothing; you'll have to pay the company thirty kopecks in Odessa."

The *Vassiliev* and the *Turgenev* ran on the same route, and the competition between the two ships, the one white, the other black, had reached a point that a ticket from Akkerman to Odessa now cost only fifteen kopecks. . . .

We thanked the officer very warmly and gave him our words that we would produce the money later, reinforcing our promises by making the sign of the cross in the direction of the Turkish fortress, since there was no church in the vicinity. Very soon, the *Vassiliev* cast off and our return to our native soil began, admittedly not under sail, but, still, on a swift, little white steamer, which was busily cut-ting its way through an unusually quiet, transparent, and beautiful Black Sea. We both were satisfied and very pleased with ourselves.

The mate was the only fly in the ointment: from time to time he came over to us and, with a sinister frown, reminded us not to forget to reimburse him the thirty kopecks on our arrival in Odessa.

We caught up the two-masted *St. Nicholas*, which with its old black sails puffed out by the wind, leisurely rode the beautiful Black Sea waves. In the stern, beside the tiny wheel, old Bondarchuk was sitting on a stool in a shirt with the collar unbuttoned and obviously brooding over the wrong done to him by the wicked bureaucrats in Odessa harbour. I waved my hat to him, but he did not notice, and our nimble little steamer soon passed the clumsy sailing-ship, skirted the snow-white harbour lighthouse with its copper bell, and entered Odessa harbour, where the warm, summer sunset was reflected in the glass of the aquarium.

Without waiting for two barefooted sailors to lower the gangway, Yurka and I jumped down onto the stone quay and, spurred on by the squeaky voice of the mate shouting "Hi boys! Don't forget to return the money!," we rushed into the town. It was already lit up by the street-lights and those in the shop-windows, this rich, cosy, beautiful, endearing town of ours with its cabs, carriages, cyclists, bustling granite pavements, and open-windowed houses from which, through the fragile green of the acacia-trees, came the sounds of pianos, violins, and passionate voices singing Italian songs, sometimes Leoncavallo's "Dawn," which always aroused a strange feeling of rapturous love inside me; love for whom, even I did not know.

Seeing the theatre-posters and hearing the clanging bells of the tramways, I sank back again into the entrancing town, and it already seemed a long time ago and dream-like that I had run off for no reason at all, slept under a gibbet amidst silver wormwood in a Turkish fortress, lain huddled-up under the tarpaulin in the *St. Nicholas,* and sat in the old salt's narrow cabin, listening to his complaints of human injustice.

We swindled the *Vassaliev's* mate, of course, and did not pay our fares, confident that the company would not suffer from it; in any case, we had no money.

As for old Bondarchuk, I kept my word and went to see my friend, whose father was port superintendent. My friend took me to see his father, in a huge office overlooking the noisy harbour, with red trucks loaded with Bessarabian wheat rolling along the pier.

My friend's father turned out to be a kind, sturdy man with a head of thick, short, silvery hair bristling like a hedgehog, wearing a civil-servant's uniform decorated, I believe, with epaulets, and with a medal round his neck. He pushed me into a very deep comfortable leather arm-chair and, completely drowning in it, I made a heated speech on the injustices that were being perpetrated by the port administration, citing the outrageous case of an old, experienced skipper, the owner of a small boat, who had been at sea for forty years and was refused the pilot's certificate he so badly needed.

The superintendent listened to me with great attention and, apparently, with sympathy. Suddenly, however, his expression changed: under his moustache, his lips curved in a strange smile—was it a scornful one or a compassionate one?—as he broke in: "Now, hold on a minute, young man. I believe I know the case you're talking about. You're referring to Bondarchuk, aren't you? The owner of a small tub, the St. Nicholas? We know him very well. You're quite right he is an excellent, experienced sailor and his boat is registered here at Odessa. But try to understand: we haven't any right to issue him with a certificate; it's definitely forbidden by law. We can't go against the law or we run the risk of being thrown into prison."

"But why? Why?" I exclaimed from the depths of the chair.

"Because, unfortunately, he suffers from daltonism," the superintendent said regretfully. "Didn't he say anthing about it to you?"

"No, he didn't."

"Well, there you are. The old man can't resign himself to this fact.

Perceiving from the expression on my face that I had not the faintest idea what daltonism was, he explained it to me: colour-blindness, the inability to distinguish one colour from another.

"So, how can we give a pilot's certificate to a man who can't distinguish a red signal-light from a green one? A collison at sea is no laughing matter: it can prove disastrous, lead to the loss of a ship and a lot of lives."

"He never told me he suffered from it," I murmured.

"Although he's an excellent seaman and a fine man, the chief continued, "he's abysmally ignorant. He doesn't believe in daltonism. He's absolutely convinced that it's a figment of the doctor's imagination, invented to cheat him out of his rights."

I had to admit that it was the first time I had ever heard of daltonism.

"But how do the unfortunate people suffering from it see?" I asked.

"They see the same as we do, only they can't distinguish colours. So, my dear young friend, to my great disappointment, I can't do anything for your protégé."

I thought of Bondarchuk and his fate during the rest of the day.

. . . To look at the world and not see its colours! Not to know that waves are blue-green and that the sun is red at sunset and sunrise, merely to see everything around in shades of grey and black! Later, I learned that dogs see the world in precisely the same way. When I lay in bed, I thanked God, tearfully, with all my heart—the God in whom I believed with all the impulsiveness of my childish soul—I thanked Him for having given me the happiness of not suffering from daltonism, of being able to see the world in all the richness of its colours.

The Blériot Model

WHEN I REMEMBER now the levity and the impulsiveness with which I harboured the queerest ideas in my mind, ideas that demanded immediate realisation, I cannot help smiling, yet in some ways I regret that I no longer have the demonic energy, the urge to take immediate action, not always sensible, but action all the same.

As an instance, take the story of the Blériot model. Why did the idea of making a model of Blériot's aeroplane suddenly crop up in my mind? A moment before, I had not even thought of it. Then suddenly, like lightning, it was there! And when it flashed into my head, I envisaged a lovely model of the famous monoplane, which had just flown over the Channel, in all its details. And that model had in some way been constructed by my own hands.

I realised at once that it would be dull to construct a Blériot model all by myself, and that I must find someone to help me. It immediately occurred to me that I could not find a better collaborator than Zhenka—not my brother, but another one, surnamed Dubastij. And then, as if by magic, he appeared at the end of the street, returning sadly home from his school, where he had got bad marks and been compelled to stay in for an extra hour after lessons.

With eyes afire, I rushed towards Dubastij and, while still ten yards away from him, shouted loud enough for the whole of Otrada to hear: "Let's make a model Blériot."

"Let's!" he replied ecstatically, although till then it had never occurred to him to make a model of any kind at all.

After a moment's reflection, when his first enthusiasm had cooled down, Zhenka asked: "Why?"

"We'll sell it to the exhibition for the aeronautics pavilion," I answered instantly, mildly astonished myself that such an idea should have come to me.

"Will they let us in without tickets?" Zhenka asked quickly.

"Of course they will when we show them the model."

"And where shall we get the model?" Zhenka asked.

"We'll make it, you idiot!" I exclaimed.

"What? Ourselves?"

"Yes. Ourselves."

"And they'll let us in with the model?"

"Of course they will."

"Then let's."

"You can do the wings and I'll do the wheels."

"All right."

Without wasting a second, we rushed to the cellar in Zhenka Dubastij's house, where we found a number of things that would be required to construct a model: a hammer, nails, string, a tin of paste, a long wire on which, in tsarist days, illuminated lanterns were hung the length of the house, pieces of wood, a saw, some calico, national flags that decorated the house on feast-days (these would be indispensable for covering the monoplane's fuselage), and, among various other things, a tube of multi-purpose "syndetikon" gum, which was very popular in those distant days.

. . . Syndetikon certainly glued together the most varied materials very thoroughly, our fingers first and foremost, so that we could scarcely tear them apart. This thick, stinking, amber-coloured glue would stretch out in terribly thin, terribly long fibrous threads that adhered to clothes, furniture, and walls, so, if you applied it in a hurry without due care, it could cause a number of minor disasters.

We had, of course, no designs or blue-prints to work from; we just knocked the Blériot model together out of hastily chopped strips of wood secured by big nails (for want of small ones). We screwed the wings made of wire, covered with white calico (we had wanted it yellow, but there was none at hand), on to the fuselage, and this heavy, clumsy structure was further strengthened with smelly threads of syndetikon, which continued to stick to our fingers and hinder the work.

By working extremely hard, we managed to construct the model in two days. The only things lacking were the wheels. Without compunction, we wrenched the wheels off the toy carriage belonging to Dubastij's small sister, Lucy, and stuck them below the frame of the fuselage. We cut out the propeller from a piece of pine-wood with a table-knife and glued it in front with the help of the same multipurpose glue.

We were enraptured by the beauty of our model, which seemed remarkably elegant to us, though it was a travesty of any known type of flying machine, leaving aside its quite unnatural proportions. It was a coarse, clumsy piece of work, and the only association it could rightly claim with a real aeroplane was that it was "heavier than air." We were immensely proud of this virtue in our model.

We waited impatiently for nine o'clock to strike and, when it did, we gingerly picked up our precious model by the fuselage, which immediately went slightly awry, and proceeded to the exhibition.

On the way, we were surprised how few passers-by paid any attention to our handiwork, which we had expected to provoke general admiration. Even the street-boys from the Novoribni district, the so-called *novoribniki*, who were playing a rather dull game by the wall of one of the houses, glanced at the Blériot model quite casually, without making any comment. I imagined they did not really grasp what it was that we were carrying.

There is no point in mentioning that we arrived at least an hour too early at the exhibtion and spent a long time near the turn-stile, restoring the model, which had suffered some slight damage on the journey. We also effected a few unimportant changes in its construction, such as bending the rear of the fuselage at a sharper angle and rounding the steering-wheel into a perfect circle.

Examining the model under a merciless sun, we regretted that we had not fitted the propeller with an elastic band so that it would have turned. But elastic bands of the kind we needed were so expensive. We had to resign ourselves to the fact that the propeller would not turn, but, after all, the model was not going to fly! It would have been better, too, if the wings had been lacquered over, but where were we to get the lacquer?

At last the exhibition's door-keeper arrived, in a special uniform, and was followed by the cashier, an elegant lady in a huge hat decorated with ostrich-feathers, and lace mittens with the fingers cut off.

We moved brightly towards the entrance, carrying the model with every precaution by its wings, but the cashier looked out of her box and asked: "Boys, where d'you think you're going without tickets? First let's see your money—then you're welcome to go in."

We explained to her that we were going to the aeronautics pavilion to exhibit our model, but the cashier turned her head away and closed the little window with a bang. We tried to pass through the turn-stile, but the door-keeper shook his finger at us and said he would call a policeman.

Depressed by our defeat, we walked along the high wall of the exhibition until we found ourselves somewhere in the back part of it. Here, Dubastij managed to climb over and I passed the model to him, damaging it slightly in the process by bumping one end of the wing against the ground: then, with fear and trembling I climbed over, too. We sat down on a pile of stones left over from the construction of the main pavilions and tried to mend our somewhat damaged model, filling in the hole which Dubastij had carelessly made with his finger in the rear section. We then proceeded to look for the aeronautics pavilion, which we found with some difficulty after plodding along miles of paths, strewn with crunching gravel, past fountains, ornate pavilions through the open doors of which we could see various strange machines, velvety green lawns, and flower-beds full of roses and other flowers. Gardeners in white aprons were watering them generously with hoses and a rainbow shone in the moist cloud of dust hanging over the greenery.

The aeronautics pavilion was a huge tent made from thick aviation silk and the entrance to it was wide open. We were on the point of going in, when we suddenly espied in front of us a young man with Max Linder moustaches, wearing a fashionable check waistcoat, riding breeches, and yellow leather leggings that admirably displayed his protruding calves. A tight, starched collar propped up his chin and a silk cravat, the colour of a peacock's eyes, with a pearl pin stuck in it, lent an air of wealth and social "chic" to his sporting appearance, enhanced by a faultless parting in his straight hair, shining with brilliantine. In his mouth was a cigar, with a great deal of ash on it and a pink glow from the inner fire: on his little finger he wore a ring with a large diamond. Up till now, we had only seen such chic young men in caricatures in the magazine *Satyrikon*.

"What are you young tramps doing here?" he asked in the accent of the Odessa suburbs, with a special stress on the last word.

"We've come to sell your pavilion a Blériot model," said Zhenka Dubastij, without the flicker of an eyelid.

"That one?" the young man enquired, pointing his burning cigar at our monoplane.

"Yes, why not?" Zhenka Dubastij demanded slightly aggressively. "Will you give us eight roubles for it?"

The young man displayed snow-white teeth, girlish dimples appeared on his cheeks and he began to laugh, releasing the cigar smoke through his nostrils. . . .

"Will you give us two roubles and a half, at least?" Zhenka grimly insisted.

Max Linder continued laughing.

"Well, then, take it for free, if you're such a miser," I said. "We're prepared to exhibit our model for nothing."

Max Linder continued laughing loudly and gaily. Finally, he stopped to take a breath, wrinkling his small, upturned nose and said: "Get out of here and don't let me see you again."

Whereupon, Zhenka Dubastij pleaded pathetically: "At least let us go round your pavilion, sir."

"Of course, if you want to," Max Linder answered benevolently. "With pleasure. Only don't take that guitar of yours in with you, and don't touch any of the exhibits."

We left the Blériot model on the grass under a rose-bush and, taking off our caps, reverently entered the pavilion on tiptoe, as though going to church.

It was a fantastic temple of the future. The morning sun, penetrating the silken material of the tent, lit with a vivid but subdued light several real, big aeroplanes with engines and fairy-like propellers of three-ply polished wood, some standing on the floor, some hanging in the air, alongside coloured designs of the different types. With trembling hearts, we saw the heavier-than-air machine belonging to the Wright brothers, resting on skids similar to skis, two of its control-flaps horizontal, two vertical; next to it, on fat little wheels with blown-up rubber tyres, stood the tall, slender biplane Farman 16, its copper fuel-tank glistening and its star-shaped, lamellar-steel Gnome motor liable to send anyone crazy by its sheer constructive, purposeful beauty: we were entranced by the wheel and stick controlling direction and height. The wings of the flying-machines, covered with tightly drawn silk material, painted over with transparent lacquer and held firmly together, despite their flimsiness, by a number of thin wires, overwhelmed us by the beauty of their design and finish. We longed to touch the carved, polished bars of the foot-controls, fashioned by highly skilled carpenters, masters of their profession, from specially selected beech, maple, or, possibly, ash. The aeroplanes were both flying-machines and musical instruments, with twanging, tightly strung steel strings. . . .

. . . But what surprised us most and humiliated us was several small models, placed on special stands. They were one of the main attractions in the pavilion and a miracle of artifice, precision, and perfect proportion. At the sight of them, Zhenka and I could not meet each other's eyes in our embarrassment and walked out of the pavilion like whipped dogs, not even glancing at our Blériot model which, oozing glue and clumsy as a botched stool, lay with a half-broken wing in the grass beneath a rose-bush, resplendent with half-open buds, in the dazzling sun.

We did not notice any of the other marvels on exhibition as we passed them on our way out: the famous wooden samovar constructed by the well-known tea-firm Caravan, the height of a four-storied house, and the tea-pot beside it with a circular balcony, from which visitors could get a view over the whole exhibition grounds; the less famous monster champagne bottle from Roederer's; the steam roundabout with sailing boats instead of carriages, and a ship's copper whistle; the Russian Marine and Trading Company's black pavilion in the shape of a steamer's bows and almost life-size, complete with bowsprit, mast, and bell.

We did not even pay attention to the mesmerising smell of hot wafers with whipped cream which were cooked in front of the public on red-hot wafer irons, heated by electricity, or to the Haberbusch and Schille sausages served on cardboard plates, with mashed potatoes and a spoonful of mustard.

Oh, what a miserable day it was!

The Central Hotel ✍

I WAS GIVEN a present of a "cobalt" camera, or one very like it. It was a square little box covered with black shagreen paper that looked like leather and emitted a special smell which I always thought of then as a "photographic" smell.

My first attempts at photography turned out unsuccessfully. I was always in a hurry and often put the plates in the wrong way round; rays from the street-lights would penetrate the imperfectly closed shutters and ruin the picture; occasionally two quite different photographs appeared on the same plate, one vertical, the other horizontal. I did not wash the little black baths for developing and fixing thoroughly enough, so that the plate turned out dirty and smudged; I mixed up the bath for tone-fixing with the developer and then the skin of the layer sensitive to light slid off; I dropped the plates in the dark-room and they broke on the floor. It was a long time, indeed, before I learned to produce photographs that I regarded as reasonably good.

And one fine day, I at last made my way to the rifle-range, where aeroplanes flew every day. To make a photograph of an aeroplane with my own camera was my dream of dreams.

Carrying the camera by its leather strap and happily reminded by the slight clattering inside that it was fully charged with plates, I went out of town to the shooting-range.

Everything augured success: a bright sun, by the light of which one could take snapshots, a clear, transparent air, and the sound of aeroplane-engines which became audible as I thrust my way through the weeds to the field.

Farman 16 was making a beautiful slow turn, high above the earth, yellow and glinting in the sun, its copper fuel-tank polished like a samovar, its engine buzzing like a bumble-bee.

Having completed the turn, the pilot switched off the star-shaped engine, which sputtered out behind his back, and began one of the most dangerous aerial stunts of those times, the so-called "mountains," when a biplane made a series of dives towards the earth, soaring up again in between them, until its wheels and sliding undercarriage touched the soil.

The descent was so beautiful that, in my admiration, I forgot all about my camera and did not have time to take a photograph; but I could scarcely have done so in any case as the sun would have been shining directly into the lens.

The aeroplane rolled along the grass and stopped very close to me. The pilot, in a leather helmet, leather jacket, and yellow leggings— the famous Odessa hairdresser Khioni, a long-standing rival of

Utochkin—passed in front of me, pulling off his big leather bell-shaped gloves and twisting up his smart black moustache, slightly dishevelled during the flight.

I noticed, in the middle of the steppe, a town carriage with a folding top. The driver, in a long dark-blue coat, was hanging a nose-bag of oats over the horse's head and his passengers—a lady in a large hat and a light gauze scarf round her neck and a bearded gentleman in a merchant's jacket cut from fine cloth—walked down the weedy road to meet the pilot; they shouted to him gaily, probably congratulating him on a beautiful flight, and the lady even applauded as if she were in a theatre.

I listened and overheard them asking the pilot to take them up in the aeroplane. The lady took off her hat, threw it in the dusty calomel, and tied the gauze scarf round her head: the man turned his merchant's cap round the other way.

I could see them climb up the rope and struts onto the lower wing and then settle down in the light wicker seat that looked like the baskets in which berries are sold at the market.

Almost fainting with fear, the lady clung to the polished bar in front of her and the man squeezed up against her as closely as he could, since the two of them, both corpulent, had to share the same seat. The pilot checked the controls, then the mechanic swung the propeller, not without some difficulty, the engine sprang into life and the propeller revolved quicker and quicker until it became an almost invisible disc, over which flashed like lightning the sun's reflection.

The Farman bumped forward over the calomel, detached itself from the earth, soared up to a height of five hundred metres, circled round, and then, with its engine switched off, executed a brilliant *vol plané*, starting very steeply and gradually flattening out. As it landed gently and ran on, the coachman and I heard the lady's ecstatic cackle and her companion's raucous laughter.

"Not bad," the driver said. "He spent all last night with his "mam-sel" in the Alcazar and now he ends up here; thought a flight might be good for his hangover, I reckon." The driver good-naturedly and respectfully added a few obscene words, shaking his head in his hard, beaver cap, with its metal clasp: he had bright metal figures of horses' heads on his leather belt. "A rich gentleman. Not from these parts. A merchant out for a bit of fun."

At this moment, the aeroplane came to a halt in front of us and the lady, red as a tomato from fear and the pleasure of the flight, caught sight of me with my camera.

"Hi, boy, take a photo of us!"

"With pleasure," I said, blushing with happiness and clicking my heels.

"Do you know how to use that thing?" the gentleman asked. "If not, you'll make such monsters of us, that our own mothers won't know us."

"Please, keep still for a minute, so that I can take a time-exposure," I said sternly and, concentrating on the small, coloured picture of the lady, gentleman, and pilot, seated in the aeroplane in my view-finder, clicked the shutter.

"Will you give us the photo?" the lady asked.

"With pleasure," I repeated, again clicking my heels on the dusty grass of the rifle-range.

"See you don't forget!" the gentleman said and, rummaging in his pocket, handed me a large visiting-card on which he wrote with a gold pencil: "Central Hotel Number 76."

When I took the card from his hands, I caught the smell of alcohol on his breath.

The gentleman then climbed down from the aeroplane and helped the lady down after him. She jumped straight into his arms, laughing and shouting: "Whoops!" After this, the gentleman took out his wallet, extracted a twenty-five-rouble note and pressed it into the pilot's glove.

"Permit me, sir, to congratulate you on your air-baptism," said the driver, taking off his hat and fumbling with the buttons on his long overcoat.

"I'll settle up with you for everything later," the gentleman said. "Now drive us as fast as you can to the Arcadia for dinner. And you, boy, whatever your name is, don't forget to bring the photo. I'll see you don't suffer by it," he added significantly, peering out of the carriage window.

And the gentleman and lady drove off. I realised that I had been lucky and could now become quite rich. It stood to reason. The gentleman had ordered me to take a photograph of his first flight in an aeroplane and was bound to pay me well. He was no miser and certainly wouldn't be if he liked the photo. If he gave the pilot twenty-five roubles for the flight—an unheard-of sum in my experience—without batting an eyelid, he surely wouldn't begrudge me five for my photo. Well, if not five, say three. And that was already something. Or, in any case, not less than two. Honestly, what could it matter to him giving a man two or three roubles? I had seen what a lot of money he had had in his wallet—masses of it. And all in twenty-five rouble notes. Never in my life had I seen such a lot of money at one time. No, he wouldn't give me less than five: his conscience wouldn't let him. After all, the snapshot would be invaluable to him. It was no joke, a first flight, and with his wife, too. And I'd be providing proof that they'd actually flown in the aeroplane. Not many people had done it. It was quite a rare event at that time —perhaps three or four people in the whole town and even that was doubtful, not counting the pilots, of course.

. . . No, for a photograph like that, even ten roubles wouldn't be too much.

Ten roubles . . . It made me shiver even to think of it. . . . A dream, an impossible dream . . . a fantasy. . . . Yet, it was quite possible. All I must do was develop the photograph as well as possible, without hurrying and taking care not to smear it with my fingers: I must make a first-class job of it.

On getting home, I could hardly wait for evening, to start developing my plate.

By the red light of the lamp—very similar, by the way, to the red lamps with the inscription "exit" on them over the doors of theatre-auditoriums which burn throughout the performance—I carefully shook the flat little bath, in which I could see the innocently flashy surface of the china plate sunk in the acrid-smelling developing-fluid. The shuttered windows were covered with blankets and the door locked. The faintest ray of light could destroy all my work and the dream about the ten roubles would vanish like smoke. I tried to penetrate the pink surface of the plate, as I waited impatiently for the first signs of an outline. It seemed to me they would never come. I had already lost all hope, thinking that I had probably forgotten, in taking the picture, to remove the black velvet cover from the lens.

I was ready to cry.

They called me to tea through the door, but I kept a dismal silence, biting my nails. Then, suddenly, when the last hope had almost gone, I saw very faint, barely distinguishable black and white stains, which gradually became more distinct and began to acquire a shape.

... It was like a night spent by the sea, when at first everything melts into a uniform, starry, silvery vacuum, but shortly before dawn the sea begins to separate itself faintly from the sky and the outlines of rocks and scows on the beach begin to appear; followed by the dim glimmer of the long coastal waves, the silhouette of the cliffs, and the first glimpse of the walls of the house on top of it, white and shiny, the black groups of sinuous trees, and the white stars of the sleepy tobacco-plants. The sky glows clearer and as dawn breaks, the landscape gradually re-establishes itself in all its details, down to the small pebbles washed by the surf's lacy foam. And the dear, sleepy face ...

What I now witnessed was much the same. The black and white spots on the plate began definitely to mean something, to display some details. After a moment, I could already see in ecstasy the negative image of black human faces with white eyes, the white, slanting struts of the biplane, and a faint outline of the fuel-tank and the control-stick. A few seconds later, I could see the surface of the wings and part of the propeller. All this was not as clear as one would have wished, but it was unmistakably a photograph, a real negative from which quite decent copies could be printed on good, glossy paper; copies for which one would not grudge me, well, if not ten, certainly five or three, roubles. ... But perhaps ten, all the same?

The printing from the negative was in itself a miracle! But it did not seem quite enough to me: I decided to stick the slightly mauve, still-damp, shiny photo inside a special passe-partout frame, so that my work would please my rich customer even more.

I wangled fifteen kopecks from my aunt and, in a photographic-materials shop, bought three grey frames, corresponding in size to the measurements of my photograph. The broad margins, decorated with decadent little designs, increased the size of my opus and made it look considerably more expensive. I stuck the clearest print on with special photographic glue and placed it under a pile of textbooks to ensure that it adhered firmly; then, in a high state of excitement, I went to bed, ready to leave for the Central Hotel first thing in the morning.

I woke shortly after seven, wrapped the passe-partout in a sheet of newspaper, put on my satchel, and departed, apparently for school but in fact for the hotel. On the way, I unwrapped the parcel several times to cast an eye over my handiwork. To tell the truth, it was not as successful as I had imagined. In my hurry, I had not kept it long enough in the fixative and it now looked rather dim, though not to the extent that one was unable to grasp what it represented. The faces of the lady and gentleman were unfortunately out of focus, and it was difficult to recognize them, but I told myself reassuringly that certain peculiarities in their clothing would still enable one to do so if one wanted to. In addition, the photograph seemed too small, even taking into account the slightly increased size lent it by the passe-partout borders. And, in spite of all my care, I had managed to smear the plate during the developing and the slightly blurred print now bore my thumb-print only too clearly.

But I did not despair, relying on the kindness and generosity of the gentleman and his wife, who must already be happy that my photograph would provide them with their sole proof that they had ever been up in the aeroplane.

I walked as fast as I could, in a panic that I should not find them still in. By a quarter to eight I was already in the hotel, asking the sleepy porter whether I could see Mr. So-and-so and his wife. The porter, dressed in a frock-coat, his eyebrows painted a lilac colour, looked down a me haughtily and explained how to find the gentleman's room, but added with a hasty smile: "I can't give you any information about his wife. You'll have to find that out for yourself."

I did not quite grasp the meaning of his remark, but headed for the iron stairs covered with a red, worn-out carpet, went up to the second floor and walked down the darkish corridor, smelling of cigar smoke, past a quantity of locked doors, in front of which stood men's and women's shoes put out to be cleaned. There was also a strong smell compounded of dust, face-powder and scent and something else, elusively vicious, possibly even criminal. Having found number 76, I cautiously knocked on the dirty-white door with gold mouldings. Nobody answered. I listened, my ear to the key-hole, and heard a reassuring scuffling noise: my customer must still be there.

I knocked again more loudly.

"Who's there?" asked a man's hoarse voice.

"It's me," I said.

"Who are you?"

"The boy you spoke to yesterday, don't you remember? I took a photograph of you and your wife in the aeroplane."

"Did I go up?" the voice behind the door inquired.

"You did," I said. "I've brought the photo."

From inside the room, there came something that sounded like good-natured swearing, then I heard the padding of bare feet, the door opened and I saw the gentleman in a long night-gown over his underpants, with a dishevelled beard, red nose, and blurred eyes.

"Here's the photo," I said, clicking my heels like a well-brought-up school-boy and handing the gentleman the passe-partout in its news-paper wrapping.

"What time is it?" he growled.

"About eight," I replied.

He unwrapped the sheet of newspaper and took out the photo-graph. After examining it for a long time, he scratched his head. "So I really did fly! How fantastic! Well, thank you."

The gentleman breathed a complicated mixture of various alco-holic fumes into my face, shut the door again, and locked it. I again heard the patter of bare feet, followed by a woman's rasping cough, muffled by the shabby, red-velvet curtains, impregnated with to-bacco-smoke.

I stood for a while outside the door and then went to school, my heart heavy with the bitterness of unfulfilled hopes.

Halley's Comet 🖋

THE RUMOUR SPREAD like lightning. From the heights of outer space, Halley's comet was heading towards the earth and some astronomers were predicting a very probable collision between that heavenly body and our planet, as a result of which humanity would perish.

The picture of perishing humanity was very vague, even abstract; nonetheless, the thought of it made my heart contract with fear, since it meant that I should perish, too. I did not experience my usual fear of death, which now and then penetrated my whole being, only to disappear without trace and be forgotten until the next sud-den onslaught, but a new fear, fear of a meaningless, blind, and in-exorable physical law of celestial mechanics, which had power over my life and the lives of everyone else inhabiting the earth; the power to destroy the earth itself, transform it into nothingness and, at the same time, one that could be foretold several centuries ahead.

I was terrified by the scientific designs in papers and journals, which all illustrated the disaster in the same way: a parabola, on which Halley's comet was represented in all the phases of its inescapable approach to the earth by a few dots with tails pointing away from the direction of the sun, with our earth depicted as a small circle at the bottom of it, already half-covered by the comet's tail.

. . . The insanity-rate increased in the town. Sinister old women appeared, sometimes carrying icons, with fierce eyes and dark circles round them. They went from house to house, cursing the inhabitants for being sunk in lewdness and vice.

The town was drenched by the scent from an unprecedented blossoming of white acacia. During the short, dark, stifling nights, the sound of Italian songs coming from wide-open windows turned our peaceful Otrada into something like Naples, or at least Sorrento; in the darkness, denser than usual, couples moved about silently, the dim red glow from cigarettes appeared here and there, and one could hear "whispers and timid sighs" in every secluded corner; the air from *The Merry Widow*—"Let's forget all our sorrows as we hide in the hollows"—whistled very softly, seemed to suggest that we were all trying to forget the same shared sorrow.

Above the sea sparkled milky summer stars, the brightest of which were reflected in the almost motionless water, casting a silvery light towards the dark horizon, whence, out of the coal-black abyss, the comet was due to appear.

In the town, one heard the horns of small, chugging motor-cars, and carriages on pneumatic tyres silently raced past, with lanterns by the coachman's seat, and carrying, I knew, rich young men and their ladies to carouse at the Arcadia or the Northern, where beauties, outside my sphere, with painted lips and mascaraed eyes, designed to give them an appearance of seductive frailty, sang songs in spangled dresses that left their white shoulders bare. And, in the theatre, *Aïda* was being given, with a blue Nile, silvery under an African moon, and sinister exclamations of "Radames! Radames!"

. . . And in a world gone mad from the expectation of atoning for its sins, willing or unwilling, the monsterous super-dreadnoughts of the American navy, their masts of interlaced steel resembling the Eiffel Tower enveloped in thick, black smoke, were furrowing the seas. And somewhere in the depths of the ocean, submarines glided along, prepared at any moment to release their Whitehead automatic floating mines. The airship *Count Zeppelin* rose over the Bodensee like a huge sharpened pencil, and light aeroplanes, soon to be equipped for dive-bombing and included in armament programmes, flew peacefully over the green meadows of Europe. There were manoeuvers everywhere, and the dreadnoughts fired with twelve-inch guns at targets floating in the divinely blue waters of seas and oceans, across which—in the present, at least—gold from Europe and America circulated freely to and fro.

In my imagination, all this was linked with the fantasies of H. G. Wells; with the howling of the dying man from Mars that chilled the marrow of those living among the heather-strewn moors of good old England; with a man who woke up with the flying-ships of the future; and with the death, decay, and destruction that earth brought with it from the fathomless depths of a cosmos man had not grasped. Halley's comet came nearer and nearer every day with its clear core and phosphorescent veil surrounding the tail turned away from the sun.

One could not see it yet.

Only a few astronomers had seen it, through their gigantic telescopes with sixteen-inch refractors.

Then photographs of it appeared in the papers, distinguished from the scattered stars around it by its nebulous tail, so short and small that it required a vivid imagination to sense the danger of a collision with this luminous tadpole with a round eye.

I stopped sleeping, terrified of the inevitable catastrophe, although an eminent astronomer declared it to be utter nonsense and the figment of ignorant journalists, since nothing would happen even if the earth were to come into the orbit of the comet's tail. The tail was composed of such fine material that the earth would easily pass through it without our being aware of it. And if the comet's core collided with our planet, nothing disastrous would happen either, because the core was only a gaseous body, slightly more condensed than the tail.

Despite this comforting assertion, I am sure, from what I saw of him, that my father was deeply concerned about the destiny of our little planet and the whole of humanity.

My aunt, on the other hand, while not excluding the possibility of a world disaster, adopted a very flippant attitude towards it.

"Well, suppose one fine day we do flare up and burn, like butter-flies, along with all our earthly civilisation, what of it? It serves us all right!"

And Aunt, having put on her hat and gloves, would then proceed with friends to hear an operetta and admire Dnieprov, who, accord-ing to rumour, had once been a monk; or go to a cinema to see Max Linder, or the famous Harrisson in the film *Nordisk*, an elegant well-fed man with an immaculate parting in his hair and a snow-white edge of handkerchief peeping out of the breast-pocket of his very modish jacket, who always played tragic characters, often a noble, wealthy man who, left by his beautiful wife, allows everything to go to ruin and finally shoots himself with a nickel revolver, his head falling forwards on his huge writing-desk.

She would go out, humming light-heartedly the air from *Ly-sistrata*: "The glow-worm flies all night/The glow-worm gives no peace. . . ."

At last, the night came when Halley's comet was to collide with the earth, cover it with its tail, or pass near-by and sink into the dark abyss, the coal-black hole in the world of space. The streets were crowded with people, armed with binoculars and telescopes. I went to Papa's chest of drawers and found Mamma's small opera-glasses. With them, I scoured the whole summer sky and found nothing. A grown-up school-boy, Serge, came out into the street with massive Zeiss binoculars, which enlarged everything twenty or even thirty times. He strolled with the snobbish listless gait of a dandy to the cliffs, where the broader horizon gave him a better view. He searched for the comet, then suddenly said: "There it is. I can see it quite clearly. The tail is pointing upwards."

I begged him to let me have a look. He gave me one of his con-temptuous, aristocratic smiles, but nonetheless took pity on me and handed over the binoculars. Again I scoured the whole sky and found nothing even vaguely resembling a comet, but as I returned the heavy glasses to Serge, I said, feigning indifference: "Well, there's nothing so striking about it. Just an ordinary star with a tail."

As I had seen no comet, yet had passionately wanted to see it, my words instantly turned out to be almost true, though they had been a straightforward lie. My imagination created a small, blue star with a long, luminous tail, a phosphorescent imitation of a young fried fish, which I saw myself examining through a microscope and discovering in the centre of its transparent flesh something resembling a luminous system of blood circulation.

At home I bragged that I had seen the comet. Zhenka said he had seen it, too—not even through binoculars but with his naked eye.

I went out into the street again, darkened by the dense foliage of the trees. One could hear whispers and timid sighs. On the benches near the gate, a couple were kissing and laughing softly.

Everyone I asked said they had seen the comet and had not found anything extraordinary about it.

A few days later, the papers announced that the comet was already a colossal distance beyond the earth and was continuing on its parabolic way. It did not leave any visible trace behind. We did not even notice any faint luminous fog around us, when her magic tail had touched the earth. Everything was exactly as it had been before. Yet, a certain anguish remained in my heart—the foreboding of a world catastrophe, which we had miraculously escaped this time, but which would certainly occur one day and destroy humanity.

. . . Halley's comet disappeared into outer space, but after a certain time I heard a new comet mentioned, an even more terrifying one, fraught with wars and revolutions . . . with a tragic name, Biella. Biella's comet . . . And again I did not see it.

In much the same way, I was wakened one night on the Atlantic by somebody knocking on my cabin-door.

"Come up on deck and bring your binoculars with you. One can see the lights of Lisbon in the far distance."

A strong wind was blowing, which made my eyes water, and hard as I tried I could not see anything. Later, I told everyone that I had seen the lights of Lisbon. And I began believing it myself. I imagined a few diamonds strewn about in the darkness in the direction where the town lay. What magic there was for everyone in those words: "The lights of Lisbon."

Expensive Toys

THE MAGIC LANTERN with its extendable funnel that slid into itself like a telescope, its motionless coloured pictures—slides, which were usually projected on a white wall or simply on light wall-paper—its kerosene lamp and reflector, its black body liable to become incandescent at any minute and send sunbeams flashing into the mirror, which reflected them onto the walls, floor, and ceiling of the darkened room, its smell of burnt paint and the soot floating up through its funnel—this traditional delight, which was a toy at home and an educational appliance at school, had become obsolete.

In toy-shops, now, you could get a new projection instrument —a bioscope. It showed, instead of still pictures, moving ones.

In appearance, it did not differ much from the old magic lantern gathering dust in a cupboard, except for the handle which had to be turned at a steady pace so that the film moved evenly from one spool to another, though all too often it got caught up on some small projection. There was the same kerosene lamp and reflector, the same sunbeams, flashing round the darkened room, and the same soot and smell of burnt paint—but what a difference in the pictures!

At first we gazed rapturously at the miracle of the moving coloured pictures on the wall—the clown in a pointed hat juggling with balls, the twirling ballerina—but soon we got tired of it: the films were short and the miracle of movement could not atone for the monotony, while the mechanical whirr of the turning handle tended to send us to sleep.

The moving pictures in the town were much more interesting, so our expensive toy presently found its way to the top of the cupboard and later to a storeroom, where it, too, gathered dust over the years.

It had no real life in it.

The small steam-engine was also considered a toy, though an expensive one, but it was, in fact, a real steam-engine in miniature, made in a proper engineering works. It possessed a steel boiler complete with whistle, pistons, and a small but heavy flywheel. The steam, unlike that in full-size locomotives, was produced by a small spirit-lamp under the boiler.

Papa bought me one of these miniature engines, not as a toy for my amusement but with a view to increasing my knowledge of mechanics and physics. It cost a lot—somewhere in the region of five roubles—but Papa was determined to spare no expense in ensuring that Zhenka and I grew up to be widely educated adults.

Why, among the hundreds of thousands of impressions gathered in my lifetime, has that small machine kept such a permanent place in my memory? That steel boiler of a special lilac hue? I do not know.

It is still an unexplained mystery of man's memory—why he remembers one thing all his life and completely forgets another. No doubt there is a regular process of memory, the laws of which are still undiscovered.

The smell of burning methylated spirits and the sight of the yellow-blue flame stay with me to this day.

The boiler took a long time to heat up. Zhenka and I would feel it every minute with the palms of our hands, but it remained cold, though not, of course, as cold as when we had filled it from the kitchen-tap.

As if we were under a spell, we waited for the transformation of water into steam. It seemed as though there would be no end to this tormentingly slow heating process. Yet, inevitably it takes place, though almost imperceptibly at first. But at last our palms begin to feel a shade of warmth on the surface of the boiler, even if a long way short of the required temperature. The boiler is getting hot, but no sounds emerge from inside it: the water is still silent.

Now the boiler begins to burn our hands, and we instinctively snatch them away almost before they have come in contact with it. Now it begins to emit waves of warmth, like a well-heated iron. We try to turn the flywheel, and it moves but stops again almost at once: the pressure is still insufficient. We bite our lower lips and listen. From the middle of the boiler a faint, mosquito-like sound is just audible. Then our ears catch the simmering music of water approaching the boil, the music turns into bubbling, and a damp puff of steam spurts from the safety-valve. Suddenly, the stationary flywheel responds to a light touch of my finger and, having started, slowly turns a complete circle without further assistance, seems to hesitate for a second, and then, as if losing its balance, starts to revolve more and more rapidly, driven by the clattering pistons. We have witnessed the miracle of the transformation of water into steam and steam into power. Quantity turning into quality. The now frenziedly circling flywheel glues our eyes to the hissing machine and we stand fascinated by the apparently simple but actually magical manifestation of a power that seems to come from nowhere.

But this was not all. The power, compressed in the red-hot steam-boiler, could be made to turn when we so wished into sound. All that was required was to turn a wooden, painted handle on the small toy copper whistle and there emerged a sound as pure and clear as the whistle of a locomotive, calling one to unknown places, to mountains, to tunnels, to bridges thrown over violent streams of melting snow, but diminished a hundred, a thousand times to fit the area of the room.

The flywheel could be linked by a belt to a contraption in a tin basin, causing a toy fountain to spring up in the middle of it. And a school-boy I knew had a steam-engine that turned a tiny dynamo, which provided sufficient current to light a lantern with a milk-white shade on the top of a pole—an exact replica in miniature of a station-lantern.

Later, we got a toy railway-engine that worked by steam. It raced round a circular track, puffing and spitting out boiling water, and the flame of the spirit-lamp heating the boiler spread its warm, intoxicating smell throughout the room.

We never seemed to tire of admiring the steam-engine in action, the station-lantern, the spurting fountain, and the railway-engine with its string of carriages: never seemed to tire, either, of listening to the steam-whistle, reminding us of dark wintry dawns, when the factory-whistle shrilled beyond the frosty window, making our hearts miss a beat.

But strange as it may be, we did tire of all this very soon, as one always tires of toys. After all, they only repeated in miniature the actions of machines which had already existed in the world for a long time, not as toys, but as grandiose, useful objects. They merely awakened our awareness of them, an awareness that lagged behind later when it came to internal-combustion engines and diesels. And this lagging behind became intolerable when it took the faint echo of a factory-whistle to awaken our imaginations and our consciences to poverty, poor housing, and other ills of humanity.

. . . And very soon the railway-engine, together with the dis-assembled tracks, found its place first in the cupboard and then in the storeroom beside the other out-dated toys, slowly to be covered with the dust of oblivion.

Theft at the Newspaper-Kiosk 🖋

WE WERE STERNLY FORBIDDEN to read the Pinkerton books. Nat Pinkerton was a famous American detective, whose adventures enthralled us. They were small books about the size of a school copy-book, so-called "serials," and each issue carried a new picture on the cover with a portrait of the eminent detective in a red circle. This coarse lithographed portrait presented Nat Pinkerton in profile. His clean-shaven, bloated face with a projecting jaw, a rather fleshy nose, and a sharp line between the nostrils and the edges of firmly closed lips, his penetrating eyes (or, rather, eye, since he was in profile), even the slanting parting in his chestnut-coloured hair and his colourful American tie—everything pointed to the fact that he was the greatest criminologist of the twentieth century, an experienced and fearless man with a will of iron and a constant menace to the American underworld, who had discovered hundreds of horrible crimes and sent more than one scoundrel to the electric chair in Sing Sing.

Nat Pinkerton had an aide, the young American Bob Rowland, who worshipped the great chief whose right hand he was: a reckless fellow and a master of disguise, he would, for instance, stick on a false beard and, masquerading as a sick old man, follow a dangerous criminal with the tenacity of a blood-hound, only abandoning the pursuit for a moment or two to ring up Pinkerton and report progress: "Hulloa, Mr. Pinkerton. It's me, Bob Rowland."

"Ha, ha, I recognized your voice at once, my boy. Well, out with it, what's new?"

"Master, I've at last got on the track of that scoundrel, Jack."

"That's fine. Get on with it. Hulloa! I'll soon be there to help you and together we'll have that fiend in the electric chair where he belongs."

What fascinated us most was the exclamation "Hulloa," which kept bursting from the great criminologist's lips as soon as he had snatched up the telephone and brought the receiver to his ear.

The pace never slackened: on every page, there were telephones, the subway, skyscrapers twenty floors high, cabs, express trains, steel revolvers, the mysterious prison Sing Sing, of which the name alone was enough to make the reader shudder, and, finally, the electric chair.

Soon after Nat Pinkerton, other detectives began to crop up in great quantities: the English criminologist Sherlock Holmes—a cheap imitation of Conan Doyle's world-famous Sherlock Holmes—then Nick Carter.

The portrait of Sherlock Holmes appeared in a canary-yellow

square. He, too, was shown in profile, with a prominent nose, slightly but elegantly hooked, and an English pipe between his teeth, which he smoked very portentously and significantly.

Nick Carter's head was placed in a bright-blue circle. He was a very young man with the back of the head adolescently elongated, thick, upstanding hair, and the high, studious forehead of a chess-player. Nick Carter's adventures were remarkably inventive; he solved the most complicated mysteries, connected with the activities of large gangs of "society" criminals, possessing a wide assortment of strange Oriental drugs, opiates, and silent weapons, skilled in the sciences of hypnosis and spiritualism, and capable of translating souls, not to mention large quantities of stolen gold and precious stones such as diamonds the size of an egg and pearls bigger than coconuts, these last an obvious plagiarism from Jules Verne's *Twenty Thousand Leagues under the Sea.*

These high-society gangs had their own steam-yachts and private trains. They committed their monstrous crimes with the incredible speed of phantoms, moving like lightning from one part of the world to the other—in Chicago today, Valparaiso tomorrow, then on to London, Paris, of course, San Francisco and Nagasaki—leaving victims everywhere, either imprisoned or killed with some secret weapon, before disappearing again without a trace.

But where was I to get the money?

The Nick Carter books appeared every Friday, two at a time, and their combined price was fourteen kopecks. They were brought by the St. Petersburg–Odessa express, which was said to attain a speed of 110 versts an hour. As soon as the train arrived, Nick Carter's freshly printed instalments with their alluring coloured covers illustrating some episode from the adventures inside were displayed in large stacks in the newspaper-kiosks.

The burning desire to buy these two new instalments was torturing me: the last one had broken off at a moment of appalling suspense, and I now had the opportunity of learning how the story of Ines Navarro—the beautiful demon—ended. . . . The even more beautiful Irma was sitting hypnotised in the arm-chair, when suddenly, behind her back, the curtain moved and Ines Navarro herself, with a perfidious smile on her lips, appeared, grasping the small revolver which discharged poisoned bullets silently.

"Ha-ha-ha!" Ines Navarro laughed melodiously, and the beautiful demon devoured with her eyes the white, marble-like face of Nick

Carter's assistant, now plunged into a hypnotic sleep. "At last I've got you in my net, you cursed blood-hound!"

With these words the demon cocked the gun, when . . . What happened after the "when" had remained a mystery to me because that was where the instalment had finished, except for the announcement: "Continued in our next . . ."

Nick Carter did not have one assistant, but several; the Japanese Tsi-Itsli, Patsy, and even a woman, the beautiful Irma, at the sight of whom the most confirmed criminal lost his head.

The various Nick Carter books cost seven kopecks each, while the Pinkerton ones were only five. The Pinkertons had thirty-two pages, the Nick Carters forty-eight.

The Pinkertons were written in coarse style and contained expressions such as: "Curst and blast him," yelled Bob, shouting at the elusive Macdonald, or "Ah, I've got you, my pet," Pinkerton said in an icy voice, slipping handcuffs on the scoundrel, "Now at last I'll put you in the electric chair."

At first this manly style appealed to us, but after Nick Carter appeared in the book-shops, Pinkerton's attraction dropped sharply. The Nick Carter books abounded in sentences that moved us to the depths of our beings, such as: "The beautiful criminal's golden hair fell down over her marble shoulders and covered her from head to foot with a luminous cloak." Or: "Dr. Dazar plunged a hypodermic needle filled with a Tibetan sleeping-draught into the naked arm of the Japanese with a devilish laugh."

These books spread the adventure of the same criminals—"Dr. Dazar," for instance, or "Ines Navarro, a Beautiful Demon"—over four or five numbers. Thus, having read one book and stopped at the most interesting spot, it was impossible not to buy the next instalment.

And there they were, these two next instalments, on the counter of the kiosk, but my pockets were empty and there was no chance of my procuring the necessary fourteen kopecks. Meanwhile, my longing to know how the story of Ines Navarro, the beautiful demon, ended increased every minute and soon became an obsession.

I was out of my mind.

With an aching heart, I tried to find some method of getting hold of those instalments, and finally decided to commit a crime. My first idea was simply to walk up to the counter, brazenly snatch the two instalments, and then ruff off as far away as possible, perhaps to the beach, where alone behind a rock I could revel in the story's climax. But I had to abandon this plan because a by no means admirable instinct for self-preservation whispered to me that the moment I seized the books, the kiosk's proprietor, a scrofulous Jew with a face completely strewn with yellow, millet-like freckles, would jump out through the back-door and raise such a hullabaloo that passers-by would stop me at once and hand me over to the nearest policeman as a wretched little thief; and what would follow after that was too awful to imagine.

The evil spirit whispering into my left ear then suggested that, unseen by the proprietor, I go round to the rear of the kiosk and fasten the back-door with a padlock. On my pointing out that I had no padlock, it proposed that I tie the two metal rings together with a wire or a piece of string. Finally, since I had no wire or string, either, and I could not bear to defer action much longer, the evil spirit advised me to secure the rings with a handkerchief.

I did have a handkerchief in my pocket, though it was far from clean, it would certainly do the trick. Tiptoeing round the hexagonal stall with my heart in my mouth and my face contorted with anxiety, I slipped the handkerchief through the rings and knotted it as tightly as I could, adding a little saliva in the hopes that the knot would contract still further. The evil spirit assured me that I could now safely approach the counter and pinch the instalments: it would not even be necessary to make a quick escape, for what could the proprietor do? He would certainly rush to the door, but, to his dismay, would be unable to open it and would find himself trapped inside the kiosk. When he finally did succeed in emerging into the street and calling a policeman, there would be no trace of me, however loudly he screamed.

Having checked the firmness of the knot, I walked up to the counter with a vague smile on my face and, disregarding the Jew's amiable question: "What would you like, my boy?," snatched the instalments and raced off as fast as I could. I was trembling with fear that, in a matter of seconds, there would be shouts, the shrill sound of a policeman's whistle, and a chase, ending in my being seized by the arm and conducted to the police-station, not as an ordinary little sneak-thief but as a burglar who had executed a well-planned raid on a commercial property.

I hared across the road and darted down a side-street which led to Otrada, pressing the damp books, still reeking of printer's-ink, to my pounding heart. I was slightly taken aback by the fact that I did not hear any hue and cry behind me.

Reaching a three-storied building under construction, I climbed up to the very top of the scaffolding and clambered into a room where the rafters were already half-covered by tiles. Here, seated on a pile of bricks, was the small, sad figure of Zhorka Somov, afraid to go home because his school-report contained two bottom marks, one next to bottom, and an extremely unpleasant comment by his form-master. His round, fat, lazy, country-bumpkin face bore faint traces of dried-up tears. I triumphantly showed him the precious new instalments and, like a couple of lunatics, we immediately plunged into the final adventures of "Ines Navarro—the beautiful demon." Blind and deaf to everything around us, we read and read till we came to the end, when we found that the attic was already becoming dark. Only then did I realize the full horror of my situation.

Zhorka plodded back home, sighing and dragging his satchel by its torn strap as though it were as heavy as lead. I followed him slowly with the stolen books carefully concealed under my jacket and an uneasy feeling that every passer-by would be aware of my raid on the newspaper kiosk. However, everything was quiet on the street and no-one paid the slightest attention to me. At home, too, everything was perfectly normal.

Was it possible, I wondered, that my theft had passed unnoticed? It seemed highly improbable that the proprietor had failed to discover that the door had been tightly tied up with a handkerchief. No, he must certainly have informed the police long ago, and now those accursed blood-hounds from the criminal investigation department would be following me; any minute now, there would be a ring at the front door and, when the door was opened, the sleuths and policemen would walk in, put steel handcuffs on my wrists, and take me in a carriage to the Odessa prison fortress, where I would be placed in solitary confinement. The bell, in fact, did ring. I nearly fainted and then rushed to lock myself up in the lavatory; but it was only Papa returning from a conference of the pedagogical council. The blue note-books under his arm reminded me uncomfortably of the Nick Carter instalments.

Papa looked at me just as usual with his tired eyes, rumpled my hair, and kissed my forehead, which led me to conclude that he had heard nothing as yet.

For this day, at least, the storm seemed to have blown over, but what of the morrow? It was dreadful to contemplate! In the morning, I would be going to school and there was no way of avoiding the newspaper-kiosk. So the proprietor, whom I had robbed, would inevitably see me and then the scandal would start.

I tried to slip past the kiosk unobserved, with my head averted, but from the corner of my eye I glimpsed the stall and the face of the proprietor behind the counter: he seemed to be regarding me with an alarming expression of irony and feigned indifference. A shudder went down my back. Ah, this gentle Jew must be plotting something against me! I felt certain he had already informed the police about my crime, and the director of the school, too, which meant I would be arrested or, even worse, expelled and black-listed.

More dead than alive, I entered the classroom after saluting the director exaggeratedly and servilely in the corridor on the way: he gave me a curt nod with his head of silvery, close-cropped hair in response. Then I sat through all five lessons on tenterhooks, expecting to be summoned to the director's study at any moment to be lectured on my sins and told my fate.

But I was torturing myself unnecessarily. The day passed peacefully and without incident: I did not even receive bad marks. On my way home, I again had to slip past the kiosk without being noticed, and again glimpsed the proprietor's eyes, looking at me with the same indifference, but somehow ambiguously, above the Odessa *Post* which he was reading. A week went by and Friday came, when the new installments of Nick Carter's adventures usually appeared in the kiosk, with new alluring pictures on the cover to whet one's appetite for the mysteries and secrets within. This time, the St. Petersburg express train brought a new serial, featuring Dr. Dazar, and I was unable to resist the temptation of passing close to the stall just to get a momentary glance at the cover.

. . . Nick Carter stood half-concealed behind a velvet curtain in a resplendent sitting-room, where the criminals of Dr. Dazar's society gang were carousing, and in each hand the great detective grasped a large Smith and Wesson revolver. The male criminals wore long beards, tails, and starched white shirts while their female colleagues were in evening dresses covered in diamonds. Nick Carter alone was dressed modestly and correctly, and his alert, adolescent face seemed to be mouthing sarcastically: "Caught, my fine gentlemen! Hands up! Now I'll pack you all off to Sing Sing and the electric chair!"

. . . "Young man! Hi, young man, just a minute!" I heard the proprietor's voice call out. "I don't understand why you keep running past me like a hare! Your papa paid your little debt for the two instalments of *Ines Navarro—the Beautiful Demon* the day before yesterday. He was buying the Odessa *News* and I reminded him that you owed me fourteen kopecks. Take the Dr. Dazar books. You don't have to worry. I'll give you credit. Or perhaps you'd like to choose one of the Sherlock Holmes stories? Try *The Speckled Band*: the boys seem to like it. Or how about the adventures of Nina Blavatsky? Or Elsa Gavronsky? Though you may be a bit young to learn about her amorous adventures. . . ."

The Children of Captain Grant ✒

THEATRE-TICKETS cost a lot of money and stalls were quite beyond my means. Therefore, on the rare occasions when I managed to go to the theatre, I always gazed at the auditorium from the low, slanting side-seats of the amphitheatre or even the gallery. From there, the famous electric chandelier, suspended from the coarsely daubed ceiling and strewn with luminous pearls like a crown—the pride of the Odessa town council—was quite close to me, while the magnificent curtain, adorned with paintings of scenes from *Russlan and Ludmilla,* seemed no larger than a picture post-card, stuck up above the tiniest of footlights and a prompter's box the size of a small seashell. In the orchestra-pit, one could see music-stands, musical instruments, and figures in tails leaning forward to examine their scores; and, as the instruments were tuned, a cacophony soared up, rasping one's nerves, yet promising soon to become the enthralling, harmonious music of an overture. When the lights in the auditorium were lowered, leaving nothing visible but the red dark-room lamps over the exits, and the curtain went up, all I could see was the front part of the stage, across which the artistes, so foreshortened as to appear short-legged and large-headed, sidled like crabs and frequently disappeared from view altogether. With the low proscenium-arch, even binoculars would have been of no help to me.

But one day, during the Christmas holidays, our whole family went to a matinée of *The Children of Captain Grant* at reduced prices, and my aunt insisted on our sitting in the stalls like decent people; and not somewhere at the back of them, but in velvet arm-chairs in the sixth row, which was considered the smart place to be. I think that my aunt was secretly dreaming of a box in the first or second tier: it would have been going too far to dream of one of the luxurious stage-boxes, with a mirror hung on its moiré-covered partition. But the sixth row of the stalls was not too bad. It is true that our seats were at the end of the row, so part of the stage was masked from us, but my view was far less restricted than it was from my usual position in the gods.

"Matinée" was a magic word that made my heart leap and my hands tremble and sent an icy shiver of excitement running from my neck, enclosed in a clean, starched collar under the stand-up one of my cloth school-jacket, down the wohle length of my spine.

We were having heavy frosts, in our part of the world, and the theatre was rather cold and empty as I enjoyed the incomparable experience of a matinée performance. The white foyer was bathed in blue day-light, filtering through the high, frosty window-panes, and the auditorium was softly lit by brocade-shaded electric lights and lamps like large, elongated pearls, set in bronze, which glimmered above the boxes.

One of the charms of the theatre—said to be the prettiest nineteenth-century theatre in Europe—lay in the fact that in the interval between the third and fourth acts, an iron safety-curtain slowly came down. It was painted to look like golden brocade with straight folds and heavy silken tassels, although one could sense the slatted iron underneath and occasionally glimpse a reddish streak of rust. The descent of the iron curtain entertained the audience so much that scarcely anyone left their seats during this interval and the refreshment-bar did little business.

The bar in the first-floor lounge fascinated us almost more than the performance on the stage. Never had I seen such big Duchesse pears, the mere sight of which made one's mouth water, such big chocolate eggs wrapped in silver paper, with surprises inside, such alluring cakes, and such exciting bottles of fizzy lemonade, which shot out their corks, as if from a pistol, leaving their necks, surrounded by the remains of the wire, smoking and exuding a moist, prickly smell of lemon. Finally, no sandwiches could have been better than those displayed on the buffet-counter, especially the small, round open ones covered with caviar, sparkling like black shoepolish, which cost twenty kopecks and our family could not afford.

Altogether, the prices in the bar were quite beyond us. I accepted, like a fairy-tale, the fact that a big Duchesse pear cost a rouble: it passed my understanding and endowed the theatre-bar with a magic aura.

We walked gingerly past the stall, afraid of slipping on the icelike surface of the well-polished parquet, with our admiring eyes glued to the resplendent buffet, resembling some magnificent symbol, taking in the candies and sandwiches exposed on its counter and the bouquets of artificial wax flowers and fern, through which peeped the salmon-pink face of the attendant: his expression was one of faint disdain towards those unable to face his prices. He seemed to be casually sizing up our clothes and shoes, from which he no doubt deducted that we were unlikely to approach him and buy anything. Here, all that was free was our reflections in the huge, cold mirrors and a sight of the ornate, plastered ceiling.

. . . Can you image one pear, even if it is a Duchesse, costing a rouble? It's day-light robbery!

Next to me in the sixth row sat another family, with a girl of about my age, in a purple velvet dress with a white lace collar, which covered half her straight, slender back, and white leather button-up shoes. Her hair was falling loose over her shoulders, which, in my eyes, made her resemble a mermaid. She smelled of eau de Cologne, and, in her excitement, kept crumpling the small handkerchief she was holding in her hand. Naturally, I was immediately drawn to her, but as I was always timid with girls and she was haughty, I did not have the courage to speak to her and we never became acquainted.

. . . As for the play, I knew the story well and was full of admiration for the convincing, true-to-life way it was presented on the stage. Lord Glenarvon was most impressive with his clean-shaven, long face and bushy, red side-whiskers; Paganel, in check trousers, with a telescope in his hand, kept stumbling and falling over things and was so absent-minded that on one occasion he put a lady's muff on his head instead of his tropical helmet, which roused the audience to gales of laughter and applause; the scoundrel, Ayrton, on the other hand, provoked general indignation. . . . The Indian fired a long rifle at a card-board eagle, which was carrying a little card-board boy—called, I believe, Robert—in its beak. We were all terrified lest he shot the boy instead of the eagle, but all went well, the eagle was killed and fell into the wings, whence, a moment later, a real, life, blond Robert appeared, none the worse for his narrow escape.

. . . I would bet now that he was a girl, perhaps even a woman! All this, of course, was very exciting, but I was even more interested in how it was done; in the actual mechanics of the performance. I expressed my theories aloud, which caused my disapproving neighbours to hiss at me and the fascinating little girl on my left to throw in some scornful glances as well.

But one scene really distressed me immeasurably; it was when the heroes reached Patagonia, smothered in antarctic icebergs, and must inevitably die of cold amidst the huge blocks of ice, sinisterly lit up by a quicksilver white polar sun. Drinking-water and food were at an end, there was no fuel, the temperature was a long way below zero, breathing had become difficult, there was no material for making a bonfire—and not matches to light it anyway.

It was a desperate situation with no apparent means of escape. They sat on a snowdrift, huddled against each other, and entrusted themselves to the hands of Providence, since there was nothing else to be done. And there they were, freezing to death, in front of the whole audience, while Providence was slow to intervene. To make matters worse, a huge iceberg was suddenly lit from within by an errie blue light and the audience gave a gasp of horror on seeing Death himself, the most awe-inspiring, true figure of Death, with grinning skull, white shoud, and scythe raised over the frozen heroes.

"How do they do it?" I wondered to myself, appalled and astonished at the same time.

It seemed now that the end had really come. Providence was too late in arriving. And then, beyond the mass of polar icebergs, on the narrow, blue strip of open sea, there appeared a dot, which became transformed into a tiny frigate, dashing with full sail to the rescue of the dying explorers. From time to time, the frigate disappeared into the wings, to emerge again much nearer and considerably larger.

Finally, it suddenly reappeared near the front of the stage, having nosed its way through the ice-floes with a life-sized bow, complete with bowsprit, anchor and three billowing jibs.

"Hurrah!" exclaimed the desperate explorers, whose lives had been hanging on a thread, and rushed into the arms of their rescuers, who had jumped from the ship onto the stage.

An indescribable delight enveloped the audience. Everybody cried "Hurrah," too, clapped, laughed, and yelled. It was a veritable triumph! And there was nothing for unhappy Death to do but lower his card-board scythe on to his shoulders and retire into the wings, unforunately getting entangled in his white shroud as he left the iceberg. As the assistant stage-manager had forgotten to switch off the blue light, the mishap was plainly visible to the audience, who watched it with malignant pleasure.

At this juncture, my aunt, wiping away her tears with her lace handkerchief, produced a box of Abrikosoff chocolates from her muff and told Zhenka, her favourite, to offer them to our neighbours. Zhenka, in short velvet trousers and long stockings, opened the box and, hypnotised by the sight of the mass of wonderful sweets, among them a particularly appetising triangle of glacé pineapple, could not bring himself at first to hand them round.

"Well, Zhenia, don't be shy, offer the sweets!"

Then Zhenia, glancing up with innocent chestnut-coloured eyes from under his soft fringe of hair, offered the box to the pretty girl and said in a trembling voice: "I don't suppose you want any sweets?" . . . and thus ended our Christmas expedition to the theatre.

Oh, that cool reflection of the bowl of oranges in the huge mirror on the first tier! Oh, those sandwiches with caviar! Oh, the little mermaid!

Catching Sparrows

A RUMOUR that it was easy to catch sparrows with vodka, just by soaking soft crumbs of bread in it and strewing them about the yard, or in spots in the meadow where the birds were accustomed to foregather, reached the boys from God knows where.

Today it seems incomprehensible to me why anyone should want
to catch sparrows, but at that age the question never arose. What
boy could resist a chance of catching a live sparrow? It was quite
unnecessary to search for a reason: all that mattered was achieving
one's object. It was, if you like, the primeval instinct to trap, which
is buried in every man.

Up till then, the simplest way of catching sparrows was considered
by us in Otrada to be as follows: you made a sort of box on the
ground from four bricks and raised a fifth one on a stick to serve
as a roof. To this stick you attached a long piece of string and put
some grain in the box as bait. Immediately the sparrow jumped
into the trap to peck at the grain, you jerked the string, the stick
supporting the top brick would fall away, and the sparrow would
be imprisoned. It was very sound theoretically, but in practice the
sparrow never seemed to be attracted by the bait: either the coarse
bricks frightened them away or the stick and piece of string led
them to suspect that all was not quite above-board. I tried to catch
sparrows by this method innumerable times and never had any
success.

The fever to catch sparrows with vodka attacked the boys in our
town like an epidemic. There were boys who swore solemn oaths,
eating earth to give them even more weight, that they had caught
sparrows single-handed with vodka. I, too, of course, fell a prey to
the epidemic.

The desire to achieve the feat became a fixation and I felt I should
find no peace until my dream had come true.

But a serious problem arose: where was I to get the vodka? We
kept none in our sober house: we were forbidden even to utter the
word. I knew that drunkards usually bought vodka in a state-owned
wine-shop and often drank it on the spot straight out of the bottle—
glug ... glug ... glug—and the fiery liquid would be trickling down
the drunkard's beard.

I knew where the nearest shop was, but had no idea how much
the vodka cost or whether they would sell it to a boy of my age, and
a school-boy into the bargain, when it was strictly forbidden by law.

I consulted the yardsman and learned that there were two different
kinds of vodka, called "white-top" and "red-top" from the colours
of the wax with which the bottles were sealed. "White-top" was considered the better distilled and consequently cost more than "red-

top." I assumed that a sparrow would not greatly care in which vodka the bait was soaked and decided to buy the inferior one, always supposing the shop would let me have it. The immediate obstacle was the money.

Oh, money, money! How often I have had to mention it in this book! But it cannot be helped: the lack of it was constantly cropping up in my life.

Where was I to get it? I looked in the drawer of the side-board, where the cook left the change from the housekeeping-money. It was empty. The door of my aunt's bedroom was locked. A search through the pockets of Papa's old trousers, hanging in his cupboard, produced nothing. What was I to do? I gazed thoughtfully out the window and saw, as though they were doing it deliberately to annoy me, innumerable sparrows hopping about on the hard autumn ground, among the bare lilac-bushes, and pecking away at any muck they could find. If I could have laid my hand on some vodka, I would have had shown them something! The sight of them inflamed me with an urgent desire to set about my catching operation immediately. But the money! What about the money?

I should mention that vodka was sold in bottles of different sizes, each with its special name: "noggin," "little villain," and so on. I understood that a noggin, which I was certain would be sufficient for at least a dozen sparrows, cost twenty-one kopecks.

I had already thought up a subtle manoeuvre to induce the shop to sell me vodka. I would shed a tear and beg pitifully, claiming that my little brother had caught cold and that the doctor had prescribed vodka to be rubbed on his chest. After that, they would surely not be able to refuse me. Now the idea suddenly came to me to approach the lodger, to whom we rented a room, for the wherewithal. The lodger was a most unpleasant individual, always grumbling and complaining. He had no work and lounged all day on his bed in a waistcoat, without a jacket or shoes, his feet, in dirty socks, propped up on the end of it. When he rented the room, he had introduced himself as the well-known explorer Jakovlev. This had made a certain impression on my aunt and, though his hairy face, dirty pince-nez, filthy, starched collar, paper dickey, and a sort of crooked, finicky, cantankerous expression had not pleased her, the explorer had been let a room.

. . . I will tell you some more about this lodger later and also about the other ones to whom we let rooms, but now I must not be detracted.

Making silly grimaces because of my embarrassment, I knocked on the famous explorer's door. The snoring coming from inside stopped, and I heard a squeaky, angry, nasal voice: "Who's there? What do you want? Come in!"

I went in and, overcoming my fear in front of this famous person, I muttered, after remembering to click my heels: "Good morning! Forgive me for waking you up. The fact is, there's no one at home and I'm in urgent need of some money to buy vodka."

"Ah, that's the trouble, is it?" drawled the famous explorer. "It's a bit early in the morning, you know. And, anyway, I haven't any money."

"I only need twenty-one kopecks," I said imploringly.

"Yes, for a noggin . . ." the explorer murmured.

"Don't worry, I'll give it back to you, I promise." I made the sign of the cross and, to convince him further, added: "May I sink under the earth if I don't."

"Hm . . ." Jakovlev muttered unpleasantly, putting on his pince-nez, which made his face even more crooked. "Hm . . . It's rather uncouth to burst unceremoniously into a lodger's room when he's resting and demand money from him. I don't . . . understand such ways!"

With these words, the famous explorer, without getting off his bed, rummaged in the pockets of his striped trousers, yellow at the seams and around the belt, clinked a buch of keys, and finally stretched out his palm to me with some change on it—exactly twenty-one kopecks.

"But, remember now, I'm giving you this money on account of my rent. And don't you bother me again!"

I retreated on tiptoe, and he locked the door behind me: then I heard the bed-springs creak and a sniffle that must have been the prelude to a snore.

The purchase of the vodka did not go as smoothly as I had hoped; still, I achieved it in the end. The employee at the state shop, who sat behind a wire grille, proved to be a powdered lady, with a widow's tearful eyes and a fat, greasy face with a lilac flush. She said to me impertinently: "Out you go! How shameful, a school-boy like you, the son of intelligent parents, beginning at your age! I'll call the police and you'll have your school-card taken away. Never let me set eyes on you again! Out!"

I jumped like a scalded cat back into the street, where a crowd of drunken coachmen and barefooted vagrants were opening their various-sized bottles. This is how it was done: first of all, the wax had to be scraped off the top by means of a tin grater driven into the trunk of an acacia-tree in a spot where the drunks could not spoil the town's flora. The bearded coachmen, with transparent blue eyes and red noses, in oilskin or card-board hats with side-buckles and blue cloaks down to their ankles, together with the barefooted tramps, literally barefooted, or occasionally wearing some kind of incredible bark shoes tied to their feet with strings, in denim trousers and torn shirts, through the holes of which one could glimpse their naked bodies—"Maxim Gorki characters," as they were called at that time—crowded round the grater, supervised by a policeman, and scraped off the wax till the grater seemed to be covered in blood. Then, after a skillful knock on the bottom of the noggin with the palms of their hands had shot out the cork, they threw their heads back and poured the pure liquid, which had a sweet, slightly narcotic smell that made my head turn, straight down their throats. When satisfied, they wiped their hairy mouths on their sleeves and bit into appetising, yellow-green salted cucumbers, from which brine and the colourless seeds spurted profusely.

I caught sight of a man with a wheelbarrow, a sack on his head, who was already slightly sozzled and lying in the barrow with its shafts down, waiting for someone to hire him. He had reddish, wet whiskers and kind, half-drunken eyes. Feeling a wave of confidence in him, I asked hom to buy me some vodka. Giving me a wink, as to a brother-alcoholic, he readily agreed and, shortly afterwards, I was running home with the red wax seal on the neck of a noggin peeping disreputably out of the pocket of my coat. Back in my room, without wasting a second by taking off my coat, I scraped the wax off on the window-sill, filled a plate with white bread, and poured the vodka over it. Then I went out into the yard and began throwing the wet, soft crumbs about under the naked lilac-bushes and the apple-trees, with their trunks already wrapped in straw for the winter.

I was surprised to find no sparrows about when, before I had bought the noggin, they seemed to be perching on every bush and tree. I hid behind the back-door and waited, confident that the sparrows would soon see the crumbs of white bread and be attracted by the bait. Yet I waited in vain. It was a good half-hour before the first sparrow appeared, a beautiful one, no longer young and already well-fed and fattened-up for the winter: its shining feathers might have been drawn skilfully and accurately with India ink on silk by some great Chinese or Japanese artist. Its eyes sparkled like the eyes of a child and its head turned in every direction as it hopped resiliently about on its tiny feet. At first, it paid no attention to the crumbs, but eventually it noticed them, picked one of them up, shook it, spat it out of its beak in disgust, and flew away out of sight. *Fr . . . fr . . . fr . .*

"What a fool!" I thought.

Soon, about five other admirable sparrows arrived and began hopping about among my bait, but for some reason paid no attention to it, preferring to peck at the earth between the crumbs without touching them.

"What's got into them? Have they gone crazy?" I wondered.

They continued to hop about among the bits of bread and then suddenly flew away, as if in obedience to some order, separating as they skimmed low above the ground like scattered beads. *Fr . . . fr . . . fr . . .*

I began to feel cold, but firmly decided not to give in before I had caught at least one sparrow. I was longing to see how a sparrow drunk on vodka would behave. From my hiding-place, I saw my aunt bring Zhenka back from the kindergarten and my papa arrive home in his heavy coat, carrying a stack of blue exercise-books tied up with string under his arm.

I remained by the back-door till it grew dark. Several flakes of snow flew past, foretelling the coming of winter.

The sparrows came and went, in flocks and alone. Some of them pecked at my bits of bread and occasionally even carried them away somewhere in their beaks; fiinally, they ate up the whole of my bait, but not one of them became intoxicated, reeled about, and collapsed—which, after all, was what I had been counting upon.

Several times I was called to through the window to come in and do my home-work and have some tea, but I did not reply, unable to accept the fact that my dream had not come true. I still believed a moment would come when another flock of sparrows would arrive, find some remnants of bread soaked in vodka, get drunk, and fall down; I would then be able to pick them up, five or six of them, as they lay completely sozzled. What a surprise that would be for everyone!

Alas, my dreams just remained dreams. The theory of being able to catch sparrows with vodka proved pure rubbish. I went inside empty-handed.

This story of one more dream of mine that was never fulfilled could stop here if a few days later the following had not happened: I had hardly had time to cross the threshold of our apartment on my return from school when Father placed himself in my path. His pince-nez wobbled on his nose, his neck kept twitching, as though confined by too tight a collar, and there was an angry flush on his cheeks.

"You worthless boy!" he screamed, his lower jaw protruding. "It seems you've taken to secretly drinking spirits!"

"Darling Papa," I sobbed. "I swear to you by whatever you like—here's my holy cross."

"Don't blaspheme," said Papa. Taking me by the shoulders, he began to shake me, muttering at the same time: "My God; My son a drunkard! A vodka-drinker!"

His beard wagged more and more violently.

"Darling Papa, how did you find out?" I asked, sobbing.

"The explorer Jakovlev paid for his room today and subtracted the twenty-one kopecks you secretly got out of him for vodka. So there's no point in lying. You're no longer a son of mine! . . ."

He went on and on in the same vein. . . .

Obviously, a man tells the truth more often when he is exercising his imagination and lies when he is trying to be truthful.

The Lecture

THE IDEA SUDDENLY came to Papa, who taught geography in the school, to ask the explorer Jakovlev to give a lecture, with a magic lantern, to the older girls. It was known that Jakovlev kept a box of slides taken by himself during his world travels in his huge check suit-case.

Jakovlev did not agree at once. With a sour expression, he first said that public lectures in a packed hall, with no proper ventilation, were too great a strain on his nervous system and caused him to suffer from insomnia for a long time afterwards. Papa promised him that the hall where the lecture would take place would be adequately ventilated and that only the four senior classes would be present. Jakovlev then expressed doubts as to the quality of the school magic lantern. Papa assured him that the lantern was quite new and up to scratch.

"And electrically lit, no doubt?" Jakovlev asked sarcastically.

Papa was embarrassed and his forehead became slightly pink.

"No," he admitted, "but we have a very strong paraffin lamp with an excellent reflector."

"I can imagine the soot and heat it'll throw out," the famous explorer said, talking through his nose.

"The soot is removed by a special suction funnel," Papa replied stiffly, hurt by this attack on the school magic lantern.

"I can just see that funnel!" Jakovlev retorted with a snort, and his concave face became even more so.

"In any case, I can safely promise there will be no soot," Papa said, this time in his official voice.

The more the explorer quibbled, the more determined Papa became to arrange the lecture with what were then called "dissolving views." He could foresee the impression they would make on the members of the governing body, particularly when accompanied by a lecture from a famous explorer like Jakovlev, not to mention the high educative value of the undertaking.

After raising a few more objections, Jakovlev finally agreed.

"You will be doing us a great favour and, at the same time, be making a truly Christian, disinterested contribution to the education of young girls in the diocesan school, whose minds are craving for enlightenment," Papa said.

A somewhat uncalled-for grimace of displeasure appeared on the famous explorer's face. However, he rummaged in his voluminous suitcase, full of dirty linen, and extracted from it a box of slides in considerable disorder.

Papa divided them into countries and chose the most impressive ones (discarding those which featured naked bathing ladies in Ceylon); then he and the explorer composed a short synopsis of the lecture and arranged the slides in the right order.

I remember that this lecture caused infinite trouble and worry. Jakovlev insisted on a special screen being made for him, categorically refusing to show his slides on the white wall of the big hall, as he considered this to be a desecration of science. This screen cost the school a pretty penny. Then, after a captious examination of the lantern, which Papa brought home for that purpose in a cab, the explorer expressed great displeasure at the slide-holder: first, his slides were too thick to fit into it and, second, slides could only be inserted one at a time. He demanded that a new sliding frame be constructed, holding two slides, so that, while a new one was being shown, the old one could be extracted and replaced, thus avoiding delays and interruptions to his narrative. This was not unreasonable, but, unfortunately, ordinary carpenters could not cope with such delicate work and, when a specialist was found, he asked ten roubles for his skill and expertise—such a large sum that the school-treasurer made a great fuss before agreeing to pay and and reproached Papa for organizing a geographical entertainment that would so vastly increase the school's capital expenditure. On hearing these words, which almost amounted to a vote of censure, Papa flushed scarlet and was within an ace of abandoning the whole undertaking, but his innate love for geography carried the day in the end.

On the day of the lecture, Jakovlev insisted on being taken to the school in a rubber-tyred cab for fear of his precious slides being broken. Papa agreed but, as the cost of a cab had not been included in the schedule of expenses, he had to pay the fare out of his own pocket.

Zhenka and I were allowed to go to the lecture on condition that we should be on our best behaviour, and we sat in the exciting darkness of the diocesan school-hall, surrounded by girls who whispered and giggled, but with, to their credit, a certain amount of restraint.

The head-mistress sat on a gilt-chair in the front row, a stern, cold figure with a gold watch hanging on a chain from her belt and the beak-like nose and protuberant chest of a turkey. The form-mistresses sat among the girls, keenly alert to ensure that nothing improper occurred: there was, after all, an unknown man within the walls of this closed institution—the explorer Jakovlev—and who could tell what his moral standards might be?

The magic lantern, already red-hot, stood on a special table, casting brilliant arrows of light on to the surrounding walls. Papa was kept busy inserting the slides into the new frame and I felt humiliation and pain at seeing him in the humble role of an attendant.

The famous explorer himself, in a long frock-coat that filled the whole hall with the smell of naphthalene and unaired linen, dominated the room from the rostrum beside the screen: he was holding a long pointer, another accessory that had to be specially ordered, which added the smell of carpenter's polish to the others. With this pointer, Jakovlev indicated various objects in the enlarged photographs that, with Papa's assistance, appeared on the brightly lit square screen: photographs of a coconut-grove on the shores of the Indian Ocean, Norwegian fjords, a Buddhist temple in the Tibetan mountains, a group of naked, white-toothed Negro women (whose appearance caused the head-mistress to shift uneasily in her chair and subdued murmurs to come from the form-mistresses), Egyptian pyramids, a camel against a background of palm-trees with an Englishman sitting aloofly on its back, a sunset on the Nile and—oh, horrors—another group of naked women, this time Egyptians, standing in water that regrettably only came up to their knees.

Even in the darkness I could see the flush that rose round Papa's neck.

And the famous explorer, languidly moving the pointer about on the screen, muttered on monotonously, always including the number of the slide:

"Number . . . hm . . . fifteen: View of the Bay of Naples with the famous volcano Vesuvius in the background. In front—a group of pretty Italian girls with tambourines dancing the tarantella. . . . Number sixteen: A market in Zanzibar. On the right, the picture of the local beauty, carrying a jug on her head. Number thirty-six: Bathers on the shore of the bay of Biscay. . . . Number forty: The world-famous marble statue *Leda and the Swan*, surrounded by admiring tourists. . . ."

To tell the honest truth, Zhenka and I were painfully bored, and when the lecture ended, at the demand of the head-mistress, we sighed with relief.

The head-mistress rose from her golden chair and, seeming to be carrying her corseted bosom in front of her, majestically and angrily retired, followed swiftly by the form-mistresses, driving their perspiring pupils ahead of them.

Papa hastily put the slides back into their boxes, as the famous explorer, rubbing his hands together, announced: "I expect to be remunerated for my lecture. Usually I charge a fee of thirty roubles, payable in advance, but as today's had the philanthropic aim of enlightening young girls from a clerical background, I'll be satisfied with twenty-five roubles."

Papa, who had naturally taken for granted that the lecture would be free, grew cold as ice.

"I must tell you . . ." he muttered.

"No, it's I who apparently must tell you," the explorer said.

"But this expense was never foreseen in the estimates," Papa went on muttering. "And I sincerely hope . . ."

"It's no use hoping," the explorer said decisively. "Every type of work, my dear sir, deserves remuneration, particularly an explorer's. And if I don't receive it, I shall go to law!"

"You're putting me in an impossible position," Papa said, his voice trembling. "I shall be forced to pay you out of my own pocket!"

"All the better!" Jakovlev exclaimed gleefully, and it was the first time I had seen a smile on his hollow face. "It suits me. I'll be able to use the money to pay you the rent I owe."

"Dear sir," exclaimed Papa, and his employment of this form of address showed the height to which his indignation had risen. "Dear sir! I have always considered that a man of science should not seek to use it as a source of profit. In any case, gentlemen don't behave in that way."

"Really?" answered Jakovlev, continuing to smile disagreeably. "I always behave in that way, and I still consider myself a gentleman."

What could Papa do?

A month later, the famous explorer left his room, having paid us nothing, loaded his check suit-case onto a cab and, surprising passersby with his black overcoat and cork helmet, disappeared to other lodgings.

. . . Possibly to another continent.

Church Wine ✍

. . . I CAN SEE, the starched cuff, emerging from the sleeve of the precentor's long frock-coat, and the small steel tuning-fork held in his

slender fingers; I can hear the pleasant note it emitted, most probably "do," seemingly resolving all possible doubts, and the harmonious
singing of the school-boy choir by the altar of our school-church,
named after St. Alexis, the guardian angel of the heir to the throne,
Alexis, the small son of the emperor and the future sovereign of the
Russian empire.

The temples of God did not exist only in parishes but were also
attached to certain institutions, sometimes even to the private houses
of rich people—the so-called "house-churches."

To have a private church in one's own home was a sign of great
wealth and piety.

There were also private churches in some schools. There was one
in the emperor's Novorossijsk University.

"Where are you going for the Easter midnight service?"

"To the University Church."

"Where will the marriage service take place?"

"In the University Church."

"Where are you taking Communion in Holy Week?"

"In the University Church."

It was considered very chic to go to the University Church. It
was a sign of good breeding.

People went there "for the Twelve Gospels"; lovers' meetings were
arranged there.

When a private church with a sanctified altar was installed in
our school, we, too, appeared to have climbed to a higher rung on
the social ladder: up till then, the school had by no means been considered a good one. It was situated in a poor district—in Novoribni
Street—where some of its windows looked out on the Kulikovo field
and the station, and it was mainly the children of the railway staff,
clerks, or even guards and ticket-inspectors who were educated there,
which caused some people to smile disdainfully and shrug their
shoulders when its name was mentioned.

Our Alexeev church had no cupola, but light streamed in from
both sides through a row of high windows, and on sunny Sundays
it looked very attractive, principally because all the religious accessories to worship were brand-new: the freshly painted icons, the
brightly gilded iconostasis, the brocade and silver gonfalons, the
silver candle-holders, the lustre—modest in size but fitted with electric—lights, the beautifully ornate chalices, the gold-brocaded altar-
cloth, the wine-coloured silk curtain that was drawn at the par-

ticularly mysterious and mystical moments of the liturgy—when the wine in the cup turned into Christ's blood and the bread into Christ's flesh, the immaculate, rigid chasubles of the priest and deacon, the yellow poplar-wood table for the sale of candles and Communion-bread, the silver collection-plate, covered with a silk, embroidered napkin, and, finally, the round jugs for donations, attached to the candle-table into which small copper coins dropped with a metallic clink.

All this was reflected in the new, yellow, highly polished parquet floor, where the azure-blue of the windows blended with the red-dish tones of the altar-curtain, the ruby tints of the church lamps hanging on broad moiré ribbons, embroidered with roses, and the flickering gold of the candles in front of the icons of the holy saints.

We school-boys were brought here in an Indian file, with the class-supervisor at the head, and arranged on the left of the choir, while the director, inspector, and teachers, in uniforms and frock-coats, with decorations and medals, stood in front of us. And in the body of the church were all the others: ladies in hats, men in frock-coats, officers in uniforms, civil servants, girls with plaits, fringes, and curls, adorned with silk ribbons—white, chocolate-coloured, and blue.

All this looked very picturesque and one's soul was not disturbed with dismal forebodings of inevitable death, as usually happened in old, half-dark, shabby churches. In our new church, there was more of a festive, wedding atmosphere than a funereal one, a spirit of joy and gaiety that was not always, I would say, an entirely chaste one, particularly when, after Communion, at the end of the liturgy, we walked up in turn to the priest to kiss the new, still-untarnished golden cross, held in his weary hand, then drink some warm red wine diluted with water out of a shallow ladle, eat a piece of the Communion-bread, and put five or ten kopecks in the plate.

The Communion itself had already brought me into a state of mild, divine intoxication. Walking up the two steps on the carpet held in place by metal rods, I stopped in front of a young priest with a sandy beard, holding a long golden spoon in one hand.

"Open your mouth wider," he said in a studied voice. "What is your name?"

"Valentin."

"God's slave Valentin is taking Communion." And with these

: 144 :

words, he swiftly scooped up a small piece of Communion-bread, softened in the red wine, and pushed the spoon into my now wide-open mouth. The wine tasted fiery on my tongue, and as I swallowed the damp piece of "Christ's flesh" on an empty stomach (one could only take Communion before one had eaten), my soul was filled with a momentary divine intoxication. And, when the deacon, with a practised and rather brusque gesture, wiped my lips with a red linen napkin, by now well-saturated with wine, I became slightly intoxicated again.

. . . Oh, how I loved that feeling of divine intoxication; how I wanted to prolong it, to experience it just once more. . . .

Though, of course, I knew that it would soon be repeated when I drank from a gold ladle some warm, sweet, exhilarating Cahors wine, which I thought must be the best in the world. This wine was entrusted to class-mates of mine, whose good behaviour had led to their being chosen to assist in the service. In brocaded cassocks, with silver crosses woven on the back, slipped on over their school-clothes, they would hand the censer to the priest, after first blowing on the red-hot coals and adding grains of benjamin, which produced lilac-white clouds of aromatic smoke, and also open the bottles of Cahors wine and mix it with hot water in a silver jug.

Next day, they would let us smell their shoulders, impregnated with incense.

The proportion in which the two liquids, the wine and water, was mixed was in their hands. They contrived to make the mixture stronger for their friends and give them not just one ladleful, but two or even three. These acolytes were friends of mine, especially Vasska Ovsiannikov, with his good-natured, round face, dimpled cheeks, and innocent, almost girlish eyes; but his innocent appearance was misleading, for he was, in fact, a rogue, who finished off the remains of the Cahors wine with gusto after the service was over.

He had a nickname—Ponchik.

As we were friends, Ponchik took pains to prepare a pretty strong mixture for me, red as blood, let me join the queue three times, and filled the ladle to the brim whenever I came up; after which my head swam delightfully, my soul experienced unearthly bliss, as though floating in clouds of incense to the accompaniment of church music, and everything around acquired a magic silky-red colour, shot through with hot, golden sunbeams reflected from the new chalices.

On my way home, I staggered, and had to use all my will-power to prevent myself lying down in the grassy meadow, in the jungle of young, wild parsley which smeared the knees of one's denim summer trousers with its sharply smelling green juice, and falling blissfully asleep, a sleep, granted me by the serene Christian religion, with its propensity to intoxicate the faithful.

. . . Perhaps the idea of catching sparrows with vodka had originated in that divine, intoxicating bliss of Communion?

The Japanese 🖊

HE USED TO COME onto the stage, make a bow, pressing his hands, palms together, to his stomach in the Japanese way, then throw off his light-grey silk kimono and reveal himself to be wearing tights. He had the small, sturdy figure of an athlete, and his bare arms displayed impressive muscles. He started his turn by piercing these arms with long pins and walking round the first few rows of the audience to give them a closer view of his expanded, transfixed biceps. Then he pulled the pins out, one by one, and threw them onto a lacquered tray handed to him by his assistant, a Japanese girl in a bright kimono with a huge bow on her back, making her look like a gracefully hunch-backed butterfly.

The astounding thing was that this feat left no trace, not the smallest drop of blood on the tight balls of muscle. His next one seemed even more painful. The Japanese girl heated a large spoon filled with pieces of metal, probably pewter or lead, on a brazier and, when the metal had melted into a white curd-like liquid, carried the steaming spoon across the front of the stage to show it to the audience. Her hair, done in geisha fashion, resembled both a black snail and, with the protruding hair-pins, the keyboard of some strange musical instrument, as she then approached the man, bowed low in ritual greetings, and proferred him the spoon. He lifted it, red-hot, up to his mouth, poured in the molten metal and, a few moments later, in full view of the audience, spat out solid pieces one after the other onto the lacquered tray.

The feat was incomprehensible, and the whole audience broke into applause, as the Japanese turned abruptly to right and left with a strained smile on his face and held his mouth wide open with his tongue hanging out and his uvula trembling like another little tongue behind it. Then, with his pearly white teeth, apparently as strong as steel, he proceeded to bite lengths off a long metal rod, which the girl showed to the audience on her small pinkish-yellow palm.

Yet his most exciting feat lay ahead.

Curtsying and bowing from the waist, the Japanese girl brought an ordinary Viennese chair onto the stage and placed it in the middle of a special wooden square, so that it would stand firm and not sway. The man sat down on it, spreading the fat knees on his short legs well apart. Then the manager appeared, wearing a top-hat, and, in a loud, portentous circus-voice, invited any member of the distinguished audience to come up onto the stage and tie the Japanese's hands and feet in any way he chose, using ropes, chains, straps, or steel wire. Furthermore, the management gave a solemn undertaking to present one hundred roubles—yes, one hundred roubles—to anyone who succeeded in tying the man up in such a way that he was unable to free himself. As proof of the genuineness of the offer, the manager drew a new, crackling hundred-rouble note out of a smart wallet and placed it for all to see on the girl's tray. A few members of the public walked onto the stage, looking slightly embarrassed, and tied up the Japanese gentleman's hands and feet with ropes and straps, one of them even using an iron chain. I realised that most of these "members of the public" were stooges employed by the management, but, despite this, the trussed figure was most impressive and convincing, especially as everyone who wished to do so was allowed to examine the strength of the ropes and the tightness of the knots for himself. Overcoming my shyness, I, too, rushed down from the gallery onto the stage in my large winter school-coat, checked the knots and straps and examined the chain, of a type used to restrain fierce dogs, with what I hoped was the air of an expert. Everything appeared to be all right: the ropes had sunk deeply into the yellowish flesh of the man's strong, muscular arms. His girl assistant then threw a large silk shawl over his close-cropped black hair, enveloping him from head to foot. The band stopped playing and one could hear the hissing of the spot-lights.

"One, two, thlee!" the girl called out in a voice that resembled the cry of a heron. The man's body stirred slightly underneath the cover and the chair creaked; next second, he had flung off the shawl with a jerk of his powerful shoulders and was standing upright in front of the stunned audience, with the ropes, straps, chain, and overturned chair at his feet. He made a small gesture of greeting with both hands and an ovation broke out, which he received with a completely impassive expression on his orange, Asiatic face, with its short, very thick eyebrows.

The manager solemnly returned the hundred-rouble note to his wallet, raised his top-hat and left the stage.

So no-one in the audience was better off by a hundred roubles!

"Damn it all," I thought to myself. "If I only try hard enough, I must be able to find a way to shackle that little Jap so securely that he'll never be able to free himself. What a pity I couldn't get hold of a pair of automatic steel handcuffs like Nat Pinkerton's! Still, I'd see what I could do!"

The piercing of the biceps with pins was an old trick, only requiring a good knowledge of anatomy, and the swallowing of the molten metal, though very effective and at first sight impossible, was easily explained, too. Papa told me that metal existed which melted at a relatively low temperature, little hotter than that of a cup of tea that anyone could retain in his mouth.

As for the tying up with chains and ropes, everyone was sure that it was a piece of jiggery-pokery perpetrated with the connivance of the management. Yet I was still obsessed by the urgent desire to shackle the wily Oriental inextricably and win the hundred roubles.

I called all my imagination to my aid and spent sleepless nights till I finally hit on a plan. It was quite a simple one.

I would unscrew the protective steel chain from the front-door, manage to get hold of a small but strong padlock, raise forty kopecks for my ticket by hook or by crook, walk up onto the stage, make the Japanese stretch out his crossed arms, wrap the chain round his wrists, fasten the ends with the padlock, and, as additional security, fill the padlock's keyhole with wax, so that the Japanese spy (he must be a spy because, at that time, all Japanese were popularly known to be spies) would not be able to open it with his spy's master key.

It is scarcely necessary to mention the main obstacle to the plan was my lack of forty kopecks for the ticket, and I will not go into details as to how I finally obtained them, beyond saying that I quickly stifled the faint voice of conscience when it whispered into my right ear that it was not entirely ethical to sell Zhenia's sandals to a second-hand-clothes shop. It was no moment to embark on an argument with my conscience: time was flying and the Japanese's engagement might come to an end any day and then farewell forever to this unique occasion of becoming rich!

With the door-chain and the padlock, its keyhole already filled with dirty wax from a household candle, stuffed into the pocket of my coat, I walked onto the stage with a few other "willing members of the public" and indicated by signs that I wanted the man to stretch out his hands, one pressed against the other.

The Japanese looked at me with his indifferent serpent-like Buddhist eyes, in the depths of which I could detect a mocking gleam, and meekly stretched out his muscular athlete's arms, which looked as if they had been blown up with a bicycle-pump, the powerful wrists closely pressed together.

While the other "willing members" tied the Japanese to the chair, surrounding him with ropes and straps, I wound our door-chain round his wrists, assuming Nat Pinkerton's malicious smile, slipped the steel padlock, stolen from my aunt, through the last links and snapped it shut. I was already anticipating the moment when the Japanese would try to insert his master key and—aha!—find the keyhole completely filled with solid wax. That was indeed something to look forward to!

At long last, the Japanese, tied to the chair and enveloped in ropes, straps, and chains, his bare arms stretched out in front of him, firmly manacled by my door-chain, was solemnly covered from head to foot by the shawl. The band stopped playing and the Japanese girl, holding the hundred-rouble note on her tray, shrieked out to the silent, spellbound audience in her piercing and at the same time childishly tender heron's voice: "One, two, thlee!"

Whereupon, shawl and chair were flung to the floor and there was the Japanese, at his feet in disarray ropes, straps, and chains—including my door-chain completely intact, looking like an enormous bracelet fastened by a padlock—making his gestures of greeting to all and sundry before disappearing into the wings to thunderous applause from the audience. He came back again to take further calls and, in the course of them, glanced at me with the mysterious Asiatic eyes and whispered in quite good Russian: "Fooled you there, boy—ha—ha!" And thus ended my hopes of acquiring a hundred-rouble note.

. . . For a long time I could not figure out how he had managed to take off my chain and began to think he really was a magician. . . .

Then, later, someone explained to me that the Japanese was able to expand his muscles to such an extent when the ropes and chains were put on that he only had to contract them for the bonds to slip off quite easily. Thus his wrists were virtually inflated when I was winding the door-chain round them and, as soon as he chose to deflate them, he could shake it off without any necessity to break the padlock or produce a master key to unlock it.

Even nowadays, as I walk in Peredelkino, I sometimes hear the cry of that Japanese heron—Hokusai's heron: "One, two, thlee!"

The Matches ✍

BEFORE I REACHED the age of four, kerosene was called petrol, and the Nobel company delivered it in tins to the various houses from light cars, harnessed to small Scottish ponies, wearing straw hats with specially cut-out holes, through which their little brown ears, pale-pink inside, peeped out. It was at this period that I once found myself standing in the empty kitchen beside a Nobel tin of petrol, with a pretty, shiny, screw-on top.

"Sweetly smells white kerosene."

It was long past midday—after dinner, and the kitchen, already tidied and washed, smelled of the warm newspaper covering the rings of the stove as usual once cooking was over. The millet broom stood in a corner on a heap of litter and wooden, polished floor and large window-sill were bathed in amber sunlight. On the window-sill lay a box of matches covered with blue paper with a canary-yellow label, decorated with medals on the top. Its contents were called "Lapshin matches" from its dark-brown striking-strip. My small, sharp eyes noticed them at once: matches had attracted me for some time. I was also attracted by the tin of petrol. There was some curious affinity between the Lapshin matches and the Nobel kerosene that I could not grasp.

I had become aware of it after hearing Papa say to Mamma that the child should never be left alone in the kitchen in case he "threw a match into the kerosene, which would burst into flame at once and set the whole place on fire."

This greatly astonished me. If one threw a match into kerosene, it would burst into flame at once!

Although I was quite small and dressed as a girl, I was not so stupid as to be unaware that if you threw a lighted match into kerosene it would flare up: that I took for granted. But Papa had not said a "lighted" match. This meant that he knew something about matches that I had never suspected. Apparently, it was enough to throw an ordinary, unlit match, with its black top unscratched, and the kerosene would flare up by itself!

This was certainly news to me!

I could not envisage fire originating from the contact of a dry, unlighted match with wet kerosene; I found it very hard to believe. Yet Papa should know better than I. Could such a miracle really happen? No wonder I was irresistibly drawn to the kitchen, where there were kerosene and matches.

I stood all by myself with the box of Lapshin matches in my hand. The whole apartment was so silent that I could hear the tick-tock of the pendulum in the dining-room clock.

I unscrewed the pretty lid from the short neck of the Nobel tin, and smelled the familiar, sickly smell of white petrol. Was it possible that in a moment I could be witnessing the miracle of fire springing up from nothing? It couldn't be true: Papa must be mistaken; I pulled a match out of the box and dropped it through the neck into the petrol-can. Although I did not believe in the possibility of a flame flaring up, I nonetheless cautiously retreated to the corner where the broom stood almost as tall as myself. However, as I had foreseen, nothing happened: there was no fire. But how could Papa have got it wrong? He had said clearly: "The kerosene would burst into flame and set the whole place on fire." Perhaps there was something wrong with the match, I thought, and dropped in another one, taking the same evasive action afterwards. Again, nothing happened. It was very odd! Either Papa had been mistaken or there was something wrong with the second match, too. I threw in a third one, a fourth and a fifth. As though mesmerised, I went on throwing match after match into the can, feeling bitterly disappointed in the wisdom of my hitherto omniscient papa and, at the same time, delighted with my own perspicacity in making the experiment. There were only one or two matches left in the box when I heard running steps and the anxious rustle of Mamma's skirt. A moment later, she was pressing me to her heart.

"You must be crazy, completely crazy!" she muttered, trying to pull the box of matches out of my clenched hand.

"I warned you, didn't I?" Papa's angry voice exploded behind Mamma's back.

They were both wearing their pince-nez, and Papa was shaking his beard, which seemed to make their anger even more alarming.

I begin to yell and kick, of course, and stammered so much through my sobs that I was unable to explain to them that I was not nearly as stupid as they had imagined.

I might only be three years old, but I would never have been such a fool as to throw lighted matches into the petrol! All I had set out to do was to disprove Papa's statement that if you threw a match into petrol, you could produce a fire. He had not qualified it by adding "lighted."

Treasures 🖋

HAVING READ *Taras Bulba*, we decided to follow the example of the Zaporozhzi and bury a treasure. The time was most appropriate; a still, hot October, the beginning of the school year, and, though it was autumn by the calendar, everything around had remained summery, without a single yellow leaf in sight. It was still warm after school and even after dinner and, with the hours dragging by interminably, it was essential to find something to do.

After wandering about in the gardens of empty villas, already closed and locked for the winter, we scrambled through knee-high weeds, which covered our black trousers with a yellow powder from their late flowering, climbed up a clay cliff and hollowed out a small niche with our penknives. Here, during the next few days, we hid everything we could lay our hands on.

Ideally, of course, a treasure should have consisted of gold and precious stones, but where were we to find them?

In the end, I came across an ornamental fly, probably from a brooch, in a little box on Aunt's dressing-table, in which she kept her loose change. In my imagination, it was made of gold and precious stones, possibly even diamonds, two microscopic ones representing the fly's eyes.

This precious fly was very small and far from impressive, but we wrapped it in several layers of paper, put it into a match-box, and carried it to the niche, where it became the most valuable item of our treasure. Then we decided that the niche should be transformed into a smugglers' cove and ransacked the junk in the attic and storeroom for suitable objects to stow away in it: among them were a broken Turkish dagger and an ancient, rusty revolver.

We should have preferred large consignments of smuggled tobacco and Oriental silk, but had to be content with producing eight kopecks between us and buying two cigars of the worst quality for three kopecks the pair. With the rest of the money we bought a small quantity of halva, comets, and biscuits (made of black bread and treacle), which had to serve as the smugglers' store of provisions. We also had a bottle of drinking-water—for what purpose, we did not quite know—but possibly in case of siege. We blocked up the entrance to our cave with lumps of clay and camouflaged it with weeds. We visited it several times a day to see if anyone had discovered our treasure: but, no, each time we found it intact.

The days passed by, very hot and tedious, and we sweated profusely during lessons in our thick winter uniforms—Zhenka in his college, I in my school. The sun shone as though it were still summer, heating the window-sills and even the chalk on the ledge of the black-board.

Zhenka Dubastij and I did not know where to go or what to do in our spare time, and we remained in this unsatisfactory frame of mind till we decided to open up our treasure and smoke some of the "smuggled" cigars.

We took a box of matches with us, extracted the cigars, and sat down among the weeds, facing the sad, blue, calm September sea, with streaks of white across it here and there and thin wisps of smoke from a steamer on the horizon. We lit up and pretended to each other that we were enjoying inhaling the dry smoke from the spicy tobacco leaf, which left a sort of rasping sensation on our tongues. Zhenka even tried to blow the smoke through his nostrils, which made him cough and filled his innocent blue eyes with tears. But he managed to splutter out: "You know, it's jolly nice to smoke a cigar. A real Havana!"

Then saliva began to trickle out of his mouth. I myself felt dizzy and suddenly became acutely aware of the height of the cliff on which we were sitting and the precipitous drop to the beach below, whence came the gently squelching sound of the sea as it swirled round crannies in the rocks and the crunch of pebbles beneath the feet of a solitary fisherman carrying two red oars on his shoulders.

With difficulty, we forced our way, staggering and queasy, through the jungle of weeds and were plodding along towards Otrada when Zhenka's father suddenly loomed up in front of us in a bowler hat, with a gold chain across his waistcoat and a bamboo stick in his hand.

"Let me smell your breath," he said to Zhenka in a terrifying voice.

"You've been smoking, you rascal," Zhenka's father said, gripped him by the ear, and led him home.

As they disappeared, the shadows of acacia-trees criss-crossed theirs. Finally, there was a clang as the garden-gate closed behind them and I heard Zhenka's tearful voice: "Don't hit me, Papa. I'll never do it again! Dear Papa, please let go my ear!"

A Piece of Phosphorus

A FRIEND AT SCHOOL gave me a small piece of hard, red phosphorus the size and shape of a tangerine-drop. I wrapped it in paper and put it in my pocket, waiting impatiently for lessons to end so that I could examine it thoroughly and investigate its properties peacefully at home.

Back in my room, I performed a few elementary tests, held it under a tap, placed it in a saucer of water, rubbed my fingers with it. I discovered that every object I covered with phosphorus began to shine in the dark. My hand and all its extended fingers shone; the water in the saucer shone; even the stream of water from the tap in the dark bathroom shone slightly as it passed over the piece of phosphorus.

I wrapped it up in paper again and hid it in my pocket; then, whistling through my front teeth, I went out into the street.

Some of the boys were already in the meadow, throwing stones at sparrows, or playing one of our silly games: we stood a building-stone on end, placed a number of smaller stones on top of it and, after moving some ten paces back, threw bricks at it to see who would knock the top stone off first.

It was the dullest of all our games, and we only played it to pass the time until all the gang arrived and we could turn to something more interesting.

I noticed at once that Nadia Zaria-Zarianitskaia was not there: no doubt she was busily engaged on her home-work.

(It is necessary for me to explain what it was that I refer to as "the meadow." For some reason, we called all vacant sites, adjoining old or new unoccupied houses and overgrown with weeds, bushes of wild lilac, or feathery vinegar "trees," meadows.)

It was on this one that I started my intrigue with Nadia, with whom I always found myself in a complicated love-hate relationship. We competed with her in everything, in every field of our street-lives: who ran faster, who jumped higher, who hid better in hide-and-seek, who whistled louder through their front teeth, who danced better, who could guess riddles quicker, who could gabble through tongue-twisters faster and so on. The main point, of course, was: who would submit to whom and admit the other's superiority?

Nadia was our queen, so to speak: none of the other girls could hold a candle to her.

Everybody but me admitted her superiority. Owing to some trait in my character, I could not resign myself to it, although, in fact, she was superior to me in everything, even in her length of days. We were the same age within a month, but Nadia's birthday was eleven days earlier than mine, and this was something I could do nothing about. She was, inarguably, older than I. Any moment she chose, she could cast a contemptuous glance in my direction and say: "Shut up, I'm the eldest!"

At that time, when we were both eleven, it seemed to her a great advantage. Sometimes we even fought, finishing by holding up our thumbs at each other, which meant that we had quarrelled forever, but it would not be long before, with shy smiles, we made another gesture: displaying a bent little finger over our shoulders as a sign of peace and eternal friendship.

Profiting by Nadia's absence from the meadow, I did my best to divert all her supporters, both boys and girls, from her side to mine. I took them down to the basement of the Fessenko house and, in the pitch-darkness of the wood-cellar, displayed my outspread hands with luminous fingers, and my face with luminous eyebrows, nose, and ears. The boys and girls were so much surprised and impressed by this inexplicable manifestation that they immediately switched sides and declared me to be their chief, all the more enthusiastically because, in response to all their entreaties to divulge the secret of my luminosity, I said that I had become the possessor of some of the secrets of the famous Elena Blavatsky, who, as was well-known, had received a number of spiritual revelations from the world beyond. I implied that Elena Blavatsky often visited me in my dreams and had turned me into a magician, which enabled me to make my hands and face shine in the dark. I also hinted that those boys and girls who became my supporters could rely on my eventually initiating them into Elena Blavatsky's secrets, when they, too, would acquire the ability to shine in the dark and might even become magicians. I was lavish with my promises. They swore allegiance to me, raising two fingers in the air above their heads to make the oath binding.

. . . I cannot understand even now why it did not occur to any of them that there was nothing miraculous about my luminosity, that it was purely a matter of chemistry. After all, they knew that such a substance as phosphorus existed which had the property of shining in the dark, and they had seen fire-flies over the sea, which was phosphorescent, too, in summer! But, despite that, they believed in the magic quality of my luminosity and that I had been initiated into secrets of Elena Blavatsky.

Their souls were thirsting for the inexplicable.

When we climbed up out of the darkness of the basement, we found Nadia hopping about the meadow on one leg, throwing a ball against the wall of the house and deftly catching it again, then bouncing it on the ground with a sharp plop and repeating the same routine.

When she saw me surrounded by all her former loyal subjects, she frowned imperiously like an angry queen, her straight golden brows, which reminded me of wheat-ears, drew together crossly and, bouncing the ball violently on the ground, so that it shot up level with the second floor, she shouted: "Come here, my loyal brigade!"

"It's no longer yours, it's mine," I said scornfully. "They've just sworn loyalty to me in the Fessenko basement."

"You've sworn loyalty to him?" Nadia asked them.

"We have," replied the former loyal subjects. And Nadia received the unwelcome news that Elena Blavatsky visited me in my dreams and disclosed all her secrets to me, including that of being able to shine in the dark.

"He's lying to you," said Nadia.

"He isn't, because we've seen him do it."

I looked at Nadia with unconcealed triumph, folded my arms across my chest and laughed insultingly in her face.

"I suppose you don't believe it?" I said.

"I don't, because you're a well-known liar."

"I swear," I retorted proudly.

"How are you going to prove it?" she asked.

"Come down to the Fessenko basement and you can see for yourself."

"You mean you'll shine?" Nadia enquired suspiciously.

"I will," I replied.

"All right, let's go!"

"Come on then!"

We went down into the basement, groped along the dark corridor, and, just to make certain all went well, I thoroughly wetted my fingers, nose, and ears with saliva and stealthily rubbed them with the bit of phosphorus.

I suddenly stopped, swivelled round and exposed my shining face and shining, upraised, spread-out fingers to her.

"Now I hope you're convinced," I said.

Nadia stood in front of me, speechless with astonishment, and I could hear her heart pounding in the darkness.

"Are you really a magician?" she asked finally.

"What if I am?" I sniggered.

We climbed back out of the basement and I was struck by the vividness of the outside world, blue, green, and yellow in turn, and gleaming so brightly that it hurt one's eyes.

Nadia stood close to me, tall, slender, and long-legged, with scratched knees, a pretty, slightly aquiline nose, golden freckles, transparent blue eyes, and tight curls, two on each side, between which peeked out the elongated shells of her small, boyish ears. There was something almost brutally boyish about her, yet at the same time tender and girlish.

There we were, side by side, eternal competitors and enemies, who were in love with each other: and I felt I was the conqueror!

She looked at me with superstitious fear, as though I really were a magician, initiated into the mysteries of Elena Blavatsky.

"Will you let me join you?" she asked timidly. "I want you to teach me Madame Blavatsky's secrets."

I pretended to hesitate, then said: "I can only divulge those secrets to someone who swears to be my obedient slave forever."

"I don't want to know *all* the secrets," she replied, looking at me with her marvellous aquamarine eyes, under the thick reddish eyelashes that somehow made her vaguely resemble an English girl. "I only want to know how you manage to shine in the dark."

"Is that all?" I retorted sarcastically. "Why, how to shine in the dark is the biggest secret of all!"

"Well, then, tell me how it's done! Pl-ease!" Nadia said in a voice filled with the sweet coquetry of an adult woman.

I looked at her and understood everything. She was burning from head to foot with such passionate, unconquerable curiosity that it would be easy now to turn her into my obedient slave. "Very well," I said, "I will. But only if you'll swear to be my obedient slave."

Nadia hestitated for a moment. "Can't you do it without all that nonsense?" she asked.

"Impossible!" I said.

"All right," she said in a low voice. "But if I do become your slave, you really will tell me the secret?"

"Yes, I promise."

"Well, then, consider I'm your slave this very minute. Will that do?"

"Oh, no," I said. "It isn't as simple as all that. You must go through the full ritual of becoming my slave in front of the whole gang. You must kneel to me and bend your head right down to the ground, and, as a sign of my sovereignty, I'll put my foot on your neck and say: 'From now on, you are my slave and I am your master.' And then I'll disclose to you the secret of a man shining in the dark, passed on to me by Elena Blavatsky."

"You give me your sacred word that you will disclose the secret after that?" Nadia asked, quivering with impatience. She was ready to do anything.

"My sacred word, and here's my sign of the cross. May I be rooted to this spot forever if I break my oath!" I said dramatically. Nadia shook all her four English curls determinedly and knelt in front of me

: 158 :

on one knee, then, after a moment's thought, decided to kneel on both.

"Good!" I said. "Now bend right down to the ground."

Nadia shrugged and rather irritably laid her forehead on the dry, reddish dust of the meadow, overgrown with shrubs already displaying dark berries. Around us, the crowd of boys and girls watched Nadia's abasement in silence.

She was wearing a sailor-suit with a short, pleated skirt. She raised her head from the ground and gazed at me with her lovely, imploring eyes.

"Perhaps it isn't necessary for you to put your foot on my neck; I'm humiliated enough as it is," she murmured plaintively.

"Just as you like," I said sternly, "but if I don't, you'll never learn the secret of the shining human body."

"Well, to hell with you, go on, put your foot on my neck. I'm not going to haggle."

I saw two little tears oozing out of her eyes. I put my foot in its shabby shoe on Nadia's neck and kept it there for a while, with my arms crossed on my chest.

"Now you are my slave!" I announced solemnly. Nadia stood up and brushed the dust off her knees.

"And now you're to tell me the secret," she said. "Now, at once!"

"Certainly," I answered with a malicious smile. "Here's the secret."

And I took out of my pocket the small piece of phosphorus.

"What is it?" asked Nadia.

"Phosphorus," I replied coolly.

"So it was nothing but phosphorus!" she snapped, pale with indignation.

"What did you think it was? Did you really imagine that it was a secret of Elena Blavatsky's? What a fool you are. You really believed me!"

The boys and girls around us burst into laughter. That was the last straw.

"You wretched little liar! You cheat!" Nadia screamed and sprang at me like a tigress.

But I managed to dodge away and raced round the meadow, hearing Nadia's heavy breathing and the patter of her long, girlish legs in boys' sandals just behind me.

She ran much faster than I did and I realised that I could not escape her. So I decided to adopt a measure that Nick Carter's junior aide always employed on such occasions. All I had to do was to stop very suddenly in front of my pursuer and go down on all fours: she would then stumble over me and fall flat on her face.

But I had not judged the distance between us correctly. I went down on all fours and remained there like an idiot, unaware that Nadia had had time to pull up. She threw herself at me, climbed on my back and hit me so hard with her strong fists that my nose began to bleed. I dragged myself home, dripping tears, blood, and mucus and covered in dust, pursued by Nadia's triumphant cries: "Now you know what happens when you cheat people, you horrid liar!"

I paused just long enough to jerk my thumb at her over my shoulder, and she returned the gesture.

However, two days later we met again in the meadow, where a sheep was grazing, tethered to a pole, and, with a certain amount of embarrassment, extended our bent little fingers to each other as a token of eternal peace.

And, that evening, I rolled up the sleeve of my school-jacket and wrote the letters "N. Z." on my arm in ink, drew a heart pierced by an arrow alongside it—and waited a long time until it had dried.

And, on the following day, I presented Nadia with half of my phosphorus, so that she, too, could now shine in the darkness like me.

The Shot from the Roof

I HAVE COMPLETELY forgotten now how the gun came to be in my hands. More powerful than a montecristo and less so than a Winchester, it was a small-calibre sporting-gun. I think it must have belonged to a boy staying with relatives in Otrada, from whom I had become inseparable over a period of two or three days. The only thing I seem to remember about this strangely faceless boy is that he had a gun and that he and I climbed up to an attic in a new, unoccupied four-storied house, where we settled down by the dormer window. There was a high wind blowing at the time, which sent clouds scurrying over the town and whistled so dismally and persistently that one was filled with indefinable forebodings.

We shot at a number of pigeons that had been strutting along the edge of the new brick roof, on their coral feet, without hitting any of them, and finally only had one cartridge left.

Out of the dormer window we had a splendid view of Otrada's four streets with their buildings and "meadows" and the good-natured policeman in his white tunic, standing at the cross-roads in the shade of an acacia-tree; of the yards behind the houses, with their sheds, their well-trodden paths through the long, wavy grass and their freshly washed linen hanging on the line; and of the stretch of grey sea beyond the roofs on one side and a section of the French Boulevard on the other, with an occasional passing carriage and the iron standards carrying the wires for the recently built electric tramway line.

From where we were, the boulevard only seemed a stone's throw away and, as he watched the new, little Belgian trams rolling down it, sending a series of sapphire sparks shooting off the humming overhead wires, it suddenly occurred to us to take a shot at one of them.

This crazy idea did not come to fruition immediately. It first flew in through the window like a scarcely perceptible breath of some distant plague, momentarily annihilating our reason, but common-sense soon reasserted itself; though we confided to each other our secret impulse to take a shot at the tram, we promptly dismissed it as foolish and, even worse, criminal.

... But we were alone in the attic, where nobody could see us, and the sloping boulevard, with its row of iron standards standing out against the whitewashed wall of the Military Academy in the background, from which sporadic bursts in rifle-fire resounded in the underground range, and its neat trams moving smoothly along their tracks, seemed alluringly close. The window-panes of the trams reflected the saffron rays of the sun and, behind them, the profiles of the passengers were clearly visible; the sun sparkled, too, along the whole length of the copper wires above them. A fresh attack of craziness possessed us.

"How about it?" I asked.

"Yes, let's have a go," he replied, that boy I can no longer recall. That he was beside me at the time, I have no doubt, but he might just as well not have been: he remains someone without face or shape; a curious gap in my memory.

"Shall I shoot?" I asked hurriedly.

"Yes, do."

I broke the gun across my knee and inserted the cartridge, longer than a montecristo's, with a conical lead bullet, into the well-oiled barrel. Then I closed the gun again, thrust the barrel out the open window, pointing in the direction of the boulevard, and cocked the hammer. At that moment, a tram appeared, but passed on out of view before I could get my foresight on it. So we had to wait for the next one—a matter of five minutes—and, far from abating during those endless minutes, my crazy determination even increased. I moved my sights slowly down the boulevard, following an imaginary tram, as my impatience rose to its peak. I was incapable of any sane reasoning: my will-power was dominated by this obsession to shoot at a tram.

As soon as the next one came into view, reddish-yellow, with the crest of the town of Odessa on its side, I pointed the black, burnished barrel at it, sighted, and pulled the trigger; and, simultaneously, I realized the full horror of what I had done. Appalled, I tossed the gun into a corner of the attic and my faceless friend and I raced as fast as we could down the back-staircase into the street, where we fled in opposite directions. I never saw him again in my life.

It was only when I found myself on my own that it occurred to me that my bullet had probably not only hit the tram but gone right through it, wounding one of the passengers or killing him on the spot.

Trying to look unconcerned, I forced myself to walk unhurriedly past the good-natured policeman, greeting him politely, and taking off my hat. But as soon as I was out of sight round the nearest corner, I started racing towards the sea, as if it alone could save me from disaster. As I tore down Otrada's shady streets and then the lanes leading to the cliffs, I pictured the boulevard somewhere behind me and a tram drawn up in front of the wall of the Military Academy, surrounded by a crowd. And from the rear-platform, a man—or, rather, a corpse—was being lifted down, its pierced skull dripping blood on to the tracks, as the crowd turned silently to look up over the trees and roofs at the window of the four-storied house, from which some unknown criminal had fired the fatal shot.

I saw vividly, in my fevered imagination, detectives climbing up to the attic, finding the gun, and examining my finger-prints through a magnifying glass; and then a police-dog picking up my scent and dashing down the back-stairs dragging a detective in dark glasses behind it on the other end of the lead. I hid in the cleft of a familiar rock, beneath which a light-green sea capped with lacy foam surged and fell back again. I listened for the sound of pursuing feet as the police, following my tracks, came panting down the slope to the beach. . . . But everything was quiet.

I stayed there until evening, struggling all the time against the temptation to steal down the dusty, deserted lane by the side of the Military Academy and take a look from afar at the blood on the tram-lines, though by now it would probably be covered with sand. Like a murderer, I was irresistibly drawn to the scene of my crime, but I was strong-minded enough to resist such a dangerous temptation, since my appearance on the boulevard would almost certainly deliver me into the hands of the detectives, who would be lying in ambush waiting for me to walk into the trap.

I got home for evening tea when everybody was already seated at table and lingered in the hall, trying to hear what they were talking about. I was certain they would be discussing the dreadful incident on the French Boulevard.

I was wrong.

The conversation ran on its normal peaceful lines. How strange! It required a considerable effort on my part to sit down in my place calmly, as though nothing had happened, and begin buttering my bread.

"Why are you so pale today?" my aunt asked, glancing at me. "Did something happen to you?"

"No, nothing . . . nothing unusual," I answered with assumed indifference.

. . . All through the night, I was tormented by nightmares in which I was the undiscovered murderer of a number of different people: now it would be a lady, in a hat with a veil, with blood pouring from her temple, where the bullet had hit her; now, the conductor, with his face covered in blood; now, a priest with a red stain on his cassock over his heart. All these murders took place in front of the Military Academy's stone wall, which muted the sinister sounds of rifle-practice on the underground range.

: 163 :

In between the nightmares, I imagined I could hear the police, coming up the outside steps, and waited petrified for the sharp sound of the door-bell to echo through the hall. . . .

Early in the morning, I tiptoed out of my room and pulled our copy of the Odessa *News* out from under the front-door. With a pounding heart, I turned to the page carrying the more sensational news, expecting to read: "APPALLING MURDER IN TRAM. Yesterday afternoon, an unknown criminal fired at a tram from the roof of a near-by house. The bullet penetrated the window and killed a third-form student instantly. The police are investigating the crime." But, no, the paper contained nothing of the kind. I could only think that the police had cunningly suppressed the news so as not to alert the murderer.

Pale and worn, I set out for schol, but an irresistible impulse made me turn towards the French Boulevard. There was nothing there to indicate that only yesterday it had been the scene of a brutal crime. Trams were running gaily up and down the lines in the bright sunshine just as usual. I looked up at the house from which I had fired the shot. It was scarcely visible among the surrounding greenery and could not be less than half a verst away from where I was standing. It was only then that it dawned on me that my bullet, little more than a toy one, could never have reached its target and must have fallen harmlessly in some garden or other along the way —possibly in the one belonging to that revered history-teacher, Professor Starozhenko.

Since then, there are times when I become obsessed by this episode and am afraid to look in a mirror lest I see the mark of Cain on my forehead, that of an undiscovered murderer—or the guilt-racked face of a Raskolnikov. But perhaps the whole thing was just a dream in the first place?

The Elephant Jumbo

THAT YEAR, everybody in our town went crazy about an operetta called *Hubby* and sang the principal song—a very silly one—here, there, and everywhere. It resounded from Alexandrovsky Park, where it was played by a military band conducted by the famous Chernetsky, who had a glass eye, wearing the full-dress uniform of one of the sharp-shooter regiments of the "iron division," which was billeted in our town.

The same little tune was also played near the open-air restaurant on the Nikolaev Boulevard, between the monument to the duke of Richelieu and the entrance to the funicular, by another band, conducted by the still more famous maestro Davinhof, who conducted seated on a fat circus mare, which tossed its mane and waved its tail continually in time to the music. The maestro, in his long linen frock-coat, white gloves, and short, spurred boots, his moustache dyed the colour of shoe-black, would rise in his stirrups from time to time and greet his admirers among the local ladies, raising his silvery-grey top-hat high in the air above his bald, impressive, showman's head. Instead of a baton, he conducted with a spray of tuberose, so that the old-fashioned Chernetsky with his glass eye could not compete with the chic, ultra-modern, almost futuristic maestro, Davinhof, though they played the identical little air from *Hubby*.

Hubby was whistled by students and school-boys as they strolled under the ceilings of intoxicatingly blossoming white acacia; the sounds of *Hubby* burst noisily out of gramophone-horns; *Hubby* was played in the foyers of cinemas on pianolas with magical, automatic keyboards.

I have to tell you all this to explain why it was to this tune that people added new words, in order to celebrate an event, which, one fine day, shook the whole town. The new words were:

> "Poor Jumbo went quite crazy
> In the Lorberbaumer Zoo
> They said it was the springtime
> That sent him all askew
> Jumbo . . . my little Jumbo. . . ."

These silly quatrains recorded the tragedy that occurred soon after Easter on the Kulikovo field after all the merry-go-rounds and other amusements had been removed, except for the circus Lorberbaum, which chained Jumbo, the elephant, to a tree in the middle of the deserted square to lure the customers in. And, suddenly, Jumbo went mad. He began to trumpet in a most sinister manner and seemed liable, at any moment, to wrench his chain away from the tree and careen down the streets of the town, destroying everything that lay in his way.

The Kulikovo field immediately became a danger-zone and only a few show-offs ventured near the Lorberbaumer tent, where the poor crazy elephant was creating an uproar. They returned with the most hair-raising stories, which were promptly repeated throughout the town.

I, personally, saw nothing, or practically nothing. The little I did see was from a safe distance. In the dusty, trampled-down square, the grey figure of the elephant stood out like a mountain: his ears flapped like enormous fans and his lowered trunk swayed to and fro in a menacing, maniacal way with the regularity of a pendulum. Probably this was a short period of melancholia, during which Jumbo, exhausted by his fits of helpless rage, sank into a gentler madness. Looking about him sadly, he rocked his enormous bulk from side to side, leaving on the black soil of the Kulikovo field, covered with the husks of sunflower and marrow seeds, the prints of his round soles and half-moon toes. These quiet moments were, in some ways, even more frightening than the fits of violence, when the elephant sat down on his tail and tried to wrench the short chain off his front foot by spinning round like a top, at the same time raising his trunk and trumpeting bellicosely to the heavens.

People avoided going past the Kulikovo field in case the elephant did succeed in breaking free and began rampaging around, goring and killing everyone in sight with his short, half-sawn-off tusks.

For a whole week, the town's attention was exclusively taken up by the elephant. Rumours spread, suggestions were made. Bulletins about the elephant's state of health appeared in all the newspapers. He was worse, he was better. Interviews with local authorities and doctors were eagerly sought. The majority of the doctors were of the opinion that Jumbo's madness had an erotic basis, that he was pining for the companionship of his beloved Emma, a she-elephant, who had been left behind in Hamburg at Hagenbeck's because the miserly Lorberbaum had refused to buy the pair.

"Africa's son languishes for his beloved," declared the headlines of the one-kopeck Odessa *News*. . . . "Faithful unto death!" . . . "Return Jumbo his better-half!" . . . "The power of love—a lesson to all of us!" And underneath there were articles beginning: "The inhabitants of our town are being exposed daily to the risk of death. What steps are the local authorities taking to deal with the situation?" etc., etc.

A strange form of love-sickness overcame me, strange because at the time I was not in love with anyone. Inflaming me like a fever, it was a love-sickness without an object. Waves of passion raged around me and in me, reducing me to a state of irresponsibility, in which I was not answerable for my actions. One might have thought that Jumbo's soul had entered into mine. My nerves were tense: I was tormented by insomnia, punctuated by brief love-dreams. I tossed about in my bed, turning the hot pillows over and over, and got up in the morning exhausted, with shadows under my eyes. I would examine myself for a long time in the mirror, from which a pair of dazed, lifeless eyes stared back at me. I began to take immense care of my appearance and, disgustedly, squeezed out the purple spots on my chin, which my aunt with a fleeting smile called *"boutons d'amour."* I persuaded Papa to buy me a pair of tight-fitting trousers with foot-straps, in which I felt a tremendous dandy. I borrowed a stick of hair-fixative wrapped in silver paper from a friend, rubbed it lavishly over my hair and brushed it well in; but when I tried to make a straight parting, like a smart, sporting Englishman's, my stiff, childish hair resisted and stuck out greasy bristles in every direction filling the air around me with the sickly-sweet smell of the fixative.

I hung a badge in the shape of a tiny tennis-racket, which was considered very fashionable at the time, from the top button of my school-jacket, raised up the crown of my hat so that it looked like a Prussian's, and wandered around the sweltering town that was sadly deserted and quiet after the noisy Easter week.

The cloth foot-straps of my trousers kept slipping off from under my heels and I had to make frequent stops to readjust them.

The boys from the Novoribni pursued me with gibes and offensive hoots of laughter.

The pink sun set behind the station, and the streets around it seemed sensuously quiet and alluring. I walked down them, my ill-fitting foot-straps dragging in the dust behind me, and tried to pick up the latest news of what was happening on the Kulikovo field.

A rumour was spreading that Jumbo had had such an attack of violence during the night that the fire-brigade had been called out from the boulevard precinct and had poured water on the rabid animal from four fire-pumps until he calmed down.

Next day the fit of fury reoccurred even more violently. The elephant managed to wrench off the chain and it took a very precarious combined effort to get it on again. The situation became increasingly tragic every hour. The papers now began printing special bulletins about the elephant's state of health, as if he were a dying monarch.

The town council went into permanent conference like a revolutionary committee. It demanded that Lorberbaum should leave the town, taking his mad elephant with him, or agree to have it destroyed.

Lorberbaum strongly objected, harping on the large losses he would suffer, but in the end had to consent to Jumbo being poisoned —there was no other solution. Full details of the elephant's imminent destruction immediately spread throughout the town. It was decided that he should be poisoned by potassium cyanide introduced into his favourite cakes. A hundred of these were bought at the town council's expense from Libeman's well-known sweet-shop: the Napoleons, filled with yellow cream, completely covered two large iron griddles. The cakes were delivered by the representative of the medical department in a cab. He wore a white overall and his uniform-hat. I was not there to see it, but I could conjure up a vivid picture of the cab arriving at the circus-tent, assistants bringing in the cakes, members of the special medical commission, together with representatives of the town council and officials delegated by the governor, pulling on black oil-cloth gloves, picking up the cyanide crystals very carefully with pincers, inserting them into the cakes, and then, even more carefully, offering the poisoned cakes to the elephant: I could picture the elephant taking them from the griddle with his trunk, dropping them swiftly one after the other into his eager mouth, resembling a small jug, his eyes surrounded by grey wrinkles of thick skin, sparkling angrily with unalloyed hatred for all mankind for having so heartlessly separated him from his beloved, and pausing every now and then to trumpet out his wrath and try once more to break the accursed chain attached to the ring round his wrinkled leg.

Having eaten all the cakes, the elephant quietened down for a time and the authorities retreated in order to watch its dying agonies from afar, before duly signing and stamping the formal death certificate.

Oh, how vividly it rose before me—and stayed with me—this obtrusive, inescapable vision of the elephant's agony and final convulsions! I moaned in my sleep and the pillow under my head seemed aflame. Nausea swept over me and I felt that I, too, had been poisoned by cyanide. I lost consciousness every other moment in my semi-slumber and thought I must be dying. I struggled out of bed and snatched that morning's edition of the Odessa *News*, certain that I would read of the elephant's death.

Nothing of the kind!

The elephant, despite having eaten all the poisoned cakes, turned out to be alive and kicking, with no intention at all of dying. The poison had had no effect on him, except, perhaps, to make him more insane. His furious trumpeting had kept the inhabitants of the eerie streets near the station awake all night and driven them almost crazy with fear. The papers considered it a miracle or, at the very least, "an inexplicable phenomenon."

The elephant continued to trumpet and witnesses reported that his eyes were bloodshot and that a misty foam was emerging from his mouth.

The town began reacting almost as if it were besieged. Some shops closed down in case some disaster should occur, locking their doors and putting iron shutters over their display-windows. Children were not allowed out of their homes. At the theatre, where *Hubby* was being played, the sale of tickets fell sharply. There was a marked increase in burglaries. The situation seemed desperate.

But as always happens in desperate situations, the army came to the rescue. The governor-general telephoned to the commander of the military district, and at dawn, roused by a sudden call to arms, a platoon of soldiers—like heroes from a fairy-tale—magnificent men of the Modlin regiment, with peakless caps pushed back at a slant, exposing a third of their close-cropped, tow-haired heads, appeared on the Kulikovo field. They wore greatcoats over their shoulders and cartridge-belts weighed down with live cartridges.

Then, from the field to the farthest suburbs, there echoed a volley from their Mossin rifles like a piece of canvas suddenly ripped in two. And that was the end.

When I timidly joined a crowd of curious idlers on the edge of the Kulikovo field, all I saw by the Lorberbaum tent was a huge tarpaulin in the shape of a mountain, covering what recently had been the alive, suffering elephant Jumbo.

. . . He had been cured forever of his uncontrollable passion.

The town was peaceful once more. The pink and white bunches of aromatic acacia were fading away and dropping to the ground like dry moths. The folly of love vanished like smoke. I began to sleep well again and dream of happy things, inspired by my guardian angel, whose little oval icon hung from the iron bars at the head of my bed above a cool pillow and a fresh pillow-case.

The Panopticon ⚔

THE MAIN ATTRACTION of this panopticon, a long boarded exhibition-booth with a canvas roof, erected on the Kulikovo field, was a special, secret section, to enter which visitors had to pay an additional sum of five kopecks.

Although children and school-boys were not allowed inside this mysterious section, the lady who sat behind a small table collecting the extra five kopecks in a saucer was occasionally prepared to turn a blind eye, and a few of my adolescent friends had already passed behind the curtain. They refused, however, to reveal anything, maintaining an infuriating silence, though they led me to infer from their mysterious, enigmatic smiles and knowing airs that they had seen something extremely interesting and possibly slightly depraved.

To all my questions, they replied: "Go and see for yourself."

My imagination, whetted by these silent, alluring hints, began to run wild, and I decided to sacrifice a part of my savings.

I conjured up exciting pictures and thirsted to learn the mysteries of love, about which I only had the flimsiest notion.

I did not feel like embarking on the adventure alone, so I invited one of my playmates, Mishka Galik, the grandson of a Malofontan fisherman, to come with me. Galik proudly declared that he would pay his share and produced from his inside pocket a huge, flattened-out five-kopeck piece, which had obviously been under the wheels of a tram. First we strolled round the main part of the booth, examining without much interest the well-known wax figures in glass cases, palely lit by the day-light filtering through the canvas roof: the murdered French president Carnot, a bearded gentleman with a decoration under his tail-coat and stains of blood on his white waistcoat; the Egyptian queen Cleopatra, raising her mechanical hand at regular intervals to press a small, twisting viper to her pink, wax breast; the Siamese twins Dodika and Rodika attached together by their breasts, with long wavy hair and glass eyes.

We approached the drawn cotton curtain, in front of which, under a notice proclaiming "Adults Only," a fully alive but equally wax-like lady with equally glassy eyes, wearing a lace hat and with lace mittens on her yellow hands, sat at a rickety table. We dropped our treasured five-kopeck pieces into the saucer and the lady, though casting a suspicious glance at the flattened coin through her lorgnette, raised as jerkily as Cleopatra's viper, nonetheless gave us a conspiratorial smile, indicating that we might enter the forbidden premises

Feeling somewhat embarrassed by each other's company, we hesitated for a moment in front of the coloured, gypsyish curtain, as though we were about to do something shameful, then curiosity took over and we slunk into the forbidden territory, scuffling our shoes in the sawdust.

And what did we see?

The walls of the room were fitted with shelves on which stood a number of glass boxes containing wax models of parts of the human body, covered with spots, rashes, and festering abscesses produced by various skin diseases. We came on a wax face with a crushed nose and lips flowering with the terrible violet blisters of lupus and examined in horror a woman's breast covered with a greyish-pink rash. We gazed at repulsive circular ulcers, yellow at the centre from suppuration, lava-purple around the hard edges, and recoiled from men's and women's heads sprouting herpetic vesicles. We stood appalled by the sight of pallid, new-born babies with unnaturally large heads and swollen stomachs, who had been stricken with illness in their mothers' wombs.

The reality was so shockingly different from what we had dreamed of seeing that we nearly fainted and it was all we could do to stumble out of the room. We became entangled in the cotton curtain, managed finally to fight our way out of its enveloping folds, and ran towards the exit, past the dying president, the beautiful Egyptian empress Cleopatra, with a black serpent on her rose breast, and the inseparable Siamese twins, followed by a slightly malicious comment from the lady with lace mittens: "So, it wasn't quite what you two boys expected, eh?"

The Heroes of the Russo-Japanese War ✍

DURING THE MORNING of the first day after Easter, my grandmother
—Papa's mother—went rummaging through her trunk, produced a
worn twenty-kopeck coin from a rolled-up pair of stockings, and gave
it to me. To the eight-year-old schoolboy I was at the time, it was a
fortune. Bubbling with excitement, I immediately headed for the
front-door to go out and spend it. In vain, my aunt leaned over the
well of the staircase and screamed down to me: "Where are you going?
It's the first day after Easter. Everything will be closed."

I pretended not to hear.

The twenty kopecks clasped in my sweating palm were burning
into it and I felt an uncontrollable urge to buy things with them,
though I was well aware, even before my aunt told me, that all the
shops would be closed. I just hoped for a miracle: maybe something
would suddenly turn up on which I could spend them.

I wandered round all the small shops I knew, but they were all
firmly locked. The town seemed to be dead. The inhabitants were
resting after the midnight Easter service, followed by the supper
at home or with friends at a table decorated with hyacinths, and
bearing *paskas, kulichi,* and cooked ham, with a mother-of-pearl
bone peeping out from the pink meat and white fat.

Oh, how dismally deserted the cleanly swept streets were! There
were not even any boys about: they would be rolling coloured Easter
eggs in their back-yards or on waste ground. My last hope was the
Kulikovo field, on which the windows of our house looked out. It
was already covered with tents, booths, merry-go-rounds, stalls, and
counters for the sale of sweets and kvass, but proved to be a broken
reed.

The festive, vivid little town, built during the last week of lent
from freshly cut planks and canvas, decorated with huge coloured
pictures of wild animals, jugglers, and clowns, was even more dead
than the real town that surrounded it. As if to emphasize the lack
of life, a tall, chalk-white flag-pole stood forlornly and unadorned
in the middle of the field, waiting for the morrow, the second day
after Easter, when, exactly at midday—not a second earlier or later
—the white, blue, and red trade flag of the Russian empire would be
hoisted as a sign that the fair was open. At that moment, everything

and everyone would spring into action: the roundabouts would start whirling round, their calliopes whistling out their hoarse music, the bells would be jangled to attract the public to the side-shows, kvass-vendors would announce their wares with sharp, staccato cries and, as the enormous crowd of townsfolk in their Sunday best moved sedately from booth to booth, the first balloon, red as a cranberry, would snap its thread and float up into the sky.

Then one would have ample opportunity to spend Grandmother's twenty kopecks quickly, reasonably, and pleasurably. But "then" was a long way away—tomorrow on the stroke of twelve! At the moment, there was nothing to do but stroll through the dead show-town on the Kulikovo field, without finding a single booth open along the way.

In the blue, windy Easter sky above me, round clouds pursued and passed each other, seeming almost to brush against the bright golden crosses and big blue cupolas of the Alfon homesteads, clustered opposite the station and fire-brigade tower of the Alexander district, where a policeman, dressed in his gala uniform, with white cotton gloves covering his fat paws, paced leisurely up and down.

Several times, I passed by open church-doors, sniffing the odour of incense, catching the sound of Easter singing, and glimpsing the golden candle-light as it fell on the snow-white and pink robes of the priests. The only places doing any business today were the churches: they were selling holy bread and candles. For a moment, I entertained the silly idea of purchasing four five-kopeck candles: it would, after all, be a buy.

I was actually on the point of entering the church when, among the respectable Easter beggars on the porch, I suddenly saw a blind man I knew: he was grey-haired and had a small piece of paper pinned to his chest, bearing the words, written in Slavonic script: "Hero of Plevna."

A town celebrity, he was one of the brave men who had fought under General Gurko. He was almost as well-known as another old warrior, whose hair was even greyer; a hero of Sebastopol, now not far off a hundred, he had fought under Admiral Nakhimov. It was the custom, as one passed them by, to raise one's hat, and I, too, would respectfully raise my new school-hat, a size too large for me, which came down over my boyish red ears and made my shaven head sweat. On this occasion, I did not have time to take off my cap, with its big silver crest in the shape of two crossed branches, before

I caught sight of a lot of blue lithographs, portraits of heroes of the Russo-Japanese war printed on glossy paper, spread out on the church-steps by the Plevna hero's feet.

The warrior, who had fought under the famous General Gurko, was selling portraits of the heroes of Chemulpo, Port Arthur, and Liolan. Each portrait cost two kopecks and I immediately bought ten of them, dropping my twenty-kopeck piece into the wooden cup, which the grey-haired soldier held in his hand.

I liked the portraits, printed in the famous Fessenko Institute, very much: the generals' rugged faces, coupled with their black, shaggy Manchurian fur hats, St. George crosses, and sabres, aroused my patriotic feelings. I was enchanted by the famous Admiral Makarov's long, parted beard and Admiral Skridlov's three-cornered hat, pince-nez, and uniform, on which two rows of decorations and medals shone so clearly and dazzlingly that just by mentioning the word "Skridlov," one seemed to hear them jingling together.

I hated General Stessel, the traitor who had surrendered the Port Arthur fortress to the enemy and had managed inexplicably to worm his way into the collection; all the more because I had inadvertently taken two portraits of the scoundrel, who was always spoken of with great contempt at home.

My first idea was to tear them up, but when I considered the waste of money, I changed my mind and decided to keep them. One of the pictures was of the scout Riabov, who fought in the Russo-Japanese war, and was famous for having penetrated to the rear of the Japanese lines, disguised as a Chinese, but was evidently caught and executed. The Japanese buried him with all military honours.

The picture showed Riabov barefooted, disguised as the Chinese, kneeling in front of the execution-post and crossing himself. I gazed, in horror and admiration, at his clenched fists and eyes, white as those of a blind man. A squad of Japanese soldiers in white spats stood pointing their Arisak rifles straight at the hero's naked breast with a cross hanging on it. The false pigtail lay near-by. Soldier Riabov was staring fearlessly into the eyes of death. I had seen the picture several times before in papers and magazines, but it still brought tears of pride and emotion to my eyes.

Having had my fill of admiring Riabov, I hid the pictures in the inside pocket of my school-jacket, alongside my pupil's card and a cheap "Comrade" note-book, convinced that I had made a wise purchase. But a worm of regret was soon nibbling at the back of my mind, and by the time I reached home, I was equally convinced that I had spent my twenty kopecks stupidly and far too hastily. If I had only waited till the following day, I could have bought so many wonderful things on the Kulikovo field: a long stick of lollipop, wrapped in a striped piece of paper with a fringe, and a durban, a sort of Jew's harp, looking like a small, Greek omega, made of steel, which one put in one's mouth, held between one's teeth, and then pulled a thin hook, thereby producing a metallic, droning twang invaluable for breaking the monotony of the last lesson. I could have gone on the merry-go-round and visited the booth where they were showing the sinking of the battleship *Petropavlovsk* on the tiny stage of the dolls' theatre. Last but not least, I could have enjoyed almonds covered in burnt sugar and eaten, from a bone spoon, out of a thick glass, thick as that of the lamps in front of icons, at least two portions of sugar ice, hollow inside, though ladled out in a heap as high as a mountain. Dammit, what a fool I'd been!

I was no longer made happy by the blazing sun, which poured through the window and lit up the beautifully decorated Easter table, nor by the sound of the church-bells that seemed to soar over the town, chasing the snow-white, rare spring clouds.

The Cinema ✍

IN THE MILITARY CADET SCHOOL, where Papa taught geography and Russian twice a week, they were giving a demonstration of a new invention—the moving pictures perfected by the Lumière brothers. Up to now, moving pictures had only existed abroad, but at last Russia, too, had discovered the secret. The military authorities, of course, were the first to become interested in it, with a view to adapting it to their own purposes. Because of this, the demonstration was, to some extent, secret, and members of the general public were not allowed to be present. But Papa had asked the director of the school if he might bring me with him, and the general had agreed, on the understanding that I should at no time disclose what I had seen. Papa warned me very seriously that I must strictly observe the general's condition and I swore to him that I would.

At last the day came when Papa and I mounted the cold front

stairs of the cadet school, passing a plaster bust of the emperor set in
a niche and a duty-trumpeter sitting in a chair with his trumpet in his
hand, and entered a huge vaulted hall. This served in turn as a church,
a dining-room, a gymnasium, and a theatre, where on a small stage,
about twice a year, cadets, made-up with wigs, beards, and moustaches, performed one-act plays by Chekhov and others, such as
The Fop and I, The Fiancé from the Pawnshop, The Bear, and *The
Proposal.* There were other entertainments, too, in which the same
cadets recited popular verses and monologues, such as "The Madman," by Apukhtin, which began with a cadet tragedian leaning on
an overturned chair, and declaiming in a false, shaky baritone:

> " 'Sit down—I'm glad to see you.
> Fear nothing: feel at ease,
> No doubt you know that recently
> I was elected king by all my people. . . .' "

He would be followed by another cadet, a comic actor this time,
not a tragedian, who, in the thick, free and easy voice of the "soul of
the company" would recite:

> " 'The sun sank slowly down behind the hill;
> The cows moved homewards through the verdant fields,
> Watched by their owner proudly from the gate:
> When, swift, a troika raced across the bridge
> With jingling bells and pulled up to a halt.
> Pressing the new arrival to his heart
> The owner cried: "Piotr Semionich,
> How God is good! I came to meet the hert
> And He sent you, the perfect substitute!" ' "

This was a poem which invariably roused Homeric laughter.
Or:

> " ' "Look at this pig," said Kolia once to Sasha,
> "I bet you he will soon be fatter than Papasha,"
> But Kolia said: "Oh Sasha, my dear Sasha,
> When has there been a pig as fat as our Papasha?" ' "

I need scarcely say that this brought the house down, the cadets
falling out of their seats with laughter, the school-inspector, a colonel,

rocking his fragile chair in the front row till it nearly broke as his stomach heaved, and the general, in an arm-chair beside him, hiding a smile beneath his dyed German moustache.

But, today, the stage had been replaced by a large linen screen hung up on the wall, which added something mysterious and full of promise to the whole atmosphere of the academy, with its smell of uniforms, boiled cabbage, and lighted gas-mantles; the two cadets standing to attention beside the flag enclosed in a black cover; and a third cadet, prepared to act as a runner, stationed behind the table at the entrance.

The place was already filled with cadets, who sat on rows of long benches at the back, while the staff occupied chairs in the front. Behind the cadets, on a wooden stand specially erected for the occasion, stood the projector, with two copper spools, on which the highly inflammable celluloid ribbon was rolled, and a complicated piece of lighting-apparatus, like a spirit-lamp, that gave off a strong smell of ether and occasionally emitted a shrill hissing sound. The projectionists were busy around it, exercising all their skill to get the machine to work. It was a long time before they succeeded. The authorities began to show their anxiety and impatience: the inspector approached the machine more than once to give various sharp instructions on the procedure to be followed should it burst into flames. Everyone, in fact, was secretly afraid of fire breaking out, as seemed highly likely, and rapidly spreading through the whole building.

Papa and I, as civilians, sat a little to one side on chairs behind the masters, but in front of the cadets. This semi-privileged position, while flattering to my childish vanity, made me feel slightly embarrassed.

At last, the situation seemed to be under control and the gaslights were extinguished. A white ray lit up the screen, on which appeared large silhouettes of hands with outspread fingers, busily working on something, and sections of shaven heads and noses; then the shadow of the celluloid ribbon on its spool made a momentary appearance, was grasped by the shadow of the hands and, presumably, from the click that followed, inserted into its proper place in the projector. Finally, someone began turning a handle, there was a soft whirring sound, and on to the lighted screen there was thrown a huge photograph of the familiar sixth station of the Bolshefontansk railway. What gave it magic was that certain objects on the photograph *moved*. A dog with a curled-up tail like a doughnut ran across the rails of the narrow-gauge railway, the leaves of the acacia-tree on the far side fluttered and, as its branches separated, one caught a glimpse of the white tents of the Modlin regiment's summer camp; on the platform, a number of passengers, their faces turned in our direction, were gesticulating as they stared at something—probably at the camera photographing them. Then, in the far distance, one could see clouds of steam emerging from the funnel of a small railway-engine, the light, open carriages with canvas curtains drew into the station and stopped, and officers in white summer uniforms, caps with white covers, and white, shiny boots, some of them spurred, jumped out and flitted past among ladies in lace dresses carrying lace parasols.

And all this had not been taken abroad—in Paris—but in our own Russia, our own familiar Odessa; it even included the soda-water stall, from behind which a black-eyed girl peered out, with a hair-do *à la* Vialtzeva, the famous gypsy singer. I felt a surge of patriotic pride in the success of our own moving pictures, mingled with regret that when they were being taken, I was not on the platform of the sixth station and consequently could not see myself, a small school-boy, on the screen.

The miracle lasted for three or four minutes—then suddenly it was all over. The gas was lit again and a triumphant voice announced: "Gentlemen—that concludes the performance."

And I found myself back again in the ordinary and, despite the gas-light, rather dismal hall of the Military Academy.

From all around me came excited chatter and exclamations of admiration. Somebody had recognised someone on the screen; one cadet had recognised himself and swore that he was the one who had gone up to the soda-water stall, bought a glass of it, and drunk it down.

And that is how I saw a miracle for the first time. It is a day I shall never forget.

The Story of the Cats and the Old General 🖋

THE RETIRED general's apartment was situated on the first floor of the Society of Apartment Owners' new house, but his wife never referred to it as the first floor but the *rez-de-chaussée*. "We live on the *rez-de-chaussée*," she used to say.

Half of the general's windows looked out on Pirogov Street, on the long stone wall of the military hospital named in memory of the great military surgeon Pirogov; the other half and the small open terrace looked out on the yard. The general's wife made jam on the terrace while the general sat in a velvet-upholstered chair reading the reactionary paper *Russian Speech.*

But he did not like remaining in one spot for long and, putting on his cap with an enormous leather peak that dated from the Turkish campaign and a pair of shabby, rubber-soled boots with big old-fashioned spurs, which produced a loud scratching noise, would make frequent sorties onto our green, provincial street, still very quiet at that time, where my cousin Sasha and I had once caught frogs.

The general would appear in frightening green glasses, the skin of his wrinkled neck, peering out of the collar of his tunic, reminding one of the crimson skin on the neck of a turkey-cock; he had a dyed moustache turning back to greyish-purple, Alexander I side-whiskers, a long summer cloak with red general's stripes and a St. George ribbon in the lapel, and a sinister dragging gait that inspired passers-by with respect, and policemen and soldiers with genuine fear.

The general was permanently obsessed with a thirst for administrative activity and seemed to feel that he was the commander of a captured enemy town, inhabited solely by Turks, who, being infidels of an inferior race, did not have to be treated with any kind of ceremony.

In a loud, sharp voice, he made critical remarks about ladies who passed by wearing hats with long, projecting hat-pins; he shouted at the municipal employee for sweeping the street inadequately; he threatened a cab-driver, with his rubber-ended crutch, who was breaking the law by driving in the middle of the street; he demanded that local house-owners should put bowls of water outside their premises to prevent pets catching rabies; he pulled cigarettes out of the mouths of smoking school-boys and stubbed them out with his boot; he punched the nose of a medical-corps officer, walking arm-in-arm with his little hat-shop girl-friend, because he did not salute him; he battled with cyclists and later, when motor-cars became the fashion, with motorists, telling them to stop making the whole of Pirogov stink of benzine with their devilish machines.

Children playing "at school" in front of his *rez-de-chaussée* were the worst sufferers. For some unknown reason, he hated this game, and the children's immature sketches, chalked on the asphalt pavement, drove him wild. Once he pulled my brother Zhenka's ears for having drawn a ship, with smoke pouring out of its funnel, in charcoal on the wall.

In short, the general was a universal calamity and there was no way of controlling him. He managed to transform the vicinity of our co-operative house and, indeed, the whole of Pirogov Street, from the French Boulevard to the Odessa Military District headquarters-building near the Kulikovo field, into a zone where scandals, insults, and dangers dogged the steps of every inhabitant. The general even found fault with the timid, local school-girls from the Bellain de Ballet school, renowned for its strict discipline. He shouted at one of them, striking the pavement with his stick: "Take that filthy hair of yours away from here, you nasty girl!"

The situation seemed desperate; yet, one fine day—or, rather, night—our general got what he deserved.

On the night in question, the whole house was awakened by a dreadful cats'-concert. Two or three of the gang of ill-bred, shabby cats that ran wild over the brick roofs of our town were sitting on the general's terrace screaming at the top of their repulsive voices. The general and his wife ran out on to the terrace several times and chased the cats away, but they had scarcely got back to bed before the cats were at it again miawling their heads off. The night was completely ruined. And the next one proved to be no better. It seemed as though not only all the Pirogov Street cats but a great number of others from the side-streets and even from the Botanical Gardens and the Voltuk villa had made their way to the general's terrace for some mysterious, inexplicable reason to indulge in bacchanalian rites. . . . A Walpurgis Night, my aunt called it.

Unruly, debauched, and shameless, without any sense of decency left, the cats and their bedragged females, as noisy as the market-women in Novoribni Street, revelled beneath the general's windows, breaking the silence of the night with high-pitched, amorous cries. They rolled on the terrace, jumped about and scratched on the balcony doors. Tufts of cats' fur and curious wisps of cotton wool flew about in the air. The general and his wife rushed out in the middle of the night and attacked the cats, hurling empty flower-pots, rolling-pins, brushes, and even dusters at them, but to no avail. The cats of both sexes had literally gone crazy. Uttering terrible curses and wearing nothing but his underpants, the general tried to shoot them with his army revolver, but the rusty old .44-calibre Smith and Wesson misfired five times in succession and the general in his fury finally threw it at them—yet the Walpurgis Night continued.

On the following morning, driven to despair, the general called on the Odessan governor to complain, petitioned the town council, appealed to the society for the protection of animals, and even visited the bacteriological laboratories in the belief that he was the victim of some strange, hitherto uninvestigated epidemic, that caused insanity among household pets.

No-one was able to understand what was happening. Everybody was preoccupied and anxious.

... Only my brother, Zhenka, and his little group of friends strolled about quite unconcerned, with secretive enigmatic smiles fluttering round their lips, swollen from a surfeit of melons.

But one morning my aunt was looking for something in her little medicine-chest and discovered that all her valerian drops had disappeared. She caught Zhenka in the corridor and grasped him by the shoulders.

"What is it, Auntie?" Zhenka asked, gazing up at her with his innocent, chocolate-coloured eyes.

"Is it you who's taken my valerian drops?" my aunt enquired.

"Yes, Auntie," Zhenka replied modestly.

"I thought as much!" my aunt exclaimed and suddenly her lips curved and she burst out laughing.

I need hardly explain that Zhenka and his friends, aware of the attraction valerian had for cats, had been responsible for all the commotion by throwing pieces of valerian-impregnated cotton wool on to the general's terrace each night. I cannot remember now how it all ended or where the general disappeared to. I believe he lived peacefully till the revolution and died in the first of it from old age. His funeral passed unnoticed, without a military band, archbishop, choir, rifle-volley, or any other such nonsense.

Bader, Utochkin, MacDonald ✒

BETWEEN THE handsome white building of the third school and the Alexandrovsk Park, there was a large town common, half of which was taken up by a cyclodrome, surrounded on all sides by a high, wooden fence. It was an elliptical wooden construction—a track where bicycle and, later, motor-car races took place—and, perhaps, the most popular attraction in the town. Thousands of people of all classes of society assembled in it on the days of important handicaps, and Uspensky Street, which led to the arena from the centre of the town, was covered in clouds of dust from the passing cabs, carriages, and motor-cars. Those first mechanical carriages, which looked like cabs but had no horses, were fitted with small red radiators, brass lamps in front, and horns blown by rubber pears rather like enormous enemas.

Dust was also raised by pedestrians on their way to the cyclodrome from the working-class suburbs, whole families of old and young, carrying food and drinking-water with them.

The idol of the cyclodrome was Utochkin, a great racing-cyclist over short distances and undisputed world champion for some years, whom the people affectionately called Seriozha and regarded as one of their greatest fellow-countrymen.

For some reason, in our time, Utochkin is only remembered as an outstanding aviator, the pioneer of Russian aviation, in fact. But he was much more than that: he was a first-class performer in every field of sport. In addition to being an aviator, he was a yachtsman, skater, swimmer, jumper from cliff-tops into the sea, diver, expert shot, runner, and also, I believe, boxer. He made several ascents in a balloon and once took his school-boy son up with him, which made all the other boys green with envy. However, he never reached the top in these activities and can be put down as a talented and fearless amateur rather than as a professional. But at cycling he was something of a genius: there was no one to touch him on a cycle-track. The best cyclists in the world competed against him, but none of them ever succeeded in defeating our Seriozha.

Rich people occupied the best seats in the front rows, opposite the thick white finishing-line. The less wealthy usually sat near the start, while the bulk of those attending filled the seats on the wooden stands, the higher the cheaper. The very poor, boys, workers, and fishermen were not given numbered seats but found what positions they could, trusting to God to protect them, at the very top of the stadium, clinging to the lattices supporting the curves of the track. The track itself was constructed of laths of the best ship's timber, which gave it something of the appearance of a yacht's deck.

I remember the day of the great race between the three best cyclists in the world: Bader, Utochkin, and MacDonald.

Those three names—Bader, Utochkin, and MacDonald—seemed to have taken possession of the minds of everyone in our town to the exclusion of everything else. ". . . Bader, Utochkin, MacDonald . . . Bader, Utochkin, MacDonald . . . Bader, Utochkin, MacDonald . . ." —that was all one heard in a crowd. It sounded like a crazy obsession, like Herman's three cards: three, seven, ace. . . .*

With considerable difficulty, my friend Boria and I managed to acquire twenty kopecks for our tickets and, almost squashed to death by the festive crowd, climbed to the very top, where we found two seats in the last row. As we could not see anything if we sat down, we stood upon the bench, clinging to each other for support, and then, above the stormy sea of caps, berets, Panama hats, and various serv-ice-caps, we were at least able to see something. The "something" consisted of a small part of the track, which, from a great height, from the gondola of a balloon, for instance, must have resembled an oval linen-basket. Below us was one of the steep curves, round which raced the pacing motor-cycles, their engines smoking and spit-ting, lying almost parallel with the ground; with the racing pedal-cycles set close behind them, they seemed to be attached. They would have to do ten, twenty, or even thirty laps.

We were familiar with the various makes of motor-cycles: Wan-derer, de Dion Bouton, Red Indian.

Particularly the Red Indian. One of these American motor-cycles was exhibited in the display-window of a shop in Richelieu Street. Beside the dull, old-fashioned windows displaying haberdashery, be-coming yellow from the sun, the one with the Red Indian in it looked like something out of the future. The scarlet Red Indian, built for speed, with just a hint of what we now call streamlining about it, seemed to be thrusting forward and about to race off through the shiny spare parts exhibited in front of it, and our admiration and reverence for the man whose technical genius had enabled him to create such a superlative machine was unbounded. We were, of course, fascinated too by the head of the redskin woman, painted on the petrol-tank, with feathers stuck in her pitch-black hair, flowing behind her in the wind; a symbol of movement . . . flight . . . and much that was to come. . . .

* From *Pique-Dame,* opera by Tchaikovsky, words by Pushkin. *Translator's note.*

Our interest in long-distance races with pacers was confined to the motor-cycles. What we were really waiting for was for Utochkin, Bader, and MacDonald to appear on the track and compete against each other for the championship of the world: this was the great attraction of the afternoon and the last event on the programme. We strained our eyes, hoping to catch a glimpse of Sergei Utochkin through the open door of the shed from which the racers usually emerged. It was sufficient to say "I saw Sergei Utochkin today" to become, for a time, the hero of the hour.

Among the motley crowd of racers, starters with their flags, judges in bowlers and top-hats, and reporters crowded together on the green plain in the centre of the cyclodrome, we tried to single out the figure of Utochkin. Rather on the short side, very broad-shouldered, bull-necked, slightly bandy-legged, his red hair parted in the English way on his faintly cubic head, he bore some resemblance to a circus-clown when he wore his American checked jacket and yellow thick-soled shoes. We suddenly heard cheers coming from the crowd of idlers outside the fence, who had not been able to afford tickets, and gathered that they must be welcoming Utochkin, who apparently had only just driven up. Next moment, the cheering was taken up by the whole cyclodrome. Utochkin had appeared on the central lawn, yet we were still unable to distinguish his familiar figure in the crowd. But it somehow came to me that on this very day the supreme happiness would be granted us; that we should find Utochkin beside us, hear his stammering voice, and feel the touch of his bare, muscular freckled arms as he brushed past us. And my presentiment was right! This is how it happened:

... The three contestants first made a careful examination of their light machines with raised saddles, which meant that their heads were low, their powerful backs bent forward, and their behinds sticking up in the air. Then, to a storm of applause, the three greatest cyclists of the twentieth century, Bader, Utochkin, and MacDonald, began circling the track, so different and yet superficially so alike in their shorts, multi-coloured pullovers, and hairy legs, working like the pistons of a well-oiled machine.

Bader—a good-natured, rather fat, pink-faced German with a baldish head, who looked as if he were a lover of good Bavarian beer and *kartoffel Salat*.

Next, our own Seriozha Utochkin, with his prominent, slightly convex, freckled forehead.

And, finally, the dry Scotsman MacDonald, with a narrow face that might have been carved out of wood, and the aquiline nose of a Sherlock Holmes above a protruding, determined chin. After a few circuits, the champions drew up at the start, where their cycles were held upright by their attendants. The starting-bell rang, the band broke into a waltz, the tricoloured flags on their white poles flapped in the wind, and Bader, Utochkin, and MacDonald were off.

They had to do three laps.

In the first lap, MacDonald, Utochkin's most dangerous rival, went to the front and led our Seriozha by at least two wheel's-lengths and, when the racers soared high up the curve, leaning over almost horizontally, he was still in front. Slightly lower down the slope, pounding away with his short, muscular legs, Utochkin was close behind him, but the German Bader, bending over the handle-bars with sweat streaming from his red face, had lost his rhythm and was nearly four full lengths behind the other two. The fact that MacDonald had taken the lead so quickly and was maintaining it plunged us into despair.

"Utochkin, Utochkin!" Boria and I shouted encouragingly, almost falling off the bench in our excitement, while the crowd of workmen around us added their own urgent pleas: "Come on, Utochkin, come on! Stick to it! Don't shame Mother Russia! Don't let the Scotsman win!"

But the Scotsman was still in front and it did not look as if any power on earth would catch him. In spite of all his efforts Utochkin, far from drawing closer, seemed to be falling farther back. The whole cyclodrome, to a man, heaved one vast sigh of distress. Some people wept unashamedly. And the military band went to pieces, the musicians' eyes on the track instead of on the scores attached to their trumpets.

Yet the real connoisseurs were not perturbed. They watched Utochkin with stop-watches in their hands, aware that Seriozha was only pretending to be going flat out. Actually, he was keeping a short way behind on purpose, saving himself for his famous spurt in the last lap, which he counted on to carry him past MacDonald just before the finish and bring him victory.

At the end of the second lap, Utochkin shot up the curve at a dizzy speed well above MacDonald, then swooped down to the level again. This brought him alongside MacDonald, and the Scotsman began to drop back almost imperceptibly as Utochkin accelerated. The whole cyclodrome broke into a roar. But, at this point, Bader, who had escaped attention running third, suddenly spurted to the front and led the other two for a good wheel's-length and a half. The crowd's roar broke off abruptly and turned into a moan.

My friend Boria, who had a well-balanced, placid, even slightly phlegmatic temperament and was something of a fatalist, stood on the bench, his arms folded across his chest, his legs trembling, and gritted his teeth to stop himself making a sound; but I, a much more emotional boy, allowed great tears to trickle down my cheeks, as I felt sorry for myself, Boria, Utochkin, our Mother Russia, and the kopecks spent on the tickets.

Then all three racers left our field of vision and only reappeared when they were half-way round the third lap, tearing down the slope of the curve towards the final straight and the three-coloured ribbon fluttering at the end of it.

The German was still in front, his fat white legs driving him on like pistons, his fair hair blown about by the wind; close behind him, came Utochkin, struggling to catch up; and third was the dangerous Mac-Donald, four lengths in the rear, with no chance now of finishing second, let alone first.

Once again, Utochkin put on his tremendous spurt, drew level with Bader, and then forged half a wheel's-length ahead of him. The yells from the crowd drowned the triumphant sounds from the band.

"Bravo, Utochkin! Hurrah for Seriozha!" broke out on all sides. Then, amid all this commotion, a childish, squeaky, very common voice suddenly piped out beside us: "That's the boy, Ginger!"

Now, I must tell you that while Utochkin was a good-natured man on the whole, he was extremely sensitive about his red hair and his stammer and was apt to lose his temper if anyone referred to them. It is very hard to understand how the word "Ginger" could have reached his ears with all the din that was going on, but it did, and something quite extraordinary happened as a result. Utochkin looked round, slowed down, drew up by the rails in front of the stand and, propping himself and his bicycle against them, began to unfasten the straps attaching his feet to the pedals, letting his bicycle fall to the ground, he climbed up the stand, his head thrust forward like a bull's, jumping over the benches and elbowing aside anyone who got in his way, till he reached the spot from which the word "Ginger" had come. His face, with its broad, protruding, freckled forehead, was extremely alarming as we watched it approach.

Pushing past Boria and me, he unerringly located, in all that crowd, the boy who had addressed him as Ginger, and grasped him firmly by both shoulders. The boy quivered with fear, tried to shrink back, and tears gushed from his glassy eyes down his cheeks and the sides of his peeling nose. "Dear Uncle," he pleaded. "I won't do it again! I promise I won't!"

But Utochkin was merciless. "S-so you're the m-marmot who c-called me G-ginger!"

He picked the boy up and held him above his head before going on: "N-never let m-me s-see you again! You're not f-fit to c-come to a d-decent race m-m-meeting!" Utochkin had particular difficulty with the final word, but once he had got it out, he casually dropped the boy over the fence: fortunately, he landed in a rubbish-pit overgrown with nightshade, its dingy black berries thickly covered with August dust. Utochkin then went back to the track, picked up his bicycle, mounted it, and strapped his feet to the pedals.

Because of this untoward incident, the judges called the race off and, after a brief conference, decided it should be rerun. Utochkin passed first MacDonald and the Bader towards the end of the last lap, finished first, and did a circuit of honour with a piece of the ribbon adhering to his chest to an ovation from the crowd and a lively march from the band; as he passed the spot on the stand where Boria and I were standing, he looked up and wagged a menacing finger.

Jurka's Papa 🖋

JURKA KOSLOV's father—Jurka was a small boy who had only recently come to Otrada—was an intelligent drunkard, a little, energetic, bearded, snub-nosed old man, who wore a bowler hat, fashionable waistcoat, and gold pince-nez, which kept slipping off his inconveniently small nose to dangle at the end of a black silk ribbon.

He used to leave by cab in the morning for some very good job, possibly in a bank, and often returned in the evening walking slightly unsteadily, with an occasional stumble, and carrying a leather suitcase. He would greet us very good-naturedly as he passed by, raise his bowler hat jokingly, exposing the snow-white silk lining and his initials in gold letters, and say gaily in a nasal voice "Hullo, children, I've laid in a store of Sanzenbacher beer to see me through the evening."

Jurka Koslov's mother was much younger than her little, old husband and Otrada in general considered her to be a smart woman. She often quarrelled with her husband and could be heard through the open door of their balcony shouting at him derisively: "You're an old, decrepit idiot! A useless rag! I despise you! *Cocu!*"

What the mysterious word "*cocu*" meant we had no idea.

From time to time, Mme Koslova, beautifully made-up, in an ostrich-feather boa and a large Paris hat, a gold-mesh bag in her hand, spreading a delicious aroma of French scent around her, took a cab and returned home very late, when she would find old Koslov in a piqué waistcoat, a smouldering cigar between his fingers, fast asleep on the sitting-room sofa with a blissful smile on his pug-nosed face.

Abandoned to the mercy of God, small Jurka Koslov, good-looking like his mother and amusing like his father, turned into a real street-urchin and knew a whole lot of things that to the rest of us boys were merely matters for conjecture. He occasionally scratched obscene words on walls with his penknife and made indecent gestures, but it seemed to me that he did it almost unconsciously, without fully realising what he was doing or why: on the whole, he struck me as a kind, congenial sort of boy.

One day, when Jurka and I were playing forfeits and I was about to climb on his back, as he had lost and had to carry me from one side of the meadow to the other, his Papa appeared on the scene in a good humor and offered, in his Moscow dialect, to take us both to watch a balloon going up.

It seemed too good to be true!

Usually, I only saw a balloon when it was already in flight, high up over the town or the sea, or caught a glimpse of it between houses before it disappeared behind roofs or clouds.

At that time, a lot of people went in for ballooning, hoping to earn a living out of it: they moved around from town to town where there were gas-works, enabling them to inflate their balloons on the spot. They usually travelled by passenger-train, third-class, and sent the envelope, netting, and gondola—a special kind of wicker basket—ahead by slow goods-train. There were so many of them about that they scarcely made any money at all, particularly as the majority of

JURKA'S PAPA

the spectators witnessed the flights for nothing: the sky, after all, belonged to everyone, or, rather, to God, and few people were prepared to spend money on tickets just for the privilege of watching the envelope being filled and the take-off. So balloonist after balloonist went broke. In order to attract more spectators, they had to resort to circus-tricks. One balloonist swung about on a trapeze; another promised, weather permitting, to make a parachute-jump; a third advertised that he would embark on the flight with his wife and children. On this particular day, there was a huge poster displaying the balloonist high in the sky, seated on a bicycle.

Despite this added attraction, there were very few people about when Jurka, his father, and I drove up in a smart cab with pneumatic tyres. The balloonist's wife, with white powdered cheeks, was sitting in a small booth selling tickets and, from her dismal expression, it looked as if the takings were small—scarcely enough to pay for the gas. Jurka's papa, a fragrant cigar in his mouth, opened his large purse, bulging with notes, silver, and even gold coins, and took three tickets in the front row, each costing seventy-five kopecks.

I had never seen so much money in one man's possession! I realized that Jurka's papa must be *very* rich and grasped what the gossips of Otrada meant when they said: "Jurka's mamma is a beauty and she married his papa—that old drunk—just for his money."

A fireman in a brass helmet was standing by the entrance to the piece of waste ground, where wooden benches for the paying public had been set up. He asked Jurka's papa to put out his cigar: smoking was strictly forbidden for fear of a gas explosion.

And then I saw something which I have remembered more clearly all my life than the actual flight of the balloon. Jurka's papa took the cigar out of his mouth but, instead of throwing it on the ground and stamping it out with his foot, he carefully put it into a special silver contraption for holding unsmoked cigars, consisting of two hinged concave sides, which snapped together like a purse. Jurka's papa bent forward and stuffed the contraption containing his cigar into the pocket of his velvet waistcoat, from which protruded the edge of a lilac-coloured silk handkerchief, and it occurred to me that there might be some truth in the tale that the young beauty had married the old man for his money.

We sat down in the front row on a miserable wooden bench that had not even been planed and was so high that Jurka's and my legs did not reach the ground, and watched the rubber pipe, which had crawled out under the gas-work's gates, snaking about from the pressure of the gas pouring through it, into the balloon's silken, resin-covered envelope, up till now spread out, flat and shapeless, inside a net, with heavy sand-bags on its edges.

The balloonist walked round the envelope as it began to stir, a leather jacket with the collar turned up thrown over his shoulders, and carefully examined the patches stuck with rubber gum over its worn sections. The inflation process, which lasted a good two hours, took far too long and was very boring; we fidgeted about on the uncomfortable bench, dangling our legs, not knowing what to do with ourselves: there was nothing in the invisible gas pouring into the envelope to hold our interest. But finally the envelope swelled out and rose, pear-shaped and light, above the launching-platform, rocking gently in its net, with the stone wall of the gas-works, grown grey with age, and a fringe of acacia-trees in the background.

... We were in a part of the town that was unfamiliar to me, somewhere at the end of Khersonskaia Street, behind the town library, where the street seemed to hang over the port and a new, beautiful view on Peresip, Zhevakhov Hill, Dofinovka, and the fields behind Dofinovka suddenly opened up. Down below, spectators were swarming like flies over the brick and iron roofs, waiting to see the flights for nothing. They were up in the trees, too, in large numbers, whereas the people on the launching-platform, where the seats had to be paid for, could be counted on one's fingers: this sad state of affairs was reflected on the thin, gloomy face of the aeronaut, as he moved about making the final preparations.

The balloon was now appreciably rounder and bigger and, to prevent it flying away, several firemen were holding on to the gondola, which was equipped with an anchor on a long rope to arrest the balloon's progress when the moment came to land.

The wind from the bay, which could be seen as clearly as the palm of one's hand, was blowing harder and harder, tugging violently at the huge balloon, so tautly enclosed in its surrounding net that it seemed liable to explode at any moment.

The balloonist threw off his jacket, removed his trousers, and appeared in faded lilac tights, like a street-acrobat. He walked round the group of onlookers with one thin arm raised high in greeting, then went off to say good-bye to his wife, who had come out of the booth. She kept a firm grip on the green metal cash-box with one hand and drew her husband to her with the other. They kissed theatrically,

though on the aging, ugly face of the wife, deeply lined from her in-
digent life, there was a genuine expression of anxiety, even of grief.
The balloonist mounted the shabby bicycle, attached to the gondola
by a long rope, and called out to the firemen: "Let her go!"

The balloon moved slowly sideways, then rose, dragging the balloonist on the bicycle up after it until he was suspended in the air
above our heads. Then it began to soar more rapidly into the clear,
autumnal sky, made still more vivid by the lemon-yellow leaves of
the acacia-trees below. The small figure of the aeronaut in his ex-
hibition-tights waved farewells and sent kisses from the air to the
retreating earth. Then he climbed from the bicycle on to a trapeze
suspended above it and performed a few simple acrobatics, already
almost over the bay, towards which the breeze was smoothly carrying the diminishing balloon with its anchor and bags of ballast.
Finally, the balloonist crawled up into the gondola and that was the
end of the show.

We stayed on to watch the balloon moving out over the open sea,
where it began to come down and eventually settled on the water. We
learned from the papers next morning that all ended well: the balloonist was picked up by a launch sent out from the harbour though
the balloon and gondola sank.

I drove home in the cab with Jurka and his father. Jurka's papa
finished his cigar and his snub-nosed face in pince-nez resembled
that of Émile Zola. But what I saw before my eyes was a picture
of the balloonist's parting from his ugly, unfortunate wife, as she
stood with one arm round her husband's bare neck and pressed the
green metal cash-box with its meagre contents to her heart with the
other. And, round us, there still seemed to be the sour smell of gas.

The Bottle ✒

It appeared that ice or, rather, water, freezing at a below-zero temperature, increases in bulk when it solidifies. I even read somewhere
that, if a hermetically sealed vessel, filled to the brim with water,
were allowed to freeze, the water, at the moment of its transformation
into ice, would shatter it, no matter how hard the metal from which
it was constructed. Actually, of course, the water is no longer water

when it does it, but has become ice. But this is of no importance. What is important is that the vessel will explode.

It was this that gave me the idea of making a shooting-bottle. It seemed quite simple: you took a bottle, filled it to the brim with water, closed it firmly with a strong cork, and put it out to freeze—then, after a certain time, it would shoot the cork out like a bullet from a gun or, if the cork proved too resistant, the bottle itself would explode like a grenade, with a terrible din. Which wouldn't be too bad, either.

I got an empty bottle of bread kvass, filled it to the very top with water, closed it with a cork, and, to ensure success, drove the cork in more thoroughly with a malachite paper-weight from Papa's desk.

It was frosty outside, but not yet cold enough for the execution of my plan. However, I presumed that the temperature would drop below zero towards nightfall. There was a flaming sunset, which augured well for a really hard frost. The evening wind had swept a snowdrift in front of the small lodge inhabited by an old lady, Jasikova, the granddaughter of the well-known poet, Pushkin's friend.

As soon as it was dark, I stealthily made my way and pointed my bottle, like a gun, straight at the old lady's window, on which the icy designs inside split up the multi-coloured lights from the lamps in front of the icons. I calculated that the cork would pop out and strike the window dead in the centre. I had nothing personal against the old lady. In fact, I liked her. She would often call me in and give me delicious halva and jam. One day, having heard that I wrote poetry, she presented me with a small silver coffee-spoon, engraved with the initial "J" in memory of her grandfather.

But I was so obsessed by my desire to explode the bottle that I gave no thought to the fact that I might break her window and frighten her to death, she, who was living so peacefully and solitarily —dressed always in black like a nun—among her Gardner and Popov tea-cups, portraits, lithographs, and icons.

When I went to bed, I dreamed of bomb explosions and saw and heard the cork breaking the old lady's window with a terrific noise. I woke up in the middle of the night and went barefoot to the window to see if the frost had increased. The rime-strewn window was sparkling with bright January stars and I was reassured: the frost was very hard.

On my way to school next morning, wrapped up in a yellow camel's-hair *bashlik,* its fleece tickling my lips, I went up to the snowdrift in which I had planted the bottle. It was where I had left it, with a long icicle peeping out of its neck: the cork was lying in the snow near-by. There had been no shot, no explosion. As it turned into ice, the water had pushed out the cork quite silently and the bottle itself, filled with ice, had a small diagonal crack.

That was all.

A weight fell from my conscience as suddenly, for the first time, I felt pity for the old lady. And she, poor soul, had no inkling of the disaster that had threatened her that night and was calmly, sadly drinking her morning coffee with cream out of a Popov ultramarine cup, which, one day, perhaps, had been used by her famous grandfather.

Football 🖋

I HAVE FORGOTTEN the Christian name and surname of that overgrown school-boy in the seventh form—I believe he was Jurka's elder brother —but I well remember his appearance: he was gaunt and narrow-chested, with red-rimmed eyes that somehow always seemed to be looking in the wrong direction, and a dribbling mouth that managed to smile arrogantly and lewdly at one and the same time. He went about without a belt, which was strictly forbidden, and when asked where it was, would reply in a simpleton's voice that he had left it last night in the ——. He uttered the coarse, soldier's word quite calmly, but we all felt a deep flush of shame rising to the very roots of our hair.

Everything about him inspired one with fear and disgust, particularly the purple spots on his neck and a slight greasyish-pink rash on his forehead.

One day, this elderly school-boy stopped me during the long break, when I was carefully carrying a glass of tea and a bun from the canteen down the corridor. As if looking casually past me through the window, he said: "*Psss* . . . Would you like to join the football-team?"

"What do you mean?" I asked.

"It's been decided that the school should raise a football-team. Have you any idea what football is?"

I replied that I had, though my idea of it, actually was extremely vague. Football had started in England some twenty or thirty years earlier but had only just come into fashion here. All I knew about it was that one kicked a large leather ball and that there were a number of football teams in existence in the country, such as the Odessa British Athletic Club eleven, called *OBAC* composed of Englishmen living in our town. I had heard, too, that there were two famous players belonging to it called Jacobs and Bates. Bates was renowned for having invented a special kick, which lifted the ball over his opponent's head and was now generally known as a "bates." "He did a 'bates' and ran round him."

Some of my friends had even been to the English football-ground, somewhere behind Malofontan, and seen with their own eyes the burst of speed Jacobs put on and the deft flick with which Bates lofted the ball.

The football germ had already infected me, and I longed to become a footballer and learn how to do a bates. The overgrown school-boy perceived my excitement and went on: "If you give me fifty kopecks, I'll put your name down."

"I haven't got it," I said.

"Bring it tomorrow, then; I can wait. Tell your parents that football's a healthy game. They'll give you the money for that sort of thing."

He proved to be right. Papa, who loved repeating *"mens sana in corpore sano,"* agreed to provide the fifty kopecks, merely expressing his fear that the game might take my mind off my school-work. I swore that it would not have this effect on me and, next morning, he handed me a silver half-rouble with the profile of His Majesty the emperor embossed on it. I, in turn, handed it to the older boy, who dropped it in a business-like way into his inside jacket-pocket, where other fifty kopecks collected earlier in the day were already jingling. He pulled out a sheet of paper and added my name at the foot of a long list, remarking that the money would be expended on the purchase of a football.

"Now, you'll have to wait a bit," he said, "but it won't be long before I get the ball and then I'll call you for a practice game."

I waited for the summons for what seemed to me rather a long time, but eventually it came.

"Be at Michael Square, next to the cyclodrome, opposite the third school, at five sharp this afternoon. Don't forget to bring your foot-ball-clothes with you."

I had no idea what he meant by football-clothes, but I did not dare admit it.

"Auntie!" I shouted, the moment I was inside the door of our apart-ment. "*Please* help me! I'm going to football-practice this afternoon and I must have the right clothes. I simply must!"

My aunt had even less idea than I had of what constituted the right clothes, but she possessed very good taste coupled with a lot of com-mon-sense, and it did not take her long to decide what I should wear for this elegant English game, bearing in mind that my garb ought to be elegant, practical, and sportsman-like. We decided that the shoes and trousers I had on would do as they were, but I replaced my shirt and jacket with a striped sailor-sweater that I happened to possess at the time. Braces were out—they did not look sufficiently sporting and, to keep my trousers up, my aunt substituted, after a few small adjustments, a wide belt of her own, made of black elastic ribbon, with a "decadent" double buckle, the sort of belt ladies wore with a blouse and a long, plain cloth skirt.

Examining myself in the mirror. I decided I looked very sporting: anyone would immediately recognize I was a football-player.

I arrived in this attire at the playground between the third school and the cyclodrome, from which came the crackling, spitting sound of motor-cycle engines, to find the game had started. But a thick cloud of dust, permeated by the rays of the afternoon sun, almost blinded me and made it difficult for me to see exactly what was go-ing on and of what the game consisted.

The older boys ran past me hither aad thither, kicking the ball as hard as they could. They were all wearing the same coloured shirts, shorts that scarcely covered their knees, woollen stockings, and special boots with hard, rounded toe-caps and leather studs attached to the soles. This, apparently, was the right football-attire.

A few younger school-boys raced after the ball in their ordinary school-clothes, their black cloth trousers covered with dust up to the knees.

I stood alone in the middle of the field, sneezing from the dust and blinking at the setting autumn sun, which caused blue shadows to swim in front of my eyes. After a while, I managed to find the elderly boy and asked him what he wanted me to do.

He glanced askance at my strange costume and spat contemptuously to one side. "What are you supposed to be, a show-girl?" he asked with one of his lewd smiles. He went on to say that I could play half-back for the time being and then he'd see, adding that I'd better come properly dressed for football next time or I wouldn't be allowed on the ground.

I wanted him to explain to me the object of the game, what a half-back was and in which direction I should kick the ball, but he had already trotted off to another part of the ground, his faded cap on the back of his head and a whistle in his wet mouth. He was, as I learned later, acting as the referee, and gave frequent shrill, cacophonic blasts on his whistle to stop the game so that he could reprimand one or another of the players for reasons that were incomprehensible to me.

The ball would sometimes roll in my direction, whereupon everyone started shouting at me simultaneously. "Kick it, you fool! Don't let it past you, you clumsy oaf!"

But as I had not the remotest idea where I was supposed to kick it and felt constricted and embarrassed in my unsuitable costume, the two hours I spent hanging about the dusty ground developed into a real ordeal.

I did, however, manage to kick the ball, which felt as hard as a stone, on one or two occasions but, to universal, hearty laughter, it always skidded off to one side and the toe of my shoe finally split at the seam. A number of times, players knocked me off my feet, and my black trousers, smothered in dust, began to look as if they were made of velvet; my striped sweater was drenched in sweat under the arm-pits and even down the back.

Next day, after my father had categorically refused to buy me a football-outfit, complete with real football-boots and real football-stockings over which people sometimes tied special shin-guards—it would have cost him a colossal sum: probably as much as eight roubles!—I approached the elderly boy during the long break and asked him to strike my name off the list of football-players and return my fifty kopecks.

He struck my name off at once, licking his indelible pencil and leaving lilac stains on his lips, and, glancing sideways over my shoulder at some distant object with his narrow, red-rimmed eyes, promised to give me back my fifty kopecks in a day or two.

He then shambled off, without a belt, as usual, having again left it somewhere the day before. I need scarcely add that I never recovered my half-rouble and all I retained from my first football-game was the memory of thick layers of September dust, on which an intolerably hot, radiant, orange sun blazed down over the roofs of the French Boulevard.

I did not know then that football should be played on smooth stretches of green: even the English footballers from the OBAC club played on a dusty ground devoid of grass. In our town, grass grew very sparsely and was scorched and dry by early spring.

The Rival 🖋

EVERYTHING WENT SMOOTHLY and happily in our street until Stasik Sologub appeared; then everything began to go wrong. The girls ceased paying any attention to us, all our games, including playing tag among the acacia-trees, stopped abruptly and Stasik became the centre of attention. He usually came out of his side-street on his new Dux bicycle, costing 110 roubles, and rode up and down in front of us, smiling condescendingly at the girls, who drooled at the sight of him sitting proudly in the saddle in his striped trousers, made by a good tailor, stiff, snow-white collar with up-turned edges, and school-cap with a glossy strap which, out of dandyism, he pulled down round his handsome chin. He was in the top form and the oldest of us all, already almost an adult, with just distinguishable side-whiskers and a budding moustache that suited his dark, olive-skinned face and kind, blue, charmer's eyes admirably.

As soon as he got off his shiny bicycle and carelessly propped it against a tree-trunk, all the rest of us boys ceased to exist as far as the girls were concerned: they just clung to Stasik. And he—as though it were the most natural thing in the world—took a cigarette out of his silver cigarette-case, stuck it between his scarlet lips, lit up, and began puffing out blue circles of smoke through his Roman nose, under meeting eyebrows, like those of the handsome Vinitzi, one of the heroes of Sienkiewicz's *Quo Vadis?*

Stasik's outstanding success with our girls caused me intense suffering because, at the time, I was secretly in love with a curly-headed girl, who had eyes like black grapes and lived next to us in the Fessenko house.

She was not the prettiest of our girls, but she was Italian, the daughter of the Lloyd-Triestino Shipping Company's agent and, in addition, bore the divine name of Julietta, so that it was impossible for me not to fall in love with her at first sight. She was about two years older than I and, though she treated me slightly condescendingly, she showed me the same sort of warm friendliness as she did to her younger brother Patrick. I, however, interpreted it as coming close to love.

Anyway, whenever my school-friends asked me why I was looking so gloomy, I used to heave a deep sigh and answer mysteriously: "I'd rather not talk about it. Her name's Julietta—that's all I can tell you."

On Stasik's appearance, Julietta ceased to notice me, and, each time she glanced at him, her face flushed like a rose or blanched like a lily.

I must give Stasik his due: he was not much interested in our girls, including Julietta. What interested him was his own appearance, the strap under his noble chin, the growing moustache, which at that stage reminded me of black eyelashes, and, most of all, riding his bicycle, which he did untiringly round Otrada's four peaceful, shady streets. He behaved very decently to us boys, occasionally allowing us to take a ride, too, on his Dux, with its intriguing pedal-brake.

Nevertheless, when I saw "my Julietta" looking at him tenderly, I nearly went crazy with jealousy and was gripped by a burning desire to wreak some terrible revenge on him. My feelings were shared by a school-boy called Sdraika—I do not remember his surname. It was he who conceived the form that vengeance should take.

Of course, as usual, we needed money to execute our devilish plan, but, by pooling our resources, we were able to obtain the ingredients we required from Korotinsky's tobacco-shop. We bought a box of the most fashionable cigarettes, Zephyrs, and three kopecks' worth of fire-crackers. We removed the tobacco from one of the cigarettes and replaced it by gunpowder from a fire-cracker. Then, to disguise the substitution, we stuffed a little tobacco back in again on top of it.

Next day, feverish with impatience and fear, we waited for Stasik to arrive on his Dux. When, finally, he turned up, Sdraika held up the blue box of Zephyrs and said in an unnaturally friendly voice: "Have one!"

"Thank you," said Stasik, with his usual politeness.

I swiftly plucked the fatal, innocent-looking cigarette out of the box and handed it to him.

Stasik said "Thank you" once again—to me, this time—stuck the cigarette into his mouth, lit it with a match kindly proffered by Sdraika, and, with a third "Thank you," pushed the bicycle away from the acacia-tree and pedalled off down the street, skilfully blowing out long ribbons of smoke through his nostrils. Just as he turned the corner, a tongue of multi-colored, predominantly green flame shot out of the cigarette with a loud bang, followed by a shower of golden rain.

Our blood turned to ice. We were certain that Stasik would tumble off his bicycle that very moment and fall to the ground with a smouldering face. We already regretted the whole foolish idea and realized its meanness. Full of repentance, we were only too anxious to rush to the assistance of our enemy. But what could we do to help him?

To our astonishment, however, Stasik not only remained in the saddle but, spitting out the smoking filter of the cigarette, continued on his way as though nothing untoward had happened and disappeared from view. Presently, he returned from the opposite direction, his aristocratic arms folded elegantly across his chest to display immaculate white cuffs and silver cuff-links. What should we do? Take to our heels? The idea occurred to Sdraika and me simultaneously, but, equally simultaneously, we realized that we should lose the girls' respect forever if we beat such a shameful retreat. We decided to stand our ground and fight Stasik to our last breath.

But Stasik apparently had no intention of revenging himself. He drew up at the nearest acacia-tree and, without dismounting, propped himself up against its grey, cracked trunk, beneath the spreading branches decked with white, aromatic flowers. He gave us a generous smile and pulled a handkerchief out of his pocket to wipe the black ashes off his Roman nose. This was the only damage he had suffered from our dirty trick.

His small, transparent handkerchief had a count's crown embroidered in the corner. . . . It seemed a pity to soil such a hand-kerchief as that! Then "my Julietta" came running to him, a scarlet ribbon in her black, curly hair, and, flushing red as a poppy, licked her own lace handkerchief, stood on tiptoe, and herself wiped Stasik's nose.

"Thank you!" said Stasik, lighting a cigarette from his silver case with its golden monogram; then, as a token of gratitude, he sat the Italian girl on the handle of his Dux and circled with her round Otrada twice or even three times.

I had the feeling—and not only I, but all of us, girls and boys—that at some point on this ride in the pale light of a large mirror-like moon, already rising above the sea, Stasik and Julietta would kiss.

My Fatal Brand

THE CENTENARY of the Patriotic War of 1812, Russia's victory over twenty nations, was approaching. A hundred years earlier, the Russian army had conquered the great Napoleon, who had occupied Moscow, the Mother of Russia. During the severest of winters, it had banished from the frontiers of our country twenty nations, Napoleon's allies, and Napoleon himself, who, shamelessly abandoning the remains of his hungry, frozen, devastated army, had raced back down the Smolensk road towards Paris in a light sleigh.

We were preparing great celebrations in our town—patriotic evenings and spectacles, concerts, lectures, and a military parade on the Kulikovo field.

Something similar had taken place three years before, when we had celebrated the victory over the Swedes near Poltava, and a wooden statue of Peter the Great in a three-cornered hat had been erected on the Kulikovo field. To the tune of the "Preobrazhensky March," the sharp-shooters' "iron brigade" and the Modlin regiment had paraded past it and then dispersed to their barracks, the soldiers singing the bravura song: "This all happened near Poltava, / Bold we marched into the fray, / With the Swedes we fought there proudly, / Peter's colours won the day."

The words of this song, which also included "He commanded all our army, brought to action all our guns," swept through our town, inspiring our unconquerable country with well-deserved pride.

I do not remember if we had a special celebration then at our school, but I do not suppose we did, as it was summer, when school would be closed for the holidays.

But now, in winter, we were looking forward to honouring the victory over Napoleon with a special, cultural matinée, during which the director was to make a speech, the history-teacher was to give a lecture on the great importance of the events of 1812, and a choir of school-boys was to sing the national anthem and other patriotic songs.

But it was another item in the programme that excited me most: the recital of poems by the school's most gifted pupils. I had a very high opinion of my artistic capabilities in this field, especially after my performance at a previous cultural evening, when I had recited the only monologue I knew really well, one of Chatsky's, with sweeping gestures and dramatic voice. When I reached the end and had angrily pronounced the famous "My carriage, please!" stamping my foot, I had rushed from the stage, clutched at the curtain and dragged it down; after which, I had been compelled to speak in a whisper for a whole week, as a result of the damage to my vocal cords.

I felt certain that this would ensure me a place in the coming programme and could already foresee my success, so my surprise was indescribable when I discovered that my name had not been included. I read through the typed list, hanging in the teachers' room, again and again: each time, I thought my eye-sight must be failing and had another look.

Alas, my name definitely was not there!

I went in search of my form-master, who principally taught Latin, and found him in the corridor. He was a Pole, Sigismund Tsesarevich, who had been given the strange, meaningless nickname of Sizik. In a trembling, ingratiating voice, I complained that my name did not appear in the list of entertainers.

Sizik listened to me benevolently, running a white hand, with a narrow wedding-ring on the third finger, through his chestnut-coloured, short-cropped hair and pointed musketeer's beard, uttered a moralising Latin proverb to the effect that a cobbler should stick to his last and added in Russian, with a strong Polish accent, that with my very modest successes and boisterous behavior I could hardly expect the honour of participating in the patriotic matinée.

I almost wept on the spot with humiliation, but clicked my heels and made a deep bow to Sizik, as school-rules demanded, before dragging myself away to the lavatory, where I could lock myself in and wipe away the tears that now were coursing down my cheeks through my clenched fist. After a while, I was seized with the urge to take steps of some kind to remedy the situation, and it occurred to me that if I were to compose a patriotic poem of my own, I would certainly be allowed to participate in the performance.

As soon as I got home, I set to work at once and by the end of the evening the poem was finished.

This is how it began:

> "When to the Russian frontier
> Napoleon moved his men . . ."

Then I added a verse or two containing the little I knew of the 1812 war in which I mentioned Kutusov and Bagration but delicately omitted any reference to the capture of Moscow—after all, what would have been the point of elaborating on it?—and ended the ode on a stirring, edifying note:

> "The war was short and glorious,
> Erased the foeman's trace
> Napoleon was conquered
> Hurrah, the Russian race!"

This sounded very concise and to the point and I felt certain that the masters forming the matinée committee would not dare to refuse so patriotic a poem.

I wrote it out in my best handwriting, making sure there were no spelling mistakes, and presented it to Sizik, who read my opus through and then asked suspiciously if I had composed it myself or cribbed it out of some periodical or calendar. I swore it was all my own work, flushing with an author's bashful pride!

"Very well," said Sizik, wrinkling his professional forehead impressively. "My congratulations! You have the making of a true patriot. This is a very laudable effort. I will bring it to the committee's attention. Go in peace and hope. *Dixi*," he ended.

And so, to cut matters short, included in the list of performers, the programme read: So-and-so "will recite the poem '1812', of which he is the author."

The cultural matinée, at which I recited my poem, has largely escaped my memory. I remember the cold school-hall with its big, round windows, beyond which there was a constant flurry of fine, dry snow-flakes, and the musical jingle of bells attached to the harness of the horses drawing light sleighs silently behind them through the snowy street. I remember two enormous, life-size oil-portraits of Russian emperors; one of the present tsar, Nicholas II, in an ermine mantle, with sceptre and orb in his hand, and a crown lying on a velvet cushion on a golden table beside him; the other, of Alexander the Blessed, Napoleon's conqueror, in a black three-cornered hat with white plumes, his long thin legs encased in jack-boots, and a telescope in his hand, standing in the shade of a romantic oak on some battle-field or other.

I remember the stern faces of the director, the inspector, the teacher of divinity, a bishop in a festive silk cassock with up-turned sleeves, and a general in the front row, wearing the silk ribbon of a decoration across his chest—all of them holding long, narrow programmes—and behind them all the rest of the audience, seated no doubt in order of importance, but to me just one many-faced whole.

Before my appearance, the history-teacher gave his long, tedious lecture, sitting at a special table, mumbling his words, as he read from an elegant, stiff-covered exercise-book, coughing the whole time and mopping his sweaty forehead with a freshly ironed handkerchief.

All around me, I was aware of the cold silence of the somnolent listeners.

I was wearing a dress-uniform, given to me by old Jasikova in memory of her beloved grandson, who had recently died of consumption, and feeling rather uncomfortable in all this splendour, since the dead boy had been both taller and fatter than I was; but, at the same time, I secretly saw myself as another Pushkin at the examination at the lycée in Tsarskoe Sielo, as he is depicted in the famous Riepin picture.

As dramatically as I could, I declaimed my poem rapidly and

clearly with only an occasional stutter, seeing nothing but my own reflection in the well-polished honey-coloured parquet floor. When I reached the impressive final lines, on which all my hopes rested, I thrust out a hand, the fist clenched, and stamped on the ground with such force that the director, sitting directly in front of me, suddenly woke up and jerked his grey, lion's head to one side, as though he thought I was about to punch his nose.

I had counted on an enormous burst of applause, but it proved to be very thin: to be absolutely honest, no one applauded at all, apart from my bosom friend Boria, who clapped and clapped frenziedly in his determination to produce an ovation; but all his efforts proved fruitless and I crept back to my seat, red as a beetroot, with sweat pouring down my neck, dismally aware of my failure.

Added to my sense of failure was one of shame that I had dared go up on the stage and declaim my own pitiful verses when other, much older school-boys had recited poetry by Lézmontov, Tiutchev, Krilov, and Majkov. Oh, how sadly mediocre I felt in the hostile, cold, white school-hall, lit by the bluish light of a winter morning, particularly when my comrades, sitting beside me on creaking wooden chairs, whispered patronising words of consolation: "You mustn't give up. You're bound to do better next time. . . ."

But the important thing that happened was that all this military-patriotic window-dressing of tsarist Russia, which up till now had gripped my immature imagination, was somehow, almost inperceptibly dispelled and, in the depths of my soul, a new, true conception of war was born.

At home, I stood for a long time in front of the window and watched the thin snow, which a storm originating in some far-away corner of our vast, immeasurable country—in the east, the Urals, Siberia, the Baikal—had been sweeping over us since the day before. From the fourth floor of the new co-operative house to which we had recently moved, I gazed and gazed till a blue veil seemed to descend over my eyes, blotting out the uninterrupted snow-fall, and Tiutchev's prophetic lines about the fatal stigma that would soon brand almost every forehead wandered persistently through my mind. I was overwhelmed by the fear of something indefinable that was threatening our world, threatening Papa, my aunt, Zhenia, and me; and I prayed to God, in whom I still had childish, naïve faith, that my forehead might not bear the fatal stigma.

And He heard me.

The Lottery ✍

PAPA USED TO SAY irritably that all these lotteries were a complete
fraud, converted philanthropy into a childish game, and only existed
to amuse rich old ladies who had nothing better to do. If anyone told
him that they were, in fact, organised to assist widows and orphans,
he would become quite angry and retort that they were a parody of
charity, and that it was quite possible to help the poor and needy
without hiring the Stock Exchange building at great expense, hanging out national flags, setting up a sort of peep-show, and arousing
the lowest instincts of an ignorant mob by offering them a vague
chance of winning something worth a hundred roubles for twenty
kopecks. Papa was a convinced Tolstoyan, though he was opposed
to vegetarianism.

The more excited he got, the more eloquent his descriptions of the
abhorrent and immoral effects of the lottery, the more I wanted
to see it, and I implored him so importunately to take me there that
he finally agreed. I had a vague suspician that he actually was quite
keen to go there himself, and try his hand at winning something for
nothing, a piano or a cow, say, for twenty kopecks. But if he did, he
was careful to conceal it and continued to smile squeamishly whenever the word "lottery" was mentioned.

The Stock Exchange building was considered one of the most
notable sights of the town, together with the monument to the Duke
of Richelieu, the gun from the English frigate the *Tiger* standing in
front of the Town Hall, the theatre, the famous stairs leading from
the Nikolaev Boulevard down to the port, and the funicular running alongside the stairs.

The Stock Exchange was a rather poor copy of the Doge's palace
in Venice, with soaring pillars, enormous stained-glass windows, yellow brick walls, a granite foundation, and a marble staircase leading
from the street into a colossal marble two-storied hall. The ice-
covered pavements near the Stock Exchange were strewn with yellow sand, tricolour flags flapped in the frosty sea-wind at the top of
their white flag-staffs, and policemen in white gloves froze by the
marble pillars at the top of the staircase. There was a long line of
cabs, the drivers, an eye out for customers, walking round their
shaggy, rime-covered horses and trying to keep warm by slapping
themselves on their shoulders, thighs, and even backs crosswise with

their gauntlets. On a corner of the street, there was a brazier with burning logs, round which other drivers and uniformed and plain-clothes police were warming themselves.

Papa and I mounted the white, scraped marble steps and found ourselves in the hall, which, despite the artificial lighting added to the dull light of an ordinary winter's day, seemed rather dingy, like a large railway-station. The floor was thickly strewn with sawdust, which hushed the sound of footsteps, and people, for some unknown reason, whispered as though in church. Altogether, it did not at all resemble the gay dance-hall I had been expecting. In the corners, there were booths, at which the lottery-tickets were sold, and be-side them were stands with the prizes spread out on wide shelves covered with red calico, rising in tiers from the floor right up to the ornate ceiling, so that the objects on the highest shelves—samovars, accordions, balalaikas, and so on—seemed very small, almost like toys.

There was no rule about taking off one's coat here, and the public crowded round the stands with the prizes in their winter coats and snow-boots, merely removing their hats as a token of respect for the charitable aims of the undertaking.

We stood for a long time, Papa and I, examining the prizes, try-ing to make up our minds as to which valuable object we should like to win. For instance, it would be nice to win the big, chiming grand-father-clock, with its lead pendulum, like a full moon, swaying to and fro in the glass case; or a pretty lamp on a tall marble stand, with a lace shade, that resembled a coquettish lady's nightcap—a magnificent lamp, which would be a most decorative addition to our modest apartment. I mentioned my hopes of our winning the lamp on a green marble stand, green as an Aivazovsky sea, to Papa, but he did not share my enthusiasm and even made one or two derogatory remarks about my philistine taste. Then he, in turn, expressed the opinion that it would not be at all bad to win an oak book-cupboard, all by itself on a special stand. We noticed, close by it, a whole din-ing-room suite, out of light-green painted wood, comprising a rather ugly, decadent side-board and a number of high and probably not very comfortable chairs. Papa, with his classic, realist taste in art, was again scornful, but I secretly thought that the painted, green furniture would be a considerable improvement on our dull side-board bought at a market and the shabby Viennese chairs, with holes in their criss-cross seats.

What a jumble of things there were at that lottery! Carpets, Kuznezov table-services, crystal carafes, silk draperies, canteens of cutlery, musical instruments, and, on another special stand, a rosewood piano—the highest peak of luxury that I could possibly imagine—not to mention pictures, oil-paintings in gold frames, silver trays, and folkloric embroideries and lace.

A not very beautiful and not even very large Chinese vase with dragons—the gift of the dowager-empress Marie Feodorovna—attracted great attention. The public filed past it with reverence and secret hopes of winning the imperial gift as the policeman in full uniform guarding it repeated monotonously every other minute: "Ladies and gentlemen, please be careful, this is really something!"

There were many more valuable objects. A huge talking doll, Nelly, with a number of different dresses in a lovely box, several bicycles, coloured garden-umbrellas, wicker garden-furniture—far too much for me to be able to remember them all! And they made me aware of the existence of a rich, luxurious life, beside which ours seemed grey and beggarly.

There was also a cow among the prizes, but it was not in the room: a printed notice announced that a Simmenthal cow named Zorka would be won by the possessor of such-and-such a numbered ticket and that the winner could take a hundred roubles instead if he or she preferred to.

"That would be quite nice, too," Papa murmured with a smile. "Not the cow, of course, but the money."

Noticing my expression, Papa tried to pass his remark off as a joke, adding that the whole thing was a romp, anyway.

However, the time had now come for the draw to begin. Papa had already firmly declared before we started out that he had no intention of buying any tickets, that we would just look around and then go home. But here he ran into a snag. It turned out that the entrance-tickets, for which Papa had paid a rouble each, entitled us to five free lottery-tickets each. It was impossible not to take advantage of such an opportunity.

Papa and I approached the glass hexahedron in which the tickets, rolled up tightly into tubes, were all mixed together. The patroness, with a boa of bird's feathers round her wrinkled neck, spun the case around and Papa and I each drew out five of the little paper tubes through a hinged window in it. Moving out of the crowd, we held our breaths so as not to "frighten our luck away," pulled off the rubber bands, and began unrolling the tubes. I unrolled the first ticket and saw the big round stamp of the charitable society on it.

"Papa!" I cried loud enough for the whole room to hear. "Look! I've got a stamp! I've won!"

Papa put on his pince-nez, looked at my ticket with its stamp and said shortly: "No number."

"What do you mean, no number?" I asked, fearing the worst.

"I mean, it isn't a winning ticket. You can throw it away."

I was reluctant to throw away a ticket with such an impressive-looking stamp on it, but I finally sent it to join a host of others scattered about on the sawdust. But I kept the rubber band—it might come in useful some time.

We hurriedly unrolled the rest of our tickets and it began to look as though they would all be losers; but, on my last one, a long, six-figured number was clearly printed in black alongside the circular, lilac stamp. My heart pounded with the same joy and hope I experienced when pulling a hooked bullhead out of the sea.

"Well done! Now you really have won something," Papa said, and we went to collect it.

A young dandy with a moustache took my ticket, consulted some lists, and then solemnly announced: "Number 666872—a Baccarat crystal drinking-glass."

With these words, he bent under the counter and handed me a small parcel with 666872 stuck on it.

"My congratulations on your win," the young man said.

I tore off the wrapping-paper and saw a small, cut-glass tumbler like those used at spas.

At first, I was so disappointed that I almost burst into tears—so many hopes, such a miserable outcome—though I tried to console myself with the thought that it was not just an ordinary glass but Baccarat.

"Papa, what is Baccarat?

"It's glass specially made with a small admixture of silver," Papa replied.

Papa's words completely restored my equanimity. Baccarat! Crystal! Admixture of silver! It wasn't every boy who had such a valuable glass! It must be terribly expensive: probably about a hundred roubles in a shop.

"Baccarat is the name of a town in France where they manufacture glass articles like that one," Papa added.

"Hurrah!" I cried, ecstatic that my glass had such an exotic origin.

. . . And so we had carried out our programme and it was time to go home. But how could one leave a room filled with such valuable prizes?

"Papa, dear Papa," I said imploringly, tugging at the sleeve of his thick overcoat, "let's buy at least one more ticket each!"

I was certain that Papa would remain implacable, but after a short hesitation and a few shakes of his head, he said: "Oh well, all right, in for a kopeck, in for a rouble!"

Papa's face was slightly flushed, and I could have sworn that at the bottom of his heart he was as much of a gambler as I, only he was going to some pains to conceal it.

Five tickets all proved to be unnumbered and we threw them away. My eyes clouded with disappointment.

"Oh, hang it all!" Papa suddenly exclaimed. "One more try and then—*basta!*"

He gave me a rouble and I drew five more paper tubes out of the glass case. One of the tickets had Number 003224 on it.

"Winning number 003224!" the young man announced and looked through his lists. "Ten pounds of lump sugar donated by the Brodsky factory." And he brought out a large packet wrapped in blue paper.

At the time, this struck Papa and me as a magnificent win. Ten pounds of sugar! A fortune! And to it had to be added a glass with an admixture of silver, which had probably cost five roubles. I tried to persuade Papa to buy five more tickets and win something really valuable: the cow, the dining-room suite, or the Chinese vase—gift of the dowager-empress.

But this time, Papa refused categorically: "We're completely broke as it is, my boy," he said, and we went out into the street, where it was almost dusk and the frost was getting really sharp.

The fires on the corners were enveloped in thick smoke, through which one could hardly see the orange-red, crackling pieces of wood. Papa acted like a ruined card-player to whom nothing mattered any more, for when one of the cab-drivers inquired whether the gentleman would care to take a ride with a fine, frisky horse, he not only accepted the offer, but, almost without haggling, agreed to a fare of forty kopecks, instead of the usual thirty. We settled down in the small sleigh, accompanied by the parcel of lump sugar kindly donated by the Brodsky company, with aromatic hay under our feet, and the driver twisted round in his seat to wrap us in a thin, worn, moth-eaten cloth rug, sparingly edged with a narrow strip of bear-skin. Then we drove up the middle of the glistening, icy street, bumping from hillock to hillock, while the driver, exhaling strong fumes of vodka into the frosty air, kept turning his bearded face with a Father Christmas nose towards us and repeating in a singsong voice: "From hillock to hillock I drive/ The gent gives no vodka to keep me alive. . . ."

Papa turned a deaf ear to these hints as he worked out the un-satisfactory balance-sheet: a debit of four roubles for the tickets and forty kopecks for the driver against the credit of our prizes, which he valued at a mere one rouble sixty—one rouble twenty for the ten pounds of sugar and forty kopecks for my little glass.

"How do you know that the glass only cost forty kopecks?" I asked Papa. "The silver in it alone must be worth three roubles."

"There's a piece of paper stuck to the bottom with the price on it —forty kopecks," Papa told me disconcertingly.

And in the pale-pink, frosty sky, above the low houses and the pil-lars of blue and lilac smoke rising from their chimneys, a full moon was beginning to shine ahead of us, cold and bright, like a silver half-rouble coin.

Addenda ✒

I WAS NOT TELLING the truth when I described at home how Utoch-kin abandoned the race at the decisive moment just before the finish and left the track in order to punish the small boy who had shouted "Ginger:"

In reality, it happened after the finish, when Utochkin had won and was doing the lap honour, so there was no question of having the race rerun.

I succumbed to the temptation of dramatising my story and

swerved away from the precise facts: the rest is more or less authentic—I beg the readers' forgiveness.

The Six-Sided Briquette

EVERY YEAR, late in the autumn, Papa went to the Odessa goods-station to buy fuel for the whole year. It was, of course, at the time when we still lived in a house with stoves.

In spite of my repeated appeals, Papa never took me with him. He said I was too young and that the road to the station was usually full of traffic, which could be dangerous for a little boy.

I always envisaged the journey to buy the fuel as a long one into an unknown, mysterious, almost fairy-tale country called the Odessa goods-station. In one respect, it was Odessa, the familiar town in which I was born and where I lived on Basarnaia Street; but in another it was a station, something connected with the railway-engines, trains, flickering signal-lights, porters, and guards, these last with wooden, pear-shaped handles of red and green flags peeping out of leather cases attached to their belts. And as the station was a *goods*-station, it also evoked a picture of a mass of different wares, enclosed in sacks, packing-cases, and tarpaulin covers bound with metal strips.

The population of this country consisted of people who were not like us and sold fuel among other things.

But where did that fuel come from, where was it stored, how was it sold, weighed, loaded, and finally delivered to the coal-shed in our yard? All these questions disturbed me and aroused such insatiable curiosity that I was shedding bitter tears as I implored Papa: "Papa, dear Papa! Why won't you take me to the Odessa goods-station? Why? I promise I'll be a good boy and obey you."

But Papa kept stubbornly repeating the same sentence about "the traffic," and I finally conjured up a picture of a long, paved street along which lorries raced, trying desperately to overtake each other, knocking down pedestrians and spreading havoc among the cabs, driving prospective fuel-buyers to the Odessa goods-station.

All this was dreadful!

But, one day, after Mamma's death, when I was older, Papa did take me with him to fetch the fire-wood. We drove for a long time in a cab through the suburbs of the town, past a large number of small one-storied houses, whitewashed like country huts, and along seemingly endless, wide, badly paved roads, covered with dry November dust and, occasionally, hay that had fallen off passing carts. At the smithy which we came across on our way, the doors were open and, in the dark caves behind them, an orange fire was burning, the red-hot iron was gleaming with a plum-coloured light, and we could hear the clang of the hammer on the anvil and the shrill neighing of horses, as their hooves were shod by blacksmiths in leather aprons.

There was nothing particularly interesting about that and, as far as traffic was concerned, I scarcely noticed any.

As we approached the goods-station, I saw an increasing number of barns full of oats or hay and, later, spotted a coloured poster on the side of a shed, depicting most realistically a wood in winter; clumps of tall, symmetrical pine-trees, their black trunks covered in dazzling white snow; and along a highway through the wood raced three chestnut horses, harnessed to a three-cornered sleigh, laden with some strange, coal-black cakes, one of which had fallen off in its mad career and lay clearly in sight in the bluish-white snow on the road. The sleigh's driver, with a broad red belt round his waist, was lashing the horses furiously, and on a patch of clear blue sky between the pines were written the words: "Sale of coal and briquettes."

. . . Oh, so that meant that those black cakes were briquettes! But what actually were briquettes? Papa explained to me that they were fuel—coal-dust compressed into six-sided tablets; tablets I had seen. I do not know why, but my imagination was sharply stimulated by that winter landscape with the black briquette lying on the white snow.

The buying of the fire-wood did not interest me much, and the return journey in the same cab, behind the carts carrying Papa's purchases, was very slow and tedious. I kept thinking about the briquettes so beautifully moulded into six-sided tablets from coal-dust. That kind of fuel was entirely new to me. But the strange thing was that the word "briquette" was familiar to me, though where, when, and in what circumstances I had heard it, I could not remember. Nevertheless, I had certainly experienced previously the same sense of surprise and admiration at the sight of that strange black object: their colour and shape had imprinted themselves on my susceptible childish brain.

But where and in what circumstances? That was the problem. And then, when the carts entered the yard and the logs were tossed out by the shed, piled one on top of the other and filling the autumnal air with a bracing, sourish smell, their coating of silver lichen seeming to presage the imminent approach of winter and flimsy snow-flakes dropping out of dark December clouds, it dawned upon me!

The briquettes were in some way connected with Uncle Misha, Papa's dead brother, a man with a strange fate. He finished his mathematical studies in the physio-mathematical faculty of Novorossijsk University, with a gold medal, his thesis being on a method of calculating a comet's orbit—I do not remember the year—but instead of remaining on at the university, for some obscure reason he joined the army's artillery brigade, billeted in Nikolaev. I believe he had some notion of bringing the light of knowledge into the dark, dreary life of the army and introducing the circle of provincial officers to clear thinking, kindly feelings, and possibly some revolutionary ideas. Perhaps it was distant echoes of the Dekabrist movement in the south of Russia, then called Novorossia, but I am by no means certain of this.

However, it ended by Uncle Misha, anxious to save a fallen human being, which was very much in the spirit of the times, marrying an illiterate girl in Nikolaev and leaving the army; he was then struck with an incurable mental disease, left his wife, and, with nothing but the suit he had on and a small bundle in his hand, turned up at our house when I was only three and Mamma still alive.

I remember well how Uncle Misha was put into the town hospital and Papa, Mamma, and I went to visit him in a huge, dismal, over-crowded ward, where he was lying under a grey hospital blanket, which reeked of carbolic. A slovenly male nurse in soldier's boots came in and placed two flat rice cutlets, covered in prune sauce, on a metal plate, beside Uncle Misha on a stool. Uncle Misha spilt some of it on his beard and suddenly burst into tears, kissing Mamma's hands and apologizing for all the trouble he was causing.

He ran away from the hospital in calico underclothes and his hospital dressing-gown and suddenly reappeared at our house, sobbing his heart out and begging us to let him live with us. A bed was arranged for him in the sitting-room, between the ficus and the piano, where our Christmas tree usually stood. Thin as a skeleton, yellow as parchment, with a thinning moustache, he breathed heavily, stared at Mamma through Dostoevsky eyes, filled with pain and gratitude, and again kissed her hand, smearing it with egg-yolk. And Mamma, hardly able to keep back her tears, smiled at him tenderly with her slightly squinting eyes, and told him he would soon recover, everything would be all right; and, to the sound of her sweet voice, he suddenly fell asleep or became unconscious and snored loudly enough to be heard throughout the apartment, his dry, rasping snore frightening me so much that I hid behind Mamma and clung to her skirt.

Sometimes Uncle Misha felt better and lay in bed, reading, or played a game with me, in which I ran close by him and he tried to raise himself, stretch out his bony arms, and catch me: sometimes he did catch me and began tickling me and I was scared to death by the cold fingers of a dying madman, by the look of the unnaturally enlarged pupils in sunken, already half-dead eyes, by the gay, loud laughter, which froze my blood.

I would tear myself out of his clutches, run into the dining-room, and hide behind Grandmother's screen.

Sometimes Uncle Misha was overcome by fits of raving lunacy, and Papa would somehow manage to tie him to the bed with a towel. We had to have a nurse for him and it was in her arms that he died one night. I only saw him next morning, washed and his hair neatly combed, in a starched shirt and black frock-coat, with bony, colourless hands pressing a small icon to his heart, a gristly nose, and closed, protruding eyes. In death, his face was beautiful as a martyr's.

I remember him in his coffin, the drawing-room full of friends and relatives, the lilac velvet head-dresses and dove-coloured mourning cassocks of the clergy, the funeral service, the clouds of incense, and the students' choir: then all this dispersed, vanished, and the room became the same old empty sitting-room, with the ficus, the piano, and the velvet arm-chairs, but without Uncle Misha and his bed, without the coffin, which I had seen for the first time in my life.

Uncle Misha's wife—"that woman"—arrived a little later from Nik-olaev; but she did not enter the sitting-room: she sat quietly in the kitchen, a country-shawl over her head, weeping softly with her mouth pursed up or drinking tea from a saucer balanced on three fingers, with a small Kiev ring on one of them. She stayed with us for two days, thanked Mamma for looking after Uncle Misha, and gave us a present; a fat, plucked hen, which she had brought with her in a basket covered with a towel. I never saw her again and it seemed odd that she should be my aunt, but, for some reason, that woman, with her kind peasant's face, made a more painful impression on me than Uncle Misha's death, which had produced neither fear nor anguish, because I was too small then to understand the meaning of death.

Uncle Misha left us a carbon copy of his thesis, "A calculation of the comet's orbit in [such and such a year]", which included a number of designs completely inexplicable to me, circles and curved lines with little drawings of a long-tailed star in its different phases. This thesis disappeared after Mamma's death, during one of our numerous moves from one apartment to another.

There was also a black, compressed, six-sided tablet, which he had brought with him in his bundle as a memento of his service as a junior officer in the artillery.

As it turned out later, it was composed of black gunpowder—a briquette used by the army before the invention of smokeless gunpowder, which had something of the appearance of dry, yellow macaroni.

But I did not understand any of this at the time: I was merely struck by its name—briquette—which now suddenly floated back into my memory when I saw the picture of the troika loaded with the six-sided cakes. To me, Uncle Misha's briquette was fuel.

It was kept in Papa's chest of drawers along with a lot of other useless junk. I shall give you a description of that chest of drawers and what it contained later—providing, of course, that I do not forget.

So it was like that! We had, in our house, a splendid briquette, a form of fuel which nobody had thought of using. Well, now it would be! I was tingling from head to foot with impatience to get home as soon as possible and see how Uncle Misha's briquette would burn in the kitchen-stove.

The rest is predictable.

Taking the black hexahedron from Papa's chest of drawers, which he had forgotten to lock, I rushed into the kitchen and, before the cook had even time to blink an eyelid, I had shifted the pan of borsch to one side and thrown the briquette into the ring. The gunpowder did not explode very violently, but, still, the whole of our dinner was destroyed and a shaft of multi-coloured smoky fire soared from the stove almost to the ceiling. By some happy chance, neither the cook nor I was injured.

Is it necessary to describe the awful dressing-down which I got from Papa and my aunt? I swore that I had had no evil intent in mind and tried to explain how I had been led astray by the resemblance of the six-sided artillery briquette composed of gunpowder to the six-sided briquette composed of coal-dust, which I had seen in the pretty poster on the side of the fuel-shed on our way to the Odessa goods-station. Alas, nobody would believe me, and my reputation of an impossible boy who would "one day destroy us all" became more definitely confirmed.

Later on, when I was already grown up, I tried to explain the history of Uncle Misha's briquette to Papa and my aunt. But even then, they would not believe me: they still considered that I had done it on purpose. Now, when neither of them is in this world, there is no-one to whom I can attempt to exonerate myself. And who would believe me, anyway?

A Short Dissertation on Lodgers 🖋

I HAVE ALREADY told you about one lodger, Jacovlev the explorer. But there were also others. It was the custom at that time for families who were not very well off to let rooms in their apartments, though "taking in lodgers" was usually referred to in a slightly disparaging way. We, too, were sometimes compelled to take in a lodger or, occasionally, even two in order to make both ends meet; thus, beside the well-established way of life of our family, there was quite frequently another one being pursued concurrently—that of a student, an explorer, a young bachelor cramming for his law examinations, or a newly married couple, who had not yet been able to find an apartment of their own. To have a respectable, solvent lodger was a big help for our modest budget. Once, we had a lodger who was almost one of the family, my school-friend Boria, whose mother had died and whose father was a teacher in a suburban village. It was with him I went to see the race between Utochkin, Bader, and Mac-Donald.

Our lodgers represented a vast variety of different types, but I have forgotten most of them: only a few have remained in my memory.

After the death of my grandmother—Papa's mother—a room became vacant, and a certain amount of internal rearrangement enabled us to free two nice rooms connecting with each other, which we let to a young couple; a doctor, who had just passed through the Medical Military Academy and was now attached to the local military hospital, and his pretty, plump, blonde wife, who sat at home during his absence and had no idea what to do with herself.

When one of us, Zhenia or myself, began making a noise outside their bedroom, my aunt would say in a hushed voice with a faint quirk of amusement round her mouth: "Boys, stop making such a row! You're disturbing the lodgers. They're on their honeymoon."

It was, indeed, a fascinating example of a honeymoon: I have never encountered anything quite like it since. All the newlyweds' possessions were brand-new, spick and span, and they themselves looked as though they had just been contrived by a first-class craftsman out of the best material: she was pinky-white, with dimples on her cheeks and arms, her hair was nicely done and everything she wore was smart and, of course, brand-new, too; dresses adorned with little ribbons and pieces of lace, transparent stockings, and shoes with French heels.

While he was working, she was bored to tears and waited for him on the balcony in a pretty dressing-gown with flounces and ruches. She kept eating chocolates from Abrikosoff and reading novels, cutting the pages with the edge of a tortoise-shell comb she pulled out of her hair. Her eyes were blue, her mouth like a cherry, and on her china-cheek was a small, round beauty-spot, cut from a black strip of plaster with her manicure-scissors.

He arrived from the hospital, also spick and span, wearing a new summer coat, a new cap with a lilac velvet peak, a new sabre on a silver belt, passing across his shoulder and held down by a new silver shoulder-strap, long, shiny boots, and small spurs. He was tow-haired as only peasant children from Byelorussia can be, and his small, flaxen moustache was twirled up at the ends into sharp points.

As soon as he appeared, she rushed into the hall and threw her

arms round his neck, the dimples on her elbows visible under the
lace sleeves and her thick wedding-ring prominent on the third
finger of her well-manicured hand. After that, they cooed in their
room, and had dinner, after which he fed her with chocolates, taking
them out of the box with little metal tongs; then they obviously
kissed. Later in the evening, she would dress in a smart frock with a
long train, put on a new hat, covered with feathers, and a cape, and
they would go off in a cab to the operetta. They came back when
Zhenia and I were already fast asleep, but they, no doubt, indulged
in some more cooing with another chocolate or two in between.

They boarded with us and I think were not entirely satisfied with
out cutlets, cabbage *koulibiakas,* borsch, and cranberry jelly with
milk, probably deeming them too simple and everyday to match
the ecstasy of their honeymoon and the indescribable happiness they
experienced under the huge, silk eiderdown on their double bed,
to match their down pillows and the much smaller touching lace pillows called "*dumkas,*" their exquisite dressing-gowns, and their embroidered bedroom-slippers, edged with swan's-down.

I am certain they were constantly irritated by our childish games,
untiring activity, shouting, laughter, and the whistling of our toy
steam-engines.

They paid about thirty roubles for the two rooms, which was the
rent of the entire apartment. My aunt once said that they were living
above their income, what with chocolates every day, theatres, and
cinemas: all this was expensive, and a young army doctor's pay insignificant. When our honeymooners left us, they settled down in
another house, this time in one room at a much lower rent.

About five or six years later, during the First World War, I met the
former honeymooner again on the French Boulevard by the Military
Academy. He was looking preoccupied as he walked past the white
stone wall I knew so well, from behind which, as before, came the
sounds of military training. He had on the same officer's coat of silvery cloth, once so smart but now showing signs of wear, the same
cap, no longer dashing, but limp and shapeless, its velvet peak faded;
his moustache was twirled up as before, no doubt from habit, but it
had lost its silky shine and reminded me of hemp. There were a few
faint lines on his sombre, dust-coloured face, and his expression somehow suggested that he was worrying about trivialities. I felt terribly
sorry that the happiness that had once seemed to him eternal and

inexhaustible should have been so quickly eclipsed. I greeted him and he raised one hand indifferently to the shabby peak of his cap, while putting the other one on top of it to keep it in place: I noticed his thick wedding-ring on his yellowish third finger, shining as brightly as before, but shining now for a vanished glory.

A company of military cadets in cocked, peakless caps passed by us on a route-march, cheerfully whistling the air of a song:

> "My neighbour has blue eyes, blue eyes,
> Their look could not be bolder,
> I shall not marry anyone, Mamma,
> Unless he is a soldier."

—Left, left, left, left.

I remember another pair of lodgers: two middle-aged, unpleasant ladies in shabby black hats with veils, worn shoes, and both of them wearing pince-nez. One of the pince-nez had black rims, the other steel ones. We were renting one room for fifteen roubles and they took it at once without bargaining, inspecting it, or showing any kind of interest in it; they just moved straight in, plumping two bags, resembling those caried by midwives at that time, down on the window-sill. For about two days, the ladies remained in their room, scarcely ever emerging from it, brewed tea on a medical spirit-lamp, and ate sausages and canned beans.

On the third day, the yardsman came to Papa and asked for the new lodgers' papers so that he could register their change of address. Papa carefully buttoned all the buttons on his coat, which he always did when he was embarrassed, and knocked on the ladies' door.

They did not answer for some time and we could hear them scuttling about the room: then, at last, there was a click from the key and the door opened. One of the lodgers, the one whose pince-nez had black rims, faced Papa. She was in a cambric blouse with a leather belt round the waist of her long, shabby cloth skirt, edged with a tape-ribbon, from beneath which peered out a pair of very old shoes with the heels worn down on one side. Her raven hair was smoothly brushed back, which made her head look small, and tied in a thick knot at the back. The black cord of her pince-nez, slipped behind her ear in the way men did, gave her an even crosser and more formidable appearance.

"What is it you want?" she asked coldly. Papa, rather uneasily, asked for their papers so that their new address could be registered. It was a usual formality, but the lodger, for some reason, flushed a fiery red and, taking a lighted cigarette out of her mouth, glared at Papa ironically in a way that was tantamount to saying: "You ask me for my passport to hand to the police and still consider yourself a member of the intelligentsia, a citizen of a so-called constitutional country!"

But instead of actually putting this thought into words, she declared dryly that at the moment they had no identity-papers, but would produce them in a few days. While this was going on, the other lodger lay on her bed wrapped in an old Shetland shawl, her face turned to the wall, reading a pamphlet in a decadent wrapper with a social-democratic title.

Papa apologised and the lodger shut the door rather loudly behind him, turning the key twice in the lock. Next day both ladies went out for a walk, taking their bags with them. During the night, there was a loud ring at the door and, when Papa opened it, the yardsman, a policeman, and the district superintendent came in. They pushed past Papa, who was standing in his underclothes with a light coat thrown over his shoulders, and quickly opened the door into the lodgers' room, which was not locked.

The room was empty.

There was some thick wrapping-paper, in which the sausages had been enveloped, lying on the table alongside a few lumps of sugar, and the flap of the stove was open, displaying a heap of burnt paper in its depths: some of the ashes, blown out by the draught, were scattered here and there on the floor. The superintendent threw an experienced eye round the room and said, with annoyance: "Too late! The birds have flown. And you, sir"—he turned sternly to Papa—"I would ask you in future to observe the instructions relating to persons staying in your apartment. I have the honour . . ."

With these words the superintendent left, followed by the other two men. I heard one of them say rather loudly on the stairs: "Let 'em get away, worse luck."

In the morning, when the escaped lodgers' room was being tidied up, I saw the medical spirit-lamp, on which they brewed their tea, lying forgotten on the window-sill. And I found a small, neat Browning cartridge on the floor under the bed.

... We had many other lodgers, but it is impossible to remember them all. ...

The Fainting Fit 🖋

I WALKED OUT of our room, which was right under the roof, with a sloping ceiling and two windows that looked out over the fields, fruit-trees, vegetable-garden, and various outhouses on this German estate in Bessarabia, on the high cliff of the Black Sea, where I usually spent my summers with Papa and Zhenia, and ran joyfully down the steep flight of stairs. All my senses were enchanted by the dazzling heat of this July morning; the time was somewhere between seven and nine o'clock, when the sun was not yet overhead, but already brilliant, striking through the leaves of the mulberry-trees and bathing everything around in a white light, particularly the paths strewn with small, green estuary shells, that took on the sheen of mother-of-pearl like dry fish-scales. I do not know why I had left our room, where it was still quite cool: I had not had any definite aim in view. But, having come down, I made a thorough tour of the house, paused for a while by the cistern, shouted into its open orifice and heard my voice come echoing back, strengthened and, as it were, multiplied. There had been no rain for a long time, so the cistern, cemented under the ground, was empty, and I was impressed and delighted by the sound of my voice as it returned from its subterranean journey.

Then I ran down the path under the ripening apricots, already quite large, but still green, hard, and rough to the touch. The hot sand, strewn with shells, scratched pleasantly against the hard soles of my bare feet. And showing here and there through the mulberry-trees, the long-faced lilac-bushes and the silvery, tousled branches of the wild olives, beyond the edge of the red-hot cliffs overgrown with wormwood, dry and silvery, too, as everything seemed to be on this strange morning, was a strip of silver sea, glinting so dazzlingly that it hurt one's eyes.

I approached the house again from the other side and was grasping the hot banisters of the wooden staircase when I suddenly felt as though the bright sunlight had blinded me; then its rays dimmed and turned in rapid succession from silver to blood-red and from blood-red to black, and there was a drumming in my ears. After that, as Papa told me later, I somehow managed to climb the steep staircase, pale-faced, with wide-open eyes that saw nothing, in a state of complete unconsciousness. As I reached the top, he picked me up and carried me to my room, though I knew nothing of this, knew nothing of anything until the darkness suddenly began to retreat, giving place to the light of day, and what had seemed lost forever slowly returned to me . . . .

. . . .The whitewashed room with windows on the world; the window-sill on which stood crabs to be added to my collection, flesh-pink with purple, seemingly inflated claws, and dried in the sun so that they were almost weightless, alongside sea-horses in a jar of formalin, the wooden box of water-colour paints, next to a glass of dirty water, in which I had washed my brushes; a sheet of paper, on which I had painted cucumbers and radishes in water-colours with what I believed to be admirable fidelity; the dead-head moth that had fallen asleep in a corner of the ceiling; the green-slatted, Italian-looking jalousies. All this wonderful world, filled with colour and sound, had returned to me, and there was my father's careful hand, with its wedding-ring grown into the skin, pressing a wet towel to my forehead, and small, frightened Zhenka peering down at me, and my own voice, saying: "What is it? Did something happen to me? Don't worry, I'm all right: it was probably just a fainting-fit."

I felt extremely well and happy and, after lying for another five minutes with the compress on my forehead, I ran to have a bathe in the sea, as though nothing had occurred, and in the course of a long life nothing of the kind has ever occurred again. Nevertheless, something of great importance had taken place; something in me had irrevocably changed. For my soul, for a short time, had become separated from my body, and been on a journey from which there is often no return.

The Wooden Soldier 🖋

IT WAS SO unbelievably long ago that it is difficult to imagine when!

I was walking with Mama, holding her hand, along a part of the street I already knew well—a tiny fragment of the town extending from the house where we lived to the nearest corner. Beyond that, as though enveloped in mist, lay another, much less familiar world, separated from us by so great a distance that my mind could not grasp it. There were places in it of which I only knew the names: Alexander Park, the cyclodrome Langeron, the French Boulevard —a frightened street, down which a steam-engine was reputed to go, rumbling, quivering, and emitting shrill whistles, as it levelled the surface with its fearsome weight.

One day, I saw that green steam-engine enveloped in steam, with the driver sitting at the back of it under a canvas tent. Smoke rose in clouds from the funnel and a copper contraption composed of two small balls whirled rapidly over the green cylinder of the boiler.

... Later, I learned that these little things were called "eccentrics," but I may have got it all wrong.

That machine terrified me, because dogs ran away at the sight of it, horses reared up on their hind legs with piercing neighs, and buildings vibrated from its evil, shattering noise.

The part of the street running from our garden-gate to the corner seemed to me very wide and long, but my small, watchful eyes took in all its details, or, rather, since my eye-level was that of a small three-year-old child, all those on a low plane; the round, well-fitting cobbles of the roadway, the hard granite of the curbs, the cast-iron grilles over the sewers in which odd rags and pieces of rubbish had stuck, the side-walk composed of three parallel rows of bluish, lava slabs, so easy to step on in my new shoes with straps and pompons, the lower-part of tree-trunks, surrounded by railings, on which were hung at regular intervals small bowls of water for the dogs, to prevent them going mad from thirst.

Mamma often took me out for walks in the street, and during them we invariably met a crippled beggar, with the tiny feet of a child, a large, adult body, and a head that might have been carved out of wood on a stiff, red neck. He was always on the watch for passers-by, to whom he stretched out a wooden bowl, as he stood close by the bright-yellow pillar-box, a familiar landmark to me, with its picture of a white envelope, five postage-stamps, and two crossed postal-horns. It seemed enormous and raised the problem, each time I saw it: how did letters dropped into it get to their destination? I finally decided that there must be rectangular tubes, running from the pillar-box into the walls of the various houses, and that it was down these that the letters were somehow mysteriously transmitted.

When we stopped by the pillar-box, I always looked up and admired it, while Mamma, in a hat with an eagle's feather and a dark veil, took a letter from her moiré bag, lifted a flap with her gloved hand, and dropped the narrow envelope with a large blue stamp into the mysterious slot; a letter to her mother and my grandmother in Ekaterinoslav. Then Mamma would take a kopeck out of her purse and put it into the crippled dwarf's wooden bowl, as I stared with compassion and pain at his bloodshot eyes and twisted eyelids and the dilated nostrils in his small, crushed nose.

One day, not far from the pillar-box, I spotted a chestnut, looking as if it were made of polished rosewood, that had fallen from the tree and was lying by the wall of a house. I picked it up and put this great treasure into the pocket of my sailor-coat; I had never seen a horse-chestnut before.

This spot by the pillar-box seemed to be an ideal one for treasure-seekers as, soon after, I saw a large, almost new wooden soldier lying there: in some details—the wooden face and the flat, planed back of the head—it reminded me of the crippled dwarf.

I was amazed to see this colourful toy all alone on the pavement without a master, belonging to no-one, although I already suspected that things could not really belong to no-one. Probably, at one time, it had belonged to someone and had had a master—some boy or other, unknown to me—but he had lost it, so now, in a sense, the toy did belong to no-one.

I looked around, there was nobody in sight, and I felt an irresistible attraction to this nobody's thing. I looked up at my mother inquiringly and tugged at her skirt: "May I?" I asked.

She smiled at me tenderly and condescendingly under her thick veil. "Yes, take it, if you want it so badly. But, you can see, his gun's broken."

It was true. I had not noticed at first that the top of the gun he carried on his shoulder had snapped off; and, besides that, the wooden stand, on which his feet were firmly stuck, was chipped. This meant that somebody had thrown him away as a broken toy, so he definitely had became no-one's. But this did not diminish my liking for him: I stooped down and picked him up. Thus, a miracle happened; he suddenly ceased being no-one's and acquired a master.

I had become his owner. I put him in my pocket, beside the horse-chestnut, and felt a rich man, the owner of two beautiful things, a horse-chestnut made by nature and a wooden soldier made by man.

Eagerly anticipating the pleasure I would get from playing with the soldier as soon as we returned home, I gaily trotted along the lava slabs beside Mamma and meditated on the truth I had already dimly perceived: all things belonged to someone.

But, then, I was disturbed by an apparent contradiction: there were, after all, things that *seemed* to belong to no-one.

"Mamma," I asked, "to whom do sparrows belong?"

"They belong to God," Mamma replied with a smile, after a moment's thought.

"And whom do I belong to?"

"You're mine."

"That's true," I reflected. "I belong to Mamma and Papa. And, perhaps, to Grandmamma and Grandpapa, too. There's no doubt about that." . . .

"And the soldier?" I went on.

"Now he's yours," replied Mamma.

"And whose was he before?"

"I don't know."

"And whose was I before?"

It seemed to me that Mamma was somewhat taken aback as she glanced at me through the thick veil that made her face look like that of a stranger.

"Before, you just weren't there," she said.

"Then I was nobody's?"

"When?"

"When I wasn't there at all?"

Mama considered this for a while and then answered I thought rather sadly: "Yes, as I told you, you just weren't there. . . ."

"So, I was nobody's?"

"Yes, you were nobody's in particular," Mamma replied. "You were God's."

Now, I presume that Mama found it difficult to believe that there was a time when I wasn't there at all.

But, from then on, I understood that, besides things that had a master, there were things without a master which were nobody's; or anyway, were nobody's at some time or other. This thought, from so long ago, has always remained with me and even now I ask myself: Whose am I? Whose little soldier am I?

And then I had a prophetic dream:

A Box ⚰

IN THE MIDDLE of the bedroom in which I slept, I saw a big square box on the floor, made of strong, solid wood, painted brown to look like oak, or, perhaps, covered with brown wall-paper looking like oak, the same kind as was sometimes used to disguise secret panels or doors.

The presence of this large box in the room where I slept with Papa and Mamma did not surprise me at all, but it gave me a strange feeling of anxiety, all the more unpleasant because, despite its thickness and apparent impenetrability, I could see everything that was happening inside it and the people present there.

Mamma and my cousin Liolia were sitting in it in uncomfortable positions. Liolia, in my eyes, was almost a grown-up, having recently celebrated her eleventh birthday. She scarcely ever came to see us, because she had a tubercular bone in her leg and spent most of her time in bed—a kind, meek, thin girl with a transparent, sharp little nose and blond hair brushed back, who looked like a princess made of wax.

One day, when I was visiting them, I saw how she moved from her bed to a chair, hopping on her good leg, while the bad one, bent at the knee, dangled helplessly under her long night-dress.

Now she was sitting with my Mamma in a box in which it was difficult for them both to find comfortable positions, because, though the box was a big one, there was not quite enough room in it for two.

They sat huddled together, with insufficient air, but there was nothing I could do to help them, to relieve their obvious torment.

Mama and Liolia were making continuous attempts to crawl out of the box into the room, dimly lit by a night-light with a red shade. There was a lid on the box, which they both tried to lift, but it was on a tight, round spring and flipped back on them whenever they managed to raise it an inch or two with their hands or heads. It reminded me of the firmly closed top of a mouse-trap.

Mamma and Liolia continued fidgeting in the box and constantly getting in each other's way. It was clear to me that they would never get out of the box together but would have to do it one after the other; but they could not understand this or did not want to. Then Mamma made one more desperate effort, suddenly stretched up to her full height in a white bed-jacket, her hair hanging loose, and at last succeeded in lifting the lid off with her head. She crawled out of the box into the room, where I was sleeping with Papa, heaved a deep sigh of relief and smiled, somehow diaphanous in a stream of light, with her stomach strangely rounded beneath her night-dress. Liolia started to crawl out of the box after Mamma, had almost done it and was preparing to smile, too, when the lid fell on her bent leg; she gave a moan of unbearable pain, or not so much a moan as a long wail that turned one's heart to ice. Nevertheless, tearing the skin off her leg she contrived to emerge from the narrow box to freedom and gave Mama a faint smile as she embraced her.

. . . And there they stood, the two of them, breathing deeply and looking radiant, though Liolia's wail seemed to continue on its own. At this point, I woke up and saw the familiar wall-paper above the chest of drawers and, standing on it, the equally familiar oil night-light, with its little red shade like an upturned bucket. But someone must have forgotten to close the shutters, for I could also see brilliant moonlight streaming down beyond the windows and the length of Basarnaia Street was green with deep black shadows cast by the bare trees and the telegraph-poles. The long, zinc-coated roof of the factory opposite reflected the silvery light and, from somewhere near by it, came the miserable wail of a dog, freezing in the cold night.

There was no longer any box in the middle of the room and beside me stood my mamma, who had just woken up—my real mamma, not the one in my dreams; she crossed over to the shutters, giving me a reassuring pat on the way, closed them, and fixed the iron bars in place. The wailing continued for a while and then gradually stopped.

I went back to sleep and saw Mamma again, no longer in her bed-jacket with her hair hanging down, looking so dear and tender, but dressed for going out in a hat with a thick, black veil, her pince-nez, and an austere black suit, with narrow sleeves and puffs on the shoulders; in one hand, she carried something resembling a black flag —I had already learned that in French it was called "*un drapeau*"— and, in the other, a half-closed umbrella, also black—called in French "*un*" or "*une parapluie.*" As though the oppressive weight of the town were bearing down on her, she leaned on the half-closed *parapluie* with its steel ribs, as if it were a stick, as she walked along the green iron roof of the Puritz shop in Richelieu Street, amidst grim clouds, making a metallic clatter with every step, like that of shutters dropping down over display-windows. She continued on her way, sinking through the corrugated-iron roof up to her knees, with the black *drapeau* held high in the air, over the green, leaden railing of the Catholic church and the shops selling jewellery and various kinds of junk; she walked faster and faster, sinking further through the roof, and the rapidity of her movement brought my dream to an equally rapid end. In its final stages, I could see dawn breaking and a ray of sunshine and could hear the rattle of horse-chestnuts in the drawer of my night-table. There were so many of them that I picked them up with a wooden scoop, like those used in grocers' shops, dipped my hands in them, rolled them over, and admired their beauty.

Then I really woke up, to bright sunlight outside the unshuttered windows, and, through the blue veiling of my cot, saw my bearded papa, whom I loved so much, in Mamma's bed with Mamma and his bed empty.

Papa and Mamma looked at me, their small son, with laughing eyes, but I did not dare tell them my prophetic dream. I hid it securely in the very depths of my heart.

Mamma died soon after that, giving birth to my brother Zhenia, and Liolia died a little later of tuberculosis.

And all this is true.

The Coin ✍

At last January sixteenth came round, my birthday, which I awaited each year with such impatience and high hopes.

Besides presents, that day brought another joy with it. I was allowed to miss school and wallow in bed as long as I liked. I woke up when everyone else in the house was still asleep and, in the faint pre-dawn light, that made everything around me look darker than it had during the night, immediately examined the wicker chair by my bed. I had hoped to find my presents, placed there as usual the previous evening while I was asleep.

There were none.

Crawling cautiously from underneath the counterpane, I went on tiptoe—warm feet on cold floor—to reconnoitre the dining-room. I now hoped that the presents would be on the side-board or on the dinner-table, but I was disappointed again. Passing my aunt's room, from which came the sound of her even breathing, I returned to our room, where Papa was snoring his pre-awakening snore and Zhenka was smacking his lips in a dream.

On the window-sills, where the dim blue light of a wintry morning penetrated the cracks of the closed shutters, there were no presents either.

Strange!

"It isn't possible that Papa and Aunt have forgotten!" I thought. "They must have decided to give me a big surprise." But this idea brought no reassurance; if anything, it left me uneasier than before. "Is it conceivable," I wondered, "that this time they've decided to leave me without any presents? It's too incredible! But who knows? One can never tell what they'll do next. Papa has an original type of mind and does not hold with the showy side of many family events, such as name-days, house-warmings, and so on, only taking part in them, when he does, to avoid offending the people involved and over-stressing his personal views. So perhaps Papa, who does not, in his heart of hearts, even approve of religious feasts or official government celebrations, though he does not say so in so many words and does everything required of a devout Russian Orthodox citizen, has decided that the celebration of birthdays is just a superstition that it is high time to break. And so he has! While it is true," I went on in the course of my meditations, "that Leo Tolstoy has had a certain influence on him, Papa is a kind man and would not want to hurt his son. But, at the same time, he is unpredictable!"

Full of doubts, I went back to bed, wrapped myself up in my blanket and waited to see what would happen next. I started to conjure up a picture of all the unpleasant consequences that would ensue if my birthday were, in fact, annulled, but fell into a long, deep sleep before the picture was completed. When I awoke, I gathered from the silence around me that everybody had gone: Papa and Aunt must have left for school, taking Zhenia with them to drop him at Mme

Tsakni's kindergarten on the way. The only sound came from the kitchen, where the cook was chopping meat for cutlets.

I had been allowed to sleep on, which meant that the birthday was still being celebrated to some extent, and this reassured me slightly. "At least I don't need to go to school: that's something!" I thought as I opened my eyes.

The room was much brighter now, though it was difficult for the morning light to penetrate the windows, which had become covered in snow during the night. The snow-storm seemed to be continuing because I heard the stove hissing and the window-panes shook as though someone outside were throwing hard January snowballs at them.

I loved this blue winter light in the empty, silent apartment during the late morning. I glanced at the chair, hoping that everything had now been put right and the presents were where I expected them. It was empty. I peered into the dining-room. Nothing there for me, either. I went back to bed to get warm again. The wood was crackling and spitting behind the stove's round iron door. It was cosy enough in the bedroom but painfully dull. I would have done better to go to school after all, where as a birthday child, I would have had my ears pinched by way of congratulation. My thoughts returned to the matter of presents, and it occurred to me that Papa might have put a present under my pillow, as was sometimes done in our family. It seemed all the more likely because I had a dim recollection of Papa approaching my bed on tiptoe in his frock-coat while I was half-asleep, giving me a gentle kiss and tickling my cheek with his beard, damp from the bath, then congratulating me on my birthday. Perhaps he had put a present under my pillow at the same time? I thrust my hand beneath it and immediately came across something that, to the touch, felt like a small bag. I turned it over and then round and my fingers came in contact wth a metal clasp with two little knobs on it. It must be a purse!

I quickly withdrew my hand from under the pillow and, sure enough, there was a small, plain purse of Swedish leather in my grasp. Opening it, I peered inside and, in the pale, late-morning light, saw a twenty-kopeck piece.

I felt as though I had been robbed. That was a fine present to give anyone! Who would have expected a small, cheap purse with twenty kopecks in it? I had never before received such a miserable, almost offensive object for my birthday! Could it possibly be meant as a comment on the poor marks recorded on my previous term's report? Or had Papa decided once and for all to stop spending money on expensive presents and given me the purse with the twenty kopecks just as a token—Aunt's favourite word.

Boredom set in and I mourned my lost hopes of buying "Nurmis" skates with sharp fronts like the prows of battle-ships. I washed and dressed listlessly, stuck the purse in my pocket, and dragged myself to the dining-room. The cook brought in my tea, congratulated me on my birthday, and produced a special cake, sprinkled with almonds and sugar, as though a snowdrift had passed over it. Having nothing better to do as I ate it with my tea, I took the purse out of my pocket and extracted the twenty kopecks. The moment I had it in my hand, it struck me as much too heavy for a twenty kopeck piece. I looked at it again and could scarcely believe my eyes: on my palm lay a bright-yellow gold coin—five roubles. There was no possibility of a mistake: it was quite light enough in the dining-room to distinguish silver from gold. I went over to the window, where the light was even better, and carefully threw the coin down on the window-sill. It gave a golden ring, unlike any other, spun round, and, with a dying tinkle, finally fell flat. Yes, it was a real five-rouble piece! I felt ashamed of having suspected Papa of intending to annul my birthday. I knew now that he loved me despite my bad marks. I was also aware that Papa considered it immoral to give children money, because of its depraving influence: he had often said so. He had even gone so far as to declare that money was responsible for all the evil in the world. Yet, in spite of all that, he had given me money, five golden roubles. And it was not the first time.

Quite recently, on my name-day, the sixth of July, he had given me three roubles—a beautiful smooth, green note that had never been folded before, which he took from between the leaves of a book, where he concealed his paper money. We were staying at the time near Budaki in a German settler's summer villa that overlooked the sea. All around, the scenery—sea and steppes—was magnificent, but there were no toy-shops in the vicinity and it was here that Papa acted against his principles for the first time and gave me the three rubles.

How clearly I remember that unforgettable sunny morning when I wandered round the whole estate with the note clasped in my hand, looking for someone to share my happiness. But, as luck would have it, there was not a living soul about: everyone was down on the shore bathing. I went to the stable-yard, where a coach that brought summer visitors over from Akkerman and took them back again was standing, unharnessed. Climbing up on to the coachman's box and sitting on his oil-cloth seat, warmed by the morning sun, I examined my note for a long time, admiring the wonderful paper with its watermark, visible against the light, and the delicacy of the rainbow-coloured netting round the figure "3," executed by a master engraver. And the fact of being in possession of a note issued by the government bank, with the facsimile of the cashier's signature on it, endowed me, in my imagination, with a special importance, as a person connected in some mysterious way with the government itself, with the whole Russian empire!

Added to this feeling was the supreme joy of being a name-day child, which happened only once a year, when one's guardian angel descended to touch one's soul, enveloping it with cool, invisible, angelic wings, and then soared back to the sky to watch over one from above with tenderness and love for a long time after.

There was only one thing that slightly marred my pleasure: that, according to the calendar, the sixth of July was not only Valentin's day but also Sissoy's. There it was, quite clearly: Sissoy and Valentin. And I did not very much like the idea that the same angel should be guarding both me and someone called Sissoy. Of course, it was possible that Sissoy had his own guardian angel, but the coincidence, nonetheless, cast a faint shadow on my name-day.

I do not remember how I spent my three roubles.

But, on this frosty January morning, it was a heavy gold coin that nestled snugly in my shammy-leather purse. I opened the purse every other minute and peered into it to make certain that the gold had remained gold, that it had not been transformed into a silver twenty-kopeck piece or vanished altogether. Finally, I took the coin out and held it on the palm of my hand, gloating over the bright yellow gleam that belonged to gold alone. And I was its owner! I could have gone on gazing at this small but heavy circular treasure of mine forever: the influence it was capable of exerting had already taken possession of my free, eternal soul! Papa had been quite right about money depraving: it had already depraved me.

Quickly putting on my coat, galoshes, cap, and, over the cap, a yellow camel's hair *bashlik* edged with a brown band, I made my way into the town, despite the heavy snowstorm, to test out gold's formidable powers. Some time later, I returned home with my *bash-lik* all covered in hoar-frost, jumped out of a sleigh and handed the driver fifteen kopecks. He asked me to add a little something for vodka and I gave him another ten kopecks. A parcel containing my purchases hung from a button of my coat: they consisted of a fret-saw, a drill, and several packets of additional slender blades for the saw. Under my arm, I carried two sheets of plywood, rolled into a cylinder and tied up with string.

It seemed to me that an eternity had gone by since I had departed to do my shopping, but, in fact, it was no more than an hour and a half. The house was empty and spotlessly clean, as always in the morning. I boasted to the cook about my purchases, promised to saw her a decorative shelf for the kitchen, and embarked on the task immediately.

To saw out pretty patterns, however, was not nearly as easy as I had anticipated: the fine blades broke, the screws attaching them to the handle proved difficult to tighten sufficiently, the drill was not sharp enough to bore the necessary holes in the plywood, and the plywood itself was hard and rough. It became only too obvious that the assistant in the timber-store at the market near the station had swindled me. After I had cut my finger, I threw all my material and the tools for sawing ancient Russian national figures out of plywood into an old trunk, where they would probably have remained to this day if the house in Otrada, where we then lived, had not been de-molished by a German bomb in 1941. All that remained of it were a few charred branches of the oak-tree, which had stood so beautifully in front of our balcony. I will not mention poor old Jasikova's lodge: that was nothing but a vague memory. As far as my purchases were concerned, the only consolation lay in the fact that they had been comparatively cheap: the change from the five roubles amounted to two roubles odd. They jingled together in the purse, but the sound they made was not to be compared with the wonderful ring of my then-unspent, heavy gold coin, as I had heard it early that morning, when I had dropped it on the cold window-sill, lit by the blue light through the snow-covered panes.

. . . Well, after that, everything proceeded as ususal: the cake, the steaming chocolate in the lovely birthday cups, the biscuits shaped like the straps on our school-overcoats, and the guests. Among the guests, the most notable was Nadia Zaria-Zarianitskaia, who sat beside me, with her long English curls and charming, straight little nose, strewn with golden, only just perceptible freckles, which, far from disfiguring her, merely enhanced her beauty.

But I still bitterly regretted my golden coin. Why, oh why, had I been in such a hurry to get rid of it?

The Tablespoon 🔾

ON OUR BIRTHDAYS and name-days, Papa's mamma, Pavla Pavlovna, used to give Zhenka and me a silver tablespoon. The old lady would appear from behind her screen, come up to the child whose celebration it was, kiss him on the forehead with wrinkled lips, and, murmuring indistinguishable words of congratulation, which sounded like a blessing, in her mumbling Viatka accent, hand him the spoon. The celebrant would use it throughout the day; then, in the evening, Grandmother would remove it surreptitiously from the dresser, take it back behind the screen, hide it somewhere, and then bring it out again when the next family celebration occurred. Everybody knew this but pretended not to and took care to use it all day until Grandmother withdrew with it behind her screen.

One day, Zhenka and I, curious about where she hid the famous spoon, rummaged through all her things and found it under the carpet behind her bed.

Every time she gave us the spoon she would tell us how to look after it; to clean it with chalk and keep our eyes open to make certain the servants did not steal it. Then she would add that, when we grew up and married, she would give us a dozen such spoons.

Poor Grandmamma!

Only one silver spoon remained to her from the days when she was the wife of a priest at the Viatka cathedral—my grandfather Vassili Alexievitch—the mistress of a large wooden house and the mother of a large family, in which my father, Uncle Misha, and Uncle Nikolai Vassilievich were once children, just as Zhenka and I now were in ours.

She probably occupied quite an important position in the ecclesiastic society of Viatka as wife of the cathedral's senior priest, a prominent figure in the hierarchy of the local provincial clergy.

I never saw Grandmother's husband, my father's father and my grandfather, because he died in Viatka a long time before I was born. Papa had a photograph, in which the stern-faced priest appeared, surrounded by his family: he had a bony nose, a huge beard, and the eyes of Saltikov-Shchedrin, whose portrait I had seen in one of the books in our small book-case. Next to him sat grandmother, his wife, Pavla Pavlovna, a short woman in a black silk crinoline dress, her hair smoothly brushed back and parted in the middle, with a small, round old-fashioned face, reminding me of a white "blessed bread," and dry, domineering little hands primly folded in her lap. Beside his little wife, grandfather with the large cross on his moiré cassock, appeared huge, overpowering, and majestic. But Grandmother did not seem overpowered or crushed: quite the contrary. Despite her diminutive stature, there was something very independent, self-reliant, even despotic about her, and it was more than possible that my grandfather was very much under her thumb.

I gathered that their family was brought up on the strict, old-fashioned principles of the Orthodox church, which insisted on proper respect for parents and devotion to the mother country and His Imperial Majesty the tsar, emperor of all the Russias.

It was difficult for me to envisage my grandparents' way of life or imagine Papa at my age; still more difficult to picture Viatka, so far removed from our southern steppe and sea, the beauty of the Ukraine and everything else that went to make up my life as a child.

I got some idea of Papa's childhood in Viatka from the short, casual reminiscences in which he occasionally indulged. Sometimes he would tell me how, in winter, they—the three boys and their father—would go to have steam-baths at the local bath-house, whip one another with birch-tree twigs, and then, steamed to a raspberry-red, run completely naked out into the frost and roll in snowdrifts: after that, they would come back to a heated bath, followed by a cold shower, dry themselves, take a rest on a pine-bench, and finally put on clean underclothes in the dressing-room adjoining the steam-bath. And there were no ill-effects, according to Papa: none of them ever caught cold.

In Viatka, Papa was brought up in the Spartan spirit then fairly wide-spread in northern Russia. One of his favourite proverbs was: "Keep your head cool, your belly hungry, and your feet warm."

Papa also told us how, in his home in Viatka, a live toad was put into a jug of milk to prevent the milk going sour in hot weather: and the milk remained cool and fresh even in a thunder-storm, which normally would have turned it.

He made it easy for me to conjure up a picture of the timbered town-house with a garden where they all lived, and the near-by bath-house, too, though I had never seen a real Russian bath-house with its brick stove, shelves to recline on, ante-room, and birch besoms. In Odessa, we had the "Isakovich baths," with separate rooms, where Papa used to take us when the apartment we were occupying was without a bath.

I remember those baths well, where we went first by horse-drawn trams, later by electric ones, in the evening when the light from the street-lamps was reflected in the wet pavements. We walked down a corridor, misty from steam, past dim, cheap mirrors that seemed to be made of metal rather than glass, preceded by a barefoot servant in a Russian shirt, with the key of the room in his hand. The subdued lighting provided by a smoking oil-lamp on the wall enveloped us in an atmosphere that for some unknown reason struck me as vaguely sinful.

Papa soaped Zhenka and me with a flannel, then, thin and naked, soaped his own neck and head. After that we rubbed each other's backs with loofahs, smelling deliciously of Lemme's chemist's shop, where Papa had brought them. After splashing about in the water, we rested on oil-cloth couches.

Papa told us that there was a Jewish synagogue near their house in Viatka, and on Friday evenings, when their law forbade Jews to do any work, Papa and his brothers were hired as 'goys,"—that is, non-Jews—to blow out the candles, since this was regarded as work: for their services, they received two kopecks each. I could easily visualize them blowing out the candles, and it surprised and rather amused me that the seminarian sons of the senior cathedral priest should perform this task in a synagogue, where Jews sat on benches with small black boxes on their heads secured by bands round their foreheads.

But Papa said that there was nothing funny about it, because every faith was welcome to God and every faith should be respected. And then I had a sudden vision of my grandfather in the cathedral in his stiff gold and silver chasuble, stole, and the rest of a priest's sacerdotal robes, standing on the steps of the altar, surrounded by lilacchalky clouds of incense and lit by candles and icon-lamps, looking handsome and immensely authorative, with his thick, broad beard and stern, faintly accusing, faintly satirical eyes.

After Grandfather died and his post in the cathedral was taken by another priest, Grandmother was left a poor widow. Her seminarian sons, Papa and Uncle Misha, for some reason of their own, but probably because they did not want to adopt a religious vocation in view of the times, went to Novorossijsk University, which they chose because of the warm climate and exceptionally low cost of living in the south of Russia.

Papa took his mother south with him and she had lived with him from then on at his expense, so that when Zhenia and I were born, she had already been installed for a long time in the dining-room behind an ugly brown screen, covered with brown "widowy" calico. By then she was very old.

Quiet, unobtrusive, useless, she went on living her modest, pathetic life as a widow, entirely dependent on her son Peter, my papa. She made no attempt to play any part in our lives when Mamma was alive or, after her death, when Aunt took over the household duties. She was a fragment of the totally different, long-since-vanished world of pre-reform provincial life in northern Russia. She did not live, she merely existed as she slowly approached the end, though always apparently remaining the same age, walking noiselessly and spreading around her the smell of her old woollen skirt and decrepit body—a typical old widow's smell. She had a small, deeply wrinkled face with high cheekbones and lips that silently chewed the air. Across the bald top of her head, she always wore a black, knitted veil, resembling a spider's web. Her nose was the shape of a button. In one way, she reminded one of a very, very old Chinese woman; in another, of an inanimate accessory to the house. When we moved, as we often did, from one apartment to another, we took her with us as we took the samovar or the ficus.

The apartments were never big enough for her to have a separate room; she always lived, with her simple iron bed, small trunk, and carpet, behind the screen in the dining-room, and, despite her silent tread and inconspicuousness, this made us uneasy and, to tell the truth, actually annoyed us. We found her mutterings in a Viatka accent particularly irritating.

As the years passed, she became miserly and petty, counting the lumps of sugar in the sugar-basin in front of the guests, watching how much people put on their plates, spying on the cook and returning to report: "She doesn't eat, she guzzles!"

We all treated her with indifference, just bore with her: Zhenka and I sometimes teased her by imitating her unfamiliar northern manner of speech. My aunt never seemed to be aware of her presence. Papa alone loved her and did his best to carry out his duties as a son to this little old woman, no longer of any use to anyone, but the mother who, years before, had brought him into the world.

Grandmother died in Papa's arms early one morning, when the rest of us were not yet awake. She seemed simply to have fallen into a sleep, from which she never woke.

Papa closed her eyes, placing five-kopeck copper coins on her eyelids and tied up her jaw with a clean napkin so that it should not drop. It happened at the one time when she had a room to herself, but she still chose to live behind a screen. When Zhenka and I had washed and dressed, Papa, his eyes red from crying, brought us to Grandmother's cold room, where, already attired in her best dress, she lay quietly on her widow's bed. I do not remember her being placed in her coffin: I only remember that it was a cheap brown one. I also remember the white hearse, too elegant for Grandmother, standing at our gate, and the horses in black cloths with circles cut out for their eyes.

Papa did not take us to the funeral. He walked alone behind the coffin, abandoning his school-classes for that day.

When he returned from the cemetery, he said: "I've buried my mother, your grandmother. Her grave is close to your mother's. When my hour comes, I wish to be laid to rest between my wife and my mother, the two women I loved more than anything in the world."

Grandmother's room was aired, washed, put in order, and let to lodgers.

. . . And the silver spoon, which was found under Grandmother's carpet, was cleaned with chalk and ammonia and joined the other silver spoons in the side-board–cupboard.

Small Street Incidents ✍

IN OTRADA, searches frequently had to be made for an escaped monkey and a fly-away parrot. These small incidents provided our lives with variety, took the place of travels to foreign lands, and brought us closer to characters from Jules Verne and Louis Jacolio.

In the course of a moment, Otrada, with her four nice, deserted streets, framed in white acacias with feathery leaves through which the green-tinted blue sky peeped so romantically; Otrada, with her villas, smooth lawns, and beds of fiery-red flowers, was transformed into a sort of Valparaiso.

At least so it seemed to us.

By a happy accident, the fluffy cockatoo, multi-coloured as the flag of some South American republic, who had grown unaccustomed to flying, shut up in his large, domed cage, suddenly found himself free. Climbing through the little door, which someone had forgotten to close, he first staggered drunkenly about the room, then jumped up on to the window-sill and from there clumsily ascended to the small, open ventilator. Scenting freedom, he plunged out, awkwardly flapping the wings that had grown stiff from disuse. Slowly, with considerable effort, he flew low over the pavement and wove his way through the tangled leaves of the acacias, emitting strange foreign exclamations from time to time in a rather silly croak.

His captive soul could not get used to freedom all at once, but his whole being was in a state of euphoria and he exerted all his strength to paddle himself through the air with his short wings and increase his distance from the cage; that odious cage with the metal ring, from which he hung, head downwards for want of anything better to do, a beautiful, useless creature with a short aquiline beak, sharp as nail-clippers, and half-closed chamois eyelids over round, inquisitive eyes, deriving no pleasure from the seeds or the drinking-water in their containers fixed to the bars.

Now that he was free at last, all roads seemed open to him and the rough rocks round the small fountain and the alluring blue sea beyond were already beckoning through the acacias. All he had to do was to soar higher, get his bearings, flap his wings still faster, and it would be—Farewell, Otrada! Valparaiso, here I come!

But that was not the way things turned out. By now, the whole street was running after him with cries of: "Catch him! Get hold of him! Don't let him fly away!"

Leading the hue and cry, in a rustling, starched petticoat, lace apron, and coquettish cap, was the maid employed by a captain in the Naval Voluntary Reserve, in whose sitting-room the cockatoo normally resided. It was she who had forgotten to close the cage-door and, only too aware of her responsibility for the whole distressing affair, she tore after the bird, her brown Ukrainian eyes wide with terror, shouting: "Cockatoo! Cockatoo! Can't you hear me? Come back to your cage this minute!"

Close behind her, holding his hat on with one hand, pounded our red-whiskered policeman, his innocent blue eyes gazing upwards from under officially frowning brows. Though he was known to everyone as "the herring," his real name was Seltzer, and he came from a family of German settlers in the village of Klein Liebentell, or, more simply, Malaia Okarzha, near Odessa. He had taken out his horn whistle with a pea inside preparatory to frightening the bird into surrender with a series of shrill blasts. After the maid and the policeman came my friends and myself, followed by the rest of those who enjoyed dramas of this kind.

Catching the cockatoo obviously presented a considerable problem, and he might well have flown off goodness knows where if the sparrow, pigeons, and local stray cats had not rallied to our assistance: as soon as they spotted the exotic bird, they joined in the chase.

The cats climbed the tree, where the cockatoo was getting entangled with the leaves, while the sparrows and pigeons dived down on him from above, animated by the hatred that all creatures feel for a handsome intruder, pecking at his head and surrounding him with angry, avian cries. Multi-coloured feathers flew in every direction as the miserable bird tried to protect himself: then, as a final insult, the most nimble and villainous cat, miaowing in a particularly sinister way, clapped a paw on him and pulled a red feather out of his tail.

"*Co—co—co—co,*" the cockatoo protested plaintively in his foreign language and promptly fell onto the pavement. Policeman Seltzer quickly picked him up and handed him with a polite smile to the maid. Wrapping the bird, now almost scared to death, in her apron, she rushed back home, her skirts billowing in the wind, and returned him to his cage.

The cockatoo was delighted to be back in his quiet, familiar surroundings, and his foolish attempt to escape now probably struck him as an act of supreme folly. In any case, he drank his water and cracked some seeds with great pleasure, then swung head downwards from his metal ring, like a trapeze-artist high up under the domed roof of a circus, uttering ecstatic: "*Co—co—co* . . ."s.

The small monkey Daisy, who belonged to Julietta Arneri, whom I have already mentioned in this book, was finally caught after her escape in this way:

When I joined the crowd, Daisy, who had managed to break the chain attached to her collar, was squatting at the top of the town's oldest acacia-tree, busily engaged in throwing down handfuls of leaves. Julietta, with upraised, pleading arms and a forced smile on her tanned Italian face, was trying to lure her down to earth again. She was surrounded by her entire family—Papa Arneri with his Borsalino hat thrust to the back of his head; Mamma Arneri with a black lace shawl thrown over her beautifully greying hair that was just as curly as Julietta's; the Arneri brothers, my friend Rafka, and small Patrick astride his tricycle; and the elder Arneri daughter, Nelly, a ravishing beauty, with an open parasol over her shoulders.

As the monkey showed no signs of being prepared to come down to the pavement voluntarily, the yardsman had to be instructed to bring a ladder. But as soon as he leaned it against the trunk of the acacia, Daisy leaped like an acrobat to the next-door tree, emitting sounds that suggested she was cracking a nut stored in her cheek. When he started shifting the ladder towards her tree, she jumped on to the projecting bar of the street-lamp, paused for a moment to search her head for fleas, and then ran along the top of the stone wall and, with the same acrobatic nimbleness, scaled the balconies and drain-pipes of Fessenko's tall brick house, finally reaching the roof: from there she cast a scornful glance at her pursuers through her half-closed, clown's eyes, beneath their azure eyelids.

"Daisy, Daisy, darling Daisy," Julietta called to her in her tenderest voice.

Had Daisy been a man, she would, no doubt, have descended from the roof into the arms of her mistress immediately, for Julietta was extremely seductive, with her rosy little mouth and tanned, pink cheeks.

But Daisy was a monkey and all that was lost on her. She seemed, in fact, to be offended by Julietta's entreaties, judging by the way she turned her back on her and waved her tail disdainfully. At this point, Stasik Sologub rode up on his bicycle, leaned against a tree, and considered the situation for a moment or two: then he dismounted and manfully started up the fire-escape towards the roof, evoking gasps of admiration from the onlookers. But he failed to reach it, because he caught his tight-fitting, striped trousers on something sharp, tearing a hole in them through which everyone could see his underclothes. Acutely embarrassed, he quickly came down again, jumped on his bicycle, and raced off home, followed by loud applause from all my friends.

The monkey created a great deal of fuss and bother. She moved from roof to roof and no-one dared make another attempt to catch her lest she jump into the garden of the Nalbandov villa, from there down on to the rocks and then—well, then, it would have been good-bye forever!

And now it was Mishka Galik who appeared on the scene.

Galik approached the crowd with his lazy Black Sea gait, glanced up at the monkey with the keen screwed-up eyes of a ship's skipper, and then informed Julietta that catching Daisy was an easy matter: all that was required was eight kopecks. After a family conference, the Arneris handed over eight kopecks to Galik, and, with a wink at Julietta, he strolled off in his lilac beaver trousers, with his bare, dusty feet peeping out at the bottom of them.

Looking down the street, the crowd saw Mishka enter Korotinsky's shop and come out a minute or two later with a large bunch of grapes wrapped up in coarse checked paper. Brushing aside any questions, he ran up the fire-escape and, when level with the roof, dangled the grapes where the monkey could see them. Daisy seemed to gulp down the remains of a nut, lolloped over to Mishka on all fours, and stretched out a brown, human little paw towards the grapes. But Mishka kept them away and began slowly climbing down again, holding up the enticing bunch, translucent in the sun, in front of her. In this way, Mishka and Daisy returned safely to the street, where Mishka grabbed her by the tail, quick as lightning, and, disregarding her angry cries and attempts to bite him, handed her back to Julietta. Then, with just one sentence—"I'll keep the grapes for my trouble"—he walked off, surrounded by a crowd shouting: "Mishka! Galik! Come on now: don't be greedy! At least, give us half!"

But Mishka was implacable.

Valuable Fossils

A BOY BROUGHT a piece of fossilised wood and a thick block of anthracite with fern-leaves imprinted on its shiny surface to school. The boy declared—and the history-teacher confirmed it—that the leaves had grown many hundreds of thousands, even a million, years ago.

The whole class crowded around the table on which the fossils lay, picking them up, scrutinising them curiously, and utttering exclamations such as: "Oho!" or "Oi—oi!" or "Ai—ai!"

But, on the whole, the ancient specimens did not arouse much interest and the boys soon returned to their seats.

But, on me, the fossils produced a shattering impression. My imagination conjured up a picture of tree-like ferns and other monstrous plants, and ichthyosauria with long, narrow heads roaming among them against a red, fiery sunset—and all this happening a million years ago. I saw improbable branches of fern, with little oval leaves on pyramid-shaped stems, flourishing before the flood, and these same leaves becoming imprinted on the surface of slabs of coal, which I knew came from tree-trunks that had been in the earth millions of years before that. It was awe-inspiring to think of.

I wanted to possess the fossils passionately, but I was certain that they must be enormously valuable and that the boy who owned them would not be willing to part with them whatever blessings I lavished on him. So I was astonished when he replied to my request for a tiny piece of the wood and a still tinier one of the anthracite with the print of the oval leaf on it by saying: "You can take the whole of them if you want to!"

"For nothing?" I asked.

"Certainly. I'm fed up with carrying them about in my satchel," he replied.

"Word of honour?" I asked.

"Why not? Papa will bring me as much as I- like from the Don Basin."

The boy's papa was a senior railway-guard. Hardly able to believe in my good fortune, I quickly thrust the fossils into my satchel and found it quite an effort to carry them home, they were so heavy.

I was thrilled to the core to have become the owner of valuable fossils, which up till now I had only seen in pictures in the natural history magazine. I could imagine Papa's and Aunt's delight and Zhenka's envy. I was even a little sorry for the boy who had given them to me; the poor wretch could have had no suspicion of how valuable they were!

However, my acquisition produced little effect either on the way home or when I got there. The boys and girls simply could not understand what I was boasting about and my aunt made a face and blamed me for bringing more rubbish into the house.

Zhenka giggled in a silly and offensive way. And all Papa had to say after examining them on his return from his classes was that similar fossils were often found in charcoal mines and pits, which was further confirmation that life on our planet had existed for millions of years. He added that imprints of shells, molluscs, and vertebrates appeared on rocks as well as those of plants: he spoke of it all as if it were the most ordinary thing in the world. I promptly visualised the imprint of a pre-flood lizard's skeleton complete with all the diminishing vertebrate of the tail.

I was momentarily crushed, though I could not believe in my heart of hearts that Papa was right about the fossils being nothing out of the way. I clung to the idea that I was in possession of treasures, for which any museum would pay vast sums. "After all," I thought, "they collect fragments of clay utensils and arrowheads that are only a few thousand years old, whereas my fossils date back millions of years." I was particularly enchanted by the piece of fossilised tree, superficially resembling a bit of ordinary wood but heavy as lead and incredibly hard: it was impossible to break a splinter off it and all its fibres, preserving their shape and structure, had been transformed into stone.

No, Papa was certainly wrong! I was convinced that such miracles of nature could seldom come to light and must be rarer than gold or diamonds.

I need scarcely say that early next morning, I carefully wrapped my fossils up in newspaper and, instead of going to school, went to the archaeological museum.

This idea had suddenly come to me in the night as being the easiest way to get rich quickly.

The attendant just inside the museum tried to make me buy an entrance-ticket, but I informed him haughtily that I was not a mere visitor but had come to see the curator on important business.

A fat little man in a frock-coat, with a university medal on his lapel, appeared and asked me what I wanted.

I silently unwrapped the fossils and with ill-concealed triumph held them up to him. "Do you see?"

"Well, yes, I see," the fat man replied. "But what do you want me to do about them?"

"Buy them for your museum," I said. Then, noticing a slightly surprised and also amused expression on his face, I added, with less assurance: "They're several million years old. Will you give me five roubles for the two?"

The fat little man took the fossils out of my hands, turned me round so that I had my back to him, opened my satchel, stuffed the fossils into it, and did up the straps. Then he led me to the huge entrance-door with its brightly polished metal handles and said: "Don't come bothering me again."

"Uncle, dear," I was astonished to hear myself say in a whining, beggar's voice, "at least let me into your museum without paying."

"That I will do," the fat little man agreed readily and conducted me across the slippery parquet floor of the huge, cold empty hall to the rooms where show-cases displayed fragments of bones, greenish, Scythian metal armour, clay lamps, arrowheads, and various other items calculated to impress visitors to archaeological museums. I passed by amphorae taller than I in which the ancient Greeks kept wine and by a lacquered case with the softened outlines of a human body, containing, I knew, an ancient Egyptian mummy, swathed in tar-black bandages—all that remained of one of the Pharaohs. I was pursued everywhere by tokens of an unbelievably distant past, while beyond the tall museum windows, with their shining metal bolts that smelled of samovar polish, I could see the panorama of our port: the quarantine-dock, the trestle-bridges, replacing those burned in the 1905 revolution, along which the red trucks of goods-trains, loaded with Bessarabian wheat, now jostled each other, drawn by a small engine whistling cheerfully and blowing out clouds of steam, and the busy winches of the cargo-vessels tied up to the quay, emitting their own peculiar *tirli . . . tirli . . . tirli*— a sound that a famous writer, Chekhov, I believe, described a long time ago. I could see, too, the white harbour-lighthouse, shaped like an elongated bell, and a yacht with bellowing sails, listing over as it neatly skirted it, leaving a foaming wash behind and the reflection of the greenish-blue aquarium furrowed by black tugs and launches. It was all so beautiful that I longed to write poetry about it, but did not know how.

Having bidden the kind fat man good-bye, I walked out under the museum's ancient Greek portal and strolled down Pushkin Street in the direction of the station and the Kulikovo field. I was weighed down by a sense of guilt towards Papa and the school because I had missed my lessons.

I was hot in my padded coat under the friendly, wintry, southern sun, and the straps of my satchel cut into my shoulders, since, on top of my books, it held the terribly heavy fossils.

I took them out, put them down on the pavement by the foot of an old, dappled plane-tree, and, heaving a sigh of relief, returned home, meditating upon time—how immeasurably long it was and how infinitely small I was compared to it, no longer than the oval leaf of a pre-flood fern, which had become imprinted on the surface of a piece of coal that, in turn, had once been part of a live tree.

And, perhaps, a thousand years from now, someone may discover a charcoal slab with the imprint of my spine on it and, alongside, a piece of fossilised oak—of the same oak that grew under our balcony in Otrada.

Mount Athos Lemon in a Carafe 🖉

I DO NOT REMEMBER how we came to have that pot-bellied carafe of thin, cheap glass with a rather narrow neck and a tight-fitting cork.

A giant lemon, surrounded by a colourless liquid we all thought was vodka, took up most of the interior.

I had never in my life seen such a huge, beautiful lemon, with a small segment of branch bearing two green leaves slanting out of the top of it.

It was difficult, almost impossible, to understand how anyone had managed to push the lemon through the narrow neck of the carafe. Perhaps the carafe had been first made without a bottom, the lemon inserted into it, and then the bottom somehow fused onto the body? But, after carefully examining it, I was convinced that the bottom had been blown simultaneously with the rest of the vessel.

There was something magic about that carafe and the lemon, something that belonged to Aladdin's cave in the thousand-and-one nights, all the more so, because, as I now recall, they had come from Mount Athos and been sold by a monk, a pedlar of delicious-smelling cypress crosses, cheap religious pictures, silver chains, and olive-oil in narrow, corrugated-iron flasks. I believe that the monk and his bag of exotic goods came off the Russian ship *Ropita,* owned by the Russian Shipping and Trading Company, which had taken on passengers and cargo in Constantinople, and that the captain bought the carafe for his son, who went to our school: it then, apparently, passed into the possession of another school-boy and, later, somehow found its way into the hands of my brother, Zhenia, who was in the preparatory division of the school.

If memory does not betray me, Zhenka won it at a card-game or swapped it for two stamps—a Sudanese and a Brazilian one. The carafe stood for a long time on the top of our side-board, always provoking general astonishment and speculations on how the lemon could possibly have been pushed through such a narrow neck.

When a ray of sunshine penetrated the leaves of the old oak that grew in front of the house and touched the top of the side-board, the carafe suddenly shone with a bright yellowish-green flame, lighting up the small, wall-papered room, as though someone had rubbed Aladdin's lamp, and it became transformed into a treasure-cave. In the night, as the green light of the moon crept through the cracks of the shutters, I dreamed I saw the dark, thin, mysterious figure of the monk from Mount Athos, in black skullcap and leather belt, slip noiselessly through the apartment, bearing the carafe with its shining lemon as though it were a sacred vessel. But the mystery still remained: how did the lemon get into the carafe? Zhenka and I racked our brains without reaching any solution and decided that the only thing to do was to break the carafe and examine the lemon more closely. Perhaps it was an artificial one?

We carried the carafe into the kitchen and Zhenka held it over the dust-bin while I mercilessly smashed its neck. The liquid poured out, filling the room with an intoxicating smell of lemon and alcohol and we were left with the lemon. It was not as large as it had appeared when seen through the glass, which had had a magnifying property, but was still far larger than any we had previously encountered. We cut it to pieces and discovered that it was real, just an ordinary lemon, with pips and separated segments, and very sour. It was slightly paler than the usual ones, but this could be accounted for by its long soaking in the vodka. We threw it away in the dust-bin without being any nearer to solving the problem.

And our destruction of the carafe was all the more pointless, because, next day, a boy at school, the captain's son to whom the carafe originally belonged, furnished the explanation. He told us that the monks on Mount Athos cultivated a special kind of giant lemon, put the carafe over one of the young ones when it was little larger than a pea, and waited for it to grow to its full size; then cut it off the tree, leaving a small twig attached to it, filled the carafe with vodka, sealed it firmly with a good cork, and sold it, along with other souvenirs from Mount Athos, to Russian pilgrims on the quays of Constantinople.

And so we lost the mysterious carafe, which engaged my imagination for such a long time and lit up our apartment so magically both in the daytime and, more especially, on moonlit nights, when the grown-ups were snoring and the children, beneath the wings of their angels, were dreaming their fairy-tale dreams.

Cartridges Thrown into a Bonfire 🖋

I LEFT THE HOUSE and walked down the familiar street that at that moment looked deserted and miserable. I was on my way to see my friend Smirnov, a quiet boy with a stammer, of whom I had only recently begun to take any notice. I do not really know how we happened to become friends, it never occurred to me to think about it or to seek to explain it: I just took it for granted.

He lived in a dull, brick house in the next street to ours, Jasnaia Street. Spotting me out of the window almost as soon as I reached the gate, he came out at once to meet me. He was wearing a winter coat and a cap with the school-crest, which seemed to me much larger than the usual one, and filled me with a curious uneasiness, accentuated by the irreproachable quality of the silver crossed palm-branches. Smirnov had a grey face, as boring and worthy as his surname, which somehow lacked any kind of euphony. His stammer made him shy and exaggeratedly silent. I must have made friends with him from self-interest: as his father was a teacher in our school and I was a very bad pupil, his father could prove useful to me at the staff's end-of-term meeting, when my progress and general behaviour would be discussed and the question of my being expelled might arise.

This thought that I had become friends with Smirnov for my own profit troubled my conscience and all the surroundings were in keeping with my secret misgivings—the grey, uncertain weather, the sky covered with exceptionally low clouds, the bare trees, and, in particular, the emptiness and the lonely atmosphere that seemed to envelop our usually gay and animated Otrada streets, with their lovely names: Otradnaia, Ujutnaia ("cosy"), Jasnaia ("clear"), and Morskaia ("of the sea").

On the asphalt pavements of these streets, there would normally be several little boys pursuing their peg-tops with small whips and a few girls playing hoopla, tossing light rings off wooden rapiers. Now they were conspicuously absent because of the cold autumn, though I think we were only at the end of September. Smirnov had turned up the collar of his overcoat, and gave me a diffident smile to indicate that all was well: he was referring to the cartridges for a montecristo, which had come into his possession and which he had promised to bring with him. Delving into his coat-pocket, he produced a round, sporting-looking, green card-board box, with a double-headed Austrian eagle, just like ours, on the lid and handed it to me. I held it up to my ear and shook it to find out how full it was: from the noise the cartridges made, rolling about inside, there did not seem to be very many of them, in fact, very few. But this did not disappoint me, since we had no montecristo gun to put them in.

We walked side by side along the sad streets towards the cliffs and then took the footpath, which had deteriorated since I had last seen it, down to the shore. Between the foot of the cliffs and the sea lay a favourite haunt of ours, a stretch of waste ground, the product of old landslides, which was now a rubbish dump covered in weeds, thorn-apples with their prickly green capsules, deadly nightshade, and tubular flowers of an unhealthy white colour. And here we spotted just what we wanted: a smouldering bonfire creeping along the weeds with a light-grey smoke. I added several handfuls of dry weeds to it and it began to burn with a crackling sound, but not very brightly: it seemed to be smothered by the low clouds that followed each other in a long line over the restless, silent, colourless sea from somewhere beyond the misty horizon. Eventually, however, an occasional flame spurted up and I considered that the time had come to throw in the cartridges.

Speaking hesitantly, with his usual stammer, Smirnov tried to dissuade me from doing it, but I employed all my eloquence to convince him that the experiment would not only be interesting but highly instructive. For some reason, I was extremely eager to carry it out, and I produced a number of additional arguments, the strongest of which was that we were never likely to have such an opportunity again during the whole of our lives.

Finally, Smirnov agreed.

I opened the box and threw the three or four very long cartridges it contained into the bonfire: then Smirnov and I ran well away from it, expecting every moment to hear the noise of the explosion behind us. But everything remained quiet, though the very quietness struck us as sinister and pregnant with the most alarming consequences.

We realised, of course, that montecristo cartridges would not explode with any enormous force, but we were afraid that bullets would begin to shoot out of the bonfire and strike our heads or backs, possibly killing us. We crawled into a hole, overgrown with nightshade, lay flat on our stomachs, and watched the bonfire from this distant observation-post.

The cartridges took so long to go off that we gave up all hope of their doing so at all, and the sky and the silent sea became darker and still more menacing. Then the cartridges did begin to explode, but with a wholly uncharacteristic rolling, crackling sound that seemed protracted both in time and space—and I woke up in darkness to an oppressive view through my bedroom window of a murky May morning and a sky overcast with storm-clouds, through which streaks of lilac lightning darted every now and then: these were followed by the rumbling of distant thunder that went for a long time and gradually became nearer and louder until it seemed as if wheelbarrows full of iron leaves were being trundled along the roof above my head. Everyone else in the apartment was still asleep and I lay lonely in the dark room that seemed slightly tinged with the deep colour of the lilac-bushes growing in the next-door garden.

As for the boy Smirnov, he had never existed at all except in my dream, though the images of him and his teacher-father come back to me and disturb me even now. . . . No, I cannot really believe that they were merely phantasms. . . .

The Thawing of the Ice

THE TEACHERS in our school were civil servants and wore uniforms; the long grey frock-coats with gold buttons of the Ministry of Public Education. In the blue velvet button-holes of their lapels glittered silver stars indicating their rank. The state counsellors had stars resembling very large snowflakes. One or two teachers chose to appear in jackets with small, smart rhomboid university badges on the chest. But as these jackets also had gold buttons and stars in their velvet button-holes, they were more in the nature of double-breasted uniform-tunics. Their wearers were usually young men who had just finished university and had not yet discarded their liberal ideas. But they soon became converted to Christianity and took to more formal blue frock-coats with blue waistcoats that displayed a triangle of immaculately white, starched shirt-front. The blue was a dark blue, though there were very slight differences in the shade.

But one teacher—the one who taught physics and geography—distinguished himself from the others by the colour of his frock-coat: admittedly it was blue, but it was a very pale, light blue. The cloth was extremely good and expensive and the uniform-buttons did not show up so much against it, being pale-lemon rather than gold, particularly the small buttons on the waistcoat and cuffs, where they almost blended with the pale gold of his cuff-links. These links used to emit a soft tinkle when Akazapov—that was the physics- and geography-teacher's name—drew from the back pocket of his coat a square, beautifully ironed, fine lawn handkerchief, with his initials on it, that spread, when he unfolded it, a pleasant scent of eau de Cologne that would have been pale golden, too, if scents could have had colours. Akazapov was a rather short, slender man with a narrow back and narrow, thinnish beard, always neatly trimmed, and also pale-gold in colour, which went well with his sly, pale-blue eyes. Rumour had it that he had done well for himself by marrying a rich merchant's widow and that he was not above taking bribes from prosperous pupils.

He gave the impression of being a total ignoramus, muddling up rivers and countries when he vaguely traced their outlines on the shabby map full of holes, and his lectures on physics corresponded word for word with chapters in Kraevich's thick text-book, which led him to start them with the words "Kraevich and I together . . ." Boris Alexeivich Akazapov had a tendency to pronounce *e*'s and *o*'s as *a*'s, so that he often referred to "gaometry" and "hydragen." Among ourselves, we called him Baris.

Yet Baris was of an easy-going disposition and gave threes—the pass mark—to the most inveterate twos, adding as he did so: Kraevich and I together decided to give you three minus."

He was totally unsuited to be a teacher and waited anxiously for the bell to save him during lessons, constantly wiping his high, narrow forehead with his handkerchief.

Experiments in physics were particularly unlucky for him; flasks exploded, test-tubes slipped out of his fingers and broke, pouring prussic acid over the books, the spirit-lamp refused to light, and the smouldering splinter of wood in a jar with oxygen showed a marked reluctance to burst into star-like brilliance as Kraevich had declared it would. The simplest experiment failed when Akazapov carried it out.

For instance, wishing to prove the existence of air-pressure, he followed Kraevich's instructions and the diagram on the right-hand page of the text-book and filled a glass to the brim with water, then covered it with a square piece of paper. The idea was, that if you turned the glass upside-down, the water would not run out, because the pressure of the air would seal the paper to the glass. Our Baris poured water into the glass fetched from the laboratory with a trembling hand, his thin, pale-gold wedding-ring clattering against the side, and his pale-gold cuff-links clinging together, then duly covered it with the piece of paper. After that, he announced in a faltering voice that the pressure of air would keep the water in the glass, turned the glass upside-down, and the paper instantly slid sideways, releasing a small waterfall over his starched cuff, his well-creased trousers and his shoes. Afraid of losing his authority, Baris embarked again on his duel with the laws of nature as set out in Kraevich's textbook on physics and again the water poured onto the parquet floor to the gay laughter of the class. Akazapov's situation was hopeless and only the bell, ringing to end the lesson, extricated him from it.

Justice compels me to mention that not all experiments failed in Baris's hands. There was one which always succeeded brilliantly. It was called: "transformation of a liquid body into a hard one and vice versa," and it was his best number, a triumph for Kraevich's *Physics*.

On the days he was due to perform it, Akazapov was usually in a good mood and walked into the classroom with a firm gait, his blue eyes sparkling, accompanied by an assistant in a soldierly, stiff, stand-up collar and creaking boots, reverently carrying a piece of ice on a saucer.

"As you probably know," Baris began solemnly, but with a faint, underlying note of flippancy, "and if you don't, you can read it in Kraevich's *Physics*, when the temperature falls to below zero on the Réaumur scale, the liquid body, water, begins to freeze and turns into a hard body, called ice. And vice versa. At a temperature above zero, the hard body, called ice, begins to thaw and gradually turns into a liquid body, water. You can easily convince yourself of this by making the experiment you can read all about in Kraevich's *Physics* [page so-and-so, diagram number so-and-so]. Now, pay attention, please, and stop making all that noise. We take a piece of the hard body—ice—and place it in a room, warmed to a temperature above zero; this room, for instance, where, as you can see, the thermometer shows a temperature above zero. . . . Monitor, what temperature does the thermometer show at the moment?"

"Sixteen degrees above zero," the monitor announced after standing on tiptoe and peering at the glass tube, and the whole class echoed him.

"Well, make a note of it," Akazapov said significantly. "Now, let's put the hard body on the saucer where you can all see it and watch the transformation take place. . . . Grigori"—he turned to his assistant—"place the saucer with the hard body up on my desk."

After Grigori, in his black uniform with one row of metal buttons, looking like Gogol's governor, had placed the saucer holding the icicle, which he had knocked off a water-pipe outside, on the front of the desk with due care and respect and had withdrawn from the classroom on tiptoe, Akazapov began the lesson, opening his watch from time to time and glancing at the icicle on the saucer, where quite a lot of water had already gathered.

By the end of the lesson, there was nothing in the saucer except water, the hard body had vanished, and Baris, triumphantly snapping down the lid of his watch, declared that the experiment had been completely successful. This time, when the bell rang to announce the end of the lesson, it seemed to be celebrating the remarkable achievement of Akazapov "together with Kraevich." The class broke out into spontaneous applause that was not permitted within the walls of the institution, and to cries of "Hurrah!," our Baris, his attendance-register under his arm, left the classroom with an elastic step and an ambiguous gleam in his small blue eyes.

I used to be disturbed by unanswerable questions. We all know, I said to myself, that at a temperature of 100 degrees above zero, water boils and is transformed into steam, that is, into a gaseous substance. But, at a higher temperature still, gas is probably transformed into something else, and that something else into something else again. What form, then, do these new transformations take, and how far does the series of transformations go?

Tossing about at night on my hot pillow, unable to sleep, I imagined an infinite number of these transformations of one thing into another, beyond my understanding, eternal, constant, and impossible for human hands to arrest.

Even now, I am disturbed by these questions.

The Home-Made Cart ✍

Now, RECALLING that fabulously distant past, the first thing that for some reason comes into my mind—I can see it in every detail—is the immense crown of a tree, a mass of flickering leaves hanging over me like a cloud, rustling in the dry steppe wind, and casting dusty, overlapping, animated shadows all around me; above, the sweltering, dazzling midday sun hurt my eyes and made the dim surface of the river Bug shine like silver. The ancient mill-wheel, covered in green slime, interminably pouring streams of seething water into the dark, almost black, magic whirlpool beneath, filled me with terror.

We were in a part of the former Russian empire, the southern steppe, Novorossia, which bordered on the Crimea, the Black Sea, and Bessarabia—in the town of Akkerman, where, it seemed to me, waves of red-hot Turkish air swept over us, as though coming from an open oven. Somewhere, close by, was the town of Nikolaev, the village of Trikhati, where we had got off the train, and the port, from which we would soon be taking a ship back to Odessa.

Time has broken my reminiscences as it might a marble grave-stone, deprived them of continuity and sequence, but at the same time preserved their details against any powers of destruction, as though they were golden letters forming the name of a man who had once, in the past, lived in this world.

And so it is a broken life, broken not morally, but "into pieces" physically, as a result of the eternal law of destruction and creation. Perhaps it is more like the Byzantine mosaics, which I saw many years later in Kiev and Constantinople, where people, objects, angels, and saints, and the whole golden background against which they are portrayed, are constructed of small, skilfully fitted, multi-coloured cubes of glass, smalto, sugar-white marble, lapis-lazuli, and many other such beautiful components.

Perhaps the heavy, multi-coloured story of my life, with all its picturesque details, was composed of various elements, first trans-formed by someone into separate multi-coloured cubes, then fitted together into one picture, eventually broken up by time, losing its form but not its colour, only to be transformed once again into one, beautiful whole.

. . . Perhaps a broken life? A mosaic?

The tree I have mentioned—perhaps a sycamore?—so enormous compared to me, with its furrowed trunk and thick, spreading branches, was then only a detail in a large mosaic now broken up into pieces, but awaiting time when some magic agency shall re-construct it into the integrated picture it once was.

I can see among the mass of separated cubes, as if it were only yesterday, patches of the tree's greenery and fragments of sugar-white cloud against a lapis-lazuli sky.

Barefooted urchins climbed that tree and brought down a nest with small fat nestlings in it. As the name for the birds was very similar to that of a weight, I envisaged the little nestlings as solid, metal circles such as I had seen in the grocer's shop, surrounded by smells of tar, kerosene, biscuits, leather, harnesses, and the earthen floor, on which warm river-water had been poured.

I believe the boys brought the nest over to my papa for my benefit, but Papa did not buy the little "weights"; he gave the boys two kopecks and told them to put the nest back, because the mother and father were flying over our heads with shrill, desperate cries in the hope of saving their children.

That summer was the first time I saw steppes, fields, and cows with their little calves, one of which, a spotty one, was standing, its legs far apart and its tail projecting to one side, as a dark-red stream poured from it and spread over the roots of the dry steppe plants. A man in a faded calico cap and dusty, well-worn boots drove up in a sulky, smelling strongly of wheel-grease, hot oil-cloth, and horses' sweat, looked at the calf and said: "Haemorrhage," and I remember how that word, pronounced in the man's coarse voice, frightened and somehow shattered me.

I do not remember now where we stayed; I only remember white, scalding, crumbling foot-paths crossing the dry steppe, which bit unpleasantly into my bare soles, and how afraid I was of stepping in cow's manure, dry outside and soft underneath.

Every now and then, we used to visit "neighbours" who had not come just for the summer, like Papa, Mamma, and me, but lived there the whole year round in a house with a green iron roof, surrounded by already faded lilac-bushes and pyramid-shaped poplars. They always had a lot of guests, and I remember the dry clay soil in front of the house and a flower-bed full of white-starred tobacco-plant and reddish-lilac evening-glory, their flowers folding up tightly in daytime, like little umbrellas. Here, among the guests, I once displayed myself in an unfortunate light. Looking into the dining-room and seeing the table laid for supper with plates of round slices of tea-sausage on it, I rushed out onto the terrace where all the guests were gathered and rushed up to Mamma, shouting ecstatically: "Mamma, let's go in at once: there's tea-sausage there!"

Everybody laughed except Mamma. She flushed red with embarrassment—I had never seen her like that, with tears in her eyes—and said quite angrily, while trying to force a smile: "Anyone would think you'd never seen tea-sausage!"

I had seen it, of course, but I was never given it, because it was considered indigestible: I generally got scrambled eggs and Hercules oatmeal, which Mamma boiled on a kerosene stove, when what I liked more than anything in the world was tea-sausage!

Also there, in the dining-room, where the juicy tea-sausage was and candles were burning with a purple light, I saw on the window-sill, in the twilight, a number of large pale-yellow apples. I picked one up and took a bite out of it, but it turned out not to be an apple at all but a dry pumpkin left to seed.

This again aroused the laughter of the guests and caused Mamma embarrassment. She said to me: "You simply don't know how to behave in society."

In those days of high summer, at the beginning of my life, I became convinced of my papa's all-powerfulness. I had become convinced of my mamma's extraordinary powers even before that, on one of the first long wintry evenings of my life, when the lighted kerosene lamp was reflected in the frozen window-panes, on which the shutters had not yet been closed. Mamma was sitting at the table, hemming a new pillow-case—though I only learned exactly what she was doing much later—with a shiny needle that nimbly pierced the material, drawing a thin, white, number forty thread after it: and as she sewed, she sang softly and sadly what sounded to me like: "Do not sew me, Mother, dear, a bright red sarafan, I do not want you, dearest one, to grant me such a boon."

This song worried me because "boon" was a new word to me and it became confused in my mind with "baboon." I pictured a baboon, with a pretty, curly tail, scrambling about on all fours after the red sarafan and trying to catch hold of its edge.

"Mamma, why was the baboon there?" I asked.

"What baboon? Who said anything about a baboon?"

"Well, the boon, then?" I persisted. "Was Mother dear sewing the red sarafan for the boon?"

Mamma tried to sort matters out, but I was unable to understand her explanation; she stopped pushing the needle through the pillow-case with her silver thimble, bolted the shutters, and decided to distract my mind from the boon by getting me to play with my cart.

It was a small, toy cart, harnessed to a tiny donkey, which had

recently been given to me as a present, and I had not yet grown tired
of it. Mamma placed the cart and donkey in front of me and began
telling me a long story about them.

She had a fantastic gift for story-telling, inventing fairy-tales of her
own, full of humor and amusing details, and I usually fell completely
under their spell, ceasing to be capricious as I was translated into her
fantasy-world.

But now the picture of the new "sarafan," so unnaturally linked
with the four-footed and probably equally bright-red animal following closely behind it, overcame the magic of Mamma's story about
the cart and the donkey and its adventures in Italy and I became
even more capricious, picking holes in every other sentence. I kept
on stubbornly declaring that the cart was not a real one, nor was the
donkey, for had they been, there would be grass in the cart and the
donkey would be eating it, so the donkey was a fake, a cheat, and
possibly even a "boon."

"Aha!" I said aggressively to Mamma. "You can't suddenly put
grass into the cart, now, can you?"

Mamma looked downcast, feeling that she had her back to the
wall. But what could she do? How could she possibly produce grass
in the middle of winter in a room with a heated stove and tightly
closed shutters? She would have to be a magician for that! And I
knew very well that Mamma was just Mamma and not a magician.

And so I became increasingly capricious, demanding from Mamma
the impossible—grass for the cart.

Suddenly, as I persisted in my naughtiness, I noticed that Mamma's
eyes were sparkling and caught a hidden smile darting across her
lips.

"Very well," she said. "If you want your grass so much, you'll
have it. We'll look for it and perhaps we'll find it."

She went to the chest of drawers, rummaged in it, and suddenly
I saw in her hands a splash of something green. Could it possibly
be grass? No, it couldn't! It would be incredible! But Mamma was
already putting the green, grass-like substance into the cart and
tenderly pressing my head to her warm breast. "Well, are you happy
now?"

I understood, of course, that it was not real grass not even hay.

It was the dry moss, painted bright green, with which we usually ornamented the roll of cotton wool we laid between the double windows in winter. Sometimes we put little glasses of prussic acid in it to prevent the panes from frosting over.

So it was not grass, but painted moss. Nevertheless, it was a miracle. I understood that the cart was not real, nor was the donkey, so the same could be said about the grass, yet for me it remained a miracle and Mamma, clearly, was a magician.

The clock on the wall wheezes, creaks, and finally strikes eight times, whereupon my eyes turn inwards. I am incapable of holding up my heavy head and do not remember, am no longer conscious of Mamma undressing me and putting me to bed. But as I fall blissfully asleep, I am convinced with all my being of my dearest, beloved magician—Mamma's all-powerfulness.

It was only some months later that I became convinced of Papa's all-powerfulness and magician-status.

It occurred on one of those sweltering days under the huge, hazy crown of the sycamore tree, and it suddenly came back to me today, during an unusually long winter in Peredelkino.

I was standing beside Papa, my head scarcely to his knee, with the mass of shifting leaves casting waves of shadows down on us. A short while before, I had seen a bullock-cart in the steppe for the first time and been fascinated by the immensely long vehicle with sides, that looked like two horizontal wooden ladders turned on their sides. I was seized with an urgent longing to possess such a cart— even a toy replica of it—and, tugging at my father's trousers, I asked him to make me one. Then the sight of our little mongrel dog, Rudko, running round us with his tongue hanging out, gave me the idea that it would be fun to harness him to a small cart like that and let him drag it along the path. I had no confidence in Papa's ability to build me a bullock-cart. I did not know then that he was all-powerful like Mamma. Nevertheless, pressing against his legs, I nagged away, demanding the immediate appearance of the cart. To my astonishment, Papa soon agreed, twinkling at me through his pincenez and shaking his dark mane of professorial hair, now damp and slightly curly after his bathe in the Bug.

"Very well," he said, "stop fussing. You'll have a magnificent bullock-cart in a minute or two."

With these words, he picked up a piece of wood lying near the shed, brought a knife from the kitchen that was usually used for chopping up meat into tiny pieces for cutlets, rapidly shaved off a number of long, thin strips, and began weaving them together. In almost no time, he was holding up the body of a cart.

Papa worked cheerfully, jerking his pince-nez off his perspiring nose and leaving it dangling on its cord. He wore a linen, Little Russian shirt, soaked through and through with sweat, with an embroidered collar and a strap for a belt, and looked far more like a skilful jack-of-all-trades than a schoolmaster. I could see how much Mamma, standing on the clay threshold of the kitchen, admired my bearded papa and his enthusiastic approach to work.

The rapidity and, even more, the simplicity with which my desire had been fulfilled somehow annoyed me, and I said grumpily to Papa: "And how will you make the wheels?"

"I'll find a way," Papa replied with a laugh.

"But how?" I insisted.

"I tell you I'll manage somehow."

From the vagueness of his replies, I suspected that Papa was merely boasting about being able to make the wheels. I could not imagine how and with what he could construct anything so complicated. What instrument would he use to make them round? How would he fix the thin rim? And the spokes? Mamma was a magician, but Papa was only pretending he could do everything. He wasn't all-powerful.

"Well, go on, do the wheels!" I said to Papa with a skeptical laugh. "We'll see how you get on with them!"

"We'll see, all right," said Papa, and the miracle of the creation of the wheels occurred so quickly that I hardly had time to gasp.

Papa threw a cursory glance around, picked up a round piece of wood, part of a thin tree-trunk, took a hand-saw off a nail in the shed, put the piece of wood on the block, held it down with one knee, and sawed off four circular sections so quickly that splinters flew all over. Before I realised the purpose of the wooden circles, Papa had found nails and nailed them to the body of the cart, where they provided four splendid wheels. He twiddled them round to ease them, then pushed the bullock-cart down the path.

And then it was I realised that my papa, as well as my mamma, was a full-fledged magician and completely all-powerful. My satisfaction knew no limits as Papa, with shavings and sawdust in his hair, caught Rudko and harnessed him neatly to the cart with some string he found in the shed.

We stood there, the three of us—Mamma, Papa, and I—so close to each other, so loving and so loved, so all-powerful, too, and watched Rudko race down the path, dragging the cart behind him; but, as he turned at the end of it, the cart bumped into the stump of a tree on which a red admiral butterfly was perching and broke into smithereens, the wheels rolling in all directions. Rudko, wagging his tail, raced farther into the bushes, dragging the remains of the bullock-cart behind him.

The Mirror ✍

THE GIRL'S NAME was Xenia, but I called her Xena or sometimes Xenka. She was a few months older than I: I was then about three and they still dressed me as a girl. She was brought to our apartment by our two mammas—hers and mine—so that we should make friends and play together. Her parents were neighbours of ours, living opposite us on the same landing.

Her papa was an army doctor, a brusque man with short-cropped hair. His hands smelled of carbolic and his uniform-jacket, with shoulder-straps and an academic medal and double-headed silver eagle on the chest, reeked of tobacco and of something alcoholic, probably the vodka which he drank before dinner, and also of mustard and pepper, smells I could not stand. I hated him and was frightened of him, especially when he caught hold of me playfully and pressed me to his hard chest and still harder medal, hurting my cheek. He liked to frighten me a little and cracked a long riding-master's whip close to my legs when he drove to his hospital in his yellow gig. The whip, made of fine wattle, always stood in a corner of their dining-room. At dinner, the orderly served a fiery, over-peppered borsch with a marrow-bone in it: salt, pepper, and a carafe of vodka stood in the centre of the table.

I did not like Xenka's mother either; she had a heavily powdered, painted face, blackened eyebrows, a strong smell of scent, false hair and over-bright eyes, a man's eyes. I learned later that she put stropin drops into them to enlarge the pupils. She dressed smartly, her silk dress rustled, her corsets squeaked, and, in comparison with my mamma, she seemed arrogantly improper, all the more so because she smoked cigarettes, flicking off the ashes into a large tropical shell on the table, alongside the family album and a lamp under a silk, lace lamp-shade.

These neighbours did not fit in at all with my quiet, non-smoking and non-drinking family, but our proximity involved a certain obligation to remain friends and visit one another from time to time.

So Xenka was brought to play with me, which indicated the desire of both sets of parents to live together on friendly terms. I did not like Xenka at all: she had thin, straggly hair, a neat little apron with the straps crossed behind her back, and well-scrubbed, large ears. There were blue shadows under the eyes in her pale little face, and I had already been informed that she had worms, against which an implacable struggle went on all the time. She had a lachrymose nature and constantly irritated me with all her whims and tears.

Both mammas—Xenka's and mine—declared that Xenka and I were like bride and bridegroom and watched us tenderly as we played. Our play consisted in sitting uncomfortably on the floor, spreading out our toys and admiring my book, which had stand-up pictures when opened. Sometimes we scrambled under the sofa, and there I looked at Xenka with hatred, as I thought of the methods employed to rid her of the worms: they gave her a garlic enema, followed by a spoonful of jam containing a special anti-worm powder, and then put her on a white china chamber-pot. I could see her sitting on it, sulking with a capricious expression on her ugly little face.

Eventually, the orderly arrived and announced to Xenka's mother that dinner was served and the master was getting cross; so then she took Xenka home, forcing her to give me a farewell kiss as befitted a bride and bridegroom. We moistened each other's cheeks, and during the night I had a dream that the two of us really were bride and bridegroom; she had long, dank hair, that aroused in me a kind of loving irritation and, at the same time, a strong desire to get rid of my unwanted bride as soon as possible.

And, at this point, there suddenly came to my assistance from God knows where a magic mirror, which had the faculty of laying bare all the hidden vices of whoever looked in it. I held the mirror up to the face of the by now quite adult Xenia, looked in it and suddenly its whole surface, which had been clear as spring-water, was covered and disfigured by black shells. Xenia's face became distorted as the little black shells of her vices covered it, too, and I realised that I had passionately hated her for a long time.

I was awakened as usual by the sunbeams from the direction of Basarnaia Street coming through the cracks in the shutters. It was a beautiful day, but it failed to dispel my disgust for Xenia, which, strange as it may seem, I feel even now, though she is surely no longer in this world.

Life on the Dniester ✍

WE SPENT one summer on the Dniester, where the hillocks around the stony foothills of the Carpathians were overgrown with couch grass, artemisia, and immortelles, with lilac, faded-looking blooms, that reminded one of cemetery flowers. Here and there were the ashes of gypsy fires, and the burnt grass surrounding them was strewn with fragments of charcoal. I picked up a piece of charcoal and my imagination conjured up a picture of the band of gypsies that had camped out there for the night; the canvas-covered carts, tents, girls in long, coloured skirts, and men with curly beards, dark-blue as blackberries. And, as it was widely rumoured that gypsies stole children, I clung firmly to Mamma's hand as I fell asleep and begged her in a blurred, drowsy voice to protect me from being kidnapped.

On the slope above the Dniester, where summer residents came to admire the sunset, a rough hearth had been constructed out of limestone; a horizontal slab as the base, two perpendicular ones for the sides, and a high, narrow strip at the back, bearing slimy traces of the small steppe-snails and glints of smoky quartz. Mamma called it a throne. From here, there was a particularly beautiful view of the sunset, flaming over the stony steppe, grey with artemisia, and every now and again a harmless snake would slither out of the dry grass, pink from the dying sun, or a friendly gopher could be seen standing by the entrance to its burrow, like a small pillar, its back turned to the pre-twilight wind. And from round, dark holes in the clay cliffs on the far side of the Dniester, martins darted out, whirling and swooping over the river's foaming rapids that attacked and eroded its step banks.

Once the sun had finally set and the first little stars appeared in the sky, we sat enchanted by the sight of the small ship, which always passed by at that hour, with thrashing paddle-wheels and showers of golden rain from its funnel. The ship circled the little island in the middle of the river, on which, I knew, there was a market-garden kept by a German, where we had gone to buy hyacinth bulbs in a much smaller boat and been tossed about in the paddle-steamer's wake. Now, as it disappeared in the darkness of the starry night, Mamma's eyes followed it dreamily and she murmured: "How lovely that ship is!"

And I repeated after her, not without a considerable effort: "Ha lovey zat sip is!"

From which it may be gathered that I was not much more than three at the time. . . .

The impression that the ship with its fiery funnel made on me was somehow connected with an event which had taken place before or soon after my birth. There had been a disaster in the Black Sea near Odessa, when two ships had collided with considerable loss of life. The high number of casualties made it a topic of conversation for several years, and I still give an involuntary shudder at the mention of the word "*Mercury*," which was the name of one of the ships. Everyone discussed the inquiry which was held to discover who was responsible for the catastrophe. It lasted for a long time, and those presiding found it a difficult matter to ascertain exactly what had happened. In this connection, I recall that Doroshevich's* name was frequently uttered by the grown-ups: he was then reporting the inquiry for the Odessa *Post*. A large number of witnesses were examined, among them a Greek who, with a strong accent, uttered the following legendary words, when trying to throw light on the affair: "The vapours had no latters, passengers drowed." Which meant: the ships had no lanterns, the passengers drowned. "Vapours" was, of course, the Greek's translation of "vaporettos." It became an oft-repeated joke.

* Russian writer of the period. *Translator's note.*

Later on, the Greek witness became mixed up with another Greek —Dimba, the owner of the sweet-shop, in Chekhov's *Marriage*.

Living close to the Dniester, I saw lots of interesting things for the first time: for instance, a stork on the thatched roof of the Moldavian hut, which we had rented for the summer. His wife sat in the nest, made from reeds and entwined branches, while he stood on guard outside on one leg, with the other one pressed against his stomach. From time to time, he disappeared, to return later with food for the family in his long beak: a small grass-snake or a green, juicy frog with four splayed-out paws.

The stork could make cracking noises with his beak, reminding me of the sharp sound of the night-watchman's rattle, which I had once heard at my grandmother's in Ekaterinoslav. Papa learned how to click his tongue with much the same effect and, to amuse Mamma and me, would often stand below the nest, his hands thrust into his belt and his beard pointing skyward, and produce sonorous, distinct cracking sounds, similar to the stork's, to lure him into conversation. Eventually, the stork would reply and they would chat to each other for quite a long time, while Mamma and I laughed till the tears poured down our cheeks and she would gasp: "Stop, Pierre, you'll kill us! You're behaving like a little boy."

Mamma called Papa "Pierre," after, I think, reading *War and Peace*, a book which was considered sacred in our house.

I shall always remember the Moldavians in their raw-hide coats, fur waistcoats, and tall bearskin hats, which they wore all the year round, even in the full heat of summer.

When rain fell and the snow melted in the Carpathians, the Dniester suddenly became dark and swollen and overflowed its banks, submerging the stone dam in front of our hut: long waves, from which the wind snatched grey wisps of foam, raced over the bushes on the river's edge, penetrated the reeds, covering them almost to the top with surging water, and formed black, deadly whirlpools. At such times, many people were drowned and, from the top of our hut, I would gaze in terror at the sinister clouds and the mass of seething water revolving like a whirligig.

After a few days, the rain would cease, the water in the Dniester fell—sometimes even below its usual level—the dam reappeared, and storks strolled about the sandy banks, picking fat, unpleasant-looking black molluscs out of their half-open shells.

I would walk over to the bank and admire the shells, with the breathing apparatus that opened and closed as if the inhabitants were gasping for air. It surprised me that they were actually alive and could breathe and even seemed to be putting out their tongues at me.

When the flood began and the dam sank under the water, Mamma and I cried out to it: *"Au revoir,* dam!"

And we greeted its reappearance when the flood ended with: "Hulloa, dam. Nice to see you again!"

Once or twice during the summer Papa had to go to Odessa for a few days on business connected with his teaching activities. It was quite a short journey, but a very uncomfortable one, involving a crossing by ferry and two changes of trains. I knew that Papa had to walk to a place called Resina, a large village or even a town, with shops and a post-office, then cross by ferry to a place called Sakharna, and from there proceed to the Ribnitsa railway station, where once, when we were going away, I had actually seen an enormous, freshly caught, white sturgeon through the railway-carriage window. It had been covered with thick salt and was being lifted by a hook in its tail onto the platform of the weighing-machine: a moment later, someone announced delightedly that it weighed sixty pounds.

We awaited Papa's return with great impatience and went to meet him every day, but he always arrived unexpectedly and, at first glance, never looked like himself. Once, Mamma and I went down the road to meet him and caught sight of a rowing-boat, borne towards us by the current from the other bank of the Dniester: there was a passenger, all in black, with long hair, seated at the stern, who might have been a young monk or a psalm-reader. We paid little attention to him at first: then Mamma suddenly waved the parasol she was carrying on her shoulder and shouted out: "Pierre! Pierre! Goodness, I never recognised him!"

And it was Papa, with the travelling-basket I knew so well stretched across his knees. As soon as he saw us, he took off his black, wide-brimmed hat with its faded ribbon. It turned out that he had got out at the previous station and, instead of taking the ferry, had decided to cross in a smaller boat, which could land him on the dam right opposite our hut, which stood so picturesquely, with the stork on its roof, on the stony hillock overgrown with artemisia.

In the few days he had been away, Papa's hair had grown down over the nape of his neck, his face was sunburned, and his black summer coat was covered with dust. Mamma kept on exclaiming, as she kissed and hugged him: "Really, Pierre, what do you look like? Let's go home quickly; you must have a good wash! Your neck is quite brown!"

Meanwhile, I was busily engaged in trying to get a peek inside the creaking basket, knowing full well that it would contain presents for me from town. Then Papa let me clamber up onto his dusty shoulder and the three of us—Mamma, Papa, and I—walked happily along the unpaved road home: there seemed to be no-one else in the whole world but us.

How we loved each other at that moment!

On another occasion, we went to meet Papa and reached the outskirts of Resina before we realised it: here we were stopped by a long, deep puddle, which we could not skirt round because there were stone walls on both sides of the road. When I looked up, I suddenly saw Papa, in his broad-brimmed hat, like Maxim Gorki's, dusty summer coat and pince-nez, with the familiar basket in his hand, making his way carefully between the stone wall and the puddle, in which the quivering sky could be seen reflected in the ripples. Placing one foot in front of the other, he walked along a narrow strip of dry soil with one shoulder brushing against the wall, which left dusty stains on his sleeves. He slowly approached, unaware that Mamma and I were watching him with bated breath, smiling happily to himself in anticipation of being united with his wife and son.

And the most astonishing thing is that about sixty-five years later, after so many changes had taken place in the world and in me, when neither Mamma nor Pappa were still alive, and all that remained of them was a tender, sad memory, I happened to find myself in Resina again and instantly recognised the place where Papa had made his way along the side of the road, brushing his shoulder against the stone wall.

Nothing at all had changed—there were even black puddles still reflecting the sky—and I would not have been surprised if I had suddenly seen my young papa, in his faded, wide-brimmed hat, a basket in his hand, bearded, dusty, kind, and carefully choosing dry spots for his feet as he made his way home to Mamma and me.

I got out of the car, touched the unchanged stones of the wall, picked a dry, silvery blade of grass growing at its foot, and, almost weeping from a nostalgic grief, went back to the car and asked to be taken back along the Dniester to Sakharna, from there to Orgeev, where, during the Kerensky regime in World War I, I was almost shot by Kornilov's men, and taken on to Kishinev, memorable to me because I met Kotovsky there in the summer of 1917. While the car was manoeuvering to take a sharp turn in the narrow road between the two stone walls, the good, old, familiar stork, hovering on wide-spread wings, his long legs hanging down, examined me carefully— such an old man now and so unlike the small boy with a round face and narrow, Mongolian eyes.

At this point, I remembered something long-forgotten of our life on the Dniester at that time. We had a friend, a local landowner, who walked about in a raincoat and peasant's boots, and occasionally came over to have tea with us. He had the most extraordinary name: "Kissel Pesakhovich, Gravedigger and Leaseholder," which was printed on the large visiting-card he handed to Mamma and Papa on his first visit.

And, then, it was here that I first saw a boy get his ears pulled. It was a terrible sight that I cannot forget even now.

The Messner family rented a hut for the summer in that delightful district by the Dniester, as we did; and, one day, I saw Mrs. Messner in the orchard doing something I could not grasp to her son, a small cadet in wide black trousers and a cotton summer shirt with hard, blue shoulder-straps. The boy was much older than I and I took him to be quite grown-up, which made what I saw all the more appalling. At first, though, I thought the two of them were playing some strange game; then, I imagined she was washing him with two sponges, since I noticed that water was pouring down the small cadet's red cheeks and nose.

This caused me some surprise.

But, as I drew closer to the hedge, along which a row of pink and red hollyhocks were lit up by the sun, I saw that Mrs. Messner was pulling her son's ears. Up till then, I had only been told that bad grown-ups sometimes pulled children's ears, but I had never seen anyone do it and, to be frank, had never quite believed it, suspecting that people only said it to frighten children and teach them to be obedient.

And now, suddenly, I realised it was true: a big boy's ears were being pulled before my very eyes. Mrs. Messner, grasping the lobes of her son's ears firmly, with practised hands, wrenched them up and down until it seemed to me I could hear the cartilages creak. The cadet's ears were swollen and crimson, reminding one of the flowers of the near-by hollyhocks.

Mrs. Messner, a sturdy, blonde German, was wearing a silk blouse, tucked tightly in at the waist, which rustled on her fat back, and a starched apron—she had been cooking one of her famous apfel-strudels on a spirit-stove: she had wicked, watery-blue eyes, a pink double-chin, and a small pince-nez on her large-pored, powdered nose trembled as her plump hands, working with the drive of piston-rods, pulled at the ears with ruthless determination. The boy's face was bathed in tears and contorted with pain.

The marvellous, luminous around me on that dewy morning by the Dniester suddenly grew dark and I almost fainted. Mamma snatched me up in her arms, pressed me to her heart, and, her face pale with indignation, carried me away from the disgraceful scene.

It remained in my mind for a long time.

In Odessa, I used to meet Cadet Messner in the street occasion-ally, when he really was grown-up. As we greeted one another, I could never tear my eyes from his rather elongated, protruding ears.

I saw him for the last time during the First World War. I was rid-ing on my ammunition-wagon and he was approaching our battery from the opposite direction, mounted on a horse and wearing a cav-alry cloak, hussar's cap, with a leather field map-case slung over one shoulder: he held an officer's cane in one of his gloved hands. It was in the depths of winter in a forest near Minsk, among trees enveloped in snowdrifts, with a red, icy sun setting in the back-ground; from somewhere near-by came the rumble of guns and the resinous smell of the soldiers' camp-fires.

Messner, now a handsome young man with a small moustache, did not recognise me and rode past, patting his horse on the neck. I watched him go, my eyes inevitably drawn to the lobes of his ears, red from the frost and slightly glistening in the dying rays of the sun. And I suddenly recalled life by the Dniester with Mamma and Pappa, and the grey ashes of the gypsies' fires on the stony ground overgrown with wormwood; recalled the pieces of charcoal and the stork hovering over us on black and white outspread wings with his long legs hanging below him.

The Mandolin ✍

I DISCOVERED that one of the boys in my class was a very good musician, for he even appeared at a school literary-musical matinée. He played a number of patriotic songs on a mandolin, which he brought enveloped in a grey flannelette bag tied up with a silk ribbon, the most successful of them proving to be a variation on the well-known "I hear the song of the lark, I hear the nightingale sing."

The director himself, and all our lady-patrons, dressed to the nines in white satin pseudo-peasant costumes, applauded the young mandolin-player enthusiastically, and this immediately fired me with an idea: I would acquire a mandolin and learn to play not only small concert pieces but also dance-music for *pas de quatres* and hiavathas.

I need scarcely say that my request to be bought a mandolin was received unsympathetically by my family. As was to be expected, my aunt pursed up her mouth in a mocking smile and was rather sarcastic about this new, unwarrantable whim of mine; Zhenka was tactful enough to remain silent, but I caught a maddeningly scornful glint in his innocent brown eyes; and Papa became quite angry, drummed his forefinger on the dining-room table and called me a waster, who got nothing but bad marks and, instead of trying to do better, now wanted to take up a vulgar instrument like the mandolin. From such a hare-brained idea, he added, nothing beneficial could possibly result: it would merely involve throwing away good money on acquiring the instrument and paying the fees of some rascal who put advertisements in the papers, announcing that he could teach the mandolin in fifteen lessons at fifty kopecks a lesson.

But knowing Papa's temperament well, I did not give up, but persisted in my appeals for a mandolin, swearing on my word of honour that I would get better marks and learn my lessons properly in future. I dwelt on the importance of my receiving a musical education, since it ennobled mankind, aware that Papa, a great music-lover, shared this opinion. I finally succeeded in convincing him that my ambition was genuine, whereupon he yielded, and we took one of the new Belgian trams to the centre of town, where he bought me a beautiful Italian mandolin for four roubles fifty. The tortoise-shell plectron cost him a further forty kopecks.

I noticed that Papa seemed rather upset as he peered into his purse after paying, but he soon recovered and gave me a brisk smile as he said: "I trust you will treat this introduction to music seriously. Remember," he added with a sigh, "that your mamma loved music and was herself an excellent musician. She always hoped her children would become musicians, too."

"I will, I promise you!" I exclaimed with fervour.

"God grant it!" said Papa.

On the way home in the tram, I pressed the mandolin tenderly to my heart, admiring the incomparably perfect shape of its light, hollow body, formed of rosewood strips, and its salient neck, narrowing so elegantly towards the finger-board; admiring all the details on the finger-board—the little mother-of-pearl circles and the spacings between the metal dividing lines, not regular like those on a thermometer but wider at the top, narrower at the bottom, in some mysterious arrangement of their own.

I wanted so much, right there and then in the tram, to cross my legs, put the mandolin on my knee, bend over it, and, manipulating the plectron like an accomplished mandolinist, draw from the paired strings an exquisite, thrilling tremolo. But I restrained myself, glancing modestly at the other passengers, who I felt must be sitting enraptured by the sight of my new, brightly polished mandolin. The future promised endless delight—possibly even fame—when the fifteen lessons had transformed me into a skilled professional.

I was burning with impatience to start the lessons with my teacher and, in preparation for them, sat down on a chair in the middle of the room at every free moment, bent over my mandolin and did my best to extract melodious sounds from it.

It seemed to me so simple!

But the plectron constantly slipped between my fingers, and the sounds that emerged were anything but melodious; they could not even be described as musical, being more in the nature of a dismal tinkle. My aunt stuck her fingers in her ears and quickly retired to her room. Zhenka paid no attention, pretending to be completely unaware of what was going on.

Then, at last, I began my lessons with the teacher—a young man, with long, fair, greasy hair pushed behind his ears, who wore blue, narrow trousers and the uniform-jacket of the Post Office Department over a Russian shirt. He reeked of tobacco and spent most of the lessons rolling cigarettes from light, golden, Asmolov tobacco and telling me about his amorous adventures, whilst scratching his pimply nose with his little-finger nail.

I turned out to be so inept at playing the mandolin that I never even learned how to play a scale. In the end, I stopped going to the teacher and loafed about the town by myself instead, with my mandolin under my arm, glad to be away from his tidy but very small room in a semi-basement, filled with all kinds of cheap bric-à-brac of no use to anyone. The young man rented this room from a Jewish tailor, who lived in the rest of the apartment, and there was a permanent smell of stuffed fish, calico, and children's nappies: the oppressive silence was only broken by the clicking noise of a pendulum and endless trills from a canary.

I spent the money I was given to pay the teacher on aerated green syrups, called "fresh hay," "rhum-vanilla," and coconut-milk; on *rahat-lukum*, "monkey-bread," and other Eastern sweets; on sickly, sugary cornets that looked as if they had been given a coating of varnish. I felt an out-and-out rascal when I returned home and placed the mandolin carefully in the black cupboard in our room, where Papa's frock-coat and our new uniforms hung. I finally grew to hate the mandolin, which had fulfilled none of my early hopes and seemed to bear silent witness to my incompetence.

Luckily for me, Papa treated my changed attitude towards music in an absent-minded way, wrote it off as a loss, and stopped giving me the fifty kopecks for the teacher.

The mandolin then remained untouched in the cupboard for a long time, wrapped in the grey flannel bag which my aunt had made for it. It got covered with dust and only reminded me of its existence by the very faint musical responses it made to the slightest sounds that reached it through the bag: the front-door bell, steps in the corridor, the flush of water in the lavatory, the clip-clop of horses' hooves in the street, the rattle of carriages, the singsong cries and clatter of a tinker like a military-band passing by a long, long distance away, the sad, clear knell of the church-bell during Lent, the barking of a dog, the scratch of a mouse shifting a lump of sugar behind the side-board, any of the ordinary nocturnal noises, even the crackling of wall-paper becoming detached from the wall.

Curiously enough, no-one but me heard these signs from the mandolin, as they floated out from the cupboard to prick my conscience. They filled me with an indefinable fear, and I was afraid to stay alone in the apartment with it, as it watched my every movement, caught my every change of expression from behind the cupboard-door and seemed to repeat all my most secret thoughts in its own musical idiom.

Sometimes I woke up in the middle of the night in a state of in-explicable anguish, and the mandolin immediately woke up, too, and began producing barely perceptible sounds from all its strings, running parallel in pairs like railway-lines. I began to suffer from insomnia and the pillow burned my cheek, as the mandolin's in-sinuating tinkle echoed Papa's snores and the blissful snuffles and smacking of lips that emerged from Zhenka in his dreams. The mandolin, lying at the back of the cupboard near the wall, was in-visible from my bed even when the late-autumn moonlight filtered through the shutters, but somehow I could see it clearly in the grey bag, resting on its convex back, with its flat face and the gentle oval of its mouth, looking like a Greek tragic-mask, exposed upwards.

But chiefly what I saw was its deep hollowness, where the most varied sounds collected and were echoed back; not only the sounds from our apartment, our street, our town, our empire, but also those from the whole world, from its past, present, and future, a sinister, scarcely audible string chorale, embracing preparations for war, mobilisation of military units, stirring marches, meetings of mon-archs, religious songs, church-bells, Te Deums, the secret approach of submarines, the cries of the plague-stricken, the approach of Armageddon, the smell of death, from which, to my defenceless, still-childish mind, there seemed no possibility of escape.

The mandolin tortured me with thousands of nocturnal fears, with torments far beyond my years, and, in the end, pressing it to my breast, I crept out of the apartment like a thief and ran down the stairs, each step accompanied by reproachful sounds from within the grey bag. I reached town and, after enduring a series of humiliating rebuffs from various little junk-shops, finally sold the mandolin for a ridiculous sum—eighty kopecks, of which one coin afterwards proved to be false, a crude, tin reproduction stamped out by local, inexperienced counterfeiters, hiding somewhere in the suburbs of Moldavanka in the catacombs.

I no longer remember on what I spent this dishonestly acquired money; perhaps I just lost it, playing *vingt-et-un* with Zhorka Sobetsky in the attic of his house, perhaps it went some other way. I no longer remember, I do not know, I do not care. But, at any rate, I was rid of that wretched mandolin, which had held out promises of ecstasy and fame and had yielded nothing but agonising musical sighs and empty, profitless sounds. . . .

Before Easter ✍

ALL OUR LODGERS had various oddities and whims. One of the last ones, for instance—a candidate for the bar—had a bird in a cage, a woodpecker or a starling, I do not remember which. I think it was a starling, but it may have been the other way round.

He came to live with us when we moved into the new Apartment Owners' Co-operative house in Pirogov Street. I was at the front, a volunteer in the artillery, at the time of his arrival. Just before Easter, I asked for a fortnight's leave without telling Papa, as I wanted to surprise him by turning up unexpectedly from our positions near Smorgon, where there was a temporary lull.

My aunt no longer lived with us. She had gone to relatives in Poltava, since she considered that Zhenka and I had completed our education and her duty to our mamma, her sister, had thus been accomplished. She was now free to enjoy a private life of her own.

When I walked into our apartment straight from the front, in my active-service gunner's cloak, with a dagger in my belt and a black knapsack on my back, there was no-one at home, apart from a new servant whom I had not seen before, busily engaged in turning out the rooms for Easter. The wide-open windows had just been washed and the spring sky seemed to be hanging on loops from their dark frames. Gusts of April wind swept through the new, four-roomed apartment, equipped with electric light and steam-radiators, and the sun coloured the squares of the well-polished parquet-floor bright yellow.

When she opened the door to me, the servant had been holding an empty cage in her hand. As we had never kept birds as pets, I realised it must belong to the new lodger, who, as Papa had told me in a letter, had rented the room left vacant by my aunt's depart-ture. Tears were pouring down the girl's frightened face and I learned that a disaster had occurred: while she was cleaning its cage, the starling had nipped out, perched for a while on the cupboard to have a good look round and get its bearings, and then flown straight out the window. And that was the last she had seen of it!

She told me that the new lodger would be ever so angry, because he adored the bird, changed its water and gave it its hemp-seed every day himself, and did not allow anyone else to touch the cage.

I had not yet had time to enjoy my own freedom and the cleanliness of our new apartment with all its signs of approaching Easter: the green hillock of freshly picked watercress, the narrow pots of hyacinth, just starting to flower, and a plate of newly coloured eggs—scarlet, green, blue, and lilac—hard-boiled in vinegar to strengthen the shells and rubbed with butter till they shone like mirrors. The window was reflected in each of the eggs and the empty packets of dyes lay on the kitchen window-sill: they bore a picture of a coloured egg, with a yellow chicken peeping out of it. And the large, multi-coloured bouquet of tulips printed on the glossy cover of the Easter number of *Seashore* on the piano in the dining-room gave the house even more of a festive air.

I had not had time to enjoy all this before there was a sharp ring at the front-door bell and the new lodger appeared—a youngish, plain-looking lad in an unbuttoned coat and a Low Courts uniform-cap, with a scarf wrapped round his strong pink neck above a turkey's Adam's apple.

Pushing aside the trembling servant and paying no attention to me, the candidate for the bar entered his, or rather my aunt's room, whistling gaily, and then there was a sudden agonising silence.

A moment later, the lodger appeared in the doorway without his overcoat, a terrifying figure, and demanded almost inaudibly, with a slight Ukrainian accent: "Frossia, where is the starling?" Frossia covered her face with her apron and sobbed. "I'm asking you, where is the starling?" he asked in a still lower voice.

Frossia continued to sob.

The lodger took another glance at the empty cage, then looked at the open window and the neighbouring roof, over which skylarks quivered in a clear blue sky—though how or why they had come to our town from the country-side, who knows? Presently, he turned round with a tragic face, fired with a determination to commit murder if necessary, and said: "I want the bird here!"

He wrapped the scarf round his neck again, threw his coat over his shoulders, jammed his cap onto his head, and walked noisily down the staircase after banging the front-door behind him. From half-way down, he repeated a shout that shook the whole house: "I want the bird here!"

And I stood in the hall, smiling, amused by the impotent fury of this young man—a future pettifogger of a lawyer—who had not smelled gunpowder, had entrenched himself safely in the rear and had no idea what it meant to endure German heavy-artillery fire in our dug-outs.

And how neurasthenic and asinine one must be to demand a bird back once it has flown into freedom. . . . "You won't get it back, my boy, whistle as much as you like. . . ."

Soon after this, I was in an empty train on my way back to the front near Smorgon, and in the Byelorussian forests there were shining lakes of thawing snow. The further from sun and sea, the calmer, the purer the heart and the greater the silence. The breath of approaching spring blowing in through the open carriage-windows as we rushed through swamps and forests seemed to foretell happiness and my spirits soared and songs sprang to my lips.

I watched the dawn through my tears, and when we stopped at stations I heard nightingales sing.

The Birth of a Little Brother 🖋

WHEN NANNY brought me back from our daily walk, took off my outdoor clothes, and I walked into the sitting-room, it was almost dark, and Mamma and another woman, sitting side by side in arm-chairs near a small table, covered by a velvet cloth, were examining a book. It was not the fat album I knew so well, with springy, metal clips and thick, white, gold-edged, card-board pages, which held family photographs. That album always lay beside the oil-lamp, with its tall stand, pretty red base for the oil and pale lamp-shade shaped like a wide-open tulip, through which the funnel emerged to send quivering currents of warm air circulating round it.

When darkness fell, the lamp was brought in already lit from the kitchen, where all the other lamps in our apartment were trimmed, and then the small sitting-room, with its old, well-cushioned furniture, seemed to me to become cosier and more fairy-like as the shadow of the ficus's oval leaves suddenly appeared very clearly on the faded yellow wall-paper. But this time, though the room was already dark, the lamp had not yet been brought in.

I recognised the woman who sat near Mamma, firstly, by the black woollen material of her clothes, which smelled pleasantly of incense and oil, and, secondly, by the white colour of her plump face, surrounded by the edge of a starched kerchief, peeping out from a nun's black coif.

She was an elderly sister from the Sturdzovsk evangelical community and had some kind of connection with our family, particularly with me, that I could not grasp. I had heard people say that she had delivered me, but, as I had no notion what "delivered" meant, I had to accept the connection as a dark, unfathomable secret. I vaguely understood that I had not always lived in this world. Originally, I was not here at all, had not existed or, if I could be said to have existed, it was in some mysterious place where I was neither alive nor dead: and it was from there that Akilina Afanasievna—that was the sister's name—had in some way or other "delivered" me, taking me, a tiny baby, into her warm, plump hands that smelt of the sweet-tasting glycerine I had once licked from the cork of one of Mamma's bottles.

Akilina Afanasievna was regarded by us as a distant relative, and she sometimes turned up on the more important of our festive occasions. One day, Mamma and I went to visit her in the community which housed her in an un-Russian building of strong, rough-hewn stone, with a clock over the entrance; and I remember a dark, narrow corridor, where a small, coloured oil-lamp, suspended on three chains, burned in the chilly twilight before an icon. A strip of carpet ran the whole length of the corridor, muffling the sound of our footsteps.

Mamma did not have time to clutch at my hand before I had pulled one of the chains off its nail; the lamp fell with a clatter to the floor, the flame went out, the wick started smoking, and the oil streamed all over the carpet. To make matters worse, at this very moment the formidable figure of the mother superior, in a black, regal mantle with a tall crozier in her hand, appeared at the end of the corridor: there was a frightening expression on her pale, gaunt face as she raised her dark eyebrows, thick as whiskers. I was so terrified, particularly by the cypress rosary hanging on her chest, that I almost fainted as she slowly came up to me, slapped my hand lightly but quite hard enough for me to feel, and murmured through clenched lips: "You naughty boy!"

I do not remember now how I got away from the community, where I had created such a disturbance, but from then on I became convinced that it was from there that Akilina Afanasievna had delivered me; from that dismal corridor with narrow, Gothic windows, the little icon-lamp smoking on the carpet, and the black figure of the mother superior stretching out her crozier towards me: and I was eternally grateful to her for rescuing me, for carrying me out of that place in her soft arms into God's daylight, into a world where the sun shone, leaves fluttered, sparrows hopped about, and gay clouds, chased by the Langeron wind, swept across the sky above the iron roof of the orphanage.

And now, in the dark sitting-room, I came on Mamma sitting beside Akilina Afanasievna, who had her leather midwife's bag on her knees. I noticed an open book lying on the table: it was unlike any of ours, so Akilina Afanasievna had probably brought it with her. Although the room was rather dark, I could see it was a picture-book and immediately climbed onto Mamma's lap to look at the pictures. I found it uncomfortable there, because I was kept at a distance by her stomach, which had grown very much larger lately, though I had not paid much attention to it. I wanted to get closer to the picture displayed on the open page, as it was difficult to make it out in the twilight from where I was. It struck me as strange and unusual because it contained none of the familiar objects—no people, trees, or houses—that I was accustomed to find in what grown-ups called picture-books.

What I saw was something that looked rather like a twisted cucumber with a large, drooping head and what seemed to me to be the sleepy half-closed eye of a child.

"What is it?" I asked Mamma.

"It's nothing for children," Mamma replied.

"Yes, but all the same, what is it?" I persisted.

"You can't see it properly in the dark," Akilina Afanasievna said with a smile, wanting to distract me. I promptly demanded that the lamp should be brought in, but when it arrived, the book had disappeared. They had hidden it from me somewhere, and the picture that had aroused my uneasy curiosity was no longer in sight.

Next morning, I felt there was something wrong in the house.

Mamma remained in bed; Papa wandered restlessly from room to room and was apparently going to miss school; and Akilina Afanasievna appeared again in the sitting-room with her bag.

I was given milk-tea, dressed up warmly in my overcoat and gaiters as though for a long walk, and, after she had kissed my forehead with dry lips, Mamma told me that the cook was going to take me for the whole day to visit some friends, who lived behind the Langeron cyclodrome, on the edge of the common, where later the new section of Alexandrovsk Park was laid out; now, covered in brown weeds, it stretched as far as the cliffs, where it seemed to overhang the stormy grey sea, and squalls bent and shook the dry tumbleweed and blew a cold dust mixed with dandelion-fluff into our faces.

I was cold in my autumn coat, which was rather small for me, and my thin woollen gaiters. Shivering, I entered an apartment I had never visited before, where two little girls came running into the hall to meet me, followed by their mamma with a welcoming smile. Behind them, I saw their papa, a colonel with side-whiskers in the uniform of the Frontier Guard. He was seated in a rocking-chair and patted my cheek benevolently with a bony hand that reminded me of the hand of my dead Ekaterinoslav grandfather, Mamma's papa, who once upon a time had given me Limonchik.

My new friends had a large, luxurious apartment with a warm, glassed-in terrace, filled with tropical plants and cages of canaries. There was a long dining-room table, surrounded by summer wicker chairs.

The girls were older than I—tall, thin, polite, and forthcoming. They tried to entertain me, as well-brought-up hostesses set out to entertain a rather boring guest. I was given cocoa and biscuits, shown a card-board toy theatre and persuaded to draw various objects on a special kind of smoked glass; and, underlying all their painstaking kindness, one could sense an obscure compassion, sadness, even anxiety.

Their mamma smoked very thin cigarettes, flicking off the lilac ash into a mother-of-pearl shell. From time to time, she called me over to her and stroked my close-cut hair, bristly on top.

(Don't forget those two crowns of mine! I was destined to be "a lucky boy.")

And her expression, too, was compassionate, sad, and, at the same time, tinged with latent curiosity.

Our cook had gone back home after I had heard the girls' mother

tell her not to worry about me—if there was a delay, I could spend
the night with them on arm-chairs in the sitting-room. But what
could the delay be?

I was suddenly filled with anxiety myself. It increased all the time
and, for some reason, was connected with Akilina Afanasievna's bag
and the picture in the book, the meaning of which I was unable to
fathom, although it seemed to me that the reason for my being in
this strange house must lie buried in that mysterious picture, in that
twisted little body with a big, drooping, sleepy head, in that strange
embryo which they would not show me by the light of the lamp
brought in from the kitchen.

Now I come to think of it, I believe her name was not Afanasievna
but Savvishna. Yes, I am sure that was it. But it does not matter
any more than it would matter if her name had been Glikeria instead
of Akilina.

The girls had a governess, and she took us for a walk in Langeron,
where a high tide beat against the rocks and the sea could be seen
turbulent and green in this October storm. I began shivering again
and the governess turned up my collar, with small anchors embroidered on it, and wrapped a worsted shawl round my neck, which
made me feel more miserable than ever.

Under the dark, low-lying clouds sweeping over Langeron, in a
patch of dry weeds near the cliff, there were a number of soldiers
belonging to the Corps of Engineers, who—according to the governess—were on a course in electric telegraphy. They launched a so-
called kite-balloon into the sky and, creaking under the persistent
squalls, it rose diagonally higher and higher towards the black
clouds. It was attached to a thin wire cable that the soldiers with their
green shoulder-straps slowly unwinched from an iron drum. Beside
them in the burdocks stood wooden boxes containing electric batteries, linked to the balloon by a black wire, from which blue flashes
sparked from time to time.

The governess explained to me that the soldiers were sending
electric-telegraph signals to the torpedo-boats driving through the
stormy waters off Langeron. I saw the small figure of a sailor on
the bridge of one of the boats waving two flags with arms that revolved like a windmill's. In all this, there was something new, something sinisterly martial, full of dark forebodings, and, as I tucked

my hands into the sleeves of my short coat, I felt as though I had become an orphan.

I spent the whole day in that house, breakfasted, lunched, and dined there, and I remember how amazed I was by the splendour of the dinner; the soldier-orderly, in regimental shoulder-straps and wearing white cotton gloves, passed round a huge dish of chicken cutlets with green peas and, on the table, there was a big piece of sweating Swiss cheese, with large holes in it, on a long china plate.

Evening came and darkness fell. A sharp wind blew from the direction of Langeron. The lamps had been lit a long time before. In the aquarium, the goldfish were asleep, floating as though hypnotised among the weeds, from which air-bubbles rose like glass beads to the surface.

The strange day, spent in a strange house and the impression left on me by the kite-balloon, with its coloured canvas envelope, as it soared into the sky, sparks flashing from its antenna, combined with the noise of the stormy sea and the rustling burdocks, had tired my brain; my eyes longed to remain closed and I began to whimper. The girls' mamma finally gave orders for me to be put to bed on two arm-chairs placed together in the sitting-room, among the branches of araucaria, bronze statuettes, and large pictures in gilt frames, one of which enchanted me and at the same time frightened me by its beauty: a painting of a black-eyed Neapolitan, with a tambourine raised in her hand. I was aghast at the idea of having to sleep—like an orphan—in a strange room, watched by the piercing black eyes of the red-corseted Italian.

But at this moment our cook arrived, gay and excited, and said to me: "Well, thank God, you've got a little brother! Come along home quickly and see your mamma. She's been worrying about you."

She had brought a large Orenburg shawl with her and wrapped it round me over my coat: it seemed to me to emit a warm, homey smell, reminiscent of my Ekaterinoslav grandmother's kitchen. Hardly able to stand on my feet or keep my eyes open, with burdock-leaves clinging to my knitted gaiters, I found myself back in our small three-roomed apartment, illuminated unusually brightly and gaily by a large number of lamps and candles.

Before I saw my little brother, who had just entered this world of ours—though I could not yet really believe it—I was aware of the smell of well-scrubbed lime-wood and boiling nappies. Then I saw Akilina Savvishna's bag in the sitting-room and finally Akilina Savvishna herself, hurrying in and out of the bedroom in her starched kerchief with her plump, white arms bare to the elbow. She was clearly in charge of the whole situation and the focus of everyone's attention. Papa flashed past me, with his jacket unbuttoned, looking proud and excited. . . .

I walked over to the lime-wood trough, standing on two kitchen-stools, which was the source of the pleasant, aromatic smell I had noticed when I came in. The bottom of the trough was covered with folded fustian nappies, and on them lay a very tiny, long, red baby, with his tummy swathed in gauze.

Akilina Savvishna carefully poured warm water on him out of a jug and gently rubbed his little hands and feet—doll's hands and feet—with her soft palms, as though destined by nature to bathe new-born children. My little brother, come from God knew where, had black hair, which was sticking to his forehead, and his eyes were screwed up as though he were displeased.

Akilina Savvishna held the child face downwards on her broad palm over the trough and Papa, not caring if he splashed his new frock-coat with silk lapels or his starched cuffs, poured water out of the jug along the new-born child's fragile body, curved like a peeled shrimp. Bubbles emerged from the tiny mouth and burst noise-lessly. I watched Akilina Savvishna dry the baby with her hands and then, laying him down on the table, swaddle him tightly, so that he became a hard, immobile doll without hands or feet; only his tiny wrinkled face, red and sweaty, remained visible as it peeped out of the bindings round his head.

Without opening his swollen eyelids, the baby gave several quite loud cries: "Qua, qua, qua!"

Then Mamma, who was lying in bed, her hair spread out on the pillow like a young girl's, smiled tenderly, through her pain, with cracked, bitten lips and murmured in a far-away voice: "Ah, my little Quassy!"

And, for a long time after that, my little brother used to be called Quassy!

When Akilina Savvishna laid the swaddled baby beside Mamma,

bringing his face close to her swollen, moist breast, with a drop of milk on the coral-brown nipple, Mamma stretched out a tanned, exhausted hand to me, stroked my head with its two crowns, and managed to whisper: "Kiss your little brother."

As I brought my lips up to "Quassy's" little, round face, as carefully and reverently as if he had been an icon, I experienced at one and the same time an inexpressible tenderness towards this miraculous work of nature and an agonising, dark foreboding that pierced my heart.

In the Higher Atmospheric Strata ⚔

MY FRIEND Boria and I tried first of all to get on to the race-course belonging to the Russian Horse-Breeding Society—or whatever it was called: I do not really remember—by climbing over the wall without paying, but Boria tore his new silk-lined summer coat and received a nasty slap on the back of the neck from an attendant who suddenly appeared and chased us off. After that, we had to buy tickets like everyone else, for which Boria cashed up with a certain amount of reluctance: I did not have a kopeck on me, but he was always comparatively well-heeled.

On this particular day, the society was not running its usual races on the course, but had made it available for flights in a Farman aeroplane by the famous wrestler Zaikin, one of the great Poddubni's strongest rivals. Zaikin was our idol and some experts considered him, technically, to be Poddubni's superior. He only became an aviator for a short time, because flying was then the fashion and it brought him valuable publicity.

Boria and I were attracted to this flight not so much by Zaikin as by the rumour that Kuprin, the famous writer, who had arrived in Odessa from Petersburg, would be going up with him. Boria was particularly keen to see Kuprin, having just read *The Garnet Bracelet*, *The Duel*, and *Captain Ribnikov*.

There were not many people in the public enclosure; most of them were simple folk like us who had paid at the gate to get in. In the members' stand, there were a lot of ladies in enormous hats,

who had come to have a look at the famous writer and about twenty
students and officers in smart uniforms, who had come on account
of Zaikin, the "Volga Champion"—and, of course, to watch the
flight as well.

There was rather a strong wind blowing and the spectators were
afraid that the flight would be cancelled owing to adverse weather
conditions, as so often happened in those days when aviation was in
its infancy. Street-urchins perched in the trees outside the race-course
were debating anxiously: would flying still be on or not? However,
before long, the wide doors of the wooden shed some way beyond
the stables were flung open and a few soldiers from the local garrison,
with peakless caps, rolled the yellow biplane on its thick rubber
tyres out on to the track. At the same time, Kuprin and Zaikin appeared from nowhere and passed slowly in front of the stands.

. . . the Volga Champion was wearing a yellow leather coat, leather
flying-helmet, and black leather gloves with large ridges on the
back; his corn-coloured moustache, twirled up in wrestler-fashion,
lent an air of determination and fearlessness to his handsome peasant's face. His friend, the famous writer, a sturdy little man with a
round, slightly Tartar face and greenish slits of eyes, walked beside
him in a short, black leather jacket—known as a "Swedish" jacket—
beneath which a thick sheaf of newspapers was just visible. The
rumour immediately spread round the race-course that, in view of
the extremely low temperature prevailing in the high atmospheric
strata to which Zaikin intended to ascend, Kuprin had decided to
increase the warmth of his Swedish jacket by padding it with some
twenty copies of the Odessa *News*. It was as a special correspondent of
that paper that he was accompanying Zaikin on his attempt to reach
a record-breaking height of three hundred metres or more, which
seemed to Boria and me an impossible feat, a veritable aviation
miracle.

"Vania, don't catch cold!" shouted Zaikin's fans from the trees outside the race-course.

"Alexander Ivanovich," excited voices called from the stands, "be
careful for the sake of Russian literature!"

Waving graciously to the spectators, Zaikin and Kuprin finally
reached the end of the straight track, where the soldiers had already
brought the Farman. The French mechanic, who had accompanied

the Gnome engine from Issy-les-Moulineaux, near Paris, was carefully inspecting the biplane, testing the height- and direction-controls and making certain the thin wire struts were firmly fastened. The spectators gazed with envious admiration at his sporty, check flying-helmet—the *dernier cri* from Paris—the brown leather leggings, enveloping his bow-legs, and his Max Linder moustache.

After giving the machine a few shakes, which made it tinkle all over like a musical instrument, Zaikin climbed into the pilot's seat. With a grunt or two, Kuprin clambered up behind him and sat down below the brass petrol-tank, resembling a samovar, in which the cold sun was reflected on this windy, unforgettable day.

The spectators began to applaud and Zaikin stood up and waved his large glove in acknowledgment: Kuprin raised his small cap with a button on top from his close-cut head of hair that left a fringe on his forehead, then replaced it with the peak at the back.

"Contact!" the French mechanic barked.

"Contact!" the Volga Champion echoed in a resounding circus voice and switched on the ignition.

Two soldiers, following the Frenchman's instructions, swung the varnished, wooden propellor several times with considerable effort, the Gnome engine sneezed and finally caught, whizzing round with a great roar and discharging drops of castor-oil, with which it had been lubricated.

Dust rose in clouds.

Boria and I pulled our school-caps down till their peaks rested on our noses and stood side by side, motionless as statues, savouring those last exciting moments before the aeroplane started running forwards, tore itself away from the earth, and reached the record height of three hundred metres, thereby glorifying forever those conquerors of the air and the force of gravity, Zaikin, the great middle-weight wrestler, and Kuprin, the famous author.

"I suppose you realise we're witnessing a historical event?" Boria muttered through his large front teeth, grasping my hand tightly.

"Do you need to ask?" I whispered in reply, tears of ecstasy hanging on my eyelashes. Yes, unquestionably, this was an unforgettable moment! That two incredibly brave men, two idols, should despise danger, ignore the strongish wind, soar above the race-course and dare to ascend to hitherto unattainably high atmospheric strata, where unforeseen dangers might well await them, must surely demonstrate to the whole world what courageous Russian men were capable of!

The soldiers who had been holding the aeroplane by its tail, stamping their feet, scattered to one side and the wind blew their caps away in a cloud of dust as the Farman started to move forward to loud "hurrahs!" from the spectators. It became air-borne, banked sharply to the right, described a quarter-circle, and came to rest gently in the second Jewish cemetery, best known, by the way, for having a marble monument with the inscription in gilt letters below the hexagonal Star of King David: "Here lies Lazar Solomonovich Weinstock, an honest card-player."

The stands gasped. . . . And, immediately, an ambulance with a clanging bell, drawn by a pair of black horses, raced down the course towards the scene of the catastrophe: behind it, galloping flat out, came a number of cabs and private carriages carrying various excited members of the crowd—the French mechanic, the police superintendent, a few elegant students with binoculars, and a lady with a boa of ostrich feathers round her neck, in floods of tears.

Boria and I, terror-stricken, strained our eyes in the direction of the second Jewish cemetery, where the two light wings of the biplane, which had landed on its side, were jutting upwards among the marble monuments. But, despite our dismal forebodings, all ended happily. The ambulance came trotting jauntily back, empty, followed, at a more leisurely pace, by a carriage in which, safe and sound but looking a trifle sheepish as they reclined against the cushions, rode the Volga Champion, Zaikin, and the eminent writer in his Swedish jacket, padded with newspapers to prevent him catching cold in the higher atmospheric strata.

Seeds 🖋

MY AUNT used to go to Werkmeister's market-garden to buy hyacinth and tulip bulbs; also seedlings and flower-seeds.

Sometimes, in early spring, I was suddenly overwhelmed by a feeling, difficult to express in words—a sort of wish to take part in that mysterious process of nature, whereby a dead seed was transformed into a live green plant. I cannot define the feeling more precisely than that.

It would penetrate my whole being, take possession of all my thoughts and desires. And then, as soon as I had managed somehow or other to lay my hands on ten kopecks, I would rush off to the Werkmeister garden on Pirogov Street, opposite the massive, white headquarters building of the Odessa Military District. On this occasion, spring work in the flower-beds behind the bare stone wall had already begun. Two German gardeners, in caps and green aprons, were tending the tall rose-bushes, digging manure in round their roots, pruning the thin stems and attaching metal discs inscribed with the names of the various varieties.

Heaps of black, well-manured earth stood in the sun, giving off a faint blue smoke; water poured from a tap into a large barrel; and, scattered about, were a number of expensive watering-cans and blue, burnished-steel spades, bought, no doubt, at the "Brothers Rauchwerger" ironmonger's shop: all of which went to show that Werkmeister's was a high-class establishment, dealing only in the very best British stock.

Seeds were obtained at the end of the garden from a small shed that was called the office. Clutching the ten kopecks in my fist, I entered the whitewashed room, where Werkmeister himself, in a cap and knitted waistcoat, took charge of sales, producing the packets out of narrow drawers, with white knobs like the stops in a harmonium, in a cupboard that occupied the whole of one wall. A small balance and weights, and several china jars filled with different seeds, stood on the counter, giving the office something of the appearance of a chemist's shop.

Werkmeister, with the head of a Johann Sebastian Bach, leisurely drew out the drawers one by one to give buyers a view of the envelopes, bearing coloured pictures of flowers far more vivid, beautiful, and perfectly formed than any found in nature: pansies, petunias, evening-glory, carnations, nasturtiums, snapdragons. . . .

They were all as yet imprisoned in dead seeds, some of them as small as motes, and it was hard to believe that anything at all could grow out of them, let alone the luxuriant blooms displayed in the pictures.

In the narrow drawers of the wooden cupboard in that one room, there were sufficient flowering plants-to-come to transform the whole of our Black Sea district into a Garden of Eden.

. . . And that, to me, spelled real magic. . . .

It took me a long time to look through all the pictures on the packets, in which the microscopic embryos rustled and slithered, but finally my choice fell on runner-beans. Werkmeister meticulously weighed me out an ounce of beans and wrapped them up in tissue-paper, securing them with a rubber band. They were large and heavy—not more than four or five to an ounce—but they had the advantage of being cheap, only six kopecks: for my remaining four kopecks, Werkmeister allowed me to gather some good garden-soil in a newspaper and threw in some careful instructions as to how the beans should be planted.

At home I immediately emptied out the loose, black, moist soil into an earthenware saucer and buried my large, flat beans in it. They were hard and lifeless, like the chocolate-coloured Langeron pebbles, gently rubbed by the surf until they shone.

Everything around was beginning to bourgeon.

In the kitchen, the hillock prepared for the Easter table was already green. It was a little wooden pyramid, tightly covered with cloth; on this cloth, sticky cress seeds, resembling caviare, were smeared, watered three times a day, and then suddenly began to grow, pushing out tiny, colourless, worm-like sprouts. Finally, the hillock became as smooth and green as a well-kept lawn and, in all its beauty and freshness, filled the kitchen with a sharp, vegetable smell as it waited for the day when it would be surrounded by painted Easter eggs. On the bare horse-chestnut trees on the French Boulevard, enormous buds, looking as if they had been thickly daubed with joiner's glue, were swelling out and getting ready to burst open.

In the cemetery, bright blades of new grass crept out of the soil and thrust their way through last year's half-decaying leaves round Mamma's grave with the white marble cross above her marble tombstone. And, everywhere, plants were waking again from their long winter's sleep.

I could hardly drag myself away from the earthenware saucer containing my runner-beans.

In front of my eyes, the resuscitation of dead seeds was taking place, that mysterious but visible process by which they were transformed into green plants. First, I saw how small, pale shoots crawled out of the motionless beans and then how, fattened by the sap of life, they curved over towards the soil, delved into its depths and began to lay roots, while the beans themselves still remained inanimate.

But this, of course, was only apparently so. I was conscious of the energy of action beginning to develop in them because I had examined one of the frail shoots under a microscope and seen the cell, enlarged a hundredfold, with its transparent protoplasm, containing seeds of chlorophyll and starch, resembling small, ribbed shells.

Peering into the microscope at that astonishing, inner plant-world, inaccessible to the naked human eye, I sensed, though I could not see, a permanent, imperceptible movement in the growing cell, an accumulation of living power, come from God knew where. This unseen power, this uncontrollable energy, seemed to be able to overcome any obstacle. For had I not observed many a time how the stem of an apparently weak, weedy plant had pressed against the asphalt pavement, pierced it, and emerged into the light of day, into the sun? Had I not seen how ivy, clinging to an old church-steeple, had crumbled away the plaster and left great cracks in the brick structure?

At that time, I already knew that this force was somehow connected with the transformation of light into energy and that the process, far beyond my mental ability to grasp, was known as photosynthesis.

Photosynthesis! As though that explained anything!

And while the water-cress hillock in the kitchen grew thicker, greener, and more vivid, while my aunt watered the tobacco-plant and petunia seedlings in their shallow, pine-wood box on the balcony, my eyes remained riveted to my earthenware saucer, where my as yet lifeless beans were buried in Werkmeister's moist soil, as though in a small, circular graveyard. Right there, in front of me, the miracle of their resuscitation was taking place. The spring sunlight, transformed into energy, suddenly turned my beans on to their edges, raised them above the soil, and split them in two, making them open up like coffins: then each fleshy part turned over again and, juicy and green, became a leaf, and the two leaves stood up on one green stem in the form of a crucifix. In my imagination, I saw my saucer as a Golgotha, in which the miracles of death, resurrection and ascension took place in miniature. . . . The twisted stem of the plant, producing further pairs of leaves and then the red earrings of the bean-flower buds, twined itself round the taut piece of string I had provided for it. And the spring sun beat down with such heat on the thick wooden window-sill that the paint burst out in blisters.

The Small Black Poodle ✒

EVERYTHING WAS WONDERFUL on that Sunday morning, everything delighted me, even the mere act of slipping out of the house by the back-stairs and walking through the yard of which I was very fond because the grass was so green by the stone wall separating us from some waste-land, where it was always possible to pick up stray bits of fire-wood. Near-by was a small bungalow where Vitia Ilyin lived: he was a biggish boy, three years older than I, who drew pictures on thick white paper of Russian battle-ships, cruisers, and torpedo-boats, their bows cutting through the waves like knives through cheese, Andreev flags at the mast-heads and their names written in Slavonic characters: *Retvisan. Eagle. Dashing. Aurora.*

Vitia Ilyin promised to teach me how to shade a drawing with a special wadded piece of paper, how to erase mistakes with an India rubber, and also how to blow a bubble of air onto a stick, forming a blister that burst with a terrific noise. I was hoping to find Vitia in the yard, but he was sitting at home, at a table under the window, bending his close-cropped head low over a sheet of drawing-paper: he was probably shading a battle-ship or erasing excessive shadows from the waves furrowed by its stern. I was not greatly disappointed, because I was looking forward to a trip by tram to Arcadia with Papa, anticipating the squeals from the brake on the sharp bends and the stealthy approach of the sea towards our shoes when we reached the beach. Perhaps, I thought, Papa and I might even have a red or yellow syrup and soda—a splendid fizzy drink that tickled one's nose and nipped one's tongue—at one of the booths in Arcadia.

In order to reach Basarnaia Street, one had to pass through a tunnel, at the far end of which one saw, as if through a telescope, the carved arch of our gate and beyond it the dazzling, almost blinding street—completely deserted on a Sunday—the centre of my world at that time.

I was about three years old and walked beside Papa without holding his hand: sometimes I even dared to precede him, which made me feel particularly daring and independent and, consequently, happier than ever. Running ahead of Papa on this occasion, I rushed out of our gate and saw the figure of a man approaching us in the glare of Basarnaia Street. Never in my life had I seen such a handsome gentleman—a real fop in a summer pith helmet with two peaks, one in front, one in the back, known as a "good-day and good-bye," and this by itself threw me into an ecstasy, since it was the first time I had seen such an elegant, original form of headgear. The gentleman wore a black, naval-type cloak fastened in front by two clasps shaped like lions' heads. In his hand, he held a bamboo stick, which, combined with his little, black, pointed beard, little, black, pointed moustache, and, the last word in fashion, a tortoise-shell pince-nez on a silk string, tucked behind one ear, took my breath away, and I immediately determined to become as handsome and elegant as that when I grew up.

Yes, I was completely dazzled.

Even my dear, beloved, darling papa whom up to that minute I had considered the most handsome man in the world suddenly seemed to me commonplace and—God forgive me!—a rather poor specimen.

Beside the handsome man trotted his smallish black poodle, perhaps even more beautiful than his master. He was trimmed in the fashion of the moment, like a lion, with a mane, a well-clipped narrow waist, pompons on his paws and bushy whiskers at the end of his tail, and wore a silk ribbon round his neck. He seemed to have stepped out of the pages of a children's book, and I stood gazing down at this miracle of nature, miracle of a barber's art.

"Come here, little doggie," I cooed tenderly.

And suddenly the poodle rushed at me, placed his front paws with their pompons on my shoulders, opened his wide, deep mouth, displaying a bright-red, wagging tongue and wicked, sharp teeth, and two black, glassy eyes stared into mine.

I turned to stone.

The poodle drummed on my shoulders with his trimmed paws and barked loudly straight into my face. My whole being was stricken with terror and I screamed in a voice that deafened me and the whole of Basarnaia Street and nearly destroyed my vocal cords.

That miraculous Sunday had lost all its attraction. I threw myself at Papa, continuing to yell and shriek as I embraced his knees with trembling arms. Although the poodle was already far away, at the other end of the street, I went on and on until I became completely hoarse and Papa picked me up and carried me home to Mamma.

Though seventy or even more years have gone by since then, my throat still seems to feel the effect of that yelling: I often get a sore throat, my vocal cords are strained, and I see in front of me, as through binoculars, the tunnel to the arched gate, and beyond it sun-drenched, deserted Basarnaia Street as it was at the end of the nineteenth or beginning of the twentieth century: down it strolls a fop in a black cloak and by his side, pomponed paws twinkling along, trots a black poodle, trimmed to look like a lion, with wide-open red jaws and wicked glass eyes.

The Cab-Driver 🖋

HORSES WERE still afraid of railway-engines, steam-rollers, and the early automobiles. They went crazy, smashed carriages, killed passengers, injured pedestrians. A panic-stricken horse in a town street is an appalling sight.

First, I heard the familiar, thin whistle of the steam-roller, which had apparently reached the cross-roads at Basarnaia Street and the French Boulevard, and, with a great deal of clanking and clatter, was running its broad front wheel that looked like a section of a huge pipe over the freshly laid surface of the roadway. Then I caught other, more disturbing sounds above those of the roller: piercing high-pitched neighs, shouts from running men, the bumps of carriages mounting the pavement, the ringing scrape of a rearing horse's hind hooves. Following Mamma, pale as death, her skirt billowing round her, and the cook, whose eyes were round with fright, I rushed out onto our metal-floored balcony, which overhung the street, where something dreadful was happening.

A policeman was running past, clutching his sabre. The yardsmen in white aprons, with plaques bearing their numbers on their chests, were trying to catch the panicking horse. I was too small to be able to see over the top of the railing and had to keep on pulling Mamma's and the cook's skirts to one side in order to get a peep through the perpendicular bars. What I saw froze me with horror and left an impression on me for life.

A horse with frenzied, squinting eyes was galloping wildly down the street, dragging a cab with a broken wheel behind it: and behind the cab, the driver, who had fallen from his seat and became entangled in the blue reins, was being dragged, too. He was a peasant in a cloth coat, with a battered face and broken teeth, and blood dripping from his bushy beard left red splashes on the roadway as though it had been daubed with a broad brush. In the blazing sun, the blood had the sheen of oil-paint, and lacy shadows from the acacias fell on the driver's body, wrapped in the reins: his eyes were wide open but already vacant, fixed in a glassy stare.

It was the first time I had seen a man die an unnatural death. And I can still see that corpse in a blue padded coat being dragged down the street by the reins, past our balcony, past the neighbouring houses, past the coal-shed, with bags of charcoal for samovars standing outside it. These bags had net tops so that customers could see exactly what they were buying. Afterwards, I was reminded of the dead driver in 1917 during an action on the Rumanian front, when we were crossing a wooded valley in the foothills of the Carpathians at dawn. It was damp and chilly and one could hear the thunder of artillery along the whole front some ten versts away and catch the flashes of enemy guns behind the crests of the low hills: bombers and observation-planes of both sides were making occasional sorties. In a hurry to take up our initial position, we were thrusting our way through bushes and stumbling over tree-roots, when we suddenly came on a strange group of motionless soldiers, sitting and lying around a newly made shell-hole. They had apparently been marching along the same route as we were taking now and a German shell had landed in the centre of them.

And there they were, motionless, some in natural, others in unnatural, positions, as calm and peaceful as wax dolls, and only the jagged holes, surrounded by dark stains, in their overcoats to testify to the tragedy that had overtaken them in the fraction of a second.

I was particularly struck by an elderly soldier in a new coat, who, possibly, had been called up from the Home Guard, with a head turned into red pulp and the remains of a bushy beard, apparently splashed with red paint: his neatly packed knapsack lay beside him, ripped by shell-splinters. Immediately I saw him, I had a vision of my far-away childhood, of Basarnaia Street, bathed in a generous sun, and of the doll-like figure of the bearded driver, wrapped in the reins, being dragged past our house by a panic-stricken horse, with white, squinting eyes, followed by the shouts of the pursuers, the general exclamations of horror, the shrill note of the policeman's whistle, and the remote rumble of the steam-roller carrying on with its routine task.

The Cannon-Ball in the Plinth

ONE OF ODESSA'S famous sights was the cast-iron cannon-ball embedded in a corner of the plinth of the Duke of Richelieu's monument on Nikolaev Boulevard, at the top of the stairs connecting the town with the harbour. The statue was in a strictly classic style, presenting the Duke of Richelieu in a toga and sandals, with one hand, grasping a scroll, stretched out towards the sea in the direction of Constantinople and the Bosphorus, a gesture that had a concealed political significance. It was referred to as "the monument to the duke," or, even more laconically, as "the duke." Hence, people would say, "We ran into him yesterday near the duke. . . ."

The cannon-ball embedded in the plinth had its place in history.

During the Crimean War, the English fleet attempted to land a force in Odessa, the harbour nearest to besieged Sebastopol, but the attack was repulsed and the hundred-gun frigate *Tiger* sunk by Russian field-artillery off Malofontan. One of the *Tiger's* guns was saved for a trophy, mounted on a wooden gun-carriage, and placed, as an eternal monument to Russian glory, on the same Nikolaev Boulevard, in front of the town duma's elegant building, designed by the architect Boffo.

Thus, strolling with my mamma under the huge, mottled plane-trees on Nikolaev Boulevard, between the gun and the duke, passing Pushkin's statue on the way, I learned that our town, now so peaceful, easy-going, and polyglot, had once gone through tumultuous days when enemy cannon-balls had flown over its tiled roofs.

I vaguely remember the story told me by my grandmother, Mamma's mamma, which she had heard from her mamma, that is, from my great-grandmother: the story of the artillery ensign Shchegolev, who had repelled the English attack and sunk the *Tiger*.

It appeared that the English frigate was equipped with long-range naval guns, while we had nothing but small field-guns set up on the cliffs, which meant that the English had the fire-power to reach us, but we were unable to reach them. Ensign Shchegolev conceived and submitted a daring plan: to mount our guns on wooden rafts, manoeuvre them out to sea till the frigate came within range, and then sink her. He was given permission to call for volunteers to carry out this scheme of his and raised a squad of dare-devils from the residents of the Odessa suburbs—Peresip, Moldavanka, Dalnik. It consisted of young artisans, labourers, stevedores, and even tramps, all of them men of immense courage, fired with patriotic zeal. With their assistance, Ensign Shchegolev constructed the rafts, mounted the light field-guns on them, put out to sea off Malofontan during the night, and rowed silently towards the frigate. By the time the sun rose, he and his men had brought their guns within range and the battle began. The Russian cannonade took the English by surprise, and a number of well-aimed cannon-balls sank the ten-times more powerful frigate, causing the transports cruising around on the horizon to beat a hasty retreat. Odessa was saved.

My grandmother, repeating what she had heard from her mother, told me that Ensign Shchegolev immediately became a national hero, and the emperor issued orders for him to be promoted to captain.

But the promotion of an ensign straight away to captain raised certain problems. Military regulations had never envisaged such a case and consequently had made no provision for it. Finally, the following solution was arrived at: the whole garrison was drawn up on the Kulikovo field, the officer commanding the Military District ordered Shchegolev to come forward, presented him with new epaulets, and promoted him to second lieutenant. Then, when Second Lieutenant Shchegolev had returned to his parade-station, he was called forward again and promoted in the same way to lieutenant. The procedure was gone through twice more to achieve the lieutenant's promotion to junior captain and the junior captain's to full-blown captain. Regimental colours flapped bravely in the wind, the military band blared out martial music, and the ceremony ended with a march-past, during which Captain Shchegolev took the salute.

. . . I myself became an ensign and even a second lieutenant, but I never got beyond that.

During my childhood, when I walked round the duke, examining the small cast-iron cannon-ball embedded in the plinth, I was puzzled by something. I understood, of course, that the cannon-ball had not become stuck in the monument by itself; it had first knocked off a piece of granite and then, later, possibly several years after the end of the Crimean War, it had been inserted into the base of the monument to remind people of the town's heroic past. But what I wondered was: what had happened to the piece of granite the cannon-ball had knocked off? The cannon-ball was there for everyone to see, but where was the granite? I was convinced that I would find it somewhere among the large, specially selected stones of the gravel strewn generously on the side-walks of the Nikolaev Boulevard and on the raised platform around the duke.

I walked, a small boy, on the crunching gravel, with my eyes glued to the smooth pebbles from the beach, hoping every moment to come on the piece of granite. The small boy had a very clear idea of what the piece would look like; long, narrow, and pink, with dagger-sharp edges. I could not believe that it had completely disappeared: it must be there, close by, possibly right in front of me. Every now and again, I thought I saw it. Here it is; I've found it! But I bent down and stretched out a hand to pick it up, it suddenly vanished and all I was left with was a palmful of gravel.

I went on searching day after day, running along the paths of the boulevard in the shadow of the century-old plane-trees, which had seen the living Pushkin and Gogol, and among the flower-beds, bright with wine-coloured flowers. Sometimes, my search took me as far as the cast-iron statue of the curly-headed Pushkin, and I used to stop and admire the long-jawed dolphins that decorated the plinth. Streams of water spurted from their mouths and dropped in an arch into cast-iron shells. But there was no sign of the piece of granite here, either.

It all took on the aspect of a vivid dream, lacking the ultimate, brightest twinge of colour, or of a once familiar word, erased forever from one's memory, leaving everything around, while not deprived of beauty, pointless and without meaning.

My childish brain could not become reconciled to the idea that the cannon-ball had been inserted into the duke's plinth long, long ago, before I or even my mamma had come into this world, but the piece of granite had somehow disappeared completely from the boulevard. I did not realise the power that time exercises over life; but, perhaps, at that age, I was unaware that such a thing as time existed at all and was in no position to be troubled by the question: Does memory destroy time, or time destroy memory? The remarkable thing about it all was that every time I passed the duke, I searched diligently for the piece of granite. And quite recently, when, as an old man, I paid a visit to my home town and went for a stroll down the boulevard, I caught myself staring down at the gravel, looking for the granite, as I walked round the duke, and I really half-expected to find it at last.

. . . And who could count the bombs, shells, and rockets that had passed over me and my town in the intervening years?

The Microscope ✒

IN THE END it suffered the same fate as so many of the valuable things that Papa bought me in response to my persistent requests. Usually, my enthusiasm cooled down very quickly, and I finished up by selling the object, which had begun to bore me stiff, for a quarter of its original price. Though always with a pronounced sense of guilt.

My relationship with the microscope followed the normal course. I started out by regarding it as a miracle of optical science and, a short time later, found it even more boring than the mandolin.

Papa bought it for me as an educational instrument, intended to broaden my concept of the world around me. By his standards, it was rather expensive—it cost about five roubles—but it magnified specimens to a hundred times their actual size. It came in a lacquered box, fastened by two brass hooks, and the austere appearance of the case alone seemed to guarantee that its contents were closely allied with science in one form or another. I took the microscope out some twenty times in the course of an hour and admired its shiny metal surface, its adjusting-screws, its eyepiece, and, most of all, its small round reflector, which turned so gently and easily on its axle, and projected light onto the tray that held the two glass slides, between which the specimen due to be examined was laid.

First of all, of course, I caught a fly, to study the construction of its wings and legs under the microscope. They looked enormous, seen through the eyepiece, the wings rainbow-tinted round the edges, the legs rough and hairy. But I had been expecting more than that: I had been expecting magic. And all I saw were small, graceful objects magnified into monstrosities. There was no magic about that, no magic in seeing a fly's eye blown up till it looked like a balloon enveloped in a membrane mat.

I decided next to investigate a fine, silky-gold hair, pulled from Nadia Zaria-Zarianitskaia's head, without her being aware of the theft. Once I had it between the glass slides, I peered into the eyepiece, hoping to see something fairy-like. At first, there was nothing but a blur in the bright circle of lights, but when I had made the necessary adjustments, I was suddenly confronted with a golden log or something that might have been the coarse stem of a plant, such as bamboo, with a white bulb on the end of it. Could this be the hair from Nadia Zaria-Zarianitskaia's head that I had brought back from school carefully enclosed in my scholar's card?

Was it possible that Nadia's lovely blue eyes, almost the colour of aquamarines, her rust-coloured lashes, and her golden freckles would be transformed under the microscope into coarse, unnatural, ugly objects, the size of an elephant?

If so, who wanted that?

I was bitterly disappointed in my microscope. It did not reveal to me any of the secrets existing in substance or matter on which I had been counting. There seemed nothing to be gained from magnifying things a hundred times over.

But there was a rich boy at school, I heard, who had a microscope that magnified five hundred times. I saw it, and by comparison mine looked pathetic.

His microscope had a special lighting apparatus—a round, crystal ball, filled with water, through which the light from an electric lamp was reflected with enormous brilliance onto the glass slides.

Its rich owner showed me the blood circulation of a tadpole. Looking into the eyepiece, I saw a section of a semi-transparent body, pierced by the ray from the crystal ball, with pulsating particles passing across it like a dotted line. The boy explained to me that they were red corpuscles or albumen tissues or something of that sort.

Now, that really was a microscope!

From then on, my cheap one, lying on my table beside the globe and the cinematograph-projector, played no further part as a scientific instrument. But when the soul of the great Mendeleev entered into my body and I performed my "dreadful" chemical experiments, the sight of the microscope inspired me.

Later, it went the way of my mandolin.

The Diamond Crown 🖋

To GET HOLD of some wire was a simple matter: there were rolls of it lying in the cellar, ready for use when the house was illuminated on the tsar's celebration days. It was stretched between the trunks of two acacia-trees in front of the building, with small, multi-coloured, hexagonal lanterns suspended from it. Christmas-tree candles were lit inside the lanterns, throwing bright, vacillating outlines of stars down onto the pavement. Alongside the cluster of lanterns, there were a number of tricolour flags in the cellar, which hung over the gate on more solemn occasions.

After snipping off a length of wire from one of the rolls, I took it up to our apartment and, with the aid of pliers, twisted it into the shape of a crown: actually, it looked rather more like a basket, but this did not really matter, as it was not the finished article, merely the framework. Then I set about preparing a salt solution, which was not an unduly complicated process. First, I poured cooking salt, fetched from the kitchen in a wooden canister, little by little into a large glass of tepid water. One went on doing this until the salt stopped dissolving, which meant that saturation point had been reached. Next, I lowered the crown carefully on a piece of string into the salt solution, so that it hung just short of the bottom of the glass, and kept it in that position, as the rules governing this fascinating experiment demanded, by attaching the other end of the string to a pencil laid across the top of the glass. Finally, having stowed away glass, salt solution, and crown somewhere safe, one had to summon up all one's patience and wait.

After three weeks or, perhaps, as much as a month, the water would have evaporated from the solution, leaving the salt, in the shape of pretty crystals, adhering to the wire, and the framework would be magically transformed into a diamond crown.

In theory, it was all quiet simple—quantity transformed into quality—but in practice . . .

In practice, the process presented certain difficulties. The greatest of them was the matter of patience. It demanded incredible patience not to disturb the glass before the right time. The sacrament of crystallisation had to take place in perfect immobility and calm.

With the greatest care, I climbed on a chair with the glass containing the framework of the crown, placed it on top of the cupboard, and pushed it well back towards the wall. In my opinion, this was the safest place in our apartment for the glass to remain untouched till the transformation occurred.

It was all I could do to prevent myself climbing up on the chair several times a day to inspect the glass, shining mysteriously in the dust covering the top of the cupboard. I warned the cook not to dust the cupboard under any circumstances, a caveat she received with the greatest of pleasure. I also begged the family to open the cupboard very gently and to pass it, when they must, on tiptoe. In return, I promised them they would witness the miracle of crystallisation.

The astonishing thing was that I managed to produce the willpower to prevent myself ruining the whole thing by over-hastiness, though I must admit that I stood on my bed several times to check from afar whether the level of the solution was getting lower, as it should. And it was; little by little, the liquid evaporated, leaving faint traces on the side of the glass to record where it had once been. But, slightly astonished myself, by the firmness and resolution I was displaying, I never actually touched the glass.

And fate rewarded me.

One splendid day, I climbed on a chair, looked at the top of the cupboard and, lo and behold, the crystallisation had taken place.

In my heart of hearts, I had always entertained doubts as to the experiment succeeding, and I could scarcely believe my eyes when, instead of the bare wire framework, I was confronted by a shining, fairy-like crown, studded with what appeared to be rock-crystal. It looked like a pavilion in a winter garden, sparkling in the rays of a January sun amid glistening, faceted fragments of ice. This impression was strengthened by the weather outside, frosty, sunny, and cloudless; with dainty, ostrich-feathers of snow on the trees in front of old lady Jasikova's bungalow, where her grandson had just died of consumption. He was a young man, with a long, thin nose and large white teeth, which projected under a scrappy moustache.

Through the windows covered in hoar-frost, one could see the multi-coloured icon-lamps and funereal candles, and I entered the old lady's small sitting-room, filled with clouds of incense, and gazed in terror at the silver coffin and the waxen face of the dead man lying in it.

My luck followed me to school. On the way there, I had a chance to swank about my salt-encrusted crown, displaying it first to Nadia Zaria-Zarianitskaia, who was wearing an elegant fur coat, her satchel on her back, and then to Zhorka Melnikov, thereby, I believed, considerably raising my stature in their eyes. And when I reached our school, which was permeated through and through by the brilliant, wintry sun, my little crown again made a great impression, despite the fact that many boys and already produced similar ones, though, in my opinion, much inferior to mine. When I took mine to the teachers' room and showed it to Akazapov, he approved of it, saying something like: "Kraevich and I both consider your experiment with the salt solution most successful. Well done! Keep up the good work!"

It was one of the happiest days of my life: I shone with triumph and joy in the same way as the little crown I had created shone like a diamond when a ray of sun fell on it.

The only thing that slightly marred my pleasure was the crown brought into class by a rich, inventive boy. His crown was rather like mine, but it was covered not with white but with bright-blue crystals, which gave it the appearance of being constructed from the purest of sapphires. It turned out that he had used copper sulphate instead of cooking salt, and by this means produced the dazzling blue colour that provoked such general admiration.

I almost wept with vexation when the sapphire crown was exhibited in the display cabinet and Baris gave its creator the highest mark; I promptly decided to make another one of my own, even more sparkling and blue than his, but was unable to do so; firstly, because I had no money with which to buy copper sulphate and, secondly, because I had no idea from whom I could procure it. Nevertheless, I think you must admit that my original one wasn't too bad.

Each time I read *Boris Godunov* and reached the spot where Marina says to her maid: "My diamond crown," I see the dark cupboard and the glass with the solution of cooking salt, already shining sufficiently to adumbrate the crown to come. . . .

And the sad snow-covered trees in front of old, little Jasikova's bungalow, where the flicker of icon-lamps and funereal candles is just visible through the frozen windows.

The Steam-Roller 🖋

THE GREEN STEAM-ROLLER, enveloped in steam, moving up and down the French Boulevard beyond the Military Academy, beyond Pirogov Street, somewhere between Baltiuk's villa and the Botanical Gardens, attracted boys, not only by its revolving flywheel, enormous power, and noisy progress, which made the windows in the houses rattle and horses run wild, but also because there were always pyramidal heaps of road-metal alongside the road where it was operating. This road-metal came from afar—from mines and quarries in the Urals, the Caucasus, the Don Basin, and Siberia.

At first sight, the heaps seemed as commonplace, uniformly grey, and uninteresting as any other piles of broken stones. But one bright autumn morning, examining a heap with my piercing, curious eyes, I discovered that each stone had its own individual colour and structure.

Some of them glowed with vermilion cinnabar, some were shot with lapis-lazuli; others were tinged with green verdigris, and everywhere among them were facets of multi-coloured granite flashing with mica and dotted with bright-blue or dark-red spots.

To the accompaniment of the steam-roller's whistle and clanking rumble, I dug in the heaps of road-metal, discovering more and more unsuspected beauty in the minerals destined to surface the roadway. To me, they seemed like precious stones, especially the small, heavy yellow ones, which shone so vividly in the rays of the dry September sun that I seriously took them to be virgin gold. There were also pieces of virgin silver, though I understand that nothing approximates to this in nature. But I dealt with the laws of nature according to my own discretion. I filled my satchel and the pockets of my black cloth school-trousers with stones and then, settling down in the scorched grass of the long-neglected Botanical Gardens, under a honeysuckle-bush or a hazel-tree, its still-green leaves warmed by the autumn sun and woven together here and there by the silk threads of a spider's web, I examined all my riches, convinced that I was holding in my hands virgin gold, silver, rock-crystal, sapphires, jasper, rubies, and cornelian.

How wonderful it was to sit there beneath the bright Black Sea sun in my winter school-suit, sweating under the arm-pits and under my collar, feeling the German silver buckle on my leather belt red-hot from the sun's rays, continually lifting my peaked cap to wipe the perspiration from my forehead, from which the summer tan had not yet disappeared, and, ecstatic with admiration, sifting through my precious, colourful collection of minerals.

Of course, at the back of my mind, I was aware that they were not actually precious stones but road-metal, only of use for paving streets, and that the real stones, gold, silver, rock-crystal, diamonds, and so on, had remained in the far-away lands of the incredibly big and rich Russian empire, eventually to find their way into the hands of prospectors, gold-miners, millionaires, industrialists, and metallurgists.

But who knew? Possibly, in the heaps of road-metal, there lurked some undiscovered gems. After all, miracles did take place in the world.

Nothing would make me believe that one piece of metal, shining so brightly and expensively in the sun, was anything but virgin gold. And I was reasonably certain that I had found a small piece of dark-blue sapphire embedded in some raspberry-coloured granite. As for a large piece of transparent stone, I had no doubts whatever that it was rock-crystal. In the end, I became convinced that luck was on my side: I was one of those fortunate people into whose hands riches are suddenly showered.

I had saved a ten-kopeck piece from the money I was given to buy candles each Sunday when I went to church. I felt so happy that I bought half a pound of the cheapest grey halva, on yellow butter, at a grocer's on the way home and ate so much of it that I felt sick and for a time lost all interest in my stones.

But when Papa returned from a meeting of the scholastic council in the evening, my stones were shining as alluringly as before in the light of the paraffin lamp. I rolled them out on the slightly moth-eaten, ink-stained, green cloth on Papa's desk, surrounded on three sides by little wooden railings, and plagued him to tell me if they were valuable. He put on his pince-nez and started examining my collection, picking the stones up one by one, raising them to eye-level and pronouncing pedantically, as he laid them aside: "Granite. Basalt. Quartz. Feldspar. Bauxite. Feldspar again. Shale. Zinc-blende."

I listened to those names, hoping that they indicated something precious, but Papa had such total indifference written on his face that my hopes of riches faded away every minute.

"Isn't that one virgin gold?" I asked when he came to the yellow mineral, gleaming under the lamp with its green shade.

Papa smiled. "I'm afraid I must disappoint you," he said. "This is ordinary copper pyrite."

"But why does it shine like pure virgin gold?" I demanded, puzzled.

"It's the shininess that tells me it isn't gold," Papa replied. "Real virgin gold has a dull colour and bears little resemblance to the gold we usually see in jewellery shops. Moreover, if it had been real gold, it would have been considerably heavier. This is definitely copper. In short," he ended sententiously, with a professional smile, "as the proverb wisely says: 'All is not gold that glitters.'"

There was one hope left: the crystal. I showed Papa a large piece of the transparent mineral, reflecting the evening lamp-light in our apartment in its facets.

"You aren't going to say this isn't rock-crystal?" I asked hopefully.

"Again I must disappoint you," Papa answered, scarcely glancing at the mineral in my hand. "That isn't rock-crystal; it's just the most ordinary quartz, a kind you can find anywhere."

I was crushed. My treasures had turned out to be a heap of stones of no value whatsoever. They suddenly grew dim, lost their former metallic qualities, and became shapeless and grey, like the cheap halva on the smelly yellow butter, on my tongue and in my throat.

Well, there was one more illusion gone. Such is life. I gathered the stones up from Papa's table in silence, took them into the kitchen, and threw them into the dust-bin, where they fell with a dull, vulgar clatter. When I came back to our combined sitting-room, bedroom, and study, Papa, in the lustrine jacket he wore at home, was already absorbed in correcting his pupils' exercise-books with a pencil that was red at one end and blue at the other. The lamp, under the green shade, shone down on his table, which for some reason we referred to as his office-desk: on it, there was always to be found a malachite desk-set. It comprised a flat slab with a wide groove in the middle, in which stood two cubical, glass ink-pots; two copper candlesticks with copper handles on malachite stands; a metal paper-knife with a malachite handle; a malachite stand for stamps and drawing-pins; and a malachite paper-weight. There had once been a malachite pen, but this had been broken in the distant past. Papa had inherited the antique set, which had been bought in Ekaterinburg in the Urals, where there were many malachite mines, from his papa— my Viatka grandfather; and he, in turn, I was told, had inherited it from *his* father—my great-grandfather.

In its time it had been very beautiful and vivid, but with the years it had grown dim, its edges had become chipped here and there, and the stearin from the candles had turned the copper candlesticks green. It no longer had its former splendour. But sometimes, on important occasions, Papa would wash and clean it himself, and then it became transformed: the copper shone brightly and the zigzagging veins in the malachite slab and stands sparkled again with the same vivid green as the Black Sea waves painted by Aivazovsky.

And I was not surprised that this family treasure was so highly prized.

The Dive of Death ✍

UNUSUALLY LARGE POSTERS stuck up around the town announced that, after the motor-cycle races run daily at the cyclodrome, that

world-famous defier of the laws of gravity, the fearless Dazarilla,
would perform his amazing DIVE OF DEATH. . . . Or words to that
effect. . . .

Half the town had seen this formidable feat before Boria and I
could raise the price for our tickets, but we managed to do so for
the final performance, even though we had to pay twice as much
since it was Dazarilla's benefit-night. On this occasion, it was announced that he would make the death-dive into fire instead of
water, which meant that flaming kerosene would be floating on the
surface.

"It can't be true. It's obviously a trick of some kind," Boria declared sceptically, screwing his lips up over two large, prominent
front teeth and pulling his cap down over his forehead, which gave
his face a particularly implacable expression. He twiddled his thumb
and long, musician's fingers in front of his small nose to emphasise
the fact that we were in for a swindle. As he was well up on many
of Sherlock Holmes's cases, he had a flair for sniffing out crimes and
cheating.

"Let's keep a close eye on him," said I.

"I'm certain they'll throw a human-looking dummy into the fire,"
said Boria.

"It's more than possible," I agreed.

The cyclodrome was packed. An uninteresting race had just finished and the winner, Efimov, after completing a lap of honour on
his sputtering Wanderer and filling the stadium with a stink of
benzine, was disappearing through the doors of the competitors'
shed.

A mast the height of a three-storied house had been driven into
the green lawn in the centre of the cyclodrome. There was a small
wooden platform without railings at the top of it, on which two
fluttering national flags lent a solemn air to the coming performance.

A little way in front of the mast, a square hole had been dug to a
depth of about six feet and filled with water: a can of kerosene or
possibly benzine stood near-by on a heap of the moist, black, excavated earth.

Wooden cross-beams, looking like the divisions on a thermometer,
had been inserted into the mast at regular intervals to enable the
fearless Dazarilla to climb up to the shaky platform on top of it,
whence he would dive into the water-filled, flaming hole.

The race-course authorities allowed the public to approach the mast and the hole to satisfy themselves that everything was above-board. Boria and I thrust our way through the crowd, tested the mast on which the fresh coat of whitewash was not yet dry, and then stepped out the dimensions of the hole: it proved to be three steps square. In addition, elbowing people aside, I managed to reach the can and examine the contents. Everything was in order: it had kerosene in it.

Boria and I stood for a while, staring up at the small, beflagged wooden platform, which seemed to be floating at an incredible height among the pink evening clouds, standing out against the background of the bright seashore sky. To dive from such a height into a small and, from above, absolutely, minute, hole, would certainly be deadly dangerous. The smallest deviation from the correct line of flight would mean missing the hole and falling to one's death. Even if one escaped this fate, one might be burned to death in the kerosene flames or, if one dived too deep, one might first break one's out-stretched arms and then the vertebrae of one's neck.

It became obvious to us that if there were no cheating, death was standing beside us, invisible but ready to tear the soul from Dazarilla's body if he missed the hole and lay spread-eagled on the grass.

We took up positions at the top of the stand behind the seats oc-cupied by richer spectators than we and stood bewitched, unable to tear our eyes away from the white mast and the platform on top of it.

Actually, the whole performance need not have lasted more than five minutes, allowing three for the climb, one for the preparations to dive, a second to light the kerosene, and a few more for the dive itself. But it was mounted according to all the best circus traditions, with deliberate delays to whet the appetite of the spectators and eventually stimulate them to deafening applause.

The military band took a long time to play a sad waltz, "The For-est Fairy-Tale," and the sound of the brass instruments, the dull thuds of the Turkish drum, and the clash of cymbals echoed back from the beautiful walls of the third school, the stone structure of the diocesan school, and the granite Alexander pillar, the bronze top of which could be seen above the trees in Alexandrovsky Park, vying in height with the top of the white mast, from which the dive was to occur.

The spectators impatiently awaited the appearance of the mysterious Dazarilla. And he lingered and lingered and nobody knew when and from where he would make his entrance. Some people thought he would arrive at the cyclodrome in a car with his beautiful wife, who would accompany him to the very foot of the ominous mast. Others maintained that he had arrived a long time before and was sitting in the cyclists' changing-room, playing dominoes with his manager.

The band finally stopped playing, having exhausted its repertoire. A tense silence fell.

Boria and I freed our sweating necks, which had become stuck to our starched collars.

And still Dazarilla did not appear.

A rumour circulated that he had fallen ill, the death-dive would have to be cancelled, and the spectators would receive their money back. This provoked an angry uproar. People did not want their money back: they wanted to see the entertainment that might end in death. It is shameful to have to admit it, but Boris and I, at the very back of our blood-thirsty minds, half-longed to see Dazarilla miss the hole: in our imaginations, we could already see his dead body lying on the green grass beside the flaming kerosene.

The wait went on and on. In desperation, the manager, in a bowler hat and dyed whiskers, gestured to the band to play something lively and they embarked reluctantly on a pot-pourri from *The Merry Widow*.

And Dazarilla did not appear.

The sight of various officials running to and fro between the cashier's booth and the changing-room suggested that something was seriously wrong. The general manager, an elderly Jew in a silk scarf, from which a hot, red neck protruded, who had organised the whole entertainment, went to join them, and another, tortured silence fell on the stadium. The band started up again for the third time with an old-fashioned waltz, "On the Hills of Manchuria," which seemed rather inappropriate to our age of steam and electricity.

The crowd grew restless and began to pass critical and insulting remarks: someone threatened to fetch the police, while a number of high-pitched voices demaded their money back.

When the band gallantly started up for the fourth time, the spectators drowned it with yells and booing. This brought the general manager out into the centre of the arena, where he pressed a mega-phone to his dyed moustache and announced in a trembling but stentorian voice that the dive would take place in exactly ten min-utes: the fearless Dazarilla had just arrived and was getting ready to make his entrance. The spectators were reassured. The band burst forth with the "Toreadors' Song" from *Carmen,* and it was to these stirring sounds that Dazarilla's carriage and pair drove past the stands and made a circuit of the race-track. He was wrapped in a black cloak and wore a black mask. Standing up in the carriage, he greeted the audience with an upraised arm in the grandiose gesture of a Roman gladiator, while his elderly wife, in a hat that had slipped onto the back of her head, wept bitterly as she clutched his free hand and occasionally kissed it.

Dazarilla's small children were in the carriage, too: two boys, one in a sailor-suit, the other one in a school-uniform, and a small, red-haired girl, with two plaits that hung down beneath her knitted hat that looked rather like a flower-pot. But nobody was paying any attention to them.

Having completed his circuit of the track to roars of applause from the spectators, Dazarilla got out of the carriage a trifle labouredly and walked over to the mast to make certain it was still firmly planted in the ground.

Then a dramatic scene took place—Dazarilla's farewell to his family. I am afraid I have not sufficient talent to do it justice: I can only say that it was so genuinely moving that it reduced a number of the spectators to tears and most of the ladies preferred to turn their heads away rather than go on looking, all this despite the fact that everyone was aware that the melodrama was merely part of what circus-folk called "building up the act."

Finally, having played havoc with the nerves of the sensitive south-ern crowd, Dazarilla slowly began to climb the mast, pausing at every cross-beam to draw breath and glance down at the members of the town council's medical board, who were obliged to be present when such a dangerous feat was presented.

Boria noticed that streams of sweat were pouring down from under Dazarilla's mask and acquiring a lilac tinge after passing through his moustache. He was far from being the intrepid, slender athletic Dazarilla, with gloomy Baudelairean eyes, whom we had conjured up after reading the description of him on the posters. The band had stopped playing and the musicans were busily engaged in shaking the spittle out of their instruments. Such a deep silence had fallen on the spectators that one could hear the steamships' whistles and the grinding of the winches down in the harbour. Now, Dazarilla had reached the top of the mast and was standing on the shaky platform between the two national flags with his long black cloak billowing out behind him. There was something hesitant about him as he stared down at the hole, where the kerosene was being poured over the surface of the water.

For a moment, Boria and I thought he was feeling giddy and was about to climb down again.

"Coward!" Boria muttered contemptuously through clenched teeth.

"Then they'll have to give us our money back," said I.

At that moment, Dazarilla flung off his black cloak with a decisive, sweeping gesture and it floated down, like an eagle with outspread wings, to the lawn below, which had suddenly taken on a more vivid, dazzling green. The spectators stirred and there was some sporadic clapping. The diminutive Dazarilla stood on the platform in a black leotard, slightly too large for him, with a big white skull and crossbones embroidered on the chest.

"Light the kerosene!" he shouted down in a weak voice, then turned to the band and added: "Drums!"

The reddish-black flame of the kerosene flared up above the hole and, simultaneously, there was a loud roll on the drums that sent shivers down my spine. Dazarilla peered down again, shook his head, closed his eyes, and then, with upraised hands, palms pressed together, dived.

It all happened so rapidly that Boria and I only came to our senses when the firemen were already extinguishing the flames and Dazarilla was being hauled out of the hole with some difficulty by his frail arms, alive and unharmed, but shivering from the cold, and wet as a drowned mouse. In the black, over-large leotard, which revealed his thin, hairy legs, and with his mask slightly displaced, he drove round the race-track to the accompaniment of a fanfare from the band. Standing up in the carriage, he clasped his wife's shoulder with one hand and with the other clumsily sent kisses towards the spectators. Boria and I thought he was crying, and the dye from his moustache streamed down his chin.

"Good man!" murmured Boria, who was severe but just. "Bravo for not missing the hole!"

All the same, we were disappointed. He was not the Dazarilla we had expected to see and we were already regretting having spent so much money on the tickets, all the more so because everything had ended so successfully!

I would have forgotten this story altogether, if, some thirty or forty years later, I had not happened to be having supper in a theatrical club in Moscow with friends of mine, the singer of comic songs, S., and the director, G. The room was filled with actors, musicians, managers, poets, and dramatists, who often met there about one in the morning after the theatre.

During a gay, desultory conversation, S. glanced into a far corner of the cellar, where a small, shabbily dressed old man, with lilac pouches under his eyes, was sitting drinking beer and puffing out clouds of tobacco-smoke.

"See that fellow?" said S. "Nothing much to look at, is he? But, actually, he's a legendary figure. A hero. Used to be a minor impresario way back: presented Dazarilla, who was quite well-known at the time, in a high-diving act from the top of a fifty-foot mast into a lighted tank of kerosene. One day, Dazarilla got so tight, he couldn't stand up, let alone do the dive. So, rather than give the spectators their money back, that fellow over there, the impresario, performed the dive for him. He'd never done anything like it before in his life: might easily have broken his neck." S. laughed and added: "As he started climbing the mast, he uttered the historic words: 'I'd rather die than return the gate-money!' "

I turned to look at the old impresario. Certainly, there was nothing remarkable about him. But, you must admit, he behaved heroically on that occasion, preferring to risk his life to the prospect of being ruined and bringing his wife and children, two boys and a girl, to destitution.

Pictures in an Exercise-Book ✍

PERHAPS THE GREATEST, most irreparable loss in my life was the disappearance of the exercise-book into which Mamma stuck pictures for me. I was probably only two at the time, but I very well remember the three-sided bottle of gum with a small cork, through which protruded the handle of the brush, covered with white, hardened streaks of the gum.

Mamma would take the flat brush out of the bottle, carefully smear the back of the picture with gum, and place it on a clean sheet of the home-made exercise-book, solidly sewn together with a white thread secured by a knot. She would then smooth the glossy surface of the coloured picture down with the dear, warm palm of her hand, fragrant from the aroma of the gum. The pages of the exercise-book were made of excellent, firm paper, which Papa had procured from somewhere or other.

Before I ever saw a real lilac-bush in bloom, I knew what it would be like—vivid, elegant, and motionless. Before I ever saw a real live cat, I had seen a picture of one—a pretty little cat with glassy eyes and a blue ribbon round its white neck. I saw an angel with a silver halo round his head and white feathery wings sprouting from his back—a beautiful, unearthly creature with long hair like a pretty girl's and the clean, white forehead of a clever boy, dressed in a pale blue robe, beneath which two bare, little, human feet were just visible.

I saw a chimney-sweep in a top-hat, with a ladder over his shoulders, standing on a roof beside a German-style brick chimney, from which New Year smoke was pouring. I saw a basket full of apples, a peacock with its tail outspread, a lace fan that took up the whole of one page and dance-favours in the shape of stars and medals attached to bright ribbons.

All these pictures thrilled me by their beauty and symmetry and made a great impression on me. But, at the same time, their immobility and silence frightened and repelled me. I turned the pages of the exercise-book, feeling frustrated by their exaggerated, unreal realism: it was rather like eating something delicious in one of my dreams and waking dissatisfied.

There was something lacking.

Mamma gave me a penetrating look and realised what it was that I missed. She fetched Papa's ink-stand and a blue, wooden pen and began writing a little, explanatory story under each picture in her small, feminine handwriting; and as she did so, she read them out to me slowly, almost in a whisper, as though she were imparting a pleasant secret: "Here is a small, furry kitten, who lost his mamma and was left all alone in the street in nasty, cold rain. He was drenched and hungry and stood shivering by a strange gate, miaowing pathetically. Some children saw him, took pity on him, and carried him to their home, where they dried him, gave him some warm milk, and combed out his soft hairs. The kitten grew quite kittenish, his eyes sparkled and he began to lick his little face with a pink tongue; then he screwed up his eyes and purred. . . . The children were delighted, put him to bed on a soft pillow and, next day, gave him back to his mamma-cat, who was outside the house, miaowing plaintively for her lost kitten. And that's the kitten there in the picture. Isn't he pretty?"

Or: "Who is that black gentleman in a top-hat, with a ladder behind his back? He's the chimney-sweep, who's climbing up on the roof to clean the chimney and then drop a big chocolate sweet in silver paper into it. The sweet will fall down the chimney and land straight in the stocking hanging at the end of the sleeping boy's bed. And the boy will wake up in the morning and—lo and behold!—there is the chocolate sweet in its silver paper. So you see what a kind, good chimney-sweep he is! In spite of being covered in soot and so very, very black outside, he has a kind, pure soul inside."

And: "Take a good look at this Spanish lace fan. It spent all yesterday evening at a ball in the hands of a beautiful lady, who used it when she sat out between dances. Afterwards, the lady was tired and so was the fan, and they both fell into a sweet, deep sleep as soon as they got home; the lady in her luxurious bedroom and the fan in the hall, on the table under the mirror, spread wide open, because the lazy beauty in her eagerness to get to bed did not bother to close it. And now try to guess this riddle: 'When the wind blows, I don't work. If I work, the wind blows. And when I work, the wind always blows away from me. What am I?' " Mamma asked the question, smiling at me enigmatically and admiring the picture of the transparent lace fan with silvery edges. After a short silence, when it was clear that I could not come up with the answer, she stroked my cheek with the palm of her hand and whispered into my ear: "A fan!"

Every evening, Mamma stuck new pictures into the exercise-book, and wrote little stories underneath them, so that we ended up with a home-made picture-book and reader. At one time so new and so firmly sewn together with the flax thread, it gradually deteriorated with constant use. The ink began to fade, thumb-prints, smudges, and stains from spilt milk cropped up here and there, the pictures lost their original glossiness, and some of them became unstuck, and the paper grew yellow, but every time I opened it, a wonderful, sad feeling of love for my mamma swept over me, first while she was still alive and then after she died so young. From early childhood, she taught me to notice and admire the world, the shapes and colours of all the things surrounding me, and invested them with another life by linking them with words and filling them with an inner, sometimes secret, meaning that challenged my imagination. She was adept at weaving them harmoniously and excitingly into her simple narratives.

After Mamma's death, the exercise-book was kept in Papa's cupboard—about which I will tell you more later, as I promised—until the time of the revolution; then, when papa died, both it and the cupboard disappeared.

Where to? I simply cannot imagine. . . . But even today, as I write all this with an aged hand, glancing out the frosted windows at Peredelkino's ice-bound January landscape turning from green to blue beneath the crystal-white rays of the sun, Mamma's exercise-book still lives vividly in all its details in my memory, which continues to defeat the passage of time.

I even remember the excellent paper from which the book was composed, and the water marks that became visible when the pages were held up to the light. Those water marks have always mystified me. How is it done? Where do they come from?

Sometimes I feel that life would have been impossible without the memory of that exercise-book, without the kitten in its blue ribbon, the bush of blue lilac with its yellow stamen, and my guardian angel with the silver halo over the pretty girlish curls.

Once, when Mamma was still alive, I wanted to create something like that exercise-book myself, and she provided me with a sheet of water-marked paper and a pencil. Then, with my elbows over the table, under the light of the hanging oil-lamp with a white shade, through which the small, raspberry-coloured tongue of flame shone dimly, I started on my task. The dining-room clock was slowly striking eight and I was already half-asleep as I drew a lot of perpendicular lines with two circles in the middle, which was my idea of a dense, mysterious forest, though I had never actually encountered one. With a painstaking effort, I scrawled a caption underneath in crooked, uneven letters:

"How beautiful this forest is
And what a bliss to be so far . . ."

Of course there was one spelling mistake after another, but what does that matter if it was at this very moment that my life as a poet began; particularly as my first literary work disappeared forever, along with Mamma's precious exercise-book?

My Aunt's Admirers

AFTER MAMMA'S DEATH, her sister, Aunt Lilia, came to live with us and she brought her tea-cup with her: it immediately attracted our attention, because up till then we had had no cups in the house and always drank our tea out of glasses.

My aunt was greatly attached to her cup, only used it on important occasions, washed it up herself, and dried it with immense care on a special towel of its own. She was in constant fear that the fine, semi-transparent Sèvres porcelain might get cracked and frequently reminded Zhenia and me of its rarity, value, and antiquity. She always took it with her, when she went away, in her bright-yellow, wicker hat-box with a strap securing the lid.

One day, when we were returning home in a second-class compartment after a visit to Grandmother in Ekaterinoslav, my aunt took out the cup, poured some sweet tea with lemon into it for me from a bottle wrapped in cotton wool and warned me not to break it. In a sad, dreaming, half-mocking tone of voice—I could not make out if she were joking or serious—she told me that the cup had been given to her by Prince Zhevakhov, an admirer of hers and even, I gathered, a fiancé. I tried to elicit further details from her, but she was unwilling to give them. I was anxious to know whether, had she married the prince, she would now be a princess. I was also mystified by the word "admirer," which I had not heard before.

"What is an admirer?" I asked.

"You'll learn when you grow up," my aunt answered with her soft laugh.

"Is it an admiral?"

"Not necessarily," my aunt said evasively, her lips curling up in an amused smile.

"Then what is it—a man?"

"An admirer is a fiancé," my aunt said to put an end to the conversation, adding: "Drink your tea up before it gets cold instead of chattering away like that. And don't break the cup!"

I drank my tea, pouring it out of the cup, with the Chinese picture on it, into the precious saucer, which looked extremely old and convinced me that I was grasping a museum-piece.

The train shook and rattled, rays of dusty sunlight came through the window, and beyond stretched the flat steppes and fields of the Novorossijsk region, with here and there a Scythian hillock or a stone image. Every now and again, rays of sunlight moved slowly round the compartment, turning from the striked ticking on the banquette to the ventilator in the ceiling and then crawling onto the lantern, in which, at night, the conductor placed a fat stearin candle. This meant that we were going round a curve and if one craned out the window, one could see the engine ahead, its wheels racing round, pistons clanking, and smoke pouring out of its funnel, while, behind, the blue, green, and yellow carriages twisted like the tail of a lizard.

But nothing could distract me from my preoccupation with my aunt's words, which had impressed me profoundly because the word "Zhevakhov" was very familiar to me. Between Peresip and Dofinovka, on the way to the Kujalnitsky estuary, travelling in a real train and not in the toy summer one that took visitors to the Big Fountain, we had passed a rather large hill, overgrown with weeds, which was known as Zhevakhova Hill, because of the Prince Zhevakhov to whom it belonged.

And Zhevakhova Hill was one of the sights of the town. . . .

Now it suddenly emerged that the owner of this famous hill, Prince Zhevakhov, was none other than Aunt's admirer-fiancé. Somehow I could not quite believe it.

"Does Zhevakhova Hill belong to the same Prince Zhevakhov that was your admirer?" I asked.

"Yes, just imagine it!" answered my aunt.

"Why didn't you marry him?" I asked.

"He was very old," replied my aunt, "and I refused him."

"But you accepted the cup just the same?" I remarked.

"Yes," laughed my aunt. "As a keepsake."

I conjured up a vivid, dramatic picture of the hill's immensely wealthy owner, the aged Prince Zhevakhov, kneeling in front of my aunt with tears coursing down his wrinkled cheeks, proffering the precious Sèvres cup and asking her to be his wife; and my aunt refusing him, but accepting the cup as a keepsake. . . .

As well as the Zhevakhov cup, my aunt brought with her to our apartment a musical box, like a small organ, and a gold watch encased in a hinged ball attached to a gold ribbon which she always wore on her belt. She was very proud of these possessions and cherished them, because they were prizes she had won at dances in Nizhnedneprovsk, near Ekaterinoslav, when she was a teacher in the neighbouring village of Kamenskoe before coming to live with us. She occasionally let us touch the watch-case and opened it to show us the enamel face and gold hands, but she allowed us to play the musical box whenever we wanted. I used to turn the stiff handle endlessly, rotating a thin metal disc with slots that plucked the tenons of a steel comb, thereby producing musical notes, which, with a certain amount of imagination, could be taken for polkas, mazurkas, or waltzes.

There were about five or six steel discs, and I would put them on one after the other. My favourite was the air of a Ukrainian song, particularly when my aunt softly sang the words to the instrument's twangy, steel music. My aunt told me one day, with her usual, slightly ironic smile, that she had received the prizes—the watch and the "aristone"—for her beauty and, by way of confirmation, she lifted her skirt, danced a few graceful steps, and sang coquettishly a few bars from *The Geisha*. But I still found it difficult to believe because, from my childish point of view, my aunt was no longer young and, though nice-looking, not at all beautiful.

Perhaps what spoiled her beauty was a small bulge at the end of her nose, which looked like a small pink strawberry; she had hurt her nose so badly as a child when she had fallen off a swing that she retained the scar all her life. I think this blemish gave her face something that was unusual, very much her own, and, therefore, charming. If she had a cold, or cried, the end of the nose became very markedly red: otherwise, she had a commanding appearance, blue eyes and, as I came to realise later, a slender, elegant figure and lovely, small feet which were always well-shod.

She was not yet thirty when she came to replace my mamma. I was unable then to appreciate what a really heroic deed it was to give up her private life, freedom, and independence at that age in order to bring us up—me and the tiny Zhenia, her favourite older sister's children, to whom she had once promised her to be a mother in the event of her early death.

She was my godmother and came from her village specially to be present at the christening of her sisters' first-born son. It amused her to relate the story of how I had wetted her pink moiré skirt; the stains had proved impossible to remove and the skirt had had to be thrown away. My godfather was one of my aunt's admirers, a lawyer called Popruzhenko, whose jacket and trousers I also contrived to wet, though these stains fortunately yielded to treatment.

My aunt took the place of my mamma, taught in the diocesan school, and became the mistress of our house. She loved little Zhenia, whom she had brought up from his first days, with a passionate, tender, genuinely maternal love. It would have been quite natural in the circumstances for Papa eventually to marry her, but apparently he belonged to the rare category of one-woman men. Other women than Mamma did not exist for him. After her death, he swore to himself that he would never marry again and he stuck to his promise. I sometimes used to think that he developed a curious distaste for women, which he had difficulty in concealing. It is possible that this was due to his ecclesiastical background. Brought up in a seminary, he was preparing to be a priest, but later followed a secular path, attending a university after the seminary and becoming a high-school teacher. However, I am certain that the "spiritual streak" remained very strong in him.

His whole way of life and his views on it were much more those of a priest's than of a layman's: he was much more a man of God than a worldly counsellor. A priest was not allowed to marry twice, and often became a monk on the death of his wife. Something monastic began to show in Papa, something which made him stern, puritanical, and immune from human temptations and pleasures, except for the theatre, of which he was very fond. But he only went to see serious plays, of course, such as those by Gogol, Ostrovsky, and Shakespeare: he particularly liked Shakespeare's tragedies.

Although my aunt was completely independent, as she combined a certain amount of clerical work with teaching junior classes in the diocesan school and shared all the household expenses with Papa, her position was regarded as somewhat ambiguous by the uncharitable. There she was living under the same roof with a widower, bringing up his children, running his house. . . . There must be something wrong!

But Papa and my aunt paid no attention to the gossip that went on behind their backs or even to hints dropped in their presence, and thereby showed their superior intelligence.

Yet—as I can understand now—my aunt's life in our home must have been far from easy. After the freedom of Kamenskoe, the Nnieper balls, the prizes for beauty, and the host of admirers among the local engineers, polytechnic professors, factory proprietors, and landowners, which my aunt had enjoyed along with the work which gave her financial independence, taking up residence in the house of a widower, bringing up two boys, and running someone else's household could scarcely fail to prove a burden. It meant, in fact, the sacrifice of her personal life. Though, admittedly, she did not entirely give up the admirers. From time to time, one of them would turn up at our house, which, I think, slightly irritated Papa, who was not accustomed to guests. But he did his best not to show it.

When Aunt came to live with us, we could not stay on in our apartment in Basarnaia Street, almost on the corner of the French Boulevard, which was old-fashioned, modestly furnished, and cheap. She needed a room of her own, so we moved to another, larger apartment, rather too expensive for us, in a smart house in Marasdiev Street, which was one of the best in town.

The old, comfortable furniture was sold, and a new lot bought, of ebony, covered with gold silk. It made our sitting-room look more elegant than the previous one, but we missed the soft, cosy armchairs with sagging springs that we had known in Mamma's days. There were a good many rooms, and we took in lodgers—"to make both ends meet," as Aunt put it.

From then on, as far back as I can remember, we constantly moved

from one apartment to another, seeking one that was more con-
venient and cheaper.

And Grandmother, Papa's mother, always moved with us, sitting
as usual on a little dais beside the ficus and living in the dining-room
behind a screen; silent, of no use to anyone and ignored by us all,
except for Papa, who loved her deeply and reverently.

My aunt dressed well, used scent, and wore modern hats that
provoked ironical smiles from Papa. Even at the diocesan school,
she wore a blue silk dress, with lace on the neck and sleeves. Unlike
Mamma, who always swept her hair, black as a crow's wing, back
from her forehead, my aunt, who was almost blonde, did hers in the
latest fashion, with a sort of small bolster in front, *à la* Vialzeva, the
famous singer of gypsy songs.

She would often sit down on the cane seat of the adjustable piano-
stool, open the lid of the piano, and play Chopin waltzes one after
the other with brilliance and verve, the small but genuine multi-
coloured precious stones in her rings sparkling as her silm fingers
flew up and down the ivory keyboard.

She must even have smoked in secret, for I once discovered a
thin, lady's cigarette in her room and detected a faint smell of
tobacco-smoke.

Aunt's "admirer-fiancés" did not turn up very often, but I remember them all well. My aunt probably received their advances
rather coldly because, after a visit or two, they did not appear again.
Barring, of course, old Prince Zhevakhov, whom I continued to picture as an old man, with a face like the painter Aivazovsky's, kneeling
in front of Aunt with a cup in his hand, the most impressive of her
admirers, in my opinion, was Baron von Helmersen, a handsome
widower.

One day, my aunt announced that an old friend of hers would be
coming to dinner on the following Sunday with his son, who went
to the Military Academy. Knowing the traditional hostility that
existed between members of our school and those of the Military
Academy, she strictly enjoined Zhenka and me to behave ourselves
and treat von Helmersen's son with proper politeness. We promised
not to fight with him, but made such grimaces as we did so that
Aunt shook a threatening finger at us.

On the eve of the visit, Aunt went out shopping. She bought a
tin of sardines, half a pound of a very expensive Moscow smoked

sausage wrapped in silver paper, some Swiss cheese, shedding a tear, and two bottles of Sanzenbacher beer, with porcelain stoppers wired to the necks.

On catching sight of the beer, Papa flushed with indignation: actually, he not only flushed but went pale at the same time, for his cheek-bones became quite white. He was a convinced teetotaler and under no circumstances allowed any alcoholic drinks in the house.

"Why did you buy that disgusting stuff?" he demanded, jerking his head, then setting his pince-nez more firmly on his nose. "I'll throw it in the dust bin."

To which Aunt replied very calmly that von Helmersen was accustomed to drink beer at dinner; that he was her guest; that one should treat one's guests with due consideration.

Papa viewed the sardines and Swiss cheese, too, with a critical expression on his face. (We never had anything like that at home in the normal course of events: we began our meal with soup.) Out on the balcony, there was a tin mould filled with orange jelly, which Aunt had prepared herself, in her admirer's honour.

Von Helmersen turned out to be a very elegant gentleman, tall, bewhiskered, and wearing an English-style check jacket, a high, starched collar that thrust up his purple cheeks, sharply pointed shoes, and grey cloth gaiters. I remember, too, that he had two wedding-rings on his finger and a monocle hanging on a black silk ribbon—something I had never seen before.

On entering the hall, he pulled off his leather gloves, threw them into his hat, and leaned his solid rosewood walking-stick, with a yellowish, cracked ivory handle, up in a corner. Just visible behind his tall figure was the small, fair-haired pupil of the Military Academy, who clicked his heels and spread a smell of regulation shoe-black through the whole hall.

Von Helmersen was a widower and always took his son out to dinner on Sundays.

What made him and my aunt become friends? Where did they first meet? These were mysteries I never solved. . . .

Von Helmersen's visit remained in my memory as a dull evening, a wasted Sunday. After dinner, while the baron, crossing one leg over the other, drank beer, smoked his cigar, and conducted a social conversation with my aunt, and Papa, who could not stand tobacco, kept waving the expensive, pretty, blue cigar-smoke away from his nose with the palm of his hand, Zhenka and I took the boy out into the street to play. It was lucky that none of our friends were in the street, especially Mishka Galia, or the three of us would have had a hellish time, for he would have ragged us to death. Von Helmersen's son proved to be exceptionally boring: he hardly talked at all, because he was so busy pulling pieces of bread he had surreptitiously grabbed during dinner out of his pockets and cramming them into his bulging red cheeks that it was almost impossible for any words to fight their way out of his small mouth. On the whole, he was a quiet, harmless fellow, but he infuriated us by ruining our Sunday.

Von Helmersen stayed on till late in the evening, beginning to show signs of age as he sat stiff as a ramrod, with a cigar in his mouth, bags under his eyes, and a bald patch on top of his head. What my aunt ever saw in him I still cannot understand. Probably, he was no more than an exciting memory of the past, of those golden days when my gay, independent young aunt, the daughter of a general, spent her summer holidays on the Riga beach, about which she often happily told me stories. If she had married von Helmersen, she would have been a baroness! That would have been quite something!

Von Helmersen never appeared again, with his Military Academician son. Why did he come? Who knows? Possibly to try his luck once more, in which case Aunt must have refused the offer of marriage as usual.

I remember Papa in his best clothes, after the guests had gone, wrinkling his nose and opening the windows to air the rooms from the cigar-smoke; then picking up the tall Sanzenbacher beer-bottles himself, and taking them into the kitchen. Instead of the beer, now there were large honeycombed blobs of froth, which intrigued and puzzled me. What were they made of? How had they suddenly appeared there?

Aunt's other admirers were of no interest. They appeared for a short time, left her with a glimpse of the private happiness she might have had, then disappeared forever—rejected. Among them, there was, strange as it may be, a shop-assistant called Mukhin, a solid, handsome, smartly dressed man, who wore a silk tie the colour of a peacock's feather and a diamond ring on his little finger. He was not just an ordinary salesman in a haberdasher's shop somewhere in Richelieu Street, measuring ribbons and lengths of elastic on a metal yardstick attached to the edge of the counter; he occupied the highest rank in the hierarchy of shop-assistants, being right-hand man to the owner of a large store. Most of the time, he acted as buyer for the firm, a job which took him to Moscow, which he called the "metropolis," St. Petersbourg, which he called "Peter," and sometimes even to Paris. He had the mock-modest manners of a man well aware of his worth, a faultless parting in his neatly trimmed hair, and a clear, terse way of speaking. At the very end of his handsome Roman nose was a slight projection, like the foresight on a rifle, and all the time that he looked at the person to whom he was talking, with his penetrating, peasant's eyes, he seemed to be taking aim, lining up the sight on his nose with an invisible target. He used French scent and, in short, was an excellent specimen of a still-young, well-to-do man in a very good position. Though he was undoubtedly our superior from the point of view of finance, we nonetheless considered him beneath us: this was due to his accent and his manner of speech that reeked of haberdashery. They proved so alien to Papa and my aunt that Mukhin was very soon dismissed, though he did take Aunt, who put on a squirrel cape and hood for the occasion, to an operetta by cab one evening.

Then there was a smart student in a German-style cap, uniform-jacket, and narrow trousers, who flashed past in an unintrusive way. He accompanied my aunt when she went out on "White Camomile Day," to collect donations to a charity for consumptives. Holding a blue velvet shield, to which celluloid badges in the shape of camomile flowers were attached, my elegant aunt would gracefully approach passers-by, with a rustle from her silk skirt, smile fascinatingly, and murmur: "I hope you won't refuse," then pin one of the artificial white flowers with yellow centres on to a man's lapel or a woman's astrakhan jacket. At the same time, the student would present a tin money-box with a wax seal over the lock, clattering the coins inside as he did so, and into the slot would fall ten-, twenty-, or fifty-kopeck pieces and, occasionally, if my aunt contrived to be particularly charming, heavy silver roubles. At the end of the day, before going to the Town Hall to hand in the receipts, Aunt invited the student home to have some tea, and I was allowed to weigh the full money-box in my mind and hold the velvet shield.

At the Town Hall, it turned out that my aunt had collected more contributions than anyone else, and she was presented with a special official letter of acknowledgment. Papa disapproved of the whole proceedings, which he stigmatised as "undignified" and "playing at charity," but he may have been partly motivated by dislike for the exaggeratedly smart student. In any case, the student never appeared again, having no doubt shared the same fate as Aunt's other admirers—been rejected.

There was also a teacher at an ecclesiastical school, with the strange name of Krivda, a Ukrainian, who wore an embroidered shirt under his teacher's uniform, and had a pumpkin-shaped head, sparsely covered with a few carefully trained hairs. He had tea with us once, got the ends of his long whiskers damp in his saucer, and was extremely cheerful, telling a series of funny stories in Ukrainian, while glancing at my aunt tenderly and delightedly, like a fat tomcat.

I remember one of his anecdotes:

A Ukrainian once began to argue with a Turk as to whose God was the better. They argued and argued and came to no conclusion. Suddenly, a dark cloud appeared and a storm broke over them, accompanied by lightning and thunder. "That's our God beating yours," said the Turk, to which the Ukrainian replied melancholically: "He deserves it for getting entangled with a fool!"

At one time, a distant cousin of Papa's from Viatka, a certain Ivan Ivanovich Tvorozhkov, inscribed himself on the list of Aunt's admirers. Like Papa, he had attended the Novorossijsk University, where he read medicine, but had been compelled to leave after four terms through lack of funds: now he was apparently looking for a rich wife in order to be able to complete his studies. He had such a strong Viatka accent that it was difficult to understand him: he always seemed to be talking through a mouthful of noodles, just like Papa's mamma. He kept rubbing his sweaty hands together, giggled in a sort of Chinese way without the slightest provocation, and drank his tea with a lump of sugar gripped between his teeth. Despite all this, he had the reputation of being unusually talented and considered brilliant by his university professors.

Of course his courtship of my aunt came to nothing, and he left forlornly, a kind, shy man with a clever, bearded peasant's face, in his shabby coat, cap with a button on top, and old, worn galoshes.

About three years later, he suddenly turned up again at our house, by now a decently dressed professor of anatomy, and introduced his wife—a middle-aged woman, the daughter of a priest, whom he had married for her dowry of three thousand roubles.

He was obviously embarrassed, and there was so much sadness mingled with the kindness etched on his typically Russian, introspective, scientist's face that we all felt sorry for him, all the more so because his wife, a woman of dull, provincial appearance, wearing a silk brown dress, behaved in a very common way; she blew her nose loudly into a handkerchief that she pulled out of her sleeve and, when stewed cherries were handed round at the end of dinner, she spat the stones out into the palm of her hand, looking, at that moment, exactly like a duck. They used to come to see us, as members of the family, from time to time, and once turned up on New Year's Eve, bringing two bottles of fizzy Don champagne with them and receiving in return an apple pie with a ten-kopeck piece hidden in it for luck. It was the first time in my life that I had tasted this Don champagne, and I must admit I liked it.

My aunt's last admirer appeared when the First World War had just begun. He was a missonary from our diocese. In my mind, his was a strange, romantic vocation, involving a terribly dangerous, dedicated life on coral islands or in tense, tropical forests, seething with poisonous serpents, tsetse flies, and wild beasts: I visualised a missionary as a saint in rough monk's clothing, his eyes alight with the eternal flame of faith as he sought to convert tribes of wild savages. But our Odessa diocesan missonary, born in Kaluga, who spent his time in religious arguments with sectarians of all types, had a very ordinary and far from ecclesiastic appearance: small and frail, he wore an old, shabby jacket, baggy trousers, and shook his small goatee beard in a very funny way. When he came to have tea with us after spending his holidays back in Kaluga, he supplied us with all the local news, which was of no interest to anyone.

He clearly stood no chance of winning my aunt's heart, particularly as he turned out to be a secret alcoholic and I once found him quite drunk, sitting on the steps of our porch. He had probably set out to call on us, but pausing to take a breather before reaching his objective, had fallen fast asleep, emitting the fumes of home-made liquor, since the sale of vodka was forbidden during the war.

Shortly after that, my aunt left us to go to Poltava, where a cousin
of hers lived, a wealthy landowner and local government-official,
Evgeni Petrovich Ganko, who had probably been another of her admirers in the past. She ran his household, replacing her dead cousin,
Zinaida. I remember Evgeni Petrovich well. He was a great sybarite
and *bon-viveur*, who liked to explore foreign countries, and always
paid us a visit, showering us with exotic presents, when the ship of
the naval voluntary reserve, in which he was returning from China,
Hong Kong, Egypt, or India, called in at Odessa. He brought us
Japanese lacquered boxes, ostrich eggs and feathers, rugs made of
the finest Egyptian straw, cigarette cases decorated with figures of
scarabs, the sacred beetle, and many other treasures.

He was powerfully built, though his excesses had made him rather
corpulent and his feet were swollen with gout, which compelled him
to wear extra-large velvet shoes, or, rather, slippers. He had a magnificent head with a Roman nose, on which was perched a somehow
particularly impressive golden pince-nez, very much in keeping with
his senatorial side-whiskers and loose-fitting suit from the best London tailor, permeated by the subtle smell of Atkinson's special scent
for men.

He had grown old by the time the war started, could hardly walk,
and sat day after day in his comfortable, Ukrainian-style brick
house, surrounded by a shady garden in Poltava, in a Voltairean arm-
chair, his legs wrapped in flannel, turning the pages of old copies of
the *Revue des Deux Mondes* or busying himself with his stamps.
I heard he was quite a famous philatelist and had a priceless collection containing one specimen which was unique—a first-issue,
local Poltavian stamp.

And it was to run his household that my aunt ended her life with
us.

She died in Poltava in 1942 during the German occupation, having
buried Evgeni Petrovich a short time before: she had been forced to
move into a tumble-down hut, where she remained completely
alone, sick, old, and a beggar. A Russian patriot, she could not bear
the humiliation of the enemy's presence on her native soil, where
years ago Peter had beaten the Swedes, and no longer wished to
live.

Neighbours found her, one morning, dead, lying on the floor beside her bed. She had apparently been trying to find her slippers

when the angel of death came to bring peace to her tender, kind, un-happy soul.

How clearly I can visualise that wintry, dark morning in Poltava, with German tanks rumbling down the street and clouds over the ruins of that beautiful Ukrainian town of white-walled, green-roofed houses and endless rows of poplars . . . and the small, withered body of that old, grey-haired lady lying stretched out on a strip of thread-bare carpet.

A Child's Conception of Death ✍

FOR SEVERAL YEARS in my childhood I was haunted by a sinister dream, which only came to me once in my life, but remained in my memory for a long time after. I constantly seemed to dream it awake and was tortured by its strange significance.

The dream was the enactment of my death. It seems to me that a moment suddenly comes to everyone sooner or later in his child-hood when he begins to gather from all the evidence that he is mortal and some day bound to die, to cease living—a thought to which it is impossible to become accustomed.

In my dream, I was running round the bare, yellow oak or per-haps pine table in our dining-room, pursued by a strange, inanimate monster, as yellow as the table and side-board. (Though, actually, our side-board was made of fumed oak, and was remarkable because it had none of the traditional decorative carvings of fruit or hares, merely two wooden circles, which reminded me of my Viatka grand-mother's round eyes.)

The monster that pursued me had the shape of a grotesque piece of wooden furniture—either a chair with an enormously tall back like a ladder or the side-board with Grandmother's eyes grown as high as the ceiling.

The terribly frightening thing about it was that, though it was an object and pawed the floor with its wooden legs—like a horse with its hooves—it was also a human, trying to seize hold of me, which would mean my end. I was out of breath and afraid to turn around: it seemed to me now and again that the thing chasing me had become a yellow skeleton with rattling bones and dry white ribs bulging out from its black thorax. At the same time, I felt that I was no longer myself, but the very skeleton with a black thorax, that was pursuing me and seeking to kill me with one quick pounce. The skeleton and I were one and the same thing, or, rather, the same human being, which meant that I was chasing myself in order to cause my own death, to rob myself of my consciousness forever.

To achieve this, it was only necessary to press down the small button, a piece of apparatus resembling an electric switch, inserted in my thorax, while there was a similar one inserted in the wall by the door: my death would then be instantaneous.

The strange part of this was that, at that time, our apartment had no electricity and I had never seen a switch; but I am ready to swear that, in that childish dream of mine, there was a switch inserted in my thorax—a black, ebony switch, conjured up in some miraculous way from the not so distant future, possibly from Ekaterinoslav, where there already was electric light. There would, I suppose, be nothing extraordinary or frightening about this phenomenon if we were prepared to believe that time does not only march on but can move backwards, too. And why should that not be the case? Since the properties of time have never been fully investigated, it may well be so.

I ran like a lunatic round the table, faster and faster. I heard behind me the stamping of the horse, which was in fact one of the chairs around the table: something or someone was trying to grab me round the waist and tickle me as Mamma and Papa sometimes did in fun when they were sitting at the table and I ran past them. But these were not kind hands that I felt, but dry, cold ones, the hands of a dying or already dead man, those of Uncle Misha, with his mad eyes and the thin, straggly beard of a saint, stretching out to reach me from the sofa in the sitting-room. The intolerable, torturing fear of death enveloped me in ice and, to be rid of it, I killed myself, pressing the switch in my thorax and thereby simultaneously switching off my life: darkness inexorably flowed into me from all sides, depriving me of sight and sound, destroying me forever.

When I woke in the morning, I was no longer the gay little boy— half-animal, half-man—I had been. I was now all man, forever poisoned by the incontrovertible knowledge that I was mortal, that nothing could save me from eventual destruction.

The Human Brain ✒

RUMOUR HAD IT that Ivan Ivanovich Tvorozhkov was a distinguished young physiologist. I think he was made of the same stuff as Sechenov, Pavlov, Mechnikov, and Mendeleev. Papa, in my opinion, also belonged to this category but, unable to devote himself whole-heartedly to science, chose a different path and became an ordinary teacher.

Tvorozhkov, who came from Viatka, too, got on very well with him: their conversation was always on a high scientific level and had nothing in common with empty, philistine talk. It embraced topics beyond my grasp, problems arising in universities, the latest scientific discoveries, and so on. Sometimes, their discussions became heated, and then Papa would begin to speak as rapidly and incoherently as Tvorozhkov and with the same Viatka accent.

Investigating the human brain in his laboratory, studying its functions and mechanism in relation to man's psychic activity, and combining the theories of a scientist with the practice of a psychiatrist, Tvorozhkov developed his own theory of heredity. I was incapable of understanding the essence of it but had some idea that it was connected with the extent to which an individual could pass on his personal idiosyncrasies to the next generation, including mental disorders, actual madness, or psychic diseases tending to cause early death. It sometimes seemed to me that he had selected our family for the scientific observations that were to confirm his theory.

My paternal grandfather, the Viatka priest, had died comparatively young, at about the age of fifty. I did not know the precise cause of his death: I had been told rather vaguely that it was from a fever. Papa's brother, my uncle Misha, about whom I have already written, died insane at thirty. Papa's elder brother, Uncle Kolia, died at the age of forty from progressive paralysis: on his way to hospital, he was said to have jumped off the stretcher, a frightening, long-bearded figure in a night-shirt down to his ankles, laughed loud enough to be heard the whole way down the street, chanted funeral prayers, and conducted an imaginary orchestra. He had completed his studies at the Moscow Ecclesiastical Academy, taught in the Odessa seminary, become a state counsellor, and been awarded several decorations, which he greatly enjoyed putting on.

Papa was the only one of the three brothers still alive: he was in perfect health, well-balanced, moderate in everything, and very rarely lost his temper. I kept on catching Tvorozhkov stealthily observing me and, every now and again, he casually asked me the apparently innocent questions that psychiatrists ask patients whom they suspect of suffering from some kind of mental disease. In the end, it became a sort of mania with him: possibly he belonged to a distant branch of our family in Viatka and was gradually losing his own mind. In any case, whenever I noticed his gentle, penetrating eyes on me, they sent shivers down my spine. Was it possible, I wondered, that he considered writing poems a symptom of incipient insanity?

One day he caught hold of my hand, put his nimble, cold, doctor's fingers on my pulse, took out his watch, and finally announced: "Yes, yes, wonderful, wonderful." Then he asked: "And how about your memory?"

"Very good," I said.

"Splendid!" he said reassuringly. "What sort of dreams do you have?"

I found it difficult to reply, because I had so many different kinds —black-and-white and coloured, including a number of erotic ones —so I just blushed and remained silent.

"So-o-o," said Dr. Tvorozhkov. "Do you suddenly get a feeling of giddiness? Irritation?"

He looked into my eyes and appeared to see right through me: I was, in fact, a hot-tempered boy, almost an adolescent. Then, with the same professional fingers, he felt the glands behind my ears, after which he produced a small, black hammer from his pocket with the deftness of a conjurer and struck me a blow on my knee-cap. My leg jumped as though galvanised.

"So-o-o," Tvorozhkov said with satisfaction, "Does your heart give you any trouble?"

"Sometimes," I said, not wanting to disappoint him.

"So-o-o. Sexual maturity . . . nervousness," he murmured and gazed at my forehead so long and intently that I thought he would open up my skull at any moment to examine it for hereditary flaws. I was convinced that he was a maniac. He kept on insisting that Papa should regularly take iodine and took it himself, pulling a small bottle out of his waistcoat pocket and pouring the thick, blackish-brown liquid into a glass of milk, which immediately turned a sinister pink. He was afraid of sclerosis and found symptoms of it in everyone.

One day he invited me to his laboratory to show me how he dealt with the human brain. Doing my best to conceal my acute fear, I went to the university clinic. The huge, massive, three-storied university buildings, with large, high windows, wide, protruding ledges, and enormous polished doors with heavy metal handles, were spread all over the town, housing the various faculties, and lent the streets a particularly impressive, academic, slightly official character.

Official buildings were usually painted a special yellow colour, but those of the university were painted a pale-green, which somehow gave them the appearance of being lit by gas even in broad daylight. They even seemed to smell of gas.

They were surrounded by iron railings, and in front of them were old acacias, plane-trees, and chestnuts, with web-footed leaves, that had perhaps been there in the times of Pirogov and Mechnikov.

In the evenings, the green light of the street-lamps shone through the windows.

The medical-faculty building was further than any of the others from the centre of the town and stood, if I am not mistaken, somewhere towards the end of Khersonskaia Street, where the town had already acquired a slightly suburban character: between the houses, one could see Perèsip, the Zhevakhov hill, and a small street of sea. The laboratory was situated in a small wing approached through a shady yard, paved with large concrete slabs: some distance away to the left was another wing, which immediately struck me as sinister. And rightly so, for, as I learned later, it contained the mortuary, or, as the students call it, the "corpse-house," where dead bodies were dissected.

Ivan Ivanovich led me to his room, furnished with old, ash cupboards, which were filled with laboratory apparatus and various instruments. In the middle was a zinc table with a microscope and a machine that looked like those that had just begun to appear in groceries for rapidly cutting ham into thin slices.

Tvorozhkov was wearing linen overalls. He took a cylindrical glass vessel, with a sheet of glass on top of it, out of one of the cupboards, put it on the table and extracted something that looked like a freshly peeled walnut, though it was the size of a head of cauliflower and appeared quite heavy: it seemed to be composed of off-white, faintly yellowish wax, and its deep convolutions immediately made me guess that it was a human brain. Its owner was no longer with us. He was dead and his body buried in the ground after the skull had been cut open; but the brain, preserved in a jar with formalin and, to all appearances, quite fresh, was here in the laboratory in Dr. Tvorozhkov's rubber-gloved hands.

Tvorozhkov put the brain into the machine and began cutting it into very thin slices, which he picked up one after the other with a pair of tongs and examined against the light. He showed me a small stain on each slide which seemed to run the whole way through the brain and was no doubt the result of a haemorrhage. Ivan Ivanovich told me that it enabled him to trace the exact position of the lesion that had caused the man's death. He placed one of the slices under the microscope and invited me to examine it, but by now I was unable to force myself to look through the eyepiece.

I was feeling sick. All I wanted was to get outside as quickly as possible with the fresh air under the acacias and chestnuts. I was being driven insane by the smell of formalin and the stink of the imperceptibly putrefying brain.

I was horrified by the thought that everything surrounding man could be reflected, live, and exist in that highly complex, frail, wax-like block of material—the whole world, the whole universe, myself, the sun, the moon, the sea, and the clouds, Pushkin, Tchaikovsky, and Nadia Zaria-Zarianitskaia, joy and sorrow and the inexplicable feeling of bitterness produced by the eternal, unrequited love, which I had been carrying in my heart for so long, which up till now had seemed to me to be immortal, but, all the time, was nothing more than a faint imprint left by circumstances on the convolutions of my brain.

It was difficult to resign myself to it, but there was nothing to be done. One had to face it!

Up to the Neck in Sand ✒

WHEN I WAS very young, Papa and Mamma took me to have sand-baths by the Kujalnitsky estuary or at Langeron during the summer to prevent my getting rickets. Papa dug a fairly shallow hole, following roughly the contours of my body, and we then had to wait a little till the damp sand at the bottom of it became dry and warm under the scalding July sun. Once this had occurred, Mamma undressed me completely and laid me down in the soft, sandy nest.

I examined my round, fat arms, with their tender, rosy skin, and enjoyed myself spreading out my fingers, patting the hot sand with the palms of my hands, picking up handfuls of it and tossing it around, giggling happily as I admired the diamond glint of the grains.

Then Papa piled sand over me up to my neck, so that I could feel it under my chin and some of it tickling my lips. I tried to free my arms and legs but it required an enormous effort to shift the heavy weight and, when Papa added another layer or two, I remained buried in the hot heap with only my head, slightly raised, peeping out of it towards the sea. I was not strong enough to offer any further resistance to the health-giving sand, pressing down on every inch of my body and completely immobilising me. The sun beat down mercilessly, so Mamma opened her parasol and stuck the handle into the sand. I was now protected by its large shade and Papa and Mamma sat beside me, admiring me or, rather, admiring all they could see of me, which was my round, black head, with its two crowns.

My eyes were only just above the level of the sea, and the stretch of sandy shore, scattered with smooth, mother-of-pearl shells and ribbons of dried reeds. My field of vision was so limited that I could only see a tiny sector of water, twinkling with dazzling white stars under the rays of the sun.

The horizon seemed quite near—just a stone's throw away—but sea and sky were fused together into a misty, mirror-like mirage that made it impossible to tell where one began and the other ended. The colours around me were so bright that my eyes grew tired and I saw everything as if faded by the burning, midday sun, in pale pastel shades. Yet smells and sounds acquired a particular acuteness and strength.

There was the smell of melting tar, which was being heated somewhere behind my back to caulk the seams of a leaking scow, the smell of the wood-pile beside the boiler, and an iodine smell from the rotting reeds and fish-scales accompanied by the scrape of a plane cutting curly strips from a pine plank, which told me that, out of my sight, carpenters were engaged in building a new fishing-vessel. There were piercing cries from the sea-gulls, too, the splash of oars from a boat, with a small iron anchor hanging from the stern, passing in front of me a short way off-shore, and the laughter of a group of girls paddling in shallow water.

Now and then, I saw Papa in his linen shirt, belted round the waist, stooping down to pick up the red-hot, flat pebbles particularly prevalent in Langeron and, with a flick of his wrist, sending them skittering along the top of the ripples. They produced a series of splashes, coming closer and closer together as they disappeared from my field of vision, which reminded me of the movement of the vertebrae in the tails of the lizards I had recently watched on a rock covered with moss and rather pathetic little lilac flowers.

Streams of sweat poured down my face, but I could not wipe them away. My body seemed to be steaming under the pressure of the sand and I was becoming exhausted by this hygienic form of swaddling. Finally, Mamma looked at her watch, which led me to hope that I would soon emerge from my hole. After a minute or two, she dragged me out, half-asleep, rubbed me down with a towel, and inserted me into my piqué dress and straw hat. Papa dug a bottle of milk out of the wet sand by the edge of the sea, the cork jumped out with a pleasant pop, and he held the bottle out to me so that I could drink straight out of the neck. Then he picked me up and carried me up the sloping beach, while Mamma followed close behind, tickling my hot, wet neck and occasionally bending down to kiss first one ear, then the other. And I smiled, silent and indescribably happy, in response to her caresses.

Thus we made our way home to Basarnaia Street. When we got to the top of the slope, Papa put me down on the pavement and I then proceeded under my own steam, slowly pattering along the lava slabs with one hand in Papa's and the other in Mamma's.

All three of us—Mamma, Papa, and I—wore straw hats of different shapes.

The Pilgrimage to Kiev

WHEN I WENT to Ekaterinoslav to stay for a while shortly after my mother's death, I found great changes. Grandmother and a number of her daughters, my aunts Natasha, Margarita, Nina, and Klionia, were installed in a large, I might say huge, rich apartment, containing a multitude of well-furnished, high-ceilinged, light rooms with par-quet floors, carpets, mirrors, and trophical plants—a luxury that Grandmother, living on her pension, and her unmarried daughters, working in various offices such as the Control Office, the Local Coun-cil, and the Ekaterinoslav railway, could not possibly have afforded on their own.

The explanation of this radical change in Grandmother's way of life lay in the fact that one of the daughters, my Aunt Nina, whom the family regarded as a ravishing beauty, had suddenly married a railway-engineer in a lofty position, which earned him what Grand-mother described as a "ministerial salary." It was after this that the magic transformation took place. Aunt Nina really was a beauty; tall, slender, and fair-haired, but in no commonplace way. She had her own particular brand of aristocratic traits, a small, aquiline nose, a regal carriage, and the sparkling eyes of a good but stern fairy. Destiny had decreed that, of all the sisters, Aunt Nina should be the one endowed with the most attractive qualities.

We treasured for a long time a photograph of all my aunts, stand-ing in profile and arranged in order of height, wearing coats and hats, muffs, and fashionable skirts with trains. Aunt Nina was un-questionably the most outstanding one, the most beautiful, and the tallest, though, admittedly, hers was a "cold beauty" with something inaccessible inherent in it.

Possibly it was precisely this that procured her such a desirable husband as Ivan Maximovich, with his "ministerial salary" and splen-did good looks in no way inferior to hers. Tall and well-grommed, with a neatly trimmed beard and moustache, close-cropped hair above a high, marble forehead, and the ice-blue eyes of a handsome egoist, he was an impressive figure in his railway-engineer's uniform-jacket, with general's shoulder-straps, and well-fitting, foreign-made shoes.

In that wealthy man's seven-roomed apartment, where Grand-mother was no longer an omnipotent proprietor but had been rel-egated to the role of a respected but poor relation, as I immediately noticed with the sensitivity and observation of a rapidly growing boy and felt very badly about—it affects me even now—in that luxurious seven-roomed apartment, I somehow never felt at ease.

Plump Grandmother, with her crown of whitish-grey hair and double chin like that of the empress Catherine the Great, the widow of a general and a magnificent provincial hostess, who had reigned over her household cheerfully and good-naturedly, now definitely took second place to Ivan Maximovich, who had become acting master of the house and family.

The whole routine was dictated by him, who had been accustomed to a Petersburg mode of life: luncheon at two, dinner by lamp-light at seven, and supper at eleven, though the supper usually took place without him. He went to his club every evening to play vint,* and returned in the early hours, at one or two: his sharp ring on the door-bell woke the whole household. Ekaterinoslav was a far more progressive town than Odessa from a technical point of view: the bell was an electric one! In addition to the bells, it had telephones, electric lighting in houses and streets, and even an electric tramway with pretty little open cars, which ran up and down the main boulevard, shooting off blue sparks, clanging bells, and producing cello-like sounds from the overhead wires. This technical progress can be explained by Ekaterinoslav's proximity to the Don Basin, with its fairy-tale riches: the head offices of the coal-mines, iron-foundries, engine-works, foreign concessions, banks, and various other trade and industrial undertakings were all situated in the city, which was suddenly transformed from an ordinary provincial town into a sort of Klondike, where gold could be dug up in the streets.

Ivan Maximovich's apartment, of course, also had electric light and a telephone, which stood on the green cloth of the ministerial desk in his study. There was nothing to remind one of the modest life favoured by my dead grandfather, when, with the early fall of dusk, the small rooms of the retired general's provincial apartment were lit by kerosene lamps and paraffin-wax candles, which dribbled onto the copper candlesticks. These candles used to be bought in fours or fives, drapped in thick blue "candle-paper," from small grocers' shops. Now, the much more spacious rooms were flooded with lifeless electric light, to which I could not get accustomed.

Sometimes the telephone rang and I could hear Ivan Maximovich answering it in his study and issuing sharp official instructions to the caller.

The long table in the dining-room was laid with ten or twelve of

* A card-game of the period. *Translator's note.*

what Grandmother called "covers." The shining silver spoons and forks were not old-fashioned like ours in Odessa, but modern ones with ornate handles: multi-coloured flashes of light sparkled from their crystal stands and the crystal salt-cellars. In the middle of the table, there was a narrow dish of trimly sliced Astrakhan herring, covered with small circles of onion resembling gypsies' earrings, and a Meissen china cheese-board with a glass top. Ivan Maximovich took the top off himself before dinner and cut the cheese with a special curved knife with two sharp prongs at the end of it as though performing some preprandial ritual: and his flawlessly starched cuffs, with gold cuff-links, made a creaking noise, very much like that of a stiffly starched napkin when one unfolded it and thrust it into the top of one's waistcoat.

On this occasion, all three of us—Papa, Zhenia, and myself—had come to stay in Ekaterinoslav. Papa had dreamed for a long time of visiting Kiev to see its sacred monuments and caves and now proposed to take Zhenia and me with him. He wanted to go there by boat up the Dnieper, which could only be done from Ekaterinoslav, since the famous rapids lower down were impassable. The plan was to spend some time with Grandmother, then take the boat to Kiev, stay a few days, return to Ekaterinoslav in the same way, and from there go back to Odessa by train. This we duly carried out and the trip was a great success: Papa was delighted at having managed to show us the grandeur of Russian nature, the most ancient Russian town, where the Orthodox church had originated, and the great river Dnieper, so beautifully described by Gogol.

Afloat on the broad river, we, too, encountered the tugs, pulling long strings of large, covered barges behind them, that inspired him to write:

"In its wide bed through a pine-forest, the river pursued its way. But destiny had decreed that the journey should be hard and the river should have much to bear. It bore the weight of heavy barges, dragged behind tugs, and sometimes their beams stretched the whole way across and there seemed to be no end to them. 'Tell me, oh river, why do you do it, why suffer your waters to carry these ships? Why do you not resist this onslaught of man?' And softly the river gives its answer: 'I flow to the sea that has no frontiers, following the hard course that destiny has laid on me. And one day the sea will reward me.'"

At times, the whole river was completely covered with tugs and

barges, which made it look like an eternally moving, timbered vil-
lage-street, with raftered cabins, smouldering wood-fires, and washing, hanging out everywhere. In other places, where there were
shoals, a barefooted sailor measured the depth of the river, plunging a pole with notches on it into the water and calling out figures
that I could not understand: "Eight! Ten! Six! Four! And four! And
four! Seven!"

And the captain, in a white tunic, kept shouting orders through a
speaking-tube from the bridge to the engine-room somewhere below,
and the paddle-wheels either whipped up the muddy, greenish,
coffee-coloured waters of the Dnieper more violently with their
red slats or suddenly stopped and went slowly into reverse: then,
silently, as though with bated breath, the ship glided over the brown
river-bed clearly visible through the thin layer of rippling water.

I was amazed, when we were about to pass under a low bridge, to
see the ship's mast and funnel bend back, all the more so because
thick smoke continued to emerge from the top of the apparently
broken funnel when one would have expected it to burst out of the
lower part and shower the deck with smuts and soot.

As soon as the bridge was safely past, the mast and funnel slowly
righted themselves, resuming their previous positions, and once
again there was nothing but the broad expanse of river ahead of us,
one bank high and steep, the other, a long distance away, green and
meadowy. Overhead, our Russian summer clouds, snow-white on
top and blue underneath, were floating about the sunlit sky and
aboard ship we listened lazily to the thud of the engines, the churn-
ing of the paddles in the water, and the stentorian voice of the captain, with his bristly Ukrainian moustache and starched tunic, shouting orders into the brass mouthpiece of the speaking-tube.

For the first time, I became aware of the greatness, the bound-
lessness, of my native land, of which I had only seen a small part—
Ekaterinoslav, the Novorossijsk steppes, and the Dnieper, with its
tugs and barges and iron, latticed bridges. Here and there on the
banks were deserted little towns and villages, thatched cottages, and
whitewashed huts, with blue clay pots on their broad window-sills
and glazed ornaments on the tops of the fence-posts; in front and
around them were saint-like sunflowers with yellow halos about their
black, round faces, hedges lined with flesh-pink, wine-red, and yellow
hollyhocks, cherry-orchards, already blood-stained with the ripe

fruit, and placid, long-horned white oxen. It was all completely new to me and aroused a hitherto latent, exciting feeling of pride in my country and its vastness, for I knew that, in addition to what I now glimpsed, there were the spacious territories of central Russia, the brittle cliffs of Finland, the walls of an ancient, dormant China; there was Archangel, the Ural Mountains, Siberia, the northern ice-bound ocean, the Sagan hills, the Baikal lake, and Vladivostok, which it took a two-weeks' train-journey to reach.

One morning remains deeply etched in my memory, when Papa woke us early and told us to get dressed quickly and come up on deck. The other passengers were already gathered on the deck, still damp from the night-dew, when we got there, looking towards the left bank of the Dnieper where a tall, wooden cross was just visible on top of a hillock. Papa took off his straw hat and said in a voice in which one could sense deep emotion: "Children, take off your caps in honour of that cross and remember it all your lives. It marks the grave of the great Ukrainian poet, Tarass Shevchenko."

Zhenia and I took off our summer caps and glued our eyes to the cross, the top of which was already bathed in the first pink rays of the rising sun, until it slowly disappeared from sight. Some of the passengers made the sign of the cross and others murmured: "To his eternal memory. . . . To his eternal memory. . . ."

Many stood with bowed heads, and the captain removed his cap, pulled a wire, and sent a long, thin, mournful hoot from the ship's siren vibrating through the summer air; its sound echoed for a long time amid the high cliffs on the right shore and, as it grew fainter, ran down the Dnieper waters.

A wave of ecstasy enveloped my soul. I had grasped for the first time in my life, felt with my whole being, what real glory the poet had achieved when, unrecognised by the government, he had nonetheless been acknowledged by the people, who had erected a tall cross over his grave, illuminated by a summer's-morning sun and seen by the whole world.

It left on me one of the strongest impressions of my childhood, at that time already beginning to pass on into adolescence.

Kiev, too, has always remained in my memory, just as I saw it that summer.

First, far away on the high river-bank, we glimpsed the tall white steeples and gold helms of the Kievo-Pechersk monastery. They came silently, dreamily, to meet us, like monastic knights, out of the wide-spread, surrounding gardens and never again have I seen such beauty, that spoke to my imagination of ancient Russia and her heroes, the feats of Prince Vladimir, the feats of Russlan, and that fairy-tale world of Russian history, from which long ago my ancestors had emerged and, eventually, myself, however strange and uncanny that might seen.

Papa took off his hat, which had left a coral scar on his high forehead, removed his pince-nez, wiped his eyes with a handkerchief, and told us that we were nearing Kiev, which, with a tender smile, as though he were talking of someone close to him, a relation, he called "Grandfather Kiev."

Before our ship drew in alongside the wooden pier, we saw, among the chestnuts in the botanical gardens on Vladimir Hill, a monument to the Godfather of Russia, Prince Vladimir, and, on top of it, dominating the river and the blue distance beyond it, a slender cast-iron cross, which moved me far less deeply than the wooden cross on the grave of Tarass Shevchenko.

The sight-seeing we did in Kiev during the few days we spent there had all the aspects of a pilgrimage to holy places that Papa had envisaged in his dreams. Despite its exhaustive and exhausting character, despite the insufferable July heat, the endless walking through a large, red-hot, stone town amid the rumble of lorries and clatter of carriages on the cobbled roadway, the huge cauldrons of melting asphalt emitting dark-blue clouds of suffocating smoke, and the scaffolding that frequently impeded our passage—Kiev was rapidly becoming a rich, commercial town, with new buildings springing up everywhere, at which we gazed with the naïvete and astonishment of provincial visitors, counting the stories and sometimes reaching double figures—despite all these disadvantages, the pilgrimage made an indelible impression on me and revived the religious feeling that had been growing weaker during my progress towards maturity. But it was no longer an elevated, pure, and naïvely childish faith in something beautiful, eternal, and divine that led to salvation; now it was my imagination that was captured by the pomp and mystery of the ritual, the almost opera-like glamour of the services, with choirs, lights, golden, ornamented altar-doors, gonfalons, lilac clouds of aromatic incense, and the priests' superbly brocaded robes. Nevertheless, none of this was to be compared with the quiet, moving Lenten evening-services in a small church with narrow windows, beyond which, sadly but tenderly, too, the spring evenings grew blue as the first tremulous star came out.

Services went on uninterruptedly in the Kiev cathedrals amid the Byzantine grandeur of their glittering mosaics. Te Deums were held by the silver coffins containing relics of the saints, and crowds of pious people came from all parts of Russia to kiss a saint's dried, bony hand or light a red or green candle to Varvara, the Great Sufferer, or St. Nicholas, or a trunkless head, reputed to yield myrrh, from which a scented oil did, in fact, drip.

Candles flickered with a gold flame in front of all the icons in their silver mounts, encrusted with rubies, sapphires, emeralds, diamonds, and large and small pearls, which made the artificial paper flowers seem out of place.

It was here I saw, for the first time, green and red church candles, wound round with strings of gold tinsel. Zhenia and I bought them, tiptoed behind Papa, crossing ourselves fervently, and, after lighting their fresh, flax wicks from other candles already lit, placed them by the silver coffins of saints or in front of the ancient icons, inserted into the brightly gilded iconostasis.

We were present at four or five Te Deums at least, and Papa presented two Communion bread-rolls to be blessed, one for the well-being of the living, the other for the peace of the dead. A tall, black monk in metal-rimmed spectacles, standing behind a small counter, gave him an ink-bottle and a pen and, in his spidery handwriting, he carefully wrote a list of the names of the living to accompany the first of the hearth-baked rolls, resembling a very ancient, single-domed church, made of white dough: ". . . Elisaveta, Maria, Margarita, Natalia, Cleopatra, Nina, Ivan, Piotr, Valentin, Evgeni . . ."

Then, his eyes sad and red, he once more carefully dipped the pen into the ink-bottle and wrote a whole column of names, for the peace of the dead to go with the second one: ". . . Eugenia, Alexei, Pavel, Michael, Ivan, Vassili," and a number of people unknown to me, who were no longer in this world, and of whom there remained no trace beyond the black, spidery letters.

After the liturgy, we got our rolls back, smelling strongly of incense, with the triangular pieces cut out, and Papa wrapped them up in a clean handkerchief.

We were staying in a special monastery hotel, where a monk

brought us a large jug of rust-coloured, very tasty monastic kvass every morning; the corridors were silent and empty, the beds in our room, which I think was really a monk's cell, were covered with grey flannel blankets and a lamp burned in front of an icon. According to one of the monks, with red hair and a freckled nose, we were to pay "whatever is within your means," and Papa gave him seventy-five kopecks for the three of us, though he need not have done even this. At four o'clock in the morning, we were awakened by the loud tolling of the church-bell, calling the monks to early service. Pyramidal poplars peeped into our windows and, beyond them, we could see the monks' black figures crossing the paved yard and small, white-washed huts with newly painted green roofs: to me, it was all strikingly new and imbued with an inexplicably sad charm.

Of course Papa took us to the famous Kiev caves, where, with a crowd of other visitors grasping thin, lighted candles, we descended into an endlessly long, very narrow, dry underground corridor, with a naturally arched clay roof: here and there in the walls—always alarmingly and unexpectedly—niches appeared containing coffins with the remains of saints, wrapped in red canvas shrouds, through which one could glimpse fossilised parts of human bodies: arms folded on chests . . . the soles of feet . . . a round head, with a sharp protruding nose, slightly raised on a red calico pillow. . . .

The guide, a monk also carrying a candle, halted by each niche and rattled off a short history of the saint for the benefit of the pilgrims surrounding him—mostly peasants in heavy boots or bast shoes and their wives with black shawls on their heads and bundles strapped to their backs.

The coffin that astonished me most was one bearing a metal plaque stating that therein lay the remains of the chronicler Nestor. Up till then, I had always believed that the famous chronicler, about whom we were taught in history-class, had never really existed but was a legendary figure invented by historians specially for us little boys. And here, suddenly, in front of me, was his large, perfectly genuine oak coffin! One only had to break open the lid and one would see with one's own eyes the dried-up body or, anyway, the skeleton, still bearing a flowing white beard, of the chronicler Nestor himself—his actual bones, his actual beard!—that ancestor of mine, who had long since become a legend and now suddenly, from the depths of past centuries, was supplying material proof not only of his own existence but of the existence of that wonderful, fairy-like but real world of primordial Russia, whence we all sprang. My feelings were echoed remarkably by Pushkin in his "Pimen":

" 'Tis not in vain that God has made of me a witness
And granted me a vision of the art of writing
That I may teach the scions of the orthodox religion
One more, just one more, final legend . . ."

A few days later, filled with new impressions and loaded with souvenirs of the Kievo-Pechersk monastery—coloured paper icons, printed by Fessenko, cypress rosaries, painted rings of St. Barbara the Sufferer, bottles of holy water, copies of the Pechersk prayer-book, green and red candles, small, blue-enamel crosses on silver chains, stereoscopes through which one could see coloured views of Kiev and the Pechersk monastery, and wooden spoons with handles carved in the shape of a hand and wrist, with the fingers curved as though administering a blessing—we returned down the Dnieper to Ekaterinoslav. Once there, I realised again, with new force, that my grandmother's home existed no more, that the smart apartment belonged solely to Ivan Maximovich, whom I had disliked on first sight and now continued to do so without any concrete reason. But though I had no real reasons, I harboured in my subconscious a picture of a repellent type of rich bully and powerful official, an acknowledged "fine figure of a man," compared with whom my papa appeared insignificant and a failure.

I began to suspect that beautiful Aunt Nina had married him for financial reasons, in order to provide for a large, impoverished family living on Grandmother's pension and the meagre earnings of my aunts. I even dramatised it and decided that she had "sacrificed herself."

But this was certainly untrue. Ivan Maximovich was a good, positive-minded husband and, as I realise now, Aunt Nina really loved him. When you come down to it, why shouldn't they have loved each other? They were a very well-matched pair—he, a handsome engineer, head of the Catherine railway's rolling-stock division; she, the daughter of a retired general, with "Her Eminence" preceding her name on envelopes addressed to her, a comparatively young beauty, still under thirty, with blue-blooded veins on her marble temples and the small, delicate hands of an aristocrat. . . .

Gramophone Needles 🖋

IVAN MAXIMOVICH, as Grandmother said, adored Nina, bought her Paris models and precious stones and took her with him on his business trips to St. Petersburg. They travelled in a first-class sleeper, with blue nets for the hand-luggage and twin beds, on a long, express Pullman train, the copper lettering on the outside of the carriages polished till it shone like the sun of the empress Catherine II, in memory of whom the railway had been built.

This first-class compartment, with velvet covers and electric light, the very name "Pullman," and the fact that this journey cost nothing —for Ivan Maximovich was entitled to free travel and even the private carriage, in which he made his rounds of inspection—aroused in me an illogical, childish hatred for the man: but everything about him irritated me, even the little combed-up fringe of fair golden hair over his forehead.

There was one oddity of his—I might say, mania—which particularly irritated me: he loved birds, bought them in large quantities without any kind of discrimination, and kept them in a large room next to his study. One day, I looked into this room and was astounded by its appearance; it was filled with innumerable birds of various species, ranging from common street-sparrows and crows to Brazilian parrots and tiny humming-birds. There was utter confusion as they flew around, hopped about the floor, screeched, pecked at their food, quarrelled, fought, and splashed each other with water. Down and feathers whirled about the room, the excellent, expensive wall-paper was smeared and torn, and the damp parquet floor was covered with husks of food and lime from the birds' excretions. A sick, dishevelled heron stood in a corner, as though sent there for punishment, a pair of turquoise-blue identical parrots circled round and round unceasingly with lunatic determination, never leaving each other's side for a second, and a kakapo screamed harshly at regular intervals. The dense atmosphere gave off an unbearable stench, that spread through the whole apartment.

Grandmother passed by me in her soft house-slippers, holding her fingers to her nose, with an expression of mingled disgust and resignation on her kind, plump face.

And, from then on, I began to loathe Ivan Maximovich even more, for forcing Grandmother and all my aunts and his beautiful wife, Nina, to suffer the consequences of his ridiculous mania. But the least hint that the birds had ruined a nice room, were making the whole apartment stink, and kept everyone awake half the night with their various piercing cries provoked him to cold, silent fury and the brush of yellow hair over his forehead seemed to become sterner and more implacable. Even Aunt Nina was afraid to say a word against the birds and meekly played the part of a dutiful wife, while I was filled with pity for her, so beautiful and so badly treated.

No doubt, Ivan Maximovich was aware of my hostility and amply returned it. I sometimes caught an uncomfortably penetrating and unkind look in his blue eyes when they turned in my direction.

All this, of course, could only end in a row.

There was a gramophone—a rarity in those times—in Ivan Maximovich's room. It was an expensive foreign one, unlike the comparatively cheap ones, with large trumpets resembling enormous petunia flowers, obtainable in the market. The nickel trumpet on Ivan Maximovich's machine was long and narrow and attached to a special, somewhat complicated stand: the box, containing the machinery, was of thick red wood and carried the label of the world-renowned gramophone firm, "His Master's Voice," with a picture on it of a terrier, peering into the trumpet in the belief that his master was sitting inside.

Sometimes Ivan Maximovich pedantically wound up his gramophone, and then the apartment was filled with the sounds of Chaliapin's bass, Sobinov's tenor, or the haunting, gypsy voice of the famous Vialtzeva, singing:

> "Drive on, troika, the snow is like down,
> With the frosty night all around.
> The moon shines like silver up above,
> And the man and the girl are in love."

: 345 :

I always pictured the "man and the girl" as Ivan Maximovich and Aunt Nina.

Of course, it was strictly forbidden to touch the gramophone, or enter the study, where a model engine stood on top of the book-case, without permission. And needless to say, the study's closed door attracted me like a magnet.

One day, snatching the right moment, I slipped inside without asking and, thinking that Ivan Maximovich was out, began carefully rummaging round. First, I turned the ribbed handle on the large telephone on the table and listened to the bell ringing, but I did not dare lift the heavy, ebony earpiece off its high, nickel prong. Then I admired the firm's trade-mark on the black box at the base of the telephone: two crossed streaks of lightning in a gilt rhomb. After that, I stood on a chair and fingered the model engine on top of the book-case. I did not risk touching the gramophone, being too afraid of breaking the circular piece of mica, which mysteriously reproduced the human voice, transferred to it from the rather scratchy, whirling, glossy-black record by a sharp needle somewhat resembling a shoe-nail. But, in the end, I did just put my finger to the tip of the needle and heard a strange, rustling sound as the mica circle magnified the friction produced by my rough skin ten times over.

New, unused needles were kept in a brass box in small black envelopes. The lid of the box also had the picture of the terrier, listening to the sound of "His Master's Voice" coming from inside the gramophone trumpet. A heap of used, blunt needles was lying in a copper ash-tray, and I wanted to check just how blunt their points had become. But as I stretched my hand out towards the ash-tray, I suddenly saw, close in front of me, Ivan Maximovich's stiff fringe and his icy eyes staring down at me from under frowning, straight brows.

"How dare you touch my things!" he thundered, then grabbed my hand and crushed it in his fist. I tried to tear myself away, but his fingers had a grip of iron. He turned my wrist over and struck it very painfully with his heavy right hand, on which he wore a thin, fashionable wedding-ring.

Nobody outside the circle of family grown-ups had ever hit me before. Such a wave of fury swept over me that I almost choked. Blood rushed to my face and pounded at my temples. I broke free from the clinging fingers and, glaring with utter hatred at his flat, bristly hair and neatly trimmed golden moustache, at the wart on his cheek, his detestable forehead, smooth as a board, and the sloping back of his head, I roared, rather than screamed—with such force that I promptly lost my voice—"You've no right to strike me, you fool!"

On hearing the last word, Ivan Maximovich grew even more purple than I, and goodness knows how the conflict might have ended if my grandmother had not rushed in, waddling like a duck, and dragged me out of the study into her room, where there was the comforting smell of a clean, kind old lady. She did all she could to calm me, stroking my head, kissing my perspiring neck, and finally ordering the cook to bring some strawberry jam and run out to the shop to buy some soda-water: she knew that I loved newly made strawberry jam in ice-cold fizzy water more than anything in the world. Shedding bitter tears and blowing out bubbles, I drank the effervescent pink mixture, covered with a light layer of delectable foam and discharging carbonic-acid gas, with an after-taste of lead, which pleasantly tickled my nose. I wiped away the tears with the palm of my hands, as I swallowed the divine drink, it was a long time before my anger with Ivan Maximovich subsided, and I felt resentful and ashamed that Grandmother had not reprimanded him and ordered him out of the house. She had not dared to, my poor, dear grandmother, who was now dependent on that horrible man! It was lucky, I decided, that my father was not there! I could imagine how his lips would have shaken, how his beard would have wagged, and how taut the skin across his Viatka cheek-bones would have become, had he known that his son had been struck. He might have done something really dreadful!

In the evening, at the dinner-table, as he cut the Swiss cheese with the large, weeping holes, Ivan Maximovich referred to the incident with artificial good humour, making out that he had given me a light slap on the hand for fear that I might accidentally prick myself on the gramophone-needles. Everyone felt embarrassed and Aunt Nina grew quite red in the face. Ivan Maximovich omitted to mention that I had called him a fool, but I knew that he would never forgive me for it, any more than I would ever forget that he had dared to hit me.

On the surface, the episode ended peacefully and was forgotten. But only on the surface. For me, Ekaterinoslav and Grandmother's house had lost all its charm. Hating Ivan Maximovich as I did, I could no longer enjoy life in Ekaterinoslav, with its rattling little tram-cars, the shady, old Potemkin garden where red admirals and other butterflies perched with folded wings on hundred-year-old tree-stumps, the Historical Museum beside which, erect and aslant, stood stone figures of Scythian women with flat, oval, mysteriously smiling faces, the steep cliffs over the Dnieper, the romantic wooden pavilion behind the house, which seemed to be suspended over the green, curving ravine, where I often went to meet a neighbour's daughter, a girl in a straw hat adorned with a blue ribbon—I no longer remember her name—the far-away, sinister, purple reflections in the dark summer sky cast by the blast-furnace in the foundry beyond Chechelevka, the sharp ring of the front door-bell when Ivan Maximovich returned from his club, the electric light and the telephone, the passing sound of the night-watchman's rattle, the small nets, like veils, sprinkled with carnation-oil, which the local inhabitants wore over their hats to protect themselves from the poisonous Dnieper mosquitoes. . . .

None of the fascinations of that life now remained for me: they had been ruined in one second by Ivan Maximovich's brutality. Later, they became broken up by time like the pictures in mosaic, discovered by archaeologists during excavations of ancient Byzantine temples. And it is many, many years after that I, by now a very old man, stare out my window near Moscow at the fog, drifting over pines, firs, and birches embedded in snow, and seek desperately to reconstruct the fragments of my life, scattered by time, into one coherent picture.

Wireless Telegraphy ✍

AND NOW, once again, I dive into the depths of my memory, passing, as it were, from one stratum of time to another. Papa arrived late one evening, when I was already in bed and pretending to be asleep. Mamma was waiting for him in the dining-room, with her elbows on the round dinner-table, reading a book, and I sensed that she was finding it difficult to conceal her impatience as she listened for his steps on the stairs. I knew that Papa had gone to the Imperial Russian Technical Society, where, twice a week in the evening, he gave lessons in Russian and geography at a "foremen's school" attended by higher-ranking workmen in charge of factories, who would now be called works-superintendents.

But today Papa had not gone to teach. Today, in the Imperial Russian Technical Society's building, an experiment in the transmission of a message by wireless telegraphy was to take place before an audience of scientists, teachers, and representatives of the town authorities.

I was very small, but I already knew that telegrams were somehow sent along wires. I had seen these telegraph-wires, stretched between poles with porcelain isolators, all over the town, and loved to watch them through the window of our compartment, as they seemed to rise and fall alongside the track when we went by train to Ekaterinoslav to visit Grandmother. I could not tear my eyes from them, hoping to see a telegram running along them—one of those envelopes containing a rectangular form, to which the printed words of the message were glued on narrow strips of paper. But I never seemed to be watching at the precise moments when the telegrams mysteriously slid along the wires wavering between the poles.

The words "telegram" and "message" had something frightening about them. I always connected them with death, with someone informing someone else that a close relative had died, remembering as I did the telegram, delivered to our house by the postman with a black pouch attached to his belt, which had brought the news of my grandfather's death from a stroke. That telegram must have somehow flown along the wires, over fields and hillocks, from Ekaterinoslav to Odessa, before landing first in the postman's sinister black pouch and then in Mamma's white, trembling hand.

In any case, I was well aware that telegrams went by wire. But I now learned something that astonished me: a new device called wireless—telegraphy had been invented and henceforward telegrams would go without wires!

How could that be?

It was so incredible that I suspected Papa of pulling Mamma's and my legs when he had told us that he was going to watch wireless telegraphy. No doubt he had gone to give his lessons in the ordinary way and would bring me back some sweets; a chocolate bon-bon in silver paper or a small pail of chocolate halva from Duvardzhoglu's sweet-shop. This did happen sometimes.

The dining-room clock struck nine—the middle of the night to me.

Mamma yawned, threw her hands up behind her head and stretched, making her corsets creak. I went on pretending to be asleep, and pretence would soon have merged into reality if there had not been a rustle from the bell-wire and then a tinkle as the door-bell bobbed up and down on its spiral spring. Mamma rushed into the hall and I heard my parents' animated voices chattering away and interrupting each other: a minute later, my father was bending down beside my bed, his dear, kind face close to mine. Seeing that I was not asleep he asked: "Why are you still awake?"

"Did they really do it without wires?"

My parents laughed, and Mamma said: "I still can't believe it, Pierre. Weren't there any wires at all?"

"Amazing, isn't it?" Papa replied: "None at all!"

Then Mamma and Papa began to argue. Mamma just could not credit that a telegram could be sent without wires, and Papa kept on assuring her that he had seen it with his own eyes and trying to explain how the experiment worked. As Papa had once taken me to the foremen's school, where I was presented with a lot of sheets of drawing-paper, I had some idea what the building, where the experiment had been conducted, looked like.

I could visualise long, official corridors, dimly lit by gas-light, and the rooms in which the classes were held. It seemed extraordinary to me that these grown-up men, some of them bearded and be-whiskered, should sit like children on school-benches and write down on slates in capital letters the words Papa dictated to them.

The experiment about which Papa was talking so enthusiastically had entailed placing a transmitter on a stool in a room at one end of the corridor and the receiving-apparatus on a stool in a room at the other. The two pieces of apparatus were not linked in any way: no wire ran between them.

"Perhaps they hid the wire somewhere?" I ventured.

Papa and Mamma laughed, and Papa went on to tell us how, as the telegraph-official typed out the telegram on the transmitter, it had been typed out simultaneously on the receiver at the other end of the corridor.

"Without wires?" exclaimed Mamma, clapping her hands.

"Without wires!" Papa replied proudly, as if it were he himself who had invented wireless telegraphy.

I pictured vividly in my mind both pieces of apparatus, with brass spools, wound with white ribbons, the Leclenché batteries pouring electricity into them, and the two telegraph-officials—one transmitting the message, the other receiving it in the shape of a row of dots and dashes on the long paper ribbon. I saw the audience, consisting of stern gentlemen in frock-coats and uniforms, with my papa among them; they were all on the alert to ensure there should be no cheating and unable to believe that the telegram had arrived all by itself without the aid of wires. . . .

They began to make a careful search, lest someone had concealed a wire under the floor or behind the wall-paper and surreptitiously connected the two pieces of apparatus. But no! There was not the faintest vestige of a wire and, to make the experiment still more convincing, it was repeated with the legs of the stools placed in special glass holders.

As Papa told all this to Mamma, her face became flushed with excitement, pride in Russian science and admiration for Popov, the naval engineer, who was first in the world to discover the principle of wireless telegraphy.

At that time, it had seemed like a miracle. Papa and Mamma drank tea in the dining-room for a long time, discussing the new discovery enthusiastically and admiring the marvels of modern science, the limitless powers of the human brain, and the genius of the Russian people, with Popov's name constantly cropping up. I was as excited as Papa and Mamma and quite unable to conceive how a telegram could fly through the air on its own from Ekaterinoslav to Odessa, over the steppes, hills, and fields of Novorossia—and not a wire to be seen through the train-window!

Infected by Mamma's and Papa's enthusiasm, I felt that an event had taken place in the world that would somehow change our whole lives. "Now, everything is going to be different!" I thought. But, awakened in the morning, as usual, by the sun slipping through the chink in the shutters, I saw that nothing had changed at all in my familiar room. There by the wall, as usual, were my two horses, Limonchik on his wheels and Kudlatka on his rockers; Mamma's dressing-table, covered with a gay chintz, stood, as usual, in one corner; the dark-brown curtains, behind which Papa's mamma lived, unheard and unseen, hung as usual in the dining-room; as usual, through the windows, one looked out on Basarnaia Street, and a net-work of telegraph-wires strung between the poles with their white china insulators.

Yet, despite this apparent absence of change, I was filled with horror at the thought of sad messages announcing deaths, winging their way across the infinite spaces of the world without any wires, entirely on their own. . . .

A Party

I SEE A LARGE tray covered with tea-glasses standing in the hall. Each glass is a quarter full of an essence, thick as tar. There is a boiling samovar there, too, emitting jets of steam from all its outlets which smother the mirror on the wall and blot out all its reflection. Soon the glasses will be filled with boiling water from the samovar, they will turn an amber-red colour, and a smell of tea will be wafted round. I can also see appetising cakes and a lot of slices of sausage dotted with white spots of lard—those delightful, succulent, pungent, moist tea-sausages, from which it was so pleasant to tear off the transparent skins. I also see a bright yellow lemon, drenched with boiling water, alongside a special little saw on a glass saucer. And I also see butter in a china dish and a pile of lump-sugar, so brightly white that it looks blue. There are a lot of heavy overcoats and black capes hanging on our small rack on the wall, but there are insufficient hooks and mountains of outdoor clothes have been heaped on tables, stools, chairs, and even arm-chairs in the sitting-room. Among the men's coats lie ladies' velvet cloaks, check Aberdeen capes, astrakhan hats and shawls. On the floor are rows of flat and ankle-high galoshes, with red cloth linings and metal clasps. From the dining-room comes a buzz of conversation from the guests, feminine laughter mingling with the deep bass, what I think of as the "bearded," voices of the men, among which I can occasionally distinguish the familiar tones of Mamma and Papa.

The cook, in a new, as yet unwashed frilly blouse and a new calico apron, hurriedly puts me to bed, blesses me, and begs me in a soft

whisper to go to sleep at once, as she has such a lot to do, what with
handing round the tea and emptying the ash-trays.

People are smoking and I find the smell of tobacco-smoke in our
non-smoking house rather disturbing. Very soon, I expect to hear
the sound of the piano coming from the dining-room, where, at the
moment, the guests are sitting around arguing about something and
noisily interrupting each other: at any rate, fresh, unused candles
have been placed in the pivoting candlesticks on each side of the
music-rest, and there is a pile of scores lying on the piano-lid beside
the wooden, pyramid-shaped metronome.

There always seemed to me something magic about this device,
which vaguely reminded me of a coffin. You only had to raise a small
metal hook, take off the thin slat of wood in front, and the metronome's simple mechanism was exposed to you—an upside-down
pendulum, with a triangular weight at the end of its narrow metal
rod to give it momentum. By giving the weight a gentle push, you
set the pendulum in motion, measuring out time with a clear, metallic, clicking sound as though regulating its course. The weight could
be moved up and down a notched scale on the rod: when it was at
the very top, the pendulum's swing was languishingly slow, as
though it were reluctant to traverse the wide arc and unnaturally
long fragments of time elapsed between the metronome's clicks. And
the lower the weight came down the scale, the faster the pendulum
swung until, with the weight on the bottom notch, it raced at the
anxious speed of a man's pulse when he has a temperature of 104.

From the day when I first became acquainted with the metronome, time, for me, seemed to lose its rhythmic uniformity, its imperceptible movement, and I began to feel it passing by either at a
wild, feverish speed or with painful slowness—depending on my
state of health or the thoughts that obsessed me. If I was ill with
influenza or any other fever, and, as Papa expressed it, "was burning,"
two metronomes seemed to start clicking in my body; one with a
very slow swing, the other with a crazily rapid one, and then my
whole body trembled like a musical instrument, on which someone
was playing chromatic scales at two different speeds, and I was tormented by this loss of any precise realisation of time, of its usual
fixed measure.

It seemed to indicate that time had many scales of measurement, that it might well be able to move both forwards and backwards—from the past into the future, or vice versa. Or perhaps there was no time at all, only an instrument measuring something that did not exit, an instrument with the strange clicking name of met-ro-nome. . . .

Lying in my bed, I tried to force my disobedient eyes to stay wide open, struggled to keep awake so that I should hear the music. I knew that, at any moment now, the virginal white candles would be lit in front of an open score, and there would be a protesting screech from the piano-stool, as its height was adjusted; and I could picture Mamma's long, outspread fingers striking the chords as they started the musical half of the party.

Until late at night—as I knew and could visualise—the conversation and arguments now going on in the dining-room would be followed by music. Music . . . music . . . music . . . but none of it reaching my consciousness.

This was always the routine in our home, when the samovar boiled in the hall and a yellow lemon, sour even to look at, shone under the mirror, misted over by the clouds of steam. But there was not a single occasion, however hard I might struggle to keep my eyes open, that I succeeded in holding my deep, childish, dreamless sleep at bay. I dropped, as it were, into a hole, and when I opened my eyes again, everything was long since over. It was morning and the apartment had been tidied up: only the stubs of candles, the streaks of turquoise-green covering the candlesticks on the piano, and the lingering smell of tobacco bore witness to the fact that there had been a party, with discussions followed by music of which I had heard nothing. And the little, upright coffin, its hook done up again, shone innocently in the rays of sunlight.

In my early childhood, when Mamma was still alive and our friends gathered in our home—when the candles were lit in front of the music-rest, the metronome clicked, stormy torrents of music flowed from Mamma's fingers as they raced over the keyboard, and the names of Glinka, Tchaikovsky, and Rubinstein were pronounced with awe and admiration—I slept the sleep of the just and heard nothing. But though I never consciously heard the music, it penetrated my being in some mysterious fashion and ever after, without coming to the surface, occupied some cell in my brain: and now, when I hear a piece of music, I am aware that I have heard it before, long ago, either when Mamma was still there and candles were burning in front of the scores, dotted with mysterious ant-like signs, or when I was burning with fever myself and, in my delirium, the metronomes clicked simultaneously, both slow and fast—at long-drawn-out intervals, and as speedily as my racing pulse registering time that does not yield to measurement, the discussions between Marxists and Populists thundering at each other over the tea-glasses, Vera Pavlovna's third dream from Chernishevsky's "What Should We Do?," Tchaikovsky's "Four Seasons," or Rubinstein's bravura sounds. . . .

We're the Gang of Agarics! 🖎

WHEN MAMMA was still alive, it was decided that I should attend a kindergarten, which was the correct thing to do at that time. Our town only possessed one, at which old ladies taught small children according to the Froebel system. I do not know the exact principles of that system. I only know that, for some reason, Mamma had great faith in it, believing it would ingrain in me a desire to work and, somehow or other, turn me into a model child.

It was just after I began to wear trousers, and it gave me great pleasure to be seen in public on my way by bus or tram to the kindergarten, situated, if my memory does not betray me, somewhere near the duke on Nikolaev Boulevard beside the Woromzov palace, with its half-moon colonnade that looked on to the funnels and masts of the ships in the harbour, the concrete break-water, the white Peresip benzine tanks, and Zhevakhov Hill, which, for some reason, always struck me as insubstantial and mysterious.

The horse tram-car was an unusual vehicle, with very small front wheels and very large back ones, and made a deafening clatter that accorded well with its slang name, "tramka," as it proceeded down Ekaterina's granite roadway. Its coachman sat on a high seat, with the handle of the cast-iron brake beside him, and sparks flew from the hooves of the pair of bony nags, wearing shiny blinkers.

In the kindergarten, we sat, dressed in special little aprons, on small, uncomfortable chairs in front of low tables and modelled various fruits and vegetables out of clay in accordance with the Froebel system—cherries, pears, apples, and, most frequently of all, mushrooms. When completed, we coloured them bright red, white, brown, and green with enamel paints. As well as modelling vast quantities of clumsy fruit and equally clumsy mushrooms, we also wove mats and baskets from strips of glossy paper, all of which was intended to instill us with proper working habits.

We also sang and danced in a circle, clapping our hands and stamping our feet, and learned French songs and verses such as: "*La bonne apporte la lampe, la petite mouche tourne autour, la flamme attire la mouche, pauvre petite mouche!*" Or, "*Un, deux, trois, allons dans le bois; quatre, cinq, six, cueillir des cerises; sept, huit, neuf, dans mon panier neuf,*" and so on. It seemed to me a lot of nonsense for several reasons—I had never seen cherries growing in a forest, for one—and the absurdities did nothing to inspire me with any confidence in the old ladies or their system.

Papa, I believe, had waxed rather sarcastic about Mamma's idea of sending me to a kindergarten and was inclined to refer ironically to my instructresses as: "Oh, those Froebelians!"

However, I continued to go to school by the tramka, modelled almost unidentifiable objects in clay, painted them in a variety of colours, and repeated like a parrot: "*Un, deux, trois, allons dans le bois.*"

I could easily have become a complete little idiot, if the head Froebelian had not conceived the great idea of furthering our artistic development by organising a public performance, in which all the boys and girls of the kindergarten would participate.

The whole thing was arranged on a grand scale. She hired the premises of a small club or dancing-school and invited Zavadsky, a former actor, now the manager of a theatrical-school, to direct the show. He was one of the celebrities of our town, like the madman Mariachez, and the ex-wrestler Foss, about whose colossal weight and no less colossal appetite I had heard grown-ups tell the most fantastic stories. They said he would go into a restaurant, where his reputation had not preceded him, order simultaneously four portions of borsch, five portions of cutlets, and eight portions of ice-cream, eat them all up, with bread and mustard, and then contrive to disappear without paying a kopeck.

Foss's sudden appearance in confectioners' shops filled their owners with a sense of imminent disaster and caused the proprietors of neighbouring food-stores to lock their doors and wait behind them, trembling, till the danger had passed.

He soon had to move to the provinces, where he was not yet known, and, in a confectioner's—so the legend went—in Tirsapol, ate fifty éclairs, after which, as though there were nothing unusual about this feat, he proceeded to the station, an alarming, elephantine, puffing figure, entered the refreshment room, and ate all the meat *pirozhki* prepared for the arrival of the next passenger-train.

The police could do nothing about Foss, as he was poor as a church-mouse and never had any money, and to throw him in the cells would have recoiled on themselves, since his Homeric, pathological appetite would have spelled ruin for any police-station.

In short, it was an era that can be summed up in one sentence: "And then came Foss, who ate up all and everything."

But I have been letting my thoughts stray. . . . Back to: "Agarics, my boys, / To war we will go!"

Unlike many of the actors of that period, Zavadsky did not lead a vagabond existence, but settled down in our town, of which he became a notable figure. You would often run across him on the boulevard or the Alexandrovsky Park and, occasionally, even in our quiet Basarnaia Street. He always surprised me by his unusual artistic attire—a flowing cloak and a broad Italian hat with the brim turned down, from beneath which a name of black hair streaked with grey fell down to his shoulders. Dark shadows lay under the tragedian's eyes in his blue, closely shaven face. Once upon a time, he had acted in our dramatic Sibiriakov Theatre and had been considered a great actor, who was idolised by the public.

I was a very small child when I first saw him on the stage at a children's matinée of *Koshchei the Eternal*.* In the last act, the evil old man writhed and squirmed in front of the kind tsarevich, Ivan, who was grasping a large duck's egg, containing Koshchei's life; he had only to squeeze the egg and Koshchei would die on the spot. The tsarevich squeezed the egg harder and harder in his great, big, powerful fist, causing Koshchei to writhe and squirm more and more painfully and stretch out bony arms towards the trunk of a card-

---

* A figure in Russian folk-lore, a wicked old man who possessed the secret of eternal life. *Translator's note.*

board oak-tree. Finally, having tormented Koshchei to the full and kept the audience in breathless suspense, the tsarevich smashed the egg to pieces on the wooden boards of the stage, and Koshchei promptly fell to the ground with an agonised cry and breathed his last, to the general delight of the children in the auditorium. After that, all ended happily: Ivan, the tsarevich, rescued the beautiful girl and married her to the accompaniment of wild applause, sending everyone home rejoicing.

The programme of our kindergarten's public matinée consisted of a few short sketches, which we had to act in French, and a huge, fairy-tale spectacle, with music and songs, called *The War of the Mushrooms*. I impatiently awaited the performance, in which I confidently expected to have a glorious success, but was so much disappointed by the actual event that I was reduced to tears. I had envisaged a magnificent auditorium like that in the town theatre, a brightly-lit stage with beautiful sets, thunderous applause in my honour, and goodness knows what else. But the performance took place in day-light, the stage looked shabby and untidy, with layers of dust in all the corners, and mice, disturbed by our unwelcome intrusion, darted hither and thither about the wings. In the almost empty auditorium, mammas, papas, grandparents, governesses, and servants, all dressed very informally, sat in rows of very ordinary wicker-bottomed chairs.

In the dark, disorderly, crowded world backstage, the magnificent, cloaked figure of Zavadsky was everywhere; with outstretched hand, on which an artificial-diamond ring sparkled, he directed the show cleverly and nimbly. It actually started without my noticing it. The short French sketches, in one of which I appeared, came first in the programme. In my role, I had to enter a watch-maker's shop with a watch in need of repair. The owner of the shop, played by one of our Froebelians, then delivered a long monologue in French, to the effect that watches should be treated carefully, after which she examined my broken watch, mended it, and returned it to me. I held it close to my ear and exclaimed ecstatically in French: *"Tic-tac, tic-tac . . .*

Then, appearing to be clumsy, I dropped it and it stopped again: the Froebelian picked it up and mended it a second time, delivering, as she did so, another lecture in French on the importance of being careful of one's watch. After receiving it back, I said politely: *"Merci, madame,"* and made my exit.

My part seemed to me to be very long, full of meaning, dramatic, and rewarding, and I foresaw a triumph in it. Just before I made my entrance, the cloaked figure loomed up and pressed into my hand the prop watch, which consisted of a case without the works.

"My boy, the main thing is not to fuss," Zavadsky said, in a deep voice: then he took me by the shoulders and, casually murmuring "Bless you," pushed me on to the stage.

Mamma was in the audience, but I failed to see her or anybody else individually for that matter: all I saw in the auditorium, meagrely lit by the day-light coming through windows overlooking a yard, was a grey blur composed of people as a whole and rows of empty chairs.

I struggled as hard as I could to keep calm and not to hurry or "fuss," but, far from succeeding, I looked around, terror-stricken, suddenly lost my head and my temper and uttered my *"tic-tac, tic-tac"* straight off, without giving the Froebelian time to say a word: then I threw the prop watch down on the stage with all my strength, so that it bounced, split in two like an oyster-shell, and shot into the audience.

I followed this up, for some reason, by stamping my foot furiously, shouting out *"Merci madame"* like a screeching parrot, and dashing off into the wings with a final incredibly theatrical gesture of wrath. I had not been on the stage for more than ten seconds, though it seemed to me that I had been there for nearly two hours, had pronounced a brilliant monologue in French, and had moved the audience to such an extent by the passion with which I had flung down the watch that it burst into a storm of applause. In fact, there had only been a few sniggers and a deep sigh from Mamma.

I remember that I was even preparing to go on again and make my bow, but Zavadsky managed to pull me back in time, and thrust me behind him into the wings: with a similar thrust of his powerful hand, he pushed forward two prettily dressed little girls in pink stockings, carrying dolls, who had a funny, short scene to act in French, while I, burying my head in some prop rags, listened with increasing bitterness to the audience applauding them as they chattered away to each other. It was only then that I realised what a failure my "début" had been.

I had set great hopes on *The War of the Mushrooms*, because one of the Froebelians had told me that I would be playing one of the main parts: though I would not actually have any lines to speak, I would have a song and occupy a prominent position downstage.

While the rest of the short sketches were going on, those of us with roles in the mushroom play put on our costumes under Zavadsky's supervision. As it turned out, only the boys playing brown-caps, russulas pine mushrooms, botulas, and other speaking parts were given pretty costumes; the rest of us, the wordless agarics, merely wore ugly-looking mushrooms, made out of crinkly coloured paper stuffed with cotton wool and attached to our backs like satchels. We were bitterly disappointed, but Zavadsky, rushing up to us like an enormous bat in his black cloak, explained that we were the real heroes of the play. The other mushrooms, for one reason and another, refused to go to war to defend the tsar, our father, whereas we agarics, daring and faithful warriors, readily answered the call and agreed to do battle, thereby displaying a patriotism worthy of the highest praise.

Although Zavadsky's explanation was encouraging, we nonetheless remained frustrated, especially when the performance began and we found the centre of the stage occupied by a richly clad tsar in a velvet hat, seated on a throne, before which passed, in Indian file, a string of other, gorgeously dressed wealthy mushrooms, including an exquisitely beautiful death-cup, each of them cravenly refusing to come to his aid.

At long last, Zavadsky pushed us, the agarics, out onto the stage, and in response to the tsar-mushroom's enquiry as to whether we were prepared to go into battle, we sang our long-rehearsed song in thin, piping voices:

> " 'We, the agarics, are ready, all of us
> To go to war without making any fuss!' "

After which we marched past him, stamping our feet, and the performance was over.

I was ready to cry—and did, in fact, cry—from sheer humiliation.

But Mamma, in a hat with an eagle's feather and a veil, took my hand and walked me home along the grey, dry, stony autumn pavement, consoling me with the assurance that I had acted far better than any of the others.

I believed her and began to feel more cheerful, though at the bottom of my heart there still remained some bitterness and resentment at having been a mere, ugly agaric, doomed to fight and die for the tsar-mushroom, alongside my fellow-agarics, while the other, richer, more beautiful mushrooms stayed safely behind in their forests.

It was a cold, overcast day in the town of stone, where empty wagons rattled down the slope to the harbour, meeting other wagons, heavily laden with cases of oranges, struggling on their way up, and the chilly, autumnal air was redolent with the delicious, essentially Christmas, smell of oranges and mandarins.

Alexandrovsky Park

A HUGE square bed of standard roses, surrounded by a wonderfully green, well-mowed lawn, and beyond a long, arched brick wall—all that remained, I believe, of an ancient Turkish fortress. . . . Visible through the arches, a stretch of sea, the bright white tower of the harbour-lighthouse, the sharp bows of a yacht . . . A warm, gentle breeze off the Black Sea, lulling one to sleep . . . Broad paths, covered with a thick layer of smooth, surf-polished gravel brought from Dofinovka in splendid barges, drawn by a chuffing tug-boat . . .

In Dofinovka, there was an endless supply of this gravel, but it is not the gravel I remember so much as the deep, moist, slow, crunching sound it made beneath the wheels of the small carriages in which we children rode. These vehicles were harnessed to two smelly goats with insolent eyes, their pupils like fig-seeds, and long nostrils that added an appearance of wickedness and arrogance. They were led by an old man with a leather purse hanging on his chest, who grasped a whip in his brown hand: the whip was purely ornamental, because the ancient goats behaved obediently, walking sedately along the crunching gravel and producing an occasional tinkle from the bells on their harness.

The small holes in the bells, the size of fig-seeds, reminded one of the goats' immobile eyes, while the narrow slits resembled their arrogant nostrils.

The smell of the lacquer on the sides of the carriages combined with the red standard roses, the lawns, and the sea glimpsed through the arches of the brick wall to fill my child's mind with an ecstatic awareness of the world in all its beauty, joys, and hopes—my own particular hope that moment being to drive behind the goats. Such expeditions in Alexandrovsky Park provided the greatest happiness of my childhood.

But they were never easy to achieve. One had, first, to acquire three kopecks—the price of one ride round the lawn, and the goats' owners were always surrounded by a crowd of children begging from mammas or nurses, with tears in their eyes, the supreme happiness of being granted a drive in one of the small carriages. These carriages had two seats for two facing each other, covered in striped calico with ornamental buttons like those in second-class compartments on trains.

For some reason, nurses, mothers, and governesses did not readily accede to the requests for rides, and the children usually had to plead desparingly for a long time before attaining permission. Thus, when they finally sat down, two on one side, two on the other, the girls in light, beribboned hats over their curls, the boys in sailor-suits, their smiles of enchantment broke out over faces bearing traces of recent tears.

At the start, the journey around the fresh green lawn, surrounded by metal arches for the climbing plants and low parapets of privet, seemed to stretch ahead endlessly as the goats proceeded slowly and sedately along, tinkling their bells and occasionally dropping black olives onto the crunching gravel from beneath their piebald tails. Nannies, governesses, and mammas walked on each side of the carriages, clinging to the children with strained expressions on their faces, as though fearing that the smallest carelessness on their part might lead to immediate catastrophe. But, alas, endless as the trip round the standard roses had originally seemed, this proved to be an illusion, as the distance separating us from our starting-point grew shorter and shorter.

The old man led his goats unhurriedly but implacably towards his objective and, had he been carrying a scythe on his shoulder instead of the long-handled whip, he might well have been taken for Chronos, firmly leading a man to his death. I had seen a picture of

Chronos, the god of time, on the front page of the *Niva*,* which we took at home, and thereafter always remained frightened by his long, thick, grey beard, blown to one side, his clothes floating out behind him, the scythe slung over his shoulder, and the hour-glass in his bony hand.

Alexandrovsky Park did not consist solely of watered lawns, standard roses, gravel paths, low privet parapets, and neatly clipped yew trees with misty-blue, tarry cones; it also possessed neglected avenues and romantic corners. In one section, an arched bridge with woven maple-branch sides crossed a small, pathetic stream, forcing its way through a jungle of weeds.

These remote places were ideal for playing at being Englishmen and Boers in the war, of which we had seen pictures in other copies of the *Niva*. The Boers were bearded, wore broad-brimmed hats, carried guns, and had bandoliers hanging all over them. I no longer remember what the Englishmen looked like, but I believe they were in regimental tunics, leggings, and tropical helmets, and some of them had pipes in their mouths. I loved the Boers and hated the English: why, I do not know. Probably because the Boers were simple, poor working-folk, devoted to their country, the Transvaal, and the rich, cruel English were trying to invade it in order to transform it into one of their colonies and enslave the rightful owners—or something to that effect. . . .

The boys who frequented Alexandrovsky Park somehow divided up into pro-Boers and pro-English. I noticed that the English side mainly consisted of officers' children, who were escorted to the park by army-orderlies instead of nannies. The children, like myself, who had civilian parents, represented the Boers.

But, heavens above, what hostility and hatred existed between us "Boers" and "them, the English"! They were excellently armed: some of them even carried their fathers' sabres with sword-knots or rusty bayonets, dating from the comparatively recent Russo-Turkish War. We were armed with toy rifles with faded canary-yellow wooden stocks and copper barrels or air-pistols firing corks on the end of a string.

To tell you the truth, no actual battles took place between the

* Russian illustrated periodical. *Translator's note.*

English and the Boers. There were only mutual threats and bel-
ligerent challenges. The officers' children took up their position on
top of a small hill, covered with slippery pine-needles, where they
constructed fortifications in accordance with the best precepts of the
art of warfare; earthen forts above which miniature flags, made from
odds and ends of medal ribbons, floated in the sea-breeze. From these
strongholds, military orders rang out and their boy-commander
threatened us from afar with a real sabre. We, the poor, needy, but
recklessly courageous Boers, expelled from our own lands by the
accursed English, adopted guerrilla tactics and imagined ourselves
to be hiding under the bridge among the weeds with a pack of mules,
loaded with cases of dynamite and machine-guns, awaiting the right
moment to blow up the bridge and attack the English from an
ambush.

As a matter of fact, though we knew that the Anglo-Boer War was
taking place in the Transvaal, we had no idea where the Transvaal
was: possibly it lay in the African desert, possibly somewhere else
altogether. In any case, this remote corner of the Alexandrovsky Park
served very satisfactorily as our Transvaal.

Unfortunately, we Boers had no chance of blowing up the bridge:
the English caught us napping. We took to our heels, but I alone was
taken prisoner and conducted up the hill to the English HQ.

"You filthy Boer, now you're going to be shot!" the commander
announced, baring his sabre. I was tied with a skipping-rope to a
small pine-tree, exuding a warm, pleasant smell of turpentine. My
sailor-suit became stuck to the thin, scaly trunk by the gummy drops
of resin.

"Bandage the eyes of that scoundrelly Boer!" ordered the commander, but I made a rejective movement of my body to signify that
I preferred to look death in the face.

The English took aim at me with the canary-yellow rifles they
had captured from us. And I mustered all my will-power and fearlessly, as became a true Boer, stared straight in front of me with
ruthless, wide-open eyes, seeing in the distance the bright blue sea
framed by the arches of the old brick wall, overgrown with moss,
the green lawn with its huge rose-bed, and two piebald goats led by
Chronos, the god of time, slowly drawing behind them a carriage full
of well-dressed children: and I could hear the tinkling of its bells

and the crunch of its wheels on the moist gravel. And I felt no fear for, at that time, I was still immune from death. . . . Mamma watched from afar and laughed.

The English could not kill me, because they had not captured our ammunition along with the guns: we had managed to hide it in the nick of time among the thick weeds under the bridge, where our imaginary mules, carrying their imaginary cases of dynamite, stood patiently in the shade. . . .

The Sinking of the Petropavlovsk ✒

THE RUSSO-JAPANESE war is connected in my mind with the black, shaggy "Mandshurian" fur hats worn by Port Arthur soldiers, returning home from Japanese captivity. They reached our town in ships of our voluntary reserve fleet.

I remember the fun-fair on the Kulikovo field, where, during Easter week, they showed *The Sinking of the* Petropavlovsk. I remember the sad, heart-rending military march "Longing for my Fatherland," which was played by a brass band on the wooden stand beside the tall, whitewashed flagstaff, flying the white and blue Russian trade-flag.

The plaintive tune, momentarily interrupted from time to time by the best of the Turkish drums, filled my own heart with sorrow for my homeland as I thought of her defeat at Tsushima and the surrender of Port Arthur. I suffered for her in her humiliation, for the Russia I had hitherto believed to be the greatest and most invincible country in the world.

In the sounds of the brass trumpets and the serpent-like fioriture of the flutes, I seemed to hear Japanese or Chinese words, alien to Russian ears, wafted somehow from the hills of Manchuria: "Chumisa, Gaolian, shimosa, liaian, chemulpo. . . .

The words evoked pictures of bloody battles against small yellow-faced Japanese in white gaiters among clay defences and ruined shrines and temples.

At the fun-fair, there were several rows of benches—rough, narrow planks nailed to pine supports driven into the ground. They were uncomfortable to sit on, as my feet did not reach the ground, strewn with the husks of sunflower seeds. A dim gleam filtered through the canvas roof, and two kerosene lamps with reflectors hung on the sides of the small stage, lighting up the curtain.

The curtain rolled up to expose the stage of the dolls' theatre and I saw Port Arthur; its quays, shrines, and, in the distance, the yellow parapets behind which the small Russian batteries were sited. But, most of all, I was fascinated by the animation of the roadstead, by the ceaseless movement of the waves, flecked by a frothing white foam. At first sight, it seemed to me a quite inexplicable theatrical trick: I was totally unable to understand how they could achieve these long rollers with curly foam that now appeared on their crests, now slid down their sides and disappeared into the depths of the ocean. However, it was not long before the movement of the waves struck me as suspiciously uniform, and I suddenly realised how the effect was produced. The billows in Port Arthur Bay were made of greenish-blue painted card-board, with a line of curly papier-mâché foam, and attached to a cylinder. When this was revolved by a stage-hand in the wings, the sea took on a tempestuous appearance, as the line of foam surged upwards and down again on what looked like rolling waves. It was the regular appearance and disappearance of the foam that led me to understand that I was not gazing at real water but at an ingenious illusion. However, this in no wise diminished my admiration for the scene, especially as the quay was filled with fascinatingly vivid, mechanical moving figures of Chinese men with long pigtails, Chinese women walking on tiny, swaddled feet, and rickshaw-boys dragging their light, two-wheeled carriages, occupied by important passengers—Englishmen wearing tropical pith helmets or Russian guard-officers in regimental caps or black Caucasian *papakhas*. Here were also a number of street-booths surrounded by groups of gesticulating customers. . . .

Beautiful singsong girls passed by in open carriages, languidly waving their oval fans, and coolies ran hither and thither, bent under the weight of the packing-cases and bundles on their backs. Just beyond the edge of the quay, boats with red sails rocked up and down on the waves. Further out, in the roadstead, between two whirling billows, lay the huge, long Russian dreadnought *Petro-pavlovsk,* with her gun-turrets turned towards the open sea. At her mast-head flew the Andreev flag, with its two diagonal blue stripes that made it look rather like an envelope.

A strong, emotional feeling of pride filled my heart, though I did not then know that this feeling was called patriotism. It made what ensued all the more appalling. There was a loud explosion, like that of a Bengal firework, from the middle of the *Petropavlovsk,* followed by a fountain of golden rain: the dreadnought's long body broke in two, her stern and bows rose in the air and she began to sink slowly into the depths of the sea between the two whirling foamy waves.

She sank quicker and quicker until all that remained of her above the surface was the Andreev flag still flying at her mast-head. Then, this, too, disappeared to the tune of "Longing for my Fatherland," played uninterruptedly on a barrel-organ.

All her crew, the pride and hope of the Russian navy, were drowned, along with Admiral Makarov and the famous painter Vereshchagin—as my aunt had already told on her way to the fair.

Tears poured down her powdered cheeks and she constantly blew her nose in a crumpled little lace handkerchief, faintly smelling of the French scent Coeur de Jeanette: for some reason, this made the sinking of the *Petropavlovsk* even more poignant for me.

Possibly, the Japanese sank the *Petropavlovsk,* possibly she was blown up by a mine. Nobody knew for certain.

Meanwhile, on stage, our land-batteries around Port Arthur had gone into action, and here and there, in the blue Manchurian sky, there rose the sinister black stars of Japanese shells. Along the quay, hissing fire-crackers leaped about, emitting showers of golden sparks and a "sun" firework spun round like a top. Finally, to the same strains of "Longing," the curtain, which had rolled up into a tube at the beginning of the performance, descended on the small stage, now filled with smoke from the gunpowder.

As my aunt and I left the theatre, the spring sunset was still faintly aglow behind the station, the air was permeated with dust, which had not yet had time to settle after the day's throng of pleasure-seekers, and the Kulikovo field was almost empty. It was the seventh and last day of Easter week and the end of the fun-fair. The flag had already been lowered and the whitewashed flag-staff stood naked and forlorn in the centre of the grounds. Beside it, a policeman was blowing sharp, angry blasts on his whistle to indicate that the fair was over. Several booths had already been dismantled and their broken planks left strewn about the site. "Longing for my Fatherland" was coming to an end. I had learned some of the words from the soldiers from Port Arthur, who prowled about the town: "I'll soon be taking the long way home, where wife and children are all alone."

A strange sense of loss filled my heart.

The Earthquake ✒

I WAS SUDDENLY awakened in the middle of the night by a rushing, mechanical sort of sound that I took, at first, to be coming from the sewing-machine in the dining-room. "Mamma" I said to myself, "is sitting at the table, busily turning the handle of the machine," which had a cast-iron body that always made me think of a statuette of an Egyptian cat standing on a lacquered wooden pedestal set in a metal base. (Though, at that time, I was unaware of the existence of ancient Egypt, its statuettes, or its sphinxes.)

The idea of Mamma sewing something so rapidly at that time of night on her Singer machine was frightening and disturbing. I raised my head, heavy with sleep, from the pillow and took a look around. Everything appeared to be quiet and peaceful by the light of the red-shaded night-light, though it seemed to me to be rocking gently on top of the chest of drawers. And Mamma was not in the dining-room: she and Papa were asleep in their narrow iron beds, decorated with brass balls, without noticing the tremor which by now seemed to be shaking the whole house and possibly even the street outside.

So, if it had not been Mamma operating the machine in the middle of the night, who could it have been? Surely not Grandmother, who lived in the dining-room behind the brown screen? No, that was not possible, because then there would have been a light, which would have penetrated the room in which we slept through the keyhole or the cracks of the door, and the dining-room was completely dark.

The shaking continued. Now all the furniture was quivering—the side-board, the chairs, the table. The lamp with the white shade above the table began swinging jerkily, its glass, insecurely held by the screws in the base, rattled, and the chain by which it was suspended from the ceiling jangled. Something strange and frightening was happening in the world.

I began to cry and, stretching my fat hand through the net over my bed, on the head of which the icon of my guardian angel Valentin was trembling, I woke up Mamma by clutching at her cheek.

"What's the matter, my boy?" Mamma asked in a whisper, so as not to wake Papa, who was snoring lightly in the adjoining bed. "What woke you up?"

"I'm frightened," I said.

"What are you frightened of?"

"Someone's sewing on the machine out there in the dining-room," I murmured in a whisper, afraid of being overheard by whoever it was who was sewing. "And they're making the lamp shake."

Mamma listened, but the strange, rushing noises had stopped. A peaceful natural silence reigned in the apartment.

"You must have imagined it," said Mamma. "Go to sleep, my darling, God bless you!"

She made the sign of the cross over me, kissed me, rearranged my blanket, and tucked me in.

I was reassured and, cupping my cheek in the palms of my hands, fell asleep; but I was soon awakened again by the same alarming sounds. Before I could start whimpering, they had ceased, though it still seemed to me that, for a time, the whole room, with the beds on their small wheels, the chest of drawers, and the faded wall-paper, dimly lit by the red night-light, continued to quiver almost imperceptibly. And I sensed that, beyond the closed shutters, not only our long Basarnaia Street but the whole of our big town, the limits of which I could not yet fathom, were quivering, too.

All nature was quivering! And then I fell asleep again, with a mingled feeling of anxiety and relief that we had safely escaped some strange danger. This feeling still remained with me in the morning when Papa and Mamma had awakened and we were sitting together at table, I on my high chair eating porridge and dipping a crust of white bread into my bowl of boiled milk, which covered it with a layer of skin.

"Our boy has terrible dreams," Mamma said to Papa and repeated what I had told her.

"It wasn't a dream!" I protested. "I *did* hear someone sewing on the sewing-machine in the middle of the night and the lamp *was* shaking!"

Mamma and Papa laughed, and Papa rumpled my thick crop of hair, black as that of a Japanese boy, took a stack of copy-books tightly tied together with a string, and went off to his lessons at the diocesan school.

Ah, how well I remember those stacks of copy-books with blue covers and pink, ink-stained blotting-paper sticking out of them. Papa used to correct them in the evenings under the lamp on his desk, its green shade trembling slightly as he wielded his pencil.

Despite the fact that Papa and Mamma did not believe that I had heard this curious rushing sound in the night, resembling the noise of a sewing-machine, and were convinced that I had dreamed it all, I remained certain that it had really occurred and that in it lay some mystery of the world in which we lived not yet revealed to me.

And I proved to be right. It had *not* been a dream.

When he arrived home that evening, Papa unfolded a cpy of the Odessa *News*, ran his eyes over it this way and that and suddenly exclaimed gaily: "Why, look, Zhenichka, our boy was right after all!"

And he proceeded to read out a paragraph stating that the seismograph at our town observatory had recorded underground tremors during the previous night, the result of an earthquake with its epicentre in Turkey on the Asia Minor shores of the Black Sea, where several villages had been destroyed.

" 'This earthquake was of a minor tectonic character and did not present any serious danger to our town, except for a few landslides in the Middle Fountain area, where a number of villages sustained light cracks.' "

When he had finished reading this final paragraph in the report of the incident, Papa turned to me, smiling: "So you've turned out to be a scientist!" he said. But Mamma's face suddenly clouded over.

"Our boy has too sensitive a soul," she said. "I'm afraid that he will have a hard life."

I did not then understand Mamma's anxieties. I was feeling exuberant because no-one but me had been aware of the objects quivering in our room with the dark wall-paper, faintly lit by the red glow of the night-light rocking about on the chest of drawers; I alone had sensed it in my sleep, awakened, and heard the rattling of the sewing-machine.

Only I did not know at the time the name of that mysterious force, uncontrollable by man, which could shake lamps, night-lights, doors and houses, bring down the roofs in Turkish villages and destroy, in one second, whole towns, countries, nations. But now I learned from Papa that the mysterious force was called an "earthquake," as dismal and frightening a word as "war," "plague," and "famine," of which I knew nothing in those far-off, happy days of childhood.

Castor-Oil ✍

WE LIVED on the second floor—which my aunt liked to refer to as the "*bel étage*"—of a large house in Kanatnaia Street belonging to Goldenhorn, and our windows looked out onto the Kulikovo field, across which the wind always blew clouds of dust.

Almost in front of our house was a big locomotive-shed, from which the small, almost toy engines of the Great Fountain railway constantly emerged. And, from morning till night, suburban trains came dashing past us, rattling the windows. No doubt, this was why our large, very comfortable apartment on the *bel étage* was so cheap.

I saw the revolution of 1905 from our windows—the militants in old cloth coats, armed with revolvers, the mounted patrols of the sixth Don Cossack regiment, and, finally, dark as a storm-cloud, the dense crowd of Black Hundred members crossing the Kulikovo field on a diagonal course from the station square to the corner of Pirogov Street, where Goldenhorn's house was situated. As the crowd approached our building in ominous silence, I noticed a lithographic portrait of the emperor with a blue ribbon across his shoulder, in a narrow gold frame, carried by two angry old men wearing merchants' overcoats.

The crowd paused for a moment, then made a concerted rush towards our corner, where there was a grocer's shop in a semi-basement, at which we always bought sugar, kerosene, macaroni, and sun-flower oil. It belonged to a Jew called Kogan. Stones flew towards the shop's windows and, in a matter of seconds, it was completely devastated. For a long time after the crowd had passed on, the pavement was strewn with spilt tea, pools of kerosene, squashed boxes of cigarette-papers, packets of Troika and Brothers Asmolov tobacco, sweets in coloured paper wrappings, and fragments of broken glass. In the deserted street, against the background of the dry, winter's dust, rising in clouds over the Kulikovo field, it was a fearsome spectacle.

Everyone refrained from touching the grocer's property, lying in front of the shop. Even the Gorki types from Romanovka village—wicked-looking devils in torn shirts, their naked feet red from the cold—managed to keep away from the tempting articles it would have been so easy and safe to appropriate as they passed by.

The street-urchins from Novoribovka, driven by curiosity, slipped into the wrecked shop across the door torn from its hinges, but none of them took a single sweet or tore the smallest piece off the block of cheap white halva, now soaked in sesame oil, which had been thrown on the floor under the broken counter alongside the cast-iron weights of the crushed scales.

The November wind blew in through the smashed basement windows, bringing with it withered acacia- and chestnut-leaves, which whirled about among the chaos.

I, too, with my heart in my mouth, went down the cracked steps and walked around Kogan's shop, crunching rice, nuts, and shattered cups and saucers under my feet.

Luckily, Kogan and his family—his wife in a black hat and lace mittens, four red-haired, freckle-faced children, their lips pale lilac from fear, the two boys in white socks, the two girls in small lace hats, and an old grandmother with a hooked nose and trembling head—had had time to hide in an apartment leased to Christian tenants, who had placed icons lit up by oil-lamps on the window-sills facing the Kulikovo field to protect themselves from attacks by the Jew-hunters.

On the floor of the shop, amidst the kopecks emptied out of the cash-box, I spotted Mr. Kogan's bowler hat, bashed in and trampled on by the dastardly boots of the "Union of the Russian People." At these moments, the world around me was terrifying.

It remained terrifying for some time after, especially on the day when Papa was coming home by cab with a folding child's bed he had bought for Zhenia, who had grown out of his very small old one. Suddenly a red car—or "self-propelling vehicle," as they were then called—swung round the corner of Pirogov Street and headed straight for the cab: the horse swerved to one side and reared up, while the cab mounted the pavement and crashed into our gate-post. Papa and Zhenka's bed were flung out, his foot got caught in the cab's step, and he was dragged some way along the pavement, clutching the bed that was threatening to crush him with one hand and resting his weight on the other. I was playing near the house at the time and could see a patch of blood on his forehead and the skin being torn off his palm.

And the red car with a brass, coiled horn, and a chauffeur in a dog's-fur coat, turned inside out, and alarming motoring goggles, which concealed his face like a mask, discharged clouds of stinking benzine and flashes like gunfire from its engine as it proceeded down the road, bouncing about in the pot-holes and causing a near-panic. Angry pedestrains shook their fists and sticks at it and shouted: "How long are they going to allow such disgraceful things to happen? What are the police up to? It's high time they stopped those stinking machines appearing on the streets, frightening the horses and injuring passers-by!"

At that time, there were only about three or four cars in the town and the towns-people considered them an invention of the devil, a menace from hell, almost the first signs of the end of the world and the Second Resurrection.

Fortunately, all ended comparatively well and Papa escaped with nothing worse than a few scratches and shock, which left his face trembling and twitching and his beard sadly dishevelled.

I cannot describe how sorry I felt for Papa, as he dragged the child's folding iron bed up the marble stairs to our *bel étage* with the help of the yardsman.

I experienced an even stronger feeling of this kind later, when we lived for a time with a priest, who was a friend of Papa's, at Gladvok's orphanage, while waiting for an apartment in the Society of Apartment Owners' building in Pirogov Street to be completed. The orphanage was surrounded by a high stone wall and at night a ferocious dog was let off its chain.

Papa had been detained at the pedagogical council and came home late, when the dog was already loose. The night was exceptionally bright and cold and the shadows of the already naked trees, with every branch sharply detailed, seemed to have been drawn with coal on the white walls of the orphans' wing. As Papa came in through the gate, the dog sprang at him like one of the black shadows, knocked him off his feet, and began to bite him.

The yardsman ran to his assistance, chased the dog away, and put it back on its chain. Papa came in with his coat all torn and covered in blood. Aunt at once set about undressing him, cutting off the sleeve of his shirt with scissors as he half-lay in the arm-chair, and I saw the dark bluish-red marks of the dog's teeth on his white shin and the blood dripping from his wounds. There was a garnet-coloured lamp in front of the icon and outside the windows shone a blue moonlit night: the flame from a candle flickered, throwing huge moving shadows on the walls, and pieces of cotton wool and gauze floated on top of the incarnadined water in the enamel bowl.

Sobbing bitterly, I embraced Papa's knees and repeated in horror and despair: "Papa, Papa, dearest, darling Papa." And my heart was ready to burst with love for this adored man, closer to me than anyone in the world. I thought that Papa was going to die there and then before my eyes, or else go mad: for who could tell whether the dog had not had rabies?

Zhenia knelt beside me close to Papa and kept crossing himself, as tears poured from his watchful, amber eyes.

Everything, however, returned to normal far quicker than we could believe. In half an hour, Papa's wounds had been painted with black iodine and bound round with sterilised bandages, from which came the reassuring smell of chemists' shops: washed and dressed in clean clothes and a dressing-gown, his damp hair carefully combed, he sat drinking tea and even managed to smile at us.

This incident inflicted such a deep inner shock on me that even now I feel distraught whenever I remember that moonlit November night, the sharp outline of the running dog, the wavering purple shadow of the candle in an unfamiliar room, and the sterilised bandages on Papa's bare arm.

And I have an idea—a vague idea—of what Papa must have gone through later on, during the two years that I was away at the front, as he waited for the letters I wrote so reluctantly and so seldom. He must surely have thought all the time that I had been killed by a bullet or shell and have pictured me, his son, his own flesh and blood, falling to the ground, a mangled corpse.

About that time, on another of those moonlit nights, there came the news that Stolypin had been assassinated in Kiev, and the two events, the dog biting my father and Stolypin in all his glory dying from a shot in his liver at the Kiev theatre, in front of the emperor, became blended in my mind into one strange picture in the dark room, beneath the garnet-coloured light of the icon-lamp.

Near the Goldenhorn house, protected by a high stone wall, stood the headquarters building of the Odessa Military District, in which we believed all the important military secrets were hidden. The exterior of the wall faced a stretch of deserted waste-land, overgrown with weeds. Even in daytime, the place was eerie, and at night we imagined all sorts of dangerous criminal acts occurring there, as the wintry wind whistled in a sinister way.

One day, we heard that a soldier on sentry-duty by the rear gates that were always kept locked had killed himself beside the striped sentry-box, in which he hung his yellow, wadded coat. I visited the spot where his death had taken place and saw the indentation in the ground made by his head, filled with a reddish-brown liquid that had not yet had time to dry. He had killed himself by the method soldiers usually employed at that time; by taking off one of his boots and pressing the trigger of his rifle with his toe, while the muzzle was jammed against the roof of his mouth.

I dreamed of that soldier for a long time, with his closely cropped hair, his bare foot and waxen toe, and his white eyes beneath wheat-coloured brows, filled with the anguish of death. Outside the wall, in the rotting weeds, I once found an old, black five-kopeck coin, covered with lichen. It somehow seemed to me to bear traces of some dark, secret vice. . . .

The evenings were long and frightening. Rumours spread of murders, burglaries, and break-ins. People talked about "Black Ravens," who attacked passers-by and haunted every corner and empty site in the town. Papa would sometimes cross the Kulikovo field in the evening to fetch the papers from the station. I used to beg him not to go, terrified that the Black Ravens might pounce on him and kill him. But he disappeared into the dark night with a fearless laugh— and always returned safely. We recognised his long ring on the door-bell, but nonetheless asked who was there before taking off the chain. "Who's there?" we demanded, and the answer invariably came: "Black Ravens with nuts."

Besides the St. Petersburg papers bulging out of his coat-pockets, Papa always brought us presents; usually hot roasted chestnuts in a paper bag or very thin sweet biscuits from Ambatiello's shop. The small biscuit-bag was made of very fine paper, which made it easy to blow up and then explode with a noisy bang by clapping it between one's hands.

We had never had chains on our doors before; now no apartment was without them. In this, too, I sensed something sinister.

But do not think that everything was sinister and terrifying around the Goldenhorn house opposite the Kulikovo field during that autumn and winter. Winter brought the snow with it and the Kulikovo field grew white. Hard frosts struck us. Beyond the station, above the blue clouds of steam, an icy sunset flamed, the engines' whistles shrilled with particular distinctness in the frosty air and the electric lights on the platforms twinkled palely and beautifully beside the red and green eyes of the signals.

After Christmas, New Year, and Nativity, the clergy of the parish and the priest of the Botanical Church, in a stiff, lilac velvet head-dress, from which his well-combed, chestnut hair fell to his shoulders, blessed everyone's house. Dipping the little brush in the silver bowl— a bowl like our soup-tureen—handed to him by the deacon, the priest sprinkled the holy water with a wide, sweeping movement of his arm as he went round all the rooms of our apartment, including the kitchen, where the sprinkled cook crossed herself repeatedly and tried to catch his hand in order to kiss it.

The Epiphany frosts formed crystal designs on the outsides of the windows that might have been painted there with zinc. Bowls of steaming cranberry kissel were put out on the balconies to grow cold. The kissel was so bright red that it seemed as though it, rather than the January sun setting behind the station, was providing the departing winter with its rich rubicund hue.

And then came Shrovetide, when blinis were baked in the kitchen and pans of melting butter hissed on the stove. The smell penetrated the whole apartment, tickling the throat and bringing tears to the eyes.

We did not celebrate Shrovetide every year, but only now and then. In this particular year, a cousin of mine, Vassia, the son of Papa's dead brother Nicholas, came to stay. He was a student at the Military Medical Academy—"within five minutes of becoming a military doctor"—a gay, witty, always lively young man with a small black moustache and a pince-nez on a black ribbon, draped behind his ear. He had something pleasantly French about him, mingling with the Russian, and was very much a Petersburg student. His mother, the widow of Uncle Nicholas, had been a governess in a rich Russian family in the Crimea, and it was there she had met and married Uncle Nicholas—a quite ordinary affair. A French-Swiss from Vevey, she adopted the Orthodox religion and transposed her name to Zinaida Emmanuilovna. Though she quickly became assimilated to Russian life, while always retaining her lively, exumerant, domineering French temperament, she never learned to speak Russian properly; her accent, together with her hats, red chignon, springy foreign pince-nez, and checked Scottish cloak, provided endless amusement for the women in the old market, where she went daily to buy provisions, since she did not trust the cook, and bargained mercilessly in her mixed Franco-Russian-Ukrainian accent, not from miserliness, but because her practical Swiss character drove her to ensure that every kopeck was well spent.

She was an excellent wife, gave birth to a number of Russian children, and proved a wise, tender mother and clever housekeeper. She worshipped her Russian husband, a teacher in the local seminary, who wore a forked dignitary's beard, through which one could glimpse the red enamel and gold of the Order of St. Stanislas, smoked fat cigarettes, and was a steady drinker, without ever losing his sense of decorum.

Vassia was her eldest son, Sasha, her youngest. Her eldest daughter, Nadia, was a beauty who had married a St. Petersburg röntgenologist, and her second daughter, Zina, was also a beauty, with a vivid face and eyebrows of sable. Her youngest daughter, Liolia, had died at the age of eleven from tuberculosis of the bones. She passed her widowhood in active concern for her children's welfare and constant preoccupation with her pension and something she called "emeritus" in the French manner, along with another French word, *"consistoire."* She uttered the two words with such respect, fear, and hope that she might have been referring to the Senate or the State Council. This was understandable, since both led to an increase in the pension, which was her only means of bringing up her children.

One day the beautiful Nadia passed through Odessa on her way from St. Petersburg to the Far East. She was travelling with her military röntgenologist husband and a new-born baby, Alla. I remember the husband's Caucasian hat and the little girl's lace-trimmed nappies when we went down to the harbour to see them off on the voluntary fleetship *Tambov*, which was to take them to Vladivostock, whence they would proceed to Khabarovsk. A military band was playing "On the Mounts of Manchuria" and "Longing for my Fatherland," and I saw the narrow cabin with its circular port-hole filled with expensive Petersburg suit-cases and hat-boxes, and the baby asleep amidst all the disorder. They were going to the Russo-Japanese war; it was all very sad and frightening, and the grey, overcast sky made it even more depressing.

Vassia turned up in his army-doctor's cloak, which still had private's shoulder-straps, though he wore an officer's sabre on his narrow, silver belt. He hung his cloak and sabre on the coat-rack, put his cap on the table under the mirror, and cheerfully adjusted his green tunic, with its two rows of medical-corps buttons, which fitted his slender, thin-waisted figure admirably. He spread around him a smell of brilliantine, a barber's shop, and a damp, frosty spring day. The smoke from the blinis cooking in the kitchen brought tears to his gay, dark eyes, rimmed by the black edges of his pince-nez.

Our other cousins, with the charming Zinaida Emmanuilovna at their head, came with Vassia. Zinaida wore a shabby, check cape with a three-cornered hood, which gave her a foreign, Swiss appearance.

There was always something invisibly Swiss about her, evoking the lake of Geneva, sail-boats, the snow-capped peak of the Dent du Midi, and the castle of Chillon.

The guests filled our rooms with gaiety, and the apartment was permeated by clouds of blini smoke. Vassia was the hero of the day, as he was shortly going to Khabarovsk, where there was a vacancy for an army doctor. He was already virtually an officer, since he would receive his promotion immediately on arrival. Though the Japanese war was over, the Fart East, where Nadia and her husband had already gone and Vassia was on the point of going, still appeared to be a theatre of war, and this served to enhance our interest in his journey and our affection for him.

Little Zhenia never left him for a moment; grasping the cuff of his tunic with his small, plump hand, he dragged him to the piano with the plea: "Vassia, pay the kickwick," which meant, "Vassia, play the cakewalk."

Vassia adjusted the cane seat of the piano-stool, drawing a protesting squeak from the iron screw, sat down, settled his pince-nez more firmly on his nose, tossed back the tails of his tunic with a neat gesture, pressed down the loud-pedal with his foot that emerged from narrow trousers with red piping, and raised his hands, preparatory to attacking the keyboard. Then he suddenly changed his mind, turned to face Zhenka, Sasha, and me, who were grouped around him, and frowned at us with beetling eyebrows, black as leeches, above the bridge of his nose, pinched by the springs of his newfangled pince-nez: "And what about your castor-oil, you young rascals?" he asked menacingly.

Sasha and I froze because we had hoped that, in the general Shrovetide turmoil, the hated castor-oil, which nearly made us sick, would somehow be forgotten. Strange to relate, Zhenka adored it and drank it down with delight, even passing his tongue over his lips after he swallowed it.

"No, no, my young patients, you aren't going to dodge your castor-oil like that! You won't get away with that trick!"

We sat down meekly side by side, aware that we were doomed. Vassia thought the nauseating bottle of yellow liquid from the kitchen, got a large silver spoon out of the cupboard—its shininess provoked almost as much revulsion as the castor-oil itself—pulled out the cork wrapped in greasy paper, and poured the heavy, transparent, disgusting liquid into the spoon, which seemed to shine even more revoltingly in his professional hands; then he approached me, held me firmly between his knees, ordered me to open my mouth, and forced me to swallow a whole tablespoonful of the castor-oil. He repeated the operation, with the brutal dexterity of a skilled surgeon, on Sasha, whose ears went quite white with loathing, while Zhenka lapped down the castor-oil with the utmost pleasure, smacking his lips.

Vassia gave us each a piece of black bread with a slice of herring
on it to take the taste away and, only after that, returned to the piano
and pounded out a cakewalk, a matchichi, and a song popular in the
Russo-Japanese War, "The Chinese Girl":

> "The poor boy was wounded badly,
> The Japs put him into jug
> Where he fell in love quite madly
> With a little Chinese mug."

This brought the house down. . . . People moved about like shadows in the smoke, which continued to bring tears to their eyes. On
the table, there was a tempting display of delicacies to accompany
the blinis—grated cheese, a bowl of melted butter, another bowl with
smetana, herring prepared in a special way, which gave it a mother-
of-pearl sheen, red caviar, and very salty, dark Siberian salmon from
the river Amur, which had come on the market after the war. The
red caviar and this type of salmon cost very little, and in less well-
to-do families took the place of the black caviar and proper salmon,
which we never bought. They were beyond our means!

Papa had also provided anchovies, which came in wicker boxes.
The main attraction of these alluring little smoked fishes was that
they had to have spirits poured over them, which was then lit before
they were handed round the table. When the yellowish-blue flame
died away, the fishes' scales came off quite easily, almost of themselves. Papa was very deft at baring the aromatically smoked flesh,
so delicious that it was as difficult to tear oneself away from it as it
was from sunflower seeds.

Then to the blinis' smoke was added the magic smell of burning
spirits and the warm aroma of the anchovies themselves, which, together with "The Chinese Girl" and the snow on the Kulikovo field,
growing grey as it melted, which we could see from the window,
made up the essence of the Shrovetide feast.

When the tall pile of steaming blinis—each of them resembling
the cratered surface of the moon—was brought into the dining-
room from the kitchen, Papa, as an exceptional gesture, poured
Vassia a small cut-glassful of vodka from a special carafe reserved
for guests, and Vassia tossed it down his throat with true Military
Academy smartness. Then we all started to twist the open-work blinis

round our forks and dip them into the melted butter and cool smetana before smearing them with red caviar, the small balls of which burst deliciously under our teeth to release the sticky liquid of the salmon embryos. The wintry windows gradually turned to blue, presaging in some way the coming of spring, and Papa performed his virtuoso act of tearing the skins from the anchovies; one's mind became gay and uncontrolled, and it was heartening to see that the two branches of the family still remained so fond of each other, though living at opposite ends of the town. This feeling of affection enveloped us all and my aunt kissed Zinaida warmly. Zinaida, who had become "Russianised" enough to be well-accustomed to the blinis, from which small dabs of smetana clung to her little moustache, complimented my aunt on them in her harsh, parrot's voice: "Good blinis! *Très bon! Vraies crépes de dentalle,* as we say!"

Vassia went back to the piano again and, glancing at my aunt, played "Oi-ra!" with great fire and feeling: "Oi-ra! Oi-ra!" . . . It led me to suspect that Vassia, too, was one of my aunt's admirers.

> "The poor boy was wounded badly,
> The Japs put him into jug . . ."

Falling Stars ✍

ON DARK, moonless August nights, we sometimes walked along to the cliffs and, although there was a bench there, we preferred to squat down on the still-warm turf, thick with calamint, artemisia, and other aromatic herbs. From there, we had a clear view over the dark sea to the distant horizon, above which there was the faint gleam of a star or the light on the mast-head of some invisible ship, that had disappeared beyond the edge of the black strip between water and sky.

The most attractive element in those impenetrable, warm nights— before the beginning of the new school year—was that one's eyes gradually became accustomed to the surrounding darkness and discovered fascinating and mysterious sources of light. In a bush of wild olives, a glow-worm would suddenly appear, lighting up an infinitesimal segment of the silvery leaf; far away in the steppe, beyond the Scythian hillocks, barely distinguishable against the background of the sea, a spark from a gypsy bonfire flew up and disappeared a second later; below, on the sandy shore, at the bottom of the cliffs, a long, phosphorescent wave rolled in, covering the beach with luminous, lacy foam.

In the black sky, amidst the large, familiar constellations of the northern hemisphere and the Milky Way, billions of stars shone out, filling the heavens with silvery sand and phosphorescent smoke, and the steppe and the sea, while still remaining dark, somehow mysteriously glimmered: the air was permeated by a subtle ethereal light, against which one saw a bat, looking like a capital W, suddenly dart past on a cluster of fluttering moths, seemingly scattering grey dust around them, or the moving silhouettes of the frontier-guards as they made their rounds, and the countryside was filled with the gay, chirping sound of crickets.

We lay down on our backs on the grass with our hands laced behind our heads, Papa, Zhenia, and I, and a few boys and girls from the German estate. Now all we saw was the vast sky, its blackness dotted with constellations and a number of separate stars, which Papa hailed by their names, like old, good friends: "There's the Great Bear and the Small Bear and the Polar Star. That's Saturn over there and Jupiter, bending low towards the horizon. And that one's Venus, a strange star, for she appears twice, both in the morning and at night. That's why she's sometimes called the Morning Star and sometimes Vesper, which means evening. There was a time," Papa added, as he continued to gaze up at the heavens, "when she was thought to be two stars and not one and the same."

. . . I do not know why, but this statement deeply disturbed me: I fancied that I had two souls—one, the morning one, all joy, and the other, Vesper, filled with gloom.

We lay with our faces to the sky, and a warm night breeze blew on us, bringing with it the mingled smells of sea and steppe. It sometimes seemed to me that I was not lying on the earth and looking upwards, but just the opposite—hanging in space, face down with the vast area of the world spread out far, far below me, limitless and immeasurable in all its August splendour. I felt that I no longer belonged to the world of continents, oceans, and countries, with frontiers between each country, guarded by guns, fortresses, and frontier-posts, like our frontier-post at Budaki on the high, steep cliffs, where armed patrols kept constant watch; countries where people spoke different languages and made war on each other, seas and oceans where dreadnoughts ploughed through the waves and shadowy submarines lurked in the depths—instead I felt that I was part of the common sky that covered everyone alike, my soul a part of one universal soul, there among the falling stars that Papa called meteors, meteorites, bolides. . . .

There were many of these falling stars in mid-August. They suddenly appeared in the coal-black darkness with a briefly lasting trial of phosphorescent sparks, like matches struck on a match-box. Meteors flew luminously in every direction, without ever crossing each other, always from the darkest segment of the sky and always unexpectedly. Sometimes they remained one of a glazier's diamond, leaving their trace with an almost audible scratch on the black glass of the universe or, to use Papa's word, the cosmos. . . .

We knew, of course, that if one whispered one's heart's desire to a falling star as it fell, one's wish would be fulfilled. So I was keenly on the watch that August for the sudden appearance of a falling star at the ends of the world, somewhere between the Dniester estuary with its old Turkish fortress and the delta of the Danube in the Budaki steppe, so that I could murmur my secret wish. But, in the end, there were so many falling stars, and my wishes were so varied and contradictory, that I still do not know whether they were finally fulfilled or not.

"Break the Padlock!" ✍

EVEN NOW, I cannot make up my mind whether that little girl wanted to incite me to commit a burglary or whether there was another mysterious meaning—a disturbing, passionate one—to her words.

I do not remember her name, but she was about eleven and one of those stray girls who were always pursuing boys, preferring their company to that of their girl-friends. None of us knew—nor, in fact, did we care—from where she had come when she turned up in Otrada. Barefoot, with very close-cropped hair, she wore a faded cotton dress buttoned up the back that was so short one could see her bruised, scratched knees. She trailed along some distance behind the boys, reminding one of a marauding cat. The boys tried to get rid of her without success: she kept on saying plaintively: "Why won't you be friends? What've I done wrong? If you like, I'll take you to Madame Vassiutinskaia's shed; there are six little kittens in the straw there that've just been born and all of them striped. May God punish me if they're not all striped!"

"Go to you know where, you and your kittens. Why do you keep bothering us? Join the other girls and leave us in peace!" the boys answered rudely.

"You'll be sorry one day!" she replied menacingly and sadly, but she did not go away. After standing on one leg for a time like a stork, she continued to follow the boys, keeping her distance.

I do not know why, but she aroused contempt. I despised her, too, and never missed an occasion to shout at her: "Why do you keep getting under our feet? Go back where you came from or you'll get a licking! We'll wring your neck for you!"

As I spoke, I could not help looking at her thin, unwashed neck and ears, showing beneath her straggly hair, which had no doubt been cut by her mother, a washerwoman, or the wife of one of the yardsmen. One day, after school, I was loitering idly about the street, as my aunt was prone to call it rather nastily, seeking company, but at that swelteringly hot post-prandial hour the street was deserted: all the other boys were probably sitting at home doing their home-work. In spite of it being the end of September, there was nothing yet to denote the approach of autumn. It was as though the southern summer were loitering, too, and it appeared to be going to stay forever.

I felt completely at a loose end, lonely and depressed. For some time, the barefoot girl—appearing from God knew where—had been silently trailing me, and I suddenly heard her whisper flatly and mysteriously behind my back: "Look here, boy, would you like me to take you to an empty, boarded-up villa? The people who lived there have gone away and the gardener is safe in a vodka-shop, so no-one will see us there. How about it, boy?"

By now, she was walking along beside me, peering up at me with a curious, unsmiling expression on her face. We were alone together in this hot, deserted, afternoon-world of Otrada, and I suddenly began to feel towards her, in addition to my ingrained contempt, something strangely disurbing, almost sensual . . . something out of gogol. . . .

"Buzz off!" I said almost automatically. "Stop bothering me!"

She paid no attention to my words: rubbing her thin, little shoulder against mine, she went on muttering monotonously: "Come with me, you won't regret it. All the lodgers have left, the whole place is empty, and the gardener is out of the way."

I felt an inexplicable excitement and, without saying anything, started following her as she led the way, striding along the hot pavement of her bare feet. Every now and then, she would look back, gazing at me with empty, expressionless eyes, her gaunt face as immobile as a mask.

After passing through a deserted Otrada, beneath a roof of dusty acacia-trees, already heavy with clusters of ripe, black pods among the small leaves, scarcely yet tinged with autumn yellowness, we found ourselves on the terrace of an unoccupied villa by the edge of a cliff, beyond which the calm sea shone blue in the September sun. We began to peer through the windows, boarded up crosswise, examining the rooms, empty except for a few pieces of furniture left there for the winter and one or two forgotten objects—a flower-vase, a brass candlestick, a kitchen-knife, a tea-caddy. . . . In one corner of the whitewashed ceiling, a large grey dead-head moth perched with its wings folded up into a triangle, while in the opposite one, a spider had woven its inticate web, along with a ray of sun, penetrating the dusty panes, rolled like a golden ball. All around, there was a frightening stillness.

An iron padlock hung on the door. The little girl came up close to me, so that I could feel her breath on my face and smell a pungent whiff of garlic. Her lips were pale and anaemic, and there were sores at the corners of her mouth like yellow raspberries. On her neck, beneath her ear-lobes, were faint stains left there by the skin of the melon she must recently have eaten. Her eyes, their pupils strained but motionless, gazed straight at me, seemingly inciting me to some illegal act.

"Break the padlock," she commanded, and looked around stealthily, like a thief.

At that moment, the gate squeaked and we heard the voice of the gardener, back from his potations: "What're you doing here on other people's property! Be off with you, or . . ."

Remaining in the same spot, he began stamping his feet, pretending to be pursuing us. In a flash, the girl disappeared, as if carried away by the wind: I just had a glimpse of her pink dress as she leaped the hedge.

With flaming ears, I ran past the grinning gardener, speeded on by a good-natured slap on my behind. I never came across the little girl again.

Fanny Markovna ✍

THERE WAS a street called Malaya Arnautskaya, which seemed to me at the time to be a long way away, but was, in fact, quite close to where we lived. When we went there, we were immediately engulfed in the world of Jewish poverty, with all its confused colours and sour-sweet smells. We entered a wooden, glass-roofed arcade that surrounded the yard. Here, Mamma had to keep her head bent the whole time to avoid breaking the eagle's feathers in her hat on some protruding object or other—garments suspended on a clothesline, or a low cross-beam supporting the arcade's rickety, boarded walls, half-destroyed by death-watch beetles. The arcade possessed innumerable windows and doors. All the windows were dirty and half of them broken. Most of the doors were open and, in the darkness beyond them, nested families of Jewish shopkeepers and craftsmen: tailors, shoemakers, watchmakers, ironmongers, dressmakers. . . . Mingled together were the sounds of hammering, the squeak of cutters' huge scissors, the sharp protest of torn calico, the screech of unoiled treadles on the sewing-machines. Pungent kitchen smells were blended with the smoke from kerosene lamps with little mica windows, which lit up the apartments so that they looked like a scene in a toy theatre, representing a town on fire with corrugated card-board tongues of flame.

We pushed our way past the curtain drawn across Fanny Markovna's smoke-blackened doorway, Mamma stooping again and protecting the feather on her hat with her narrow, leather-gloved hand. Fanny Markovna met us with a smile of greeting on her thin, anaemic face, covered with black spots of acne: her smile revealed the absence of one of her side teeth. If it had not been for those defects and the flabby skin on her neck, she would have completely met my notions of a lady. She wore a jacket rather like Mamma's and a similar skirt with a train, edged with velvet, but hers were shabbier. She did her hair in quite a different way. Mamma's lustrous, coal-black hair was always brushed smoothly backwards and ended in a bun on the nape of her neck, filled with hair-pins, while Fanny Markovna had a modish hair-do, with a false pad on her prematurely-wrinkled, low forehead, which gave her the appearance of wearing a red wig. Now I come to think of it, it probably was a wig.

A chest of drawers, the colour of a beetle, stood out in the semi-darkness; it was covered with a canvas cloth, on which a small plaster vase filled with paper roses was reflected in a frameless mirror on an ashwood stand.

Mamma gave Fanny Markovna a paper parcel, containing material to be made up into a light woollen cape for the spring season. Fanny Markovna unwrapped the material and took it out into the arcade to get a better look at it. Mamma sat down on a warped, Vienna chair of a black Jewish colour and, as she pressed me to her and kissed me on the neck, I could feel how much her stomach was swollen.

Then Fanny Markovna returned, expressing her approval of the quality of the material and praising Mamma's good taste. She put the material down carefully on a round table covered with a velvet, tasselled table-cloth, then took Mamma behind a screen to fit a previously ordered rustling, lilac silk underskirt and a pair of whale-boned corsets. I sat for a long time in the centre of the room on the vacated chair, alternately examining the design on the sewing-machine's cast-iron treadle and observing how, from time to time, Mamma's bare arm or Fanny Markovna's head, the mouth crammed with pins that hovered over her upper lip like a bristly black mous-tache, would appear above the top of the bamboo screen. It seemed to me that its cracked oil-cloth cover, decorated with rose and grey flowers, extended Arnautskaya Street's smell of humanity and poverty, as though it had become permeated with the scrofulous atmosphere. I was filled at one and the same time with repulsion and a tormenting pity for that poor race, condemned to live in such crowded and ugly conditions among the two-wheeled carts with curved handles and the shops selling evil-smelling kerosene in barrels, small sacks of coal, rust-coloured salted herrings, bottles of olives, glass jars of cucumbers in clouded, milky water, bunches of dill, and halva that looked like blocks of window-putty.

I fidgeted on the black Viennese chair, waiting impatiently for the moment when the fitting would be over and, accompanied by Fanny Markovna's sweet smiles and restrained farewells, Mamma and I would finally leave for home, away from that mean, sad, unjust, terrible world of Malaya Arnautskaya Street.

Mamma in the Street ✍

I GOT TIRED tramping along the street, holding onto one of Mamma's fingers in her leather glove, and implored her to carry me, but, I remember, she always gave me the same answer: "Aren't you ashamed of yourself? Such a big boy and you haven't yet learned to walk properly!"

She often called me, affectionately, "My little Chinese boy" or "Li-Hung-Chang."

And so I went on dragging my feet along the granite pavement, and we would cross the road, ever taking prudent precautions, in front of the chemist's shop I now knew well, which had two huge, brightly lit glass decanters, one filled with lilac liquid, the other with green, standing in its broad windows; and, behind, you could see black shelves, holding big white china jars, on which were written sinister words that I could not read.

Mamma was quite a different person in the street from what she was at home. At home, she was soft, pliable, warm, and usually without a corset—just an ordinary, cosy mamma. But in the street she was a severe, even slightly disagreeable lady, with a black-spotted veil over her face, and a dress with a train, which she held up to one side with her hand, on which hung a little moiré bag, embroidered with spangles; this bag opened with a squeak and contained a yellow wooden box with pills for her migraine and a sort of wax pencil, smelling of camphor, which made your skin feel cool when you rubbed it on your forehead.

Mamma suffered from migraines, which affected me, when I had one, as though someone were striking the bass notes on the piano hard with both hands, while keeping the loud-pedal down.

In her pince-nez, visible through the veil, her thick eyebrows raised towards her temples, and the eagle's feather quivering in her hat, Mamma sometimes seemed to me a completely strange woman; not my mamma at all, but "madam," as she was addressed in shops or by someone inadvertently brushing against her on a narrow pavement: "I beg your pardon, madam."

Mamma would proudly incline her head, as a sign of forgiveness, and pass on, dragging me by the hand and murmuring: "What a clumsy bow! He doesn't even know how to walk in the streets. . . ."

Dwarfs ✍

"DWARF" WAS a surname. People said: "I must go to the Dwarfs to get some braid for my skirt."

The Dwarfs were not dwarfs at all: they were an ordinary middle-aged couple, a husband and wife—Mr. Dwarf and Mrs. Dwarf. Mamma used to buy all the material for the dresses which Fanny Markovna made for her in their shop. For me, she bought crayons, India rubbers, sticking-plaster, transfer-pictures, and just ordinary coloured pictures, pegged onto a washing-line above the counter display-case, covered with thick, none-too-transparent glass and protected from customers' elbows by metal rods.

The two Dwarfs were never in the shop together. They sold in turn, either Mr. Dwarf or Mrs. Dwarf. Mamma and I were known to them as "regular clients." I believe that Mamma first went to the Dwarfs' shop soon after having married Papa to buy some canvas and two skeins of wool, one red, one black, with which to decorate Papa's shirt with an embroidered Ukrainian design. The design had a special meaning, as Papa had finished his studies at Novorossijsk University in the historical-philological faculty with a silver medal for a paper on Byzantine influence on the national art of the southern Ukraine, or, as it was called then, Little Russia.

The summer of his last year as a student, Papa had gone on a walking-tour through many Ukrainian villages with an exercise-book, into which, with his characteristic earnestness and attention, he copied national designs on towels and shirts with red and blue pencils.

I can vividly picture Mamma finding these exercise-books and, as a surprise, secretly embroidering a summer, linen shirt for Papa in red and black cross-stitch. As far as I can remember my childhood, Papa's shirt with Mamma's embroidery on the neck and sleeves was always in use. It seemed to be immune from wear and tear and, after being washed and ironed innumerable times, the cross-stitches never lost their vivid colours: obviously the Dwarfs sold excellent wares.

Apart from that shirt, I remember a grey, unbleached pillow-case which was always put on a pillow when there was a journey in view. This travelling pillow-case was also embroidered in wool, but in quite a different spirit from that employed on the shirt. Here Mamma gave full liberty to her fantasy without displaying any signs of Byzantine influence. Using green and light and dark blue wool as well as the black and the red, she embroidered a remarkably beautiful bunch of flowers in satin-stitch, among which one could easily discern roses, carnations, and violets. I remember the bone buttons, slightly yellowed from time but still intact, with which the pillowcase was fastened. I am certain they had also been bought at the Dwarfs, as were the mother-of-pearl buttons for my shirts, which were sold by the dozen, sewn to white sheets of card-board, lying under the dim glass in the show-case, alongside reels of white and black number forty thread and black envelopes, from which protruded rows of shiny needles.

Hooks, press-buttons, erasers, paint-brushes, and the water-colour paints themselves, little circles stuck to a card-board palette or neat squares in wooden boxes—all these could be bought at the Dwarfs', and Mr. and Mrs. Dwarf always smilingly presented me with a small, alluring bonus in the shape of a blue steel nib, with the curly head of Pushkin on it, or an India rubber decorated with a white elephant. Naturally, I was always delighted when Mamma took me with her to the Dwarfs' shop. I might perhaps add that Mr. Dwarf always wore a bowler hat, reminding one of a junkman, since all the junkmen in our town wore bowler hats.

The Chemist ✍

IN THE CHEMIST'S shop, my attention was immediately caught by the number of collection-boxes for contributions to various charitable societies. They hung on the walls beside the cashier and also stood on his desk. I think there were more of them than in the church porch or on the church elder's counter. Apart from the Red Cross box, which could be seen everywhere, one noticed the Jewish Charity Organisation's box, adorned with the blue Star of David, the box of the Orphans' Charity, under the patronage of the dowager-empress, sporting a pelican with wings outspread to protect a nest full of hungry birds with gaping beaks, and, most riveting of all, the Life-boat Society's box in the shape of a snow-white boat with a red hull, bearing the society's emblem—two crossed anchors against the back-ground of a life-belt. They were all secured with small padlocks and an official sealing-wax stamp. When they got their change, customers would often drop copper or even silver coins through the slots. As their visits to the chemist's were usually connected with illness of some sort, possibly a dangerous one, they became superstitious and made their donations in much the same spirit as primeval people offered up sacrifices to propitiate the dark forces controlling the world.

Whenever Mamma bought phenacetin for her headaches, she always dropped her change into the boxes and even crossed herself as if she were in church: under the veil, her face took on a frightened and foreboding look, as though she sensed an imminent death.

The golden double-headed eagle over the chemist's sign gave him a sort of official status, suggesting that higher authorities had granted him power over the health and lives of everyone in the neighbour-hood coming to his shop for protection.

Standing on tiptoe so that I could see over the counter, I used to peep timidly into the room at the back of the shop through the open door. Here, the medicines were prepared and poured into bottles through a glass funnel, ointments were pounded in large, porcelain cups, and pills were rolled on a rectangular sheet of glass; some-thing that appeared to be covered in green dust was being weighed on the chemist's scales with its miniature weights and a Bunsen burner was alight, its flame scarcely visible in the daylight. There was a strong smell of iodine and balsam, and the labels on the bottles were stamped with the same double-headed eagle, which filled my child's mind with respect and even a tinge of fear.

I was particularly frightened of the oxygen-filled pillows, which I occasionally saw the pharmaceutist himself bring from the back-room and hand over to a customer, half-dazed with anxiety and grief, his eyes wandering blindly round the shop and his lips trembling. With fumbling fingers, he would throw money down on the circular rubber pad in front of the cashier and then, grasping the weightless pillows with their rubber tubes for inhaling the oxygen, race out into the street. Everyone would make way for him, as though he were an angel of death, and I was engulfed with fear lest the pillows should come too late for the moribund patient, making his last swallowing movements of lips and throat: I could even hear his dry, hoarse breathing, in which I sensed a dark, terrible premonition, a prophesy of things to come. . . .

The Drowned Girl ✍

AN EXTRAORDINARY thing happened to me in my early childhood, when Mamma was still alive.

For a long time, my family had kept, by way of a curiosity, a large, creased visiting-card, inscribed in capital letters by the local printer: "KISSEL PESAKHOVICH, GRAVEDIGGER AND LEASEHOLDER."

They showed it to their friends, who found it difficult to believe that anyone could have such an unusual name.

We got to know him when we spent the summer on the shores of the Dniester, near Resina, a small place, for which Ribnitza was the railway-station. I see vaguely before me the figure of a man in a cloth dust-cloak, a white, greasy cap, and peasant's boots, who not only leased several vineyards near Sakharna but also owned a small shop, which Mamma and I sometimes visited. We also hired a carriage from him to take us to Ribnitza, when we had to go back to Odessa in August for the beginning of the school year. I remember him as a very active, rather fussy man, always ready to help, with frightened eyes and a kind, slightly obsequious smile.

I do not know what business brought him there, but he often visited us in the whitewashed hut in which we lived high above the impetuously rushing Dniester. I think he was the leaseholder of several small houses, which he sublet to summer visitors, coming from Odessa and Kishinev: this may have been why he was always so well up in all the village-gossip. Every winter, as spring approached, he would send us a post-card, in which he reminded us of his existence, begged us not to forget him, and told us to be sure and let him know if we intended to come to the Dniester again so that he could send a carriage to the station to meet us.

One evening at home, when it was already dark and our lamps cast a dismal light on the flowered wall-paper, while outside there raged a wintry storm, always strangely depressing in town, and torrents of rain poured down Basarnaia Street, descending like waterfalls through the grilles inserted over the drains in the gutters alongside the granite pavements, there came through the wall the sound of footsteps climbing the stairs. For some reason, I was sure that it was "Kissel Pesakhovich, Gravedigger," coming to see us and bringing bad, even terrible news.

. . . The door-bell rang. . . .

I could hear Mamma's voice as she opened the door, then Papa's, and before I had had time to rush into the hall and see Kissel Pesakhovich in a mackintosh with a hood on the back, darkened by the rain, I *knew* that Marusia was drowned.

She was one of the workers in the vineyards leased by Kissel Pesakhovich. I had only seen her two or three times as she ran down to the Dniester with the other girls to bathe.

For some reason, I remembered her very clearly, her brown, chestnut-coloured eyes, gay Moldavian smile, and loud but agreeably musical voice that rose from the shore as the girls undressed and then, in their long petticoats, threw themselves noisily into the Dniester's tempestuous waves, broken by the occasional ink-black funnel of a whirlpool. The girls' petticoats, inflating like bubbles, floated on the surface of the water as the inshore current bore them down the river amid the reeds uprooted during a flood somewhere upstream, originating perhaps in the very spurs of the Carpathians.

"Marusia is drowned!" I cried out, trembling with fear.

This outburst, prompted by second-sight, alarmed Mamma and, growing pale, too, she tried to console me, saying that I was letting my imagination run away with me. But, when we were sitting down drinking tea and Kissel Pesakhovich was regaling us with all his local news, he confirmed that, shortly after our departure the previous year, Marusia, one of the wine-workers, had, in fact, been drowned while bathing in the Dniester, exceptionally swollen by the summer rains in the Carpathians. She was swept into a whirlpool, where the wind wrapped her inflated petticoat round her pretty head and she was smothered in the turbulent waters. The current carried her body into the middle of the river, and it was only after a search with boat-hooks lasting two days that it was found some ten versts from Resina.

After that, I kept seeing the swollen, dark-as-lead waters of the Dniester, carrying the drowned girl's white body, with the face wrapped in her thin petticoat, further and further downstream past the clay cliffs that seemed to glimmer faintly through the seething river, purple with rage.

Thus, this dead beauty drifted past me and has continued to do so unceasingly throughout my life, frequenting all my dreams— beautiful and frightening, like Gogol's drowned woman, her hair spread over her and water pouring from it in streams. And, early in the spring of 1944, when our bombers flew through the gorges above the Dniester, past the clay cliffs, from which flocks of disturbed martins suddenly emerged, and we dropped bombs on the Germans while their shells burst in red stars all around us, I seemed to glimpse, floating on the water of the swollen river, flowing tempestuously below me wreathed in mist, the beautiful, white body of the drowned girl, with her hair streaming out behind her. . . . And above us flew a flock of storks, returning to their Moldavian home from faraway lands.

The Magic Horn of Oberon 🎺

AT THAT TIME, pedlars would turn up at fairs and markets with bast boxes, covered with home-woven unbleached linen, filled with cheap books of popular songs and stories. I had just learned to read, or rather spell words out, when my grandmother, Papa's mamma, came across one of these pedlars and bought me two books. I imagine that the old lady was unaware of the existence of any book-shops in the town. One of these books has somehow completely escaped my memory, as though I had never possessed it at all, though I am certain that I did and that it had a beautiful coloured picture on the cover.

The other book was called *The Magic Horn of Oberon,* and on its cover there was a vivid, shiny picture of a king, or maybe a knight or magician, riding on a richly caparisoned horse through a thicket in a fairy forest. He had raised a curved hunter's horn on a gold chain to his crimson mouth above his chestnut beard, and I seemed to hear the resonant brass instrument filling not only the forest, bright with green ferns and white lilies-of-the-valley, with its magnificent music, but the whole of Basarnaia Street as well.

I read the book slowly, forming letters into syllables and syllables into words, but its contents impressed me much less than the picture on the cover. I have no recollection at all of the contents of the book, printed indistinctly on bad paper, but its title has remained with me all my life: *The Magic Horn of Oberon.*

And so has the vivid picture on the cover, which at the time was a substitute for all the world's paintings, of which I had not yet the remotest conception.

To all this was added an immense pride of possession: the book was *mine,* my property alone, and I hid it under my pillow, vaguely aware in my dreams of the smell of the print mingling with the mouldy, woollen smell of the small, elderly priest's widow, my grand-mother—the mother of my papa—who, unknown to herself, had made a gift of the words "The Magic Horn of Oberon," thereby, perhaps, awakening the poet in me.

The Laxative 🖋

"HE'S BURNING!" Papa said with a trembling voice, his hand on my forehead. "Zhenia"—he turned to Mamma—"just feel, he's on fire!"

Mamma came up to my bed, and, pushing her hand through the gauze net, touched my forehead with her cool palm, then my cheek and neck. "For God's sake, get a thermometer, Pierre!" she said.

Then began a frenzied search for the thermometer: I heard a squeak from each of the drawers in Mamma's chest of drawers and then the sharp click of the special lock on Papa's top drawer.

I lay with closed eyes, but the blood-red light of the lamp brought in from the dining-room still penetrated my eyelids. Papa came up to me with the thermometer in his hand and I opened my eyes. The thermometer gave out zigzag flashes like lightning, and Papa's starched cuffs clapped like thunder; he was shaking down the mercury. Then he pushed the thermometer under my arm, for a second, the touch of the glass against my skin felt like an icicle. My shoulder was bare and Papa carefully pulled the edge of the warm blanket up over it.

I felt sick, I was burning, and I experienced an unpleasant phenomenon I had suffered before. The condition or, rather, the physical reaction caused my wrists seemingly to become filled with lead, begin to swell, and turn into enormous weights, while, at one and the same time, they grew smaller and smaller until they were no larger than a pin-head. This simultaneous internal struggle with something incredibly large that was growing larger and larger all the time and something microscopically small, diminishing still further all the time, filled my heart and my dimmed consciousness with unspeakable despair, fear, and hallucination. I kept seeing a long, endless corridor, down which, far away, someone was approaching me with short taps from metal heels; the steps grew more and more rapid but never got any closer, somehow contriving to move and remain rooted to the same spot. This caused me as much anxiety as the struggle between the leaden weight and the pin-head.

I did not feel the thermometer being removed from under my arm, but I heard two voices—Papa's and Mamma's—mingling with the sound of the running, static footsteps far down the corridor.

My world had no beginning and no end. . . .

The mercury, seeming to fill the thermometer alarmingly up to its smooth, rounded end, shone so vividly that it hurt my eyes.

"Good God, Pierre!" Mamma exclaimed. "His temperature's two degrees over forty!"

"I don't know what we should do," Papa said agitatedly.

"Fetch a doctor, quickly!"

"Yes, yes, I'll go."

"Take a cab. Bring Litvarev!"

I was burning with fever and had lost all conception of time; my eyes were dimly aware of the light from the lamp, shaded from me by a book, while my ears still heard the sinister footsteps running down the corridor. These steps faded away with the arrival of Litvarev, the famous children's doctor, who spread out the fingers of his white hands, on which his wedding-ring glinted, and pressed them against the tiles of the stove to warm them. Then his gold watch suddenly opened with a click, like the sound made by beetles' hard wings preparatory to flying, and his strong fingers closed round my wrist as he took my pulse. He had stern brows over even sterner eyes, enlarged by the lenses of his spectacles, and a smell of iodoform came from his very long frock-coat.

I do not remember Dr. Litvarev disappearing from my bedside: he left a prescription with Mamma, which he had no doubt written out at Papa's desk in the dining-room. I only remember the cook, awakened from her sleep, hurriedly putting on her coat, tying a shawl over her head, and rushing off to the chemist's opposite the Dwarfs' shop.

And time now raced, now stopped, now ceased to exist entirely: I dropped into a motionless vacuum in which I alternately soared up and plunged down, unconscious of everything but the horror of this ceaseless flight. Then I suddenly started perspiring, so strongly that sweat collected in my arm-pits, my hair was damp, and my night-shirt stuck to my body; as the blanket slipped down onto the floor, I felt a delicious breath of cool air. My temperature fell as unexpectedly and quickly as it had risen.

I lay, blissfully weak, and looked at Papa and Mamma, who were examining a pretty box wrapped in gold paper, which the cook had just brought from the chemist's. The box had a label on it, stamped with the double-eagle, on which the dispenser had copied out the Latin prescription in his fine penmanship, adding instructions for the dosage in Russian.

"I'm quite well again," I said in a weak voice. "I've started sweating."

Papa came over to me, ran his hands over my cool, wet body, and stuck the thermometer under my arm again. I waited patiently for fifteen minutes, till Papa removed the thermometer and held it close to the lamp.

"His temperature's down to normal."

"No! How wonderful!" Mamma exclaimed.

She rushed across to me, kissed me, and changed my night-shirt, and there I was, lying in bed, dry and cool, delighted by my quick recovery.

I do not know why, but in my youth and adolescence, my temperature often jumped up to forty degrees and even higher, then suddenly dropped back to normal again, so that after a few hours' illness, which threw the household into a panic, I was fully restored and cool as a cucumber.

"All the same, Pierre, we must give him the powders," Mamma said.

"What for?" Papa asked.

"What for! Because it was Litvarev who prescribed them," Mamma replied, pronouncing the doctor's name as if he were a god. And Litvarev, a very expensive and fashionable children's doctor, was indeed almost regarded as a god by a lot of people.

"Oh, that Litvarev!" Papa exclaimed, all his Tolstoyan lack of faith in doctors suddenly aroused. "Doctors only kill people."

"Pierre, you're a real nihilist!" Mamma declared. "One either has faith in a doctor or one hasn't!"

"I have faith in medicine," Papa persisted stubbornly, "but I don't have faith in doctors. Particularly not in those of Litvarev's type. He charges five roubles for a visit and prescribes some rubbish or other —and the child recovers all by himself. Nature won the day!" he added solemnly. "Still, give him a powder if you want to. I only hope it won't harm him."

Mamma brought a glass of boiled water and opened the little box, but, at this point, Papa put on his pince-nez and began reading the prescription. His face grew purple.

"Calomel!" he cried out in indignation.

"Well, what about it?" Mamma asked.

"It's one of the strongest and most dangerous laxatives! Almost poison!" Papa replied. "I refuse to allow my child to be given poison!"

"Pierre, be sensible!" Mamma begged. "Litvarev prescribed it, and he's the best specialist for children's illnesses!"

Papa continued raving. "You call him a specialist! He's nothing but an ignorant quack. He ought to treat cows, not small children. Just think of it—prescribing a horse's dose of calomel for our son!"

"All the same, I'll give him just one powder," Mamma said.

"You'll do nothing of the kind! Not even half a powder!" Papa shouted. "I won't let my son be poisoned. Chuck the powders into the fire, the whole lot of them!"

Before Mamma even had time to gasp, Papa, his frock-coat flying out behind him, rushed over to the stove in a fury, unscrewed the copper bolt and flung the flap open; then, his angry face illuminated by the flaming wood-blocks, he threw the chemist's box with Litvarev's powders into the crackling fire, which transformed them in a matter of seconds into a ball of ash that flew up the chimney.

Closing the cast-iron flap again and securing it with the bolt, Papa, now his calm self again, approached Mamma a trifle guilty. "Forgive me, Zhenichka, but I swear to God I was right."

I did not hear Mamma's reply because I was already fast asleep, my cheek cupped as usual in my folded hands.

Papa's Lunch 🖋

WITH A WHITE APRON round her waist, Mamma was cooking cutlets. I can still see the flat, pink, raw cutlets, moulded from minced meat, expanding and becoming covered with a brown crust: then, when Mamma stuck a fork into them to see if they were ready, hot, meaty juice hissed out, filling the kitchen with such a delicious smell that my mouth watered. Mamma was a great expert in cooking cutlets and liked to do them herself, particularly if they were intended for Papa's lunch.

Twice a week, Papa gave lessons at the Military Academy, and we sent him his lunch with my governess or, to put it less pretentiously, my nurse, a blonde girl from Riga, whose name was Amalia. Our guests often jokingly called her "Mammalia," which brought a blush to her face and made Mamma shake her finger in rebuke at the culprit.

Mamma would spread out a stiff, starched napkin, with our name embroidered in one corner, on the table and then, very carefully, as though performing an important and pleasant ritual, wrap in it the plump, still-hot cutlets, placed between two loves of white bread, which quickly absorbed the juice.

After tying the napkin's ends into a knot, Mamma confided Papa's lunch to Amalia, standing ready in her hat and cloak, before inserting me into my coat—I could never get my arms into the sleeve holes or my chubby fists out the other end. She fastened the tight hook at the neck and, to ensure I was adequately protected, encased my legs and feet in high, cloth boots with rubber soles. Amalia took a rolled-up umbrella with her for further protection and off we went down the French Boulevard, then still called Middle Fountain Road, to the Military Academy, hurrying along so as not to be late for the long break, announced by a trumpet-call, which resounded around the big, dismal, official building, painted in unattractive barrack-room yellow, which filled my heart with gloom and bred in me a hatred of everything military.

At that time, there was no drill-square or sports-ground in front of the academy as there is now, only a stretch of waste-land and a shallow ravine, covered with weeds and filth from the street. The harsh wind of late autumn or very early spring raised clouds of cold dust, which beat so strongly into our faces that we were sometimes compelled to walk backwards, and Amalia had to clutch her big Riga hat with her lace-gloved hand to prevent it soaring into the sky, grey from the dust-storm, where kites, flown by small boys from Novoribni Street, dived and somersaulted. But she could not stop her starched skirt blowing up and flapping round her. . . .

A mote, a grain of dust or sand, would often get in my eye, irritating my eyelid and was subsequently removed in one of two ways: either Mamma would turn up my eyelid and carefully lick the speck out with the tip of her tongue, while I felt her warm, moist breath fanning my face, or Amalia would fill a glass with boiled water to the brim and I would dip my eye into it as deeply as I could and hold it there till the speck was washed out.

And, my God!—what a relief it was after the hellish tortures inflicted on my eye by that sharp grain of sand from the Military Academy waste-land.

We entered the college through the heavy front-door and climbed the two flights of the marble staircase, passing on our way the white plaster bust of the reigning emperor, Nicholas II, which stood on a marble shelf, set in the wall. Dust had gradually settled on the plaster head of the emperor, with its side-parting, so that it had become slightly darker than the beard and cheeks beneath the motionless radiant, majestic eyes, and lent the face a strange expression of neglect and doom. . . .

In 1917, on the day of the February revolution, an earthquake occurred in the region of Otrada and Malfontana: no damage was done to property except for the massive building of the Military Academy. A deep crack appeared in the front main wall and split the bust of the emperor in two, which was regarded at the time as an evil omen, foretelling the end of the Romanov dynasty's three-hundred-year reign. I myself saw the cracked bust, threatening to fall from the shelf at any moment.

But, at this particular moment in my childhood, the tsar's bust was still intact and Amalia and I passed by it, up the staircase's red plush carpet, with respect mingled with awe, seeing in Nicholas II something akin to an earthly divinity.

At the top of the stairs were a number of glass doors, behind one of which the student on duty sat on a stool, wearing a regulation white undress shirt with blue undress shoulder-straps. He announced our arrival to the duty-officer and we were ushered into the waiting-room, where Amalia, had to remain; but an exception was made for me, the small son of a teacher, and I was allowed to go out into a long, broad corridor where the duty-trumpeter was already sounding the long break. Surrounded by students, Papa emerged from one of the rooms, carrying a pointer and with a rolled-up map under his arm. I went up to him to deliver the luncheon prepared by Mamma, and he, strikingly different from the military around him in the new jacket that gave him a peaceful, civilian appearance, took the napkin, then picked me up and kissed me, tickling my face with his whiskers and beard.

The students, with bayonets in leather sheaths attached to the back of their belts with the brightly polished eagle insignia, started teasing me, tickling me under the arms and butting me with their hard, hairy heads. I fought back and laughed so loudly and infectiously in that huge, grim military corridor, that even the colonel-commandant, in his parade-uniform with shoulder-strapes and decorations, at whose approach the students froze to attention, waggled his long arrow-like whiskers and smiled at me indulgently through his gold pince-nez, as he pinched the fat bridge of his nose. He wished to show that, though he did not wholly approve, he was loath to forbid his pupils to play with a child, who had brought home-made cutlets to his civilian papa.

While Papa, settling down on the window-sill, ate the still-warm lunch prepared by Mamma's dear hands with due appreciation, trying not to drop any crumbs, I timidly examined the objects surrounding me: firing-range targets hanging on the wall, a training-rifle on a special stand, and, finally, a dummy three-inch field-gun that particularly attracted and frightened me. It rested on green wheels, which were secured by triangular blocks of wood to prevent it rolling about the parquet floor. Beside it were a number of real artillery-weapons, disinguished by their smoothly polished steel and the shining copper of what a student, with close-cropped bristly hair and a moustache, explained to me were ammunition-belts.

All this, accompanied by the usual barrack-smells of polished floors, uniform-cloth, leather, shoe-black, cabbage-soup, buckwheat, gas-mantles, and gun-oil, depressed me and seemed to be warning all us civilians, living quietly and peacefully in the world beyond the confines of this military establishment, of some distant but inevitable disaster.

I noticed that the other teachers, all army instructors, ate their lunches of bread and sausage standing up and cast envious glances at Papa, feasting on delicious home-made cutlets, laid out on the broad window-sill on an immaculate, white, starched napkin, with one corner hanging down and displaying Mamma's neat embroidery.

And then the long-drawn-out tragic wail of the brass trumpet announced the end of the break.

Recovering the napkin, with the feeling of a duty well-accomplished, I rejoined Amalia, who was flushed from a flirtatious conversation with the duty-officer, and we returned to the waste-land, where we were once more assailed by the dry, harsh wind that got under Amalia's skirts and enveloped us in sinister clouds of dust beneath the grey, south-Russian skies of late autumn or very early spring.

Lent Butter ✍

THERE WAS no-one in the apartment: I was all alone. Who has not experienced in their childhood that blissful feeling of limitless freedom, coupled with fear, when left alone in an empty apartment amidst an unfamiliar, overwhelming silence, that dins in one's ears like a waterfall and is intruded upon from time to time by a mysterious creak from the furniture or a loud drip from the tap in the kitchen.

I walked around the furniture and other objects in the silent, empty rooms, feeling the complete master: I could do what I liked.

: 402 :

If I wanted to, I could bring over a chair and climb up onto it to reach the top shelf of the cupboard, holding the tightly wrapped jars of jam, sent by Grandmother from Ekaterinoslav. If I wanted to, I could try to open the top drawer of Papa's chest; I could remove the glass topper from my aunt's curiously shaped scent-bottle and sniff her scent; I could raise the lid of the piano and play the tune of the song about the drunken sparrow with one finger; I could go to the kitchen and examine all the shelves and drawers, in which there were always interesting things to be found, or even peep into the cook's mysterious, little trunk and see what she had hidden there.

It was in the afternoon, and the sun was already low, but still bright enough to fill our apartment with yellow light; the kitchen was particularly sunny, warm, and silent. I had not yet decided which of the alternatives I would adopt when my eye suddenly fell on a tea-glass on the window-sill, with a half-eaten piece of bread beside it. The glass was half full, too, and the tea in it, pierced by the sun-rays, shone like amber. It had, apparently, gone cold, and I loved cold, sweet tea, which always reminded me of our train journeys to Ekaterinoslav to see Grandmother, on which my aunt always gave me such tea, poured from a special bottle into her Zhevakhov cup.

My mouth watered and, though I had been strictly forbidden to go into the kitchen and touch anything there, I picked up the glass: it seemed to me unexpectedly heavy but, anticipating the pleasure to come, I drained it greedily. Almost simultaneously, I realised that there had been a dreadful mistake; the glass had been full of sun-flower-oil, instead of the sweet, cold, aromatic tea, I had swallowed in one go a greasy fluid, that left its nauseating taste lingering on my tongue.

The whole of my mouth, teeth, and throat were coated with vege-table-oil and I was almost sick. I let the glass drop and it broke, then I rushed to the kitchen-tap and tried to rinse out my mouth, but with no effect: it was not as easy as that to rid oneself of the clinging taste of sunflower-oil. My chin, cheeks, hands, and, for some reason, even my ears were covered in it. I began to soap my hands with Kazan kitchen-soap—grey with blue streaks—but it did not lather and the Lent butter would not go.

At that moment, my aunt walked into the kitchen on her return from town, holding Zhenia by the hand. Before she even crossed the threshold, she exclaimed: "I said that naughty boy couldn't safely be left alone in the house! Now, he's gone and drunk the sunflower-oil. Next time, it'll be the vinegar-essence. And then we'll have to call an ambulance." Turning to me, she went on: "Your eyes are too greedy and your hands much too ready: you grab hold of everything you see. One day, you're going to land in real trouble!"

"Oh, Aunt, you don't understand anything about it," I said bitterly.

And Zhenka burst out laughing.

It was scarcely worth while trying to explain my mistake. She would not have believed me anyway. . . .

The Glitter of Christmas Lights

IN THE HOUSE of a boy I knew, I once saw a Christmas tree that amazed me, because it seemed to be standing in a heap of real, glittering snow, and the same real snow appeared to be covering the branches.

The explanation was quite simple: the bottom of the tree had been wrapped in ordinary cotton wool with boracic-acid crystals strewn over it. The crystals glittered, making the cotton wool look like a bank of snow, touched by Christmas frost. When the Christmas-tree candles were lit, the artificial snow then threw out multicoloured sparks and was incredibly beautiful.

Consumed with envy, I determined to have the same snow round our Christmas tree in the following year: of course, this resolution was forgotten almost as soon as made and only came back to me on Christmas Eve, when the tree was already standing in the sitting-room, supported by a rough, criss-cross, wooden structure, sawed and nailed together by the versatile yardsman, Piotr. As the tree's frozen branches gradually unfroze in the warm room, they spread out to form a lovely transparent green pyramid and filled the air with a tarry, Christmasy smell. The previous year's decorations had been unwrapped and were lying on the large table—splendid, feather-weight glass balls, paper chains, gold and silver nuts, candle-holders with spring clips, packets of different-coloured paraffin-candles, lengths of silver tinsel twinkling in the lamp-light, treacle-biscuits, covered with white sugar, in the shape of stars, fitted with little gauze loops, and a host of card-board objects that made one keenly anticipate the approaching feast. I immediately appropriated the change the cook had left from her marketing and rushed off to the chemist's to buy some cotton wool: the whole of the money went for several rolls of it, wrapped in blue paper bearing the stamp of the Red Cross and securely tied together with string. I decided that it was unnecessary to buy any boracic, since we always had some at home for medicinal purposes.

When I got back to the apartment, the decorating was in full swing. Standing on a bench, my aunt was flinging paper chains over the top-most branches, along with a string of miniature flags of all nations: my favourite was the Siamese, displaying a white elephant on a red background.

I assisted my aunt, Zhenia, and Papa in decorating the tree, saying nothing about the shiny snow, which I decided to arrange on my own as a pleasant Christmas surprise. By the time the tree was adorned from top to bottom, it was late and everyone was exhausted: Zhenka had fallen asleep on the floor under the lower branches, with a rustling paper chain dangling down to the parquet beside him. Aunt picked him up and we all went to bed but, early in the morning, when the frosty windows hardly let in the blue light of dawn, I stealthily made my way, barefooted on the cold floor, to the sitting-room, where the Christmas tree with its shiny glass balls and silver tinsel was only visible in the half-light, and got to work.

I spread the cotton wool on the wooden structure, in which the tree stood, strewed some more below it, and tossed small pieces upwards to make the "snow-white wisps on the branches" which Pushkin mentions in his poem. After admiring my handiwork—the wisps and the splendid carpet of snow—I went into the kitchen to fetch the boracic-acid, which was always kept on a lower shelf. But there was none there. Silently, I searched through the whole apartment, where no-one yet stirred, went back to the kitchen, where by now the sleepy cook was pushing burning wood-splinters into the narrow opening of the samovar, thereby producing a greenish smoke, and peered into the storeroom. There was no boracic anywhere; no doubt, it had all been used for gargling and Aunt had forgotten to buy a fresh supply. What was I to do?

Then I suddenly noticed a box of naphthalene on the window-sill in the kitchen-corridor, and it occurred to me that naphthalene and boracic actually had a lot in common, both being white and possessing a frost-like sparkle: indeed, naphthalene might prove even more realistic than boracic. Hastily returning to the sitting-room, I spread the napthalene over the cotton wool.

Dawn had already broken and a pink sunrise was peeping into the room through the frosty windows; in its light, the cotton wool, covered with fragments of naphthalene, glistened magically, throwing out multi-coloured sparks, and was just as beautiful as genuine Christmas snow bathed in genuine sunshine.

Satisfied with the effect I had produced all my own, I tiptoed back to our room, crawled silently under the blanket, and pretended to be fast asleep as I waited impatiently for the moment when everybody would get up, go into the sitting-room, and suddenly see the tree glittering with snow.

I did not have long to wait. . . . I heard Papa wake up in the bed next to mine and begin to dress, making strange noises through his nose as he did so. Half-opening my eyes, I realised that he was sniffing at something and turning his head from side to side in bewilderment. Then he walked out of the room, and I could hear his footsteps receding down the corridor: he was heading for the sitting-room, led there by his acute sense of smell. He would become aware of the faintest and most distant smell—for instance, that of a lamp beginning to smoke—before anyone else had noticed it.

After a time, I heard his muttering and, a moment later, loud exclamations from my aunt as she joined him. I assumed they must both be looking at the Christmas tree.

"Well, you've certainly gone and done it this time!" Zhenka observed. He had just awakened and was staring at me with his luminous, chocolate eyes through the bars of his cot.

I paid no attention to this strange remark. I imagined that Aunt and Papa were admiring the fruits of my handiwork—the glamorous, snowy adornment I had added to the tree. I quickly started to dress, anxious to hear them praise my inventiveness and artistic taste, but I had not even laced one shoe when Papa burst into the room, purple with rage, and began screaming at me in the high-pitched tones of a cock: "Was it you who committed this outrage? No, hold your tongue! You don't need to tell me! God must be punishing us for having brought you up so badly! Perhaps you'll explain to me where you got the idiotic idea of putting two pounds of naphthalene on the Christmas tree. Do you realise what you've done? You've made the whole apartment stink, poisoned the air for all of us! I can't breathe! I'm stifling! You've ruined our whole Christmas!"

I tried to explain what I had hoped to achieve, quoting Pushkin's poem in the process, but Papa broke in, yelling loud enough for everyone in the apartment to hear: "Don't you dare blaspheme by mentioning Pushkin's name! And thank your lucky stars my convictions prevent me from giving you a good hiding!"

With these words, Papa gripped me firmly by the shoulders and, thrusting out his lower jaw, began to shake me, repeating as he did so: "I'll show you Pushkin!"

He shook me until I realised my foolishness and burst into tears of penitence, whereupon the incident ended.

But the Christmas-tree celebration, which with us took place on the third day of the festival, was sadly impaired, because the whole apartment was filled with the heavy, not at all Christmas-like fumes of naphthalene. We had not got rid of the smell even by Easter, so Easter, too, was not as enjoyable as it should have been.

It was only during the summer that the fumes disappeared completely.

Curd-Cakes with Raisins 🖋

UP TO THE AGE of twenty or even later, up to the time of the civil war or even Papa's death, I had no idea that I had once been in the Caucasus. I was quite certain that I had not and that my impression of it was derived from Lermontov's books, which had left me with a mental image of blue, cloud-topped hills. Then, one day, suddenly and unexpectedly, I remembered that in the far distant past I *had* once been in the Caucasus.

I had heard the word "Essentuki" mentioned on a number of occasions, and it had merely evoked a bottle of mineral water—I could see its label with hills and a black eagle in all its details—just once it conjured up an incomplete but very vivid picture, motionless and limited in time and space like that projected by a magic-lantern slide, of a wide, shady path, strewn with yellow sand, on which unfamiliar trees, with slatted benches beneath them, cast lacy, lilac shadows. In the distance were pale-green valleys, blue in the shimmering summer air, and, beyond them, low, lavender hillocks, blue hills, and a few fleecy clouds in the sky above.

To and fro along the path walked ladies and gentlemen and officers in snow-white starched jackets, with two rows of gold buttons, and caps with white covers. Every now and again, we would be passed by an elderly invalid in a wheel-chair, his legs covered with a Scots rug, and I would be frightened by the deathly pallor of his lifeless face and toothless mouth. Well-bred dogs, wearing collars, ran about with their tongues hanging out. A pyramid-poplar, rising like a green cloud of smoke, resembled the ones I saw later in paintings by Lermontov, reproduced in his books. This pleasant spot was known as "the waters."

It appears that Papa, Mamma, and I went to "the waters" together when I was little more than two. I remember a yellow-painted kiosk in the middle of the path, with counters facing in each direction, where one could buy soda-water, syrup, and curd-cakes. It was in this alley, which seemed to me without beginning or end, like eternity, that I set eyes on curd-cakes for the first time. I was too small to see what lay on the counter while standing on the sand, but when Papa, in his felt Caucasian hat and Ukrainian embroidered shirt, lifted me up by my elbows and sat me on his hot shoulder, the first thing that came into view were the cakes, which struck me as very appetising.

Though many things in the world have changed since then, the cakes have not: they merely became proportionately smaller as I became bigger. But to the tiny boy with narrow Chinese eyes that I was at the time, they seemed incredibly large.

I remember their soft, curved edges, their middle, filled with mouth-watering, juicy sweet-curd, and something transparent on top that particularly attracted me. I stretched my hand out for one, and Papa, laughing, took a two-kopeck piece, stamped with a dark double-eagle, out of his purse, threw it on the zinc counter, then stooped lower so that I could seize my prize.

I can savour even now the rich taste of that cake, the first in my life, as I drove my milk-teeth into it. I believe Mamma, under her lace sunshade, disapproved of Papa buying it for me, and I have a vague recollection of my stomach being disturbed later, throwing them both into a panic. However, all turned out well in the end and, on the horizon, as before, stretched out the blue hillocks, behind them the hills, and behind them still more hills, and in the foreground rose the slender Lermontov poplar with its curly outline.

Oil for the Icon-Lamp ✒

SOMETIMES AFTER Mass on Saturday evenings, we went with Papa to buy some oil for the lamp which always burned in our room in memory of Mamma, in front of the icon of the Saviour.

I do not know why this is always connected in my mind with dark, very misty nights in late autumn or early spring. It happened more often on the eve of some great feast, after the priest, at the end of a long service, had held out the cross for his parishioners to kiss and then, with a little brush, smeared their foreheads with holy, sweet-smelling oil. I remember Papa, as we left the church, rubbing the oil into his high forehead, which then seemed to become even more sculptural and fragrant. We walked with Papa down the street in the twilight, lulled by the low, harmoniously blended voices of the choir, which gradually faded away as we rounded the corners of the church, where two or three coloured lamps burned in front of very dark icons, the faces of the saints indistinguishable in the dusk. We contrived to rub the oil into our foreheads, filling the misty air with the smell of balsam. (We had been told that one drop of the oil cost its weight in gold.) I enjoyed looking at Papa's shining forehead, his meek eyes behind the pince-nez, and his beard moist from the dampness of even-tide.

Our goal was the shop selling ecclesiastical supplies, which was situated in the building housing the Mount Athos refuge, where pilgrims to the holy places stayed while waiting for a ship to take them to Athos and Jaffa, whence they would proceed to Jerusalem, Calvary, and the Garden of Gethsemane.

Papa said that Gogol had once gone on a pilgrimage to Jerusalem and returned by boat via Odessa. But Odessa was in the grip of a plague-scare at the time, and he was compelled to spend nearly a month in quarantine. I could picture the mad Gogol, with his long, beak-like nose, standing on the deck of a sailing-ship in his flapping coat, as it rounded our white lighthouse, and then passing long days in Odessa's gloomy quarantine-building. His thoughts turned to the obscurantism of the Pagan orthodoxy of the church.

The shop, which was approached by a number of cast-iron steps, did not look like a trading-establishment: it seemed more like a quiet annexe to the church, with its lamp burning permanently in front of a new icon. The shelves were exceptionally tidy and it was hard to believe that they did not hold holy relics rather than things you could buy for money, such as crosses from Kiev and Mount Athos and cypress spoons with their handles carved in the shape of human hands, with the fingers curved for administering a blessing.

The monk who sold these things was a tall man with a red beard, pockmarked face, sunken chest, and a narrow, fish's back: he disappeared through a cypress-wood door, with polished handles and inlaid with crosses, and returned obsequiously with a slim bottle of Mount Athos oil, which was olive-oil obtained, not from the soft part of the fruit, but from its hard stones. It was as transparent as a tear-drop and burned without giving off any smoke. It was this oil that Papa poured into a saucer and rubbed on my chest with the palm of his hand when I caught a cold.

With a certain reverence, Papa placed some money in the monk's outstretched hand, then tucked the bottle away in the inside pocket of his light overcoat, by now damp from the mist.

Sometimes, as well as the oil, he bought a cork float for our lamp, with a match-hole in the middle, through which a waxed wick could be drawn. The wicks were also obtainable at the shop, and Papa bought a box of them twice a year. In my eyes, they, too, held something holy.

When we got home, Papa reverently filled the lamp with oil to the brim and carefully changed the old wick, whereupon the lamp shone brightly and gaily, as though aware that today was Saturday and the morrow Sunday—when there would be no school.

A shadow from the dry palm-tree branch, folded like a Chinese fan, that stood behind the icon, lay softly on the wall-paper and ceiling of the room containing three beds—Papa's, Zhenia's, and mine—and always reminded me of Lermontov's poem "Palestine Branch."

If these are all merely fragments from the picture of my life, disrupted by time, maybe Oberon's horn possesses the magic power, not only of summoning elves to do his bidding, but also of uniting these fragments, separated and dispersed in no sort of order, into one integrated whole, beautiful as a Byzantine mosaic. . . . Who knows?

The Celluloid Duck

MY AUNT BOUGHT her favourite, Zhenia, a paraffin-wax duck in Deribasov Street. It was a street in which there was a lot of under-the-counter dealing. Barefooted pedlars in torn trousers prowled along outside the well-lit windows of expensive shops, offering to sell ladies and gentlemen small, long-eared puppies of allegedly impeccable breeding, which, three months later, proved only too clearly to be very ordinary mongrels.

Peasants from Byelorussia with flaxen hair, on which their small shabby fur hats were often askew, stood outside grocers' shops, stamping their feet, in well-made bast shoes, to keep them warm in the frosty air, and offering passers-by masses of a vivid green grass, "zubrovka," which, they said, "only grew in the virgin Bialowiezh forest,"* and which some connoisseurs inserted into bottles of vodka: in the days preceding Christmas, ragamuffins sold a sort of golden rain for Christmas trees—little wired sticks, half-covered with a thick, grey, cement-like substance, which burned with a red glow, throwing out gold sparks, long as knitting needles and ending up with a burst of quickly fading stars. These stars flared up here and there along the street, lit by the ragamuffins to attract customers, and, as they died away in the crisp pre-Christmas air, I was always reminded of the little girl in Hans Andersen's fairy-tale who froze to death on Christmas Eve in a gay Danish town, with brightly lit houses and spires on Gothic roofs.

Young, nervous Jews in short Jewish coats, girdled with string,

* Where one could still find bisons—in Russian called "zubr." *Translator's note.*

rushed about in the crowd, shouting out: "What a wife gets up to when her husband's not there"—a hundred spicy stories! Or *The Kreutzer Sonata* and *The Living Corpse*—Count Leo Tolstoy's banned works; only twenty kopecks the two—special discounts to students and school-boys!

Here, too, a fat woman in a warm woollen shawl sat on a small stool, selling celluloid ducks, with bright-yellow beaks and feet, which followed the movement of the magician's wand, covered in coloured paper, that she held in her hand, as they floated serenely in a blue-enamel bowl. And now one of those ducks was swimming in a bowl of water on our dining-room table, covered with an oil-cloth, beneath the warm light from the hanging lamp. The reflection of the white lamp-shade quivered in the water, where the duck was frenziedly dashing and whirling in obedience to the magic wand, while my aunt played one Chopin waltz after another, diamonds flashing on her fingers as they ran over the keyboard, releasing inexhaustible streams of sounds that filled the room with the almond-bitterness of a spring shower, the rustle of wet leaves, and the gurgle of rain-water, rushing along the gutters and foaming round the narrow grille above the drain.

I realised that there was a magnet in the magic wand, which drew the duck, bobbing about on the surface of the water, like an empty egg-shell, towards it: what completely baffled me was how a magnet could attract celluloid. Zhenia was as bewildered as I was. Magnets were supposed only to attract iron and steel—objects like drawing-pins, needles, pins, and nails, which would cling onto them in long garlands. How, then, could a magnet compel a duck made of cel-luloid, a substance not subject to magnetic power, to obey its will? We finally decided that the duck's almost weightless, semi-transparent shell must hold some secret, that it was vital for us to discover. So, powerless to resist, Zhenia and I took appropriate action.

Exchanging sly glances, we pressed our fingers into the duck's frail body. It burst in two, into two half-shells, which had nothing inside them except the air, which enabled it to float so easily on the very top of the water. We were surprised. Where we had expected to uncover a secret, we found nothing but a vacuum. We had destroyed the pretty, snow-white, semi-transparent body, recently rocking so proudly in the bowl, in vain.

Then it suddenly occurred to us to examine the rest of the duck closely and, as we broke it in pieces, we came on a tiny strip of metal beneath the yellow beak. We had discovered the secret! But, alas, we had lost the duck itself forever and had to throw its remains into the dust-bin. All we were left with was the magnetic wand, wrapped in paper with magic signs on it, and we spent the rest of the evening picking up needles, pins, and other small objects. It was quite fun but no substitute for the duck, which had moved through the water as lightly as a ship, turning its yellow beak, almost as though alive, towards the magic wand that possessed a power of attraction, not yet, I believe, fully explained by scientists.

Papa's Chest of Drawers

THERE WERE two of them, one Mamma's, the other Papa's. Mamma's was an ordinary one and did not make much impression on us, except that the red night-light always stood on it. But Papa's was a very valuable antique one, made to order from the finest rosewood, and was fitted with some kind of mechanism that, at the touch of an almost invisible button, threw the front panel of the top drawer back and converted it into a writing-desk covered with a green cloth. At the back of the drawer were a number of boxes, some secret, some open, filled with a lot of things that made the chest particularly attractive to me.

It was indeed beautiful, that well-built, highly polished, yellowish-red chest, and had been given to Papa by my grandfather—Mamma's father—as a wedding-present, along with the piano, which was meant for Mamma, who had taken piano lessons at the School of Music, now the Odessa Conservatoire, after leaving the diocesan school.

Papa's chest had solid, well-fitted steel locks, which were opened by a special key, unlike the ordinary ones. It was large, with intricate grooves and projections and a prominent top in the shape of a Greek omega. It required to be turned twice to lock and unlock, emitting a resonant click that could be heard all over the apartment.

Papa usually carried it in his pocket, but, sometimes, in a fit of absent-mindedness, he left it on the table and then, if I happened to be at home alone, nothing exceeded the bliss of opening the chest and admiring and playing with the objects kept in it from time immemorial. . . .

It is impossible to describe all the things I found in Papa's chest!

For instance, there was a collapsible, silk *chapeau-claque*—sometimes called an opera-hat—which was an essential part of a bridegroom's outfit. When folded, it was just an oval, flat disc, with a white silk lining, on which the hatter's name was stamped in gold. Papa never put it on or even opened it up, but the tradition of the time demanded that he should hold it in his hand at the wedding, just as it compelled him to appear in tails, white tie, and white leather gloves. Papa did not possess any tails and had to borrow someone else's for the ceremony. His white tie was also in the chest and, like the top-hat, had stood the passage of time very well: they would both have looked new had they not become a little yellow with the years. This brought to my mind the bitter reflection that human life, with all its joys, is, in fact, as short as that of the material possessions we treasure, our bodies equally subject to the slow process of aging, to the same inexorable deterioration or, anyway, transformation into something else—into the dust which ancient poets chose to call ashes.

Papa's wedding-gloves lay in the chest, alongside Mamma's long ones. These, too, had grown yellow and dry, had become lifeless from losing forever the warmth of the hands they had enveloped so smoothly on the day of the wedding. They had even lost their exciting leather smell and had shrunk, so that I found it impossible to pull them onto my childish hands, with the bitten nails, though I tried them both: Papa's short ones, Mamma's long ones. I could not put Papa's tie round my neck, either: the elastic band would no longer stretch.

The tie was dead. . . .

There were also my parents' two wedding-candles, with scorched wicks and wax tears congealed on the stems, which were decorated with gold ribbons, as faded and dead as the gold letters in Papa's top-hat.

Usually, widowers wore both wedding-rings on their third fingers, but Papa could not do this because Mamma's ring would not fit him. Her hands were too small.

Sometimes, I took out Mamma's ring and slipped it easily onto my small finger. I pressed the edges of the *chapeau-claque*, which sprang open with a sharp click, turning into a long black tube. When I put it on my head, with its closely cropped hair, it proved much too big for me and slipped down to my ears.

Imagining myself to be a bridegroom, I went into the hall, where there was a mirror. I admired myself and pulled a series of faces, but none of them had the effect of making me look like a bridegroom; I looked more like a chimney-sweep.

Here, let me say a few words about chimney-sweeps. . . . I found a New Year's greeting-card in Papa's chest, with a picture of a chimney-sweep, bearing all the traditional paraphernalia: a black top-hat, a ladder over his shoulder, and a rope with a cast-iron ball on the end, encircled by a brush, to drop down the dirty chimney and dislodge the soot. The chimney-sweep in the picture looked very smart and quite unlike the live one, who came to bring us good wishes on New Year's Eve. The printed one had a gay, Teutonic face, with a curly, upturned moustache, whereas our live one had a distinctly dismal, Russian appearance, as he sat on a stool in the kitchen, waiting for his traditional New Year tip.

He usually brought a printed greeting-card with him, bearing a verse in German on one side and in Russian on the other. I do not remember the actual verse, but its import was that while other people were sleeping quietly in their warm beds, chimney-sweeps were awake and vigilant, risking their lives as they cleaned chimneys to save the populace from possible fires. It concluded with greetings and a request that we should not forget our friends, the chimney-sweeps.

Apparently these traditional greetings originated in Germany, where a guild of chimney-sweeps had existed since the Middle Ages; from there, too, came the traditional costume—the burgomaster's top-hat, the narrow trousers, and the sharp-pointed shoes. . . .

In one of the secret drawers, there was a withered branch from a wild pear-tree, bearing some dried-up, unripe fruit. Papa told me that this had been broken off in Piatigorsk, near the famous hollow where Lermontov was killed in a duel. Papa and Mamma adored Lermontov and, during their honeymoon in the Caucasus, had picked the branch as a memento of their honeymoon, their favourite poet, and the place of his death. The branch had since withered and become ugly and small, but its unripe fruit—two tiny pears—had turned to stone, as though time had not dared to touch it.

Beside the "Lermontov branch," there was another family relic wrapped in tissue-paper; an artificial spray of orange-blossom with wax buds like tears. During the wedding-ceremony, the spray had been pinned in Mamma's hair under her long white veil, while Papa had worn another in his button-hole.

It required a considerable effort on my part to picture Papa's and Mamma's wedding, which took place in Novomoskovsk, a small town, unknown to me, near Ekaterinoslav: the service was celebrated in a military church, following the wishes of Grandfather, who commanded a regiment that was in camp not far from Novomoskovsk at the time. I found it particularly difficult to envisage my parents as bride and bridegroom, standing in the middle of a field-church under canvas, exchanging rings and then kissing in front of everyone .

Mamma's silk wedding-shoes were also in the chest, scarcely worn but showing traces of time, but for some reason I took little interest in them. On the other hand, I was fascinated by Mamma's fan and the click it made when opened and shut: I liked to fan myself with it and feel the gentle stream of cool air, bringing with it a faint whiff of Mamma's scent that had not yet quite vanished. . . .

Side by side with these lovely things that now had had their day, were ugly, uninteresting, coarse objects such as a large Eismark jug with a rubber tube with an ebony end for enemas, and a pair of old, blue spectacles which Papa had worn before I was born, when he had some kind of eye trouble. I had a pathetic vision of poor Papa as a young man, all alone, in an empty apartment with an eye infection, wearing those spectacles tinted a sinister blue like that of the glass receptacles in chemists' windows.

It was even more difficult to visualize Papa shaving, also before I was born, with the razor that still reposed in its original case. I would take it out very carefully, half-open it, and timidly examine the steel handle and hinged blade, so sharp that a hair falling on it would be split in two in the air. It frightened me and I would quickly put it back, imagining a human throat, cut from ear to ear in one fell swoop by a mad barber, with streams of crimson, shiny blood pouring from the open, moon-shaped wound.

A broken lorgnette that I discovered among the rest of the junk suddenly changed my vision of Mamma as a bride and a young mother into that of a stern lady, with a black moiré bag in her hand.

Then, equally suddenly, Mamma-the-lady turned back into a young girl again, with an oval, Japanese face, first a pupil at the diocesan school and then a music student, taking lessons at the Music School, with a medal on her chest, received in recognition of her exceptional musical talents. This medal, made of copper in the shape of a lyre and attached to a red moiré ribbon, was also in the drawer, and the sight of it always evoked in me visions of Tchaikovsky and Anton Rubinstein. And from somewhere, emerging from the mysterious depths of childhood dreams, I heard loud but exquisitely harmonious sounds, coming from Mamma's extended fingers, all of them firmly bent, from the little one to the big, as they ran up and down the keyboard; sounds once heard in a silent, darkened room, dimly lit by a red night-light standing on Mamma's table.

And it was in one of the secret drawers that I found the mysterious, gunpowder hexagon that Uncle Misha left behind when he died. . . .

There were also two copy-books in the chest: one that I knew well, filled with the pictures Mamma had stuck in for me, the other containing Papa's speech to a distinguished audience gathered to celebrate the centenary of Pushkin's birth, written in his spidery, schoolmaster's handwriting in ink that had faded with the years. It was a family tradition that Papa's speech had made a great impression with its profound reflections on a writer's freedom, coupled with, at the same time, his duty towards his fellow-citizens and the state. Papa received a large, silver, commemorative medallion, specially struck for the great poet's centenary, as a reward. Heavy and very beautiful, it was encased in its original flat box. I would open the box and gaze at this Pushkin medallion, lying on a blue velvet cushion: to extract it from the hollow in which it rested, one had to pull up the end of a silk ribbon peeping out from underneath it. I liked to hold it in my hand and look down at the three-quarter portrait of Pushkin's inspired face, beautifully curled side-whiskers, and wonderful eye, resembling an inverted letter *A*, as it stared into the distance.

The sun of Russian poetry . . .

There were other family relics in the chest. The ones that impressed me most were the crosses awarded in bygone days to army priests instead of medals. They belonged to my great- and great-great-grandfathers, in whose existence I found it difficult to believe. But they certainly had existed, had been army priests, and had been awarded these copper crosses—Great-grandfather, his on a St. Anne ribbon, for his services during the War of 1812; and Great-great-grandfather, his on a St. Vladimir black and red ribbon, for services

A MOSAIC OF LIFE

in a Russo-Turkish war that took place, I think, in the reign of Catherine the Great. The latter's was almost black from age and slightly damaged by enemy fire: when I held it in my hand, a sort of superstitious fear invaded my feelings of reverence and of pride in my heroic ancestors.

Papa himself had been awarded two decorations—the orders of of St. Anne and St. Stanislas. They lay in little red boxes, but Papa never wore them, regarding decorations, ranks, and other signs of merit as trivial and unworthy of a man with self-respect, who should work for the good of society and the state without seeking medals or other forms of reward. I opened the red boxes and admired the as-yet-untarnished, cherry-red enamel crosses, edged with real gold, and the small gold double-eagles on each side of the St. Stanislas cross.

Sometimes, I pinned them onto my school-shirt and stood in front of the mirror in the hall, unable to understand how Papa could despise them and never wear them. In his place, I would have worn them all the time. Papa used to say that they represented nothing but expense, because you had to buy them yourself at a jeweller's and then travel to Petersburg, paying your own fare, for the investiture.

There was a story in the family that Papa's attitude towards the decorations provoked the following incident or, in some people's opinion, scandal:

A new archbishop had been appointed to our diocese and Papa, along with the other teachers at the diocesan school, had to be presented to him. Papa had already been awarded the orders at the time but, because of his convictions, went to be presented in his ordinary suit without wearing his decorations. The new archbishop was furious, called Papa a nihilist and even, I believe, an anarchist, publicly reprimanded him and, as Papa's decorations had been awarded by the ecclesiastic authorities, considered himself to be in a position to remove them. But the best part of the story is that the military authorities, who, by long tradition, were always on bad terms with the ecclesiastical ones, returned the unfortunate decorations to Papa a short time later, in his capacity as an instructor at the Military Academy, through the Ministry of War. In doing so, the commandant of the Military Academy was able to cock a snook at the archbishop, whom he disliked.

People said that this incident was a topic of conversation for a long

time in local scholastic circles, and that Papa had thereby acquired
the reputation of a liberal, which was pleasant enough in one way,
but less so in another. Anyway, Papa had behaved very courageously,
though it was rumoured that Mamma had not wholly approved of his
behaviour. But I cannot throw any light on this: it all happened before I was born.

Zhenia's and my christening crosses, attached to blue silk ribbons,
were also kept in the chest, wrapped up in cotton wool in much the
same kind of boxes as Papa's decorations. Had we been girls, the
ribbons would have been pink. We never wore these grand gold
crosses, hanging, instead, the popular, blue-enamelled, silver Kiev
crosses round our necks on silk cords.

I was particularly attracted by a small bronze figure of a child
with one leg raised in the air, which I discovered among broken
cuff-links, hair-pins, capsules, and buttons of every colour and size
in a long yellow wooden box with metal edges, in which Mamma
also kept the gloves she wore when going to the theatre or a concert,
a tiny pair of opera-glasses, and the programmes of Rubinstein's
concerts.

The bronze infant was found near Akkerman when a Scythian
burial-mound was being excavated, and Papa bought it for twenty
kopecks from a Moldavian boy. As there was a small hole in the
bronze infant's raised leg, it seems probable that the figurine—a gay,
dancing little god resembling a wingless cupid—had been suspended
from some Scythian object as a decoration. Anyhow, that was my
conjecture. . . .

I was very much excited by the thought of those ancient times,
when Scythians were still living on the shores of the Black Sea,
and the survival of the roughly modelled bronze statuette of the
child, no bigger than my little finger. The features had been rubbed
away in the course of all those centuries, and the extended arms
and dancing feet were damaged, but there was such gay movement, such a curiously clumsy gracefulness in this product of the
jeweller's rather than a blacksmith's art, that I felt quite faint as I
gazed at the little ghost from the depths of the past; a past when
herds of wild, long-maned horses, ridden by stocky men with sticks
in their hands, urging them on with inarticulate shouts, raced across
the steppes of the future Novorossia, almost hidden in the long grass,
turbulent as the waves of the sea and fragrant with the smell of
artemisia and stepa, while the huge pagan sun set beyond the edge

of the Budaki steppe, pouring its melting, red, copper rays over the whole countryside.

It occurred to me that some of those Scythians might have been ancestors of mine. . . .

I used to put the Scythian infant into various positions, turning him over so that he was on all fours and seemed to be crawling along in front of me—a child, and possibly an ancestor. . . . When I put the Scythian child back in Mamma's lacquered box, once a bright-lemon colour but now faded, the magic picture of the Scythian steppes conjured up in my imagination vanished with the sharp clack of the closing lid.

And perhaps the bronze infant was not of Scythian origin at all but had been brought from ancient Greece, a cupid ornamenting a jar of wine, to our Novorossijsk steppes, where in times immemorial the whole coast was dotted with Greek and Genovese fortresses, of which only a few ruins, smothered in weeds and burdock, remain.

I continued to rummage through Papa's chest, not wholly satisfied with all the relics and treasures that I had discovered there. It seemed to me that there must be some particularly precious treasure, as yet unrevealed to me, lying hidden in one of the secret drawers. I sensed its presence without being able to find it.

But it began to look like a figment of my imagination, because the things that I did come across were very ordinary and long forgotten: half a stick of sealing-wax, which, when lit, burned with a smoky flame, dripped bullock's blood onto the floor, and made the apartment smell like a post-office; small boxes and bottles of dried-up, useless medicines, some with corks blackened from the iodine they had once contained; a packet of manganese crystals, which still retained the power to turn water almost instantaneously into every shade of violet, starting with a faint, almost aquamarine tinge and ending with a dark purple that became rusty-black: Papa's saving's-bank passbook, which showed that he had withdrawn all his money at the time of Mamma's illness and death; Mamma's withered veil with the black spots and the eagle's feather from her hat; doctors' prescriptions dating from her last illness; and, finally, packets of letters tied up with ribbon and tape. These last occupied every corner of the chest.

I can see all those envelopes, as if it were today, bearing big, blue, seven-kopeck stamps and the post-marks of various Russian towns; narrow, elegant, snow-white envelopes from the nineteenth

century, which required the note-paper to be folded three times before insertion.

It was Papa's and Mamma's correspondence during their engagement and also their correspondence with their parents, friends, and
fellow-students at school and university and a number of pupils
with whom Papa did not want to lose contact.

One can imagine what a lot of important thoughts, philosophical
arguments, views on life, discussions of a moral and political nature,
and criticisms of the works of Turgenev, Tolstoy, Dostoevsky and
the beginning of the struggle between Marxists and the People's
Party were contained in those letters; how much love and friendship,
and what absorbing news of births, successes, and minor family
problems.

Partly because of my childish dislike of reading, but, more so,
because we had been brought up never to eavesdrop, spy on people,
or read their letters, I never read the ones I found in the chest—and
I now regret it. Because I might well have learned from them a great
deal about the spiritual life not only of my parents but of their con-
temporaries among the educated class, of which I can now glean
nothing from the original source.

The letters strangely deceased in numbers, which was explained
when I returned home one day shortly before the First World War
and found Papa destroying what remained of them. He was standing
in front of the open chest, rereading the letters one after the other
and then tearing them up into small bits until the whole floor was
covered with scraps of paper. Unaware of my presence, Papa continued with what he was doing, his eyes brimming with tears so that
he had to pause from time to time to take off his pince-nez and wipe
the lenses.

Suddenly, he snatched up the few packets left, walked briskly
into the kitchen, and threw them into the burning oven. Then, turning round, his cuffs covered in soot, he finally noticed me and gave
me a pathetic, helpless smile, as though asking me to forgive him.

And, without knowing why, I, too, burst into tears.

I mentioned some way further back that my Viatka grandmother
—Papa's mother—gave me two books when I was a young child;
one called *The Magic Horn of Oberon* and one that had vanished
from my memory without trace. And now, suddenly, this very minute, it has come back to me: it was *The Sleeping Beauty*. On its
cheap, glossy cover there was a coloured picture of a palace over-

grown with wild pink roses, and the Sleeping Beauty lying amid their prickly, flowering branches with a handsome young man, in a velvet costume and a cap adorned with a pheasant's feather, bending over her. His lips had just touched her pink cheek and, slowly awakened, she was gazing at the world with enraptured eyes.

Everyone now knows how the fairy-tale goes, but then I learned it for the first time. And sometimes it seems to me that it is a story about my soul. In my early youth, perhaps in my childhood, it pricked itself on the wicked fairy's spindle and fell asleep; and went on sleeping until someone fought his way through the thick, wild-rose jungle and touched it with his warm lips.

And then my soul awoke. . . .

Ah, how long I must have been asleep before everything suddenly came to life.

. . . At the dawn of the second day, I was awakened by the sweet songs of nightingales. Enough of sleep, they said, it's time to wake up and look at the world. You've forgotten you were born to love. You've forgotten that, after the spindle's prick, you lay in a wonderful paradise and then were told: You must kill! You must hate and despise—never love! All the time while I slept and did not breathe, devoid of longings, sensations, and the power of speech, my poor, blind soul went wandering through the darkling streets of my dreams, stumbling on and on. But it was to love that I was born, not to kill . . . not to kill . . . not to kill. . . . That, I cannot do. Then I woke up and lay still, very still, with my cheek reposing on my hand. Oh, how long, indeed, my sleep must have been and how strange to find myself, alive and not dead, in a world full of love where the wild birds sang! A world filled, too, with happiness, goodness, and the joy of life!

As I lay half-asleep and in tears, the sun-rays danced in the woods; dawn's fingers stretched out to me through the pines, and dawn's lips pressed themselves to mine. . . .

The Bomb

DESPITE A RUMOUR running through the town that anarchists intended to throw a bomb at the diocesan school, Papa, Aunt, and I went to our Christmas-tree celebrations—leaving Zhenia at home with his nanny.

It was only recently that the diocesan school had started celebrating Christmas with a tree, because the tree was considered to belong to an ancient German pagan feast alien to Orthodox Christianity. However, the decision was finally taken to introduce a tree, though it was still regarded as a somewhat frivolous German practice.

We decided to go after a certain amount of discussion. My aunt thought it would be better not to, but Papa firmly declared that the bomb rumour had been invented and spread about by a lot of frightened ignoramuses and that he did not believe for a second that the most extreme anarchist would want to throw a bomb at so peaceful an institution as the diocesan school, particularly during Christmas, when the majority of the pupils were spending the holidays in their fathers' parishes in the country and only the orphans who had nowhere to go remained behind in the school.

"But the archbishop will be present," my aunt murmured significantly.

"What difference does that make?" Papa asked.

"They'd enjoy blowing him up," my aunt replied.

"What nonsense! They don't kill archbishops, they kill governors," Papa retorted with immense conviction, as though he knew exactly which targets the anarchists intended to aim at.

I suddenly lost my eagerness to go to the party, though I had awaited the evening with great impatience. I had been looking forward to drinking special Christmas tea out of thick diocesan mugs in the company of the young girl pupils, among whom there were a lot of pretty ones in spite of their baldly fitting coarse blue uniforms, boys' shoes with rubber soles, and hair combed severely back from their foreheads and gathered into dark, mousy-coloured nets on the napes of their necks, attached to round combs that opened up their girlish foreheads.

In the cold, semi-basement, dining-room, approached down a narrow iron staircase, there would be long tables without cloths on which, beside each mug of sweet tea, would be a cotton bag containing all kinds of sweets, rosy Crimean apples, and mandarins, the skins of which, if squeezed hard enough, produced small drops of aromatic oil.

Though my aunt was still hesitant, it was finally agreed we should go, leaving Zhenia behind, and she put on her best blue silk dress with Valenciennes lace, smelling fragrantly of French scent and flowering elder; Papa wore his full-dress uniform. And I, in starched cuffs and a stiff collar with turned-up points, which agreeably cooled my well-scrubbed neck, a dab of eau de Cologne on my handkerchief, forgot all about the danger threatening us and merely felt a pleasant dizziness as I waited restlessly for the clock in the dark dining-room, where a cold, greenish moonlight was already shining on the parquet floor, to chime out seven o'clock.

It was a lovely, crisp night; columns of smoke rose straight up from chimneys, casting floating shadows down on the roofs, wearing their white, woolly snow-caps. Christmas stars twinkled benignly in the dark sky and the moon was as clear and magically resplendent as if it had come to us straight out of the pages of Gogol's "Night before Christmas."

The galoshes of families and their friends, going to the celebrations on foot, made crunching noises in the snow, while every now and again sleighs rushed past with a soft creak from their runners: their small bells tinkled like glass in the sharp, frosty air, which gently nipped one's ears, and mingled with the harmonious resonance of the larger ones attached to the lively horses' harnesses.

I occasionally glimpsed the shadows of potential bomb-throwers, lurking in dark side-streets leading down to the sea, and I recoiled in terror, bitterly regretting that we had not stayed at home. But once we reached the school, everything appeared to be quite normal, starting with the customary wait for the important guests in the headmistress's private quarters. She was a grand, haughty-looking lady, with a sharp nose and protuberant bosom, ensconced for the occasion in purple silk, which had earned her the nickname of "the turkey."

My pride suffered as always because, in her sumptuous sitting-room, with soft, silk-covered arm-chairs, elegant foot-stools, and standard-lamps with lace lamp-shades, standing among the high dignitaries who arrived late, close to the archbishop, with a cross on his chest mounted in an oval frame inset with precious stones, which sparkled particularly brightly against the background of his black cassock, close to the stout general, with broad epaulets and the red ribbon of the order of St. Anne hanging diagonally from his shoulder, close to the ladies wearing magnificent hats and ostrich-feather boas,

Papa and Aunt looked like poor relations condescendingly invited for this one special occasion.

I surreptitiously rubbed my brand-new shoes on the carpet to make them less slippery, bowed politely right and left, and even kissed the archbishop's plump hand when I went up to him for his blessing. With a forced smile, he looked down at me or, rather, at my bristly hair, plastered down with thick grease and parted on one side, and said: "I trust that, in these troubled days, you will prove a loyal servant of your emperor and the Orthodox church."

I scuffled my feet on the thick carpet and moved away, with a lingering taste of glycerine-soap on my lips.

Finally, the head-mistress invited us all into the large white assembly-hall where the modestly decorated and as yet unlit Christmas tree rose almost to the ceiling. The girls, in white aprons and pelerines, were ranged along one of the walls, beneath three enormous, sinister-looking, black windows, with rounded tops, that yawned into the darkness. They looked out onto the school-gardens, where trees gleamed in the moonlight, their branches transformed by the frost into white coral. When she noticed that the curtains had not been drawn, the head-mistress flushed with indignation and her nose actually became as purple as a turkey's beak. With an imperious gesture of her small hand, she summoned the girl on duty over to her and hissed into her ear: "Don't you know that they might throw a bomb here? Draw the curtains immediately!"

The poor girl, growing pale, her ears aflame, glided over the parquet floor as if she were on skates and swiftly pulled the curtains together. As they met, with a jangle from the sliding rings, they blotted out the windows, separating the white world of the cold assembly-hall from the black world surrounding the school outside. The head-mistress sat down between the archbishop and the general and waved her lace handkerchief. The school-caretaker, his hair glistening with icon-lamp oil, put a match to the end of the impregnated string and, in a flash, a flame spiralled round the tree from top to bottom, lighting the hundreds of candles and producing the effect of a high, flickering bonfire. The cold air in the assembly-hall became perceptibly warmer, the high voices of the girls' choir broke into song, and the celebrations began, causing everyone to forget about the bomb.

The smallest pupil took two paces forward and, folding her little

hands, declaimed the traditional Christmas poem in a loud, boyish
treble:

> " 'Snow has covered up our street,
> Winter's giving us a treat.
> Here's the tree she's brought along
> Which we greet with mirth and song . . .' "

I do not remember how it went on.

Then everything was a repetition of the year before: the rush
along the dimly lit corridors, peeping into cold, dark, empty classrooms, where the frosted windows sparkled mysteriously in the
moonlight, the large mugs of tea and the cotton bags filled with
sweets, my pleasurable embarrassment at finding myself sitting between two of the prettiest little pupils, perspiring under their arms,
the juice from the mandarins that we squirted at each other before
eating them and squeezing the oil out of their skins, and the grace at
the end of the meal, quickly muttered by the cheekier of my small
companions.

On the night in question, on my way down the iron staircase, I
slipped into the office where my aunt worked as a clerk to take another admiring look at the antique writing-set made from baked
clay—or, as they would say today, a product of ceramics. What
particularly attracted me was the sand-caster, from which, before
blotting-paper came into existence, one shook fine grains of golden
sand onto the letter one had just written; then, when one returned
the sand to the caster, the ink would prove to be quite dry. (Another
method of drying the ink was to hold the sheet of paper close to
the glass of a lighted lamp.)

In one of the drawers were a number of sharpened goose-quills,
which had not been in general use since the days of Gogol. The
splintered ends of these gnawed, ragged pens still bore traces of black
Indian ink from the last century, made in solid form from lamp-black
and glue and dipped in water when required. They evoked in my
imagination the world of Gogol's clerks, scratching away with their
goose-quills, surrounded by cedar cupboards full of the records of
old cases, from which came a smell of sealing-wax, mice, and archives
peculiar to old, pre-reform offices. . . .

All ended happily. No bomb was thrown. And as I walked home

with Papa and Aunt along the frosty street, I stealthily smelled my hand, which still retained a whiff of eau de Cologne, after clandestinely squeezing a soft, girlish hand.

And the stars in the black, by now night, sky seemed to be twinkling in a particularly frolicsome manner as the cold bit sharply into my cheeks. . . .

Hot Lard 🖋

FAMILY HISTORY has it that when I was only two years old, I made my way into the kitchen, where Mamma was about to make pastry and the lard was melting in an iron pan on the red-hot stove. No one knows how I did it, but I managed to reach up to the pan, overturn it, and pour the boiling lard all over myself. I yelled so piercingly that anxious neighbours the whole way down Basarnaia Street flung their windows wide open, as they always did when some disaster occurred.

I screamed uninterruptedly for at least five minutes, while my panic-stricken mamma poured water over me, covered me in talcum-powder, smeared me with vaseline, and tried to pull off my dress, soaked by the streams of lard.

My end seemed to be at hand. Both Mamma and the cook, who had seen the panful of boiling liquid tip over me, were convinced that nothing could save me. But a miracle had happened. In some mysterious way, the lard had shot past my head, and only one drop had fallen on my skin—by my throat—causing me unbelievable pain. Though the pain did not last long, I have a scar on my throat to this day. And ever since I started shaving, the slightest carelessness in my handling of the razor removes the skin from it, so that I have to staunch the bleeding with cotton wool or alum.

As soon as Mamma realised that I was safe and sound, she kissed my throat, put some vaseline on it, and topped this with rice-powder, then remarked with her characteristic Ukrainian humour: "Now you're my little marked boy. And God only marks rogues. . . ."

She attributed my miraculous salvation to the two crowns on my head. As I mentioned before, two crowns are supposed to be a sign of exceptional luck. I would not, myself, say that my life had been outstandingly lucky. Inevitably, it has contained a number of failures and reverses. But I am prepared to admit that, by and large, I have lived it, as a close, greatly missed friend of mine once observed, "in a happy mist."

I will admit, too, that I have been close to death on several occasions and only escaped by some extraordinary piece of luck. For instance, when I was on the Rumanian front in the foothills of the Carpathians during the First World War, a German shell exploded literally under my feet and hurled me into the air. When I picked myself off the ground, there were five dead soldiers lying round me. The raincoat I was wearing was torn to rags and full of holes from shell-splinters; my steel helmet was bent and dented—but I was uninjured except for a slight flesh-wound at the top part of my right thigh.

Those two crowns of mine had saved my life. . . .

As I lay on a balcony, shaded by acacia-trees, in an Odessa hospital not far from Basarnaia Street, I remembered my violent screams, like those of a stuck piglet, and Mamma's face, distorted by panic, when the boiling lard poured over me from the pan and I escaped with nothing more than a small scar on my throat—rather like the one on the top of my right thigh.

Boborikin ✍

SOMETIMES MY COUSIN, the son of Papa's elder brother, Nikolai Vassilievich, would be brought to spend the day with us.

Sasha was a year older than I and began to wear proper trousers instead of dresses a year before I did. As if by magic, they immediately transformed him into a boy. For a whole year, I envied Sasha his trousers, and closely cropped hair, but, at long last, I became four, too, the dress that made me look like a girl was removed and replaced by trousers and my hair was cut short like his.

Now, he no longer had any reason to treat me condescendingly, and we seemed to become the same age. The trousers had united us. Sasha was a genial, kindly boy, with our family's ironic smile. He was not mischievous, as I was, but neither was he meek and boringly obedient. He was five, I was four. We played all day, running about the apartment from room to room, turning the furniture upside down, seeing who could jump farther, splashing each other with water in the kitchen, crawling under the sofa in the sitting-room, and, after drawing moustaches and beards on our faces with a lump of coal, we pretended to be actors and performed swiftly improvised plays, which called for a lot of gesticulation and chasing after each other.

I remember that we deliberately broke a thermometer and had great fun playing on the floor with the quicksilver, dividing it into a number of small, shiny balls, which rolled about like beads in every direction, then crawling after them on our knees and reuniting them again into one bigger one. We were astonished by this quality of quicksilver to split up into several pieces, which retained their spherical shape and so readily merged together again into the original whole, and came to regard it as a magical liquid. When someone told us that it was not a liquid but a metal, we found it hard to believe. And, to tell you the truth, I do not really believe it even now....

I need scarcely add that we got a good scolding for breaking the thermometer, but we bore it stoically, feeling that we had somehow been introduced to one of the great mysteries of science.

I well remember another of our games, which we called "doing a Boborikin." We had often heard the grown-ups, when arguing about modern literature in the sitting-room, utter the funny word "Boborikin," but neither of us had the least idea that it represented the surname of a famous contemporary writer. To us, "Boborikin" became associated phonetically with the sounds made by the Viennese rocking-chair that stood in the sitting-room beside the ficus when turned upside down.

Papa would sit in it when he was reading a book or the paper: to him and the other grown-ups, it was just a piece of furniture. But to Sasha and me, the chair, with its yellow wicker seat, curved arms and rockers, became transformed, when we turned it upside down, into a swing, a wooden machine, a boat, an oven, or a summer-house. When its worn rockers were in the air and it was resting on its resilient beech arms, it could be made to rise slightly off the floor and come down again with the "bo .... bo ... bo ..." sounds that had given our game its name. The game itself consisted in throwing a small carpet over the rockers, thereby creating a dark, mysterious tunnel between carpet and seat, through which we had to crawl on our stomachs, sneezing from the dust which fell on us out of the carpet.

Usually, we crawled through the tunnel, one close behind the other, laughing, wriggling, and kicking and, on emerging into the world again, rolled head over heels and screamed out, in a curious, violent sort of ecstasy: "Boborikin! Boborikin!"

Dear Sasha departed this world a long time ago, and the rocking-chair has disappeared, too, along with all the other furniture of my childhood, but even now, when I see a chair like it, a voice from the depths of my consciousness cries out: "Boborikin! Boborikin!"

The Black Month of March ✍

As soon as we got close to the Alexandrovsky pillar, Mamma sat down on a bench near the rose-garden while I ran up the small hill and began to climb the slippery, rose-granite steps to the polished, labradorite socle of the pillar, so as to look down on the distant stretch of sea. Then the weather suddenly changed: a northern wind began to blow, the sun became hidden as the clouds piled up, the sea was covered with white horses, and Dofinovka disappeared into a mist.

I immediately lost all desire to climb up the socle and, lying flat on my stomach, slid down the steps' wide granite banisters, though I know this is not the correct architectural description of them.

I saw Mamma snatch at her hat, which was threatening to fly away, taking her veil with it: a whirlwind of cold dust hit me in the face. When I ran up to Mamma, she was sitting hunched up rather pathetically in her black autumn coat with mother-of-pearl buttons, and the wind was shaking the train of her long skirt, which she was pressing between her knees. In her lap lay the moiré handbag, containing a spare pair of my underpants, tidily folded in four. I was already a big boy—nearly six—but prudent Mamma knew that when we went for a walk together anything was liable to happen, and she wanted to be in a position to exchange my wet pants for dry ones, as had often been necessary in Alexandrovsky Park.

For some time after the birth of my brother, Zhenia, Mamma,

devoting herself to the care of her new child, had stopped taking me out. But now that Zhenia was a little older and stronger and could be left in charge of a specially hired wet-nurse, Mamma had decided to take me to Alexandrosky Park again so that I could get a breath of bracing sea-air.

She chose a sunny day, but March often proved to be a treacherous month. When the weather changed unexpectedly, Mamma was far too lightly clad in just a coat and skirt, without her warm cape.

The park looked empty and unfriendly; the famous oak-tree, surrounded by iron railings, which had been planted by the emperor Alexander III, seemed to become still blacker and its branches even barer when swept by the cold wind, and the yellow previous-year's grass at its foot was strewn with lonely acorns.

My sailor-coat was not sufficiently warm and I was bored and wanted to go home, but Mamma decided to wait a little hoping that the sun would come out again. In our part of the world, the weather changed several times a day during March. But that March turned out to be a particularly evil month. While Mamma was waiting for an improvement in the weather, I ran round the rose-garden, where the roses were bent in an arc to the ground, as though it were still winter: metal labels, with the names of the different varieties printed on them, hung from their thin, coral stems.

The black, naked trees, the black earth, and the dark clouds, driven low over an angry sea by the north wind from Dofinovka, combined to produce a sinister atmosphere, and Mamma's bent figure, the ostrich-feather quivering on her hat, her lips ashen-grey under her veil, strengthened my foreboding that something terrible was about to strike our family.

After sitting for a while on the bench without any improvement in the weather, Mamma changed my wet pants for dry ones and we went home, doing our best to keep our back to the sharp March wind.

I woke up during the night, because the house seemed all astir and the samovar had been put on to boil. Papa, fully dressed, sat on a chair beside Mamma's bed, holding her hand and pressing his hand every other minute to her cheek. "Oh, God, Zhenicka, you're burning with fever!"

He shook the thermometer, put it under Mamma's arm, pulled it out after a few minutes, shook it down again and replaced it under her arm. She lay there in her night-dress, tossing about on the bed, and Papa drew the slipping blanket back over her. Then he stretched his winter coat over the blanket, but she continued shivering. I could hear her teeth chatter.

Papa slid a pillow under Mamma's back and she struggled exhaustedly to sit up and sip through burning lips the hot liquid he held out to her in a spoon.

I fell asleep but was constantly awakened by my brother Zhenka's crying, or someone's careful, anxious tread, or Mamma's dry, heart-rending cough, or a lamp being moved from one room to another, or the flickering, purple tongue of the night-light. Once I heard the clock strike two.

In the morning, Mamma was worse.

Everything in the house was at sixes and sevens. Nevertheless, Papa went to the school, though he returned earlier than usual.

"Zhenia's burning!" Papa kept repeating like an invocation, not knowing what he could do to help. "She's burning! Burning!"

Late that night, when I was already asleep, the nurse, summoned from the Sturdzovsk community, decided to apply cupping-glasses to Mamma. I woke up at the moment when, with her sleeves rolled up and a white kerchief on her head, she was bending over a small spirit-lamp, which burned with a sinister flame and threw strange, dancing shadows onto the wall-paper. I could see the flame licking the inside of the round cupping-glasses, which then seemed to stick of their own accord to Mamma's bare back, sucking in her brown flesh till the vacuums were completely filled. After a while, the nurse tore the cups off with the sound of a popping cork, leaving Mamma's back covered with purple circles, and Mamma gave a moan as they turned her over and the cups were applied to her chest and sides, while the strange, fleeing shadows cast by the spirit-lamp continued their eerie dance over the faded brown flowers on the wall-paper.

Papa hoped that Mamma would begin to feel better after the cups, but she was as bad as ever. She lay with her eyes half-shut and her hair spread out over the pillow, wrapped in two blankets, with her cloak and Papa's coat over them.

Her heavy breathing seemed to force itself out of her dry, cracked lips.

Day followed night, the day became evening, and the light from candles and table-lamps again passed from room to room. Papa was applying a spirit-compress to Mamma, and I saw the effort it cost her to smile at him tenderly and murmur, almost inaudibly, as she sought to reassure him: "Don't worry, Pierre. I just caught a chill in that treacherous March wind. I think I'm better. . . ."

But she got worse and worse.

Doctors began to appear in the house. The cook kept running to the chemist's and returning with more and more new medicines. I completely lost all sense of time.

A second doctor followed the first and then I heard the frightening word: "consultation."

My bed was taken from the bedroom to the dining-room and put by the wall opposite the screen, behind which Grandmother lived. Here, too, the sofa brought in from the sitting-room, little Zhenia was swaddled and had his slightly inflamed eyes bathed with boracic-acid. I watched, fascinated, as his wet-nurse unbuttoned her blouse, extracted from it a large breast that looked like an udder, and pushed into Zhenia's tiny, sad little mouth a coral-coloured tit, which appeared to sprout out of the brown circle of rather coarse skin.

Then a stranger utttered the words: "Inflammation of the lungs."

I heard them from behind the door, close to our small spirit-stove, on which something was kept boiling the whole time in a copper bowl for making jam.

Nobody except me went to bed that night. I do not remember whether I had dinner or not: I think I snatched whatever I could find in the kitchen. The whole apartment was placed at the disposal of the doctors. Plates, glasses, and saucers, in which there was some kind of acid and cotton wool, lay on the tables, chest of drawers, and even the chairs. Basins were constantly being carried in and out. A round vessel with a handle appeared and I could only guess to what use it was put.

Papa never washed or changed his clothes. He wore his new frock-coat the whole time, and it seemed to grow old before my eyes, as it became crumpled, stained, and dusty. His cuffs, always so immaculately white, were grubby, his hair dishevelled, and his beard uncombed: his pince-nez kept falling off his nose and swinging like a pendulum on the end of the cord, their lenses flashing from the reflection of the paraffin-lamp.

The doctors kept coming and going, bringing their medical bags with them, in which one could hear the clatter of surgical instruments.

Something was being done to Mamma all the time, but I had no means of knowing what it was. The doctors, with their shirt-sleeves rolled up, held their hands in a basin and Papa poured water over them out of a jug, splashing his trousers and shoes. I remember an evening when the sitting-room was transformed into something like an operating-theatre, with a candle in a copper candle-stick, covered with green wax-drippings, burning on the album table, and pretty little glass ampoules and tiny syringes with copper plungers and steel needles lying on a plate beside the forceps and scapel. I was told that the ampoules contained something with a slightly alarming, magical name: chlorethyl.

The young doctor beckoned me over to him with his finger, obviously feeling sorry for me and wanting to divert my thoughts. He squirted a few dew-like drops of chlorethyl from a syringe into the flame of the candle and it crackled and flared up in a misty rainbow, reminding me of the drops of oil, squeezed out of mandarin peel, that I used to drop on our Christmas-tree candles. But the doctor's drops produced an unappetising smell of ether.

He left me the syringe with a little chlorethyl still in it and, for a while, I occupied myself by squirting drops into the flickering candle, which was immediately surrounded with a crackling rainbow aura that gave the sitting-room, with all its furniture moved around, a sinisterly festive air.

Later, I learned that the doctors had decided that there must be an abscess in Mamma's pectoral or abdominal cavity—or possibly somewhere else—which required lancing at once to let the pus out. They tried to do so repeatedly, but were unable to locate the source of infection. In all, they made eleven deep surgical punctures, none of them successful.

Since then, the number eleven has always had a sinister connotation to me.

I do not know whether it was late at night or early in the morning that I saw one of the dark-grey oxygen pillows being taken into the bedroom. They had been fetched several times from the chemist's, always by cab, though his shop was only a stone's throw away. Papa kept on opening his desk and taking money to give to the doctors, nurses, cabmen, and cook.

From the bedroom, to which Mamma had been carried back from the sitting-room, I heard a strange, hoarse sound. Walking up to the door-way, with fear in my heart, I peeped in at her. Her wheezing mouth was pressed round the black, rubber tube protruding from the oxygen-pillow, which the nurse was folding over and over as it grew emptier in order to squeeze out the remainder of the life-saving gas while the cook fetched another tautly expanded pillow.

Mamma's dry, hoarse breathing continued to force its way out of her mouth. The light from the lamp on the chest of drawers was screened by a volume of Brockhaus's encyclopaedia, and its shadow lay on Mamma's face, merging with her flowing hair. I had supreme faith in the healing properties of such a very costly remedy as those dark, weightless pillows, which had been fetched at regular intervals by cab during the last two days. I was certain that Mamma would recover, all the more so because the doctors had left, taking with them their rattling medicine-bags.

The house was quiet again, and I undressed and went to bed, still hearing in the few minutes before I fell asleep Mamma's heavy breathing and the hissing of the oxygen-pillow's rubber tube coming from the bedroom.

I woke up late. The shutters in the dining-room, where I was sleeping, had already been opened and a March, pre-Easter sun shone through the window. There was a strange, unnatural silence in the apartment. Smartly dressed in a new blouse, her hair exceptionally neat, the cook came in and told me to get up: she pulled my long woollen stockings over my legs and helped me do up my shoes with a button-hook. Then she tucked in my shirt, which had recently been made from woollen material left over from Mamma's winter skirt. I was surprised that she had not taken me into the kitchen first to have a wash and began to feel uneasy at the unusual silence, like that on a Sunday, by which I was surrounded. The cook looked at me sadly, crossed herself, and said: "God has taken your mother to be with Him. Your mamma is dead. Come along with me. . . .

She took me by the hand and led me into the silent, freshly tidied bedroom, where an icon-lamp was burning on a stool at the head of Mamma's bed. Mamma lay with her eyes shut, her hair smoothly combed back, and her head slightly inclined to one side, a faint smile on her lips, darkened by the medicines, and an oily gloss to her forehead, which reflected the gentle, unflickering, almost transparent flame from the burning icon-lamp.

Papa stood beside Mamma's bed without his pince-nez, his tired eyes looking down at her with infinite sorrow. I went up to him, conscious of the loud tread of my still-very-new shoes.

He put his hand on my shoulder and said: "Well, your mamma is no longer with you."

I looked at Mamma, at her immobile, slightly Japanese face, at the long black eyelashes on her closed lids, with a last tear still wet on them, at the red icon-lamp at the head of her bed, at her body covered up to the waist with a blanket, somehow already no longer concerned with this world, yet, at the same time, so much the same, still earthly and as I had always known her, and, though I perfectly realised that Mamma was dead, I could not conceive that she would remain in this state of death forever.

I experienced neither horror nor grief; my heart was not yet prepared for any deep suffering. All I felt was that something dreadful, though commonplace enough, had happened in our family.

I remember that Papa, lost and not knowing what to do during those first silent, static hours, sat rocking in his favourite chair, staring blindly into the distance, into the world outside the windows, where, almost unbelievably the residents in our streets continued to lead their everyday lives just as usual, amid the rattle of cabs, the heavy footsteps of pedestrians, the cries of old-clothes men, and the squeak of wheelbarrows.

As I have said, I understand that Mamma was dead, but did not yet understand that it was forever: there she was, right beside us, ours, with her tanned, shiny forehead, her faint and, despite its immobility, seemingly fleeting smile.

One of the grown-ups, possibly Mamma herself, had once told me about experiments with a dead frog, which had been made to move its paws by subjecting its muscles to electric shocks. I even knew that movements of this kind were called galvanic.

I sat down on Papa's knees and, rocking with him in the chair, asked whether Mamma could not possibly be revived? Surely there must be some means of doing so?

With a heart-breaking smile, Papa stroked my hair with an ice-cold hand and said, with a deep sigh, that, alas, no such means existed.

"What about electricity?" I asked, unaware of the terrible pain I was causing him.

"Alas . . ." replied Papa.

I still insisted: "But it works on dead frogs! They make galvanic movements. Oh, please, Papa!" I pleaded desperately. "Do ask someone to try it on Mamma. Then she'll open her eyes and be alive again."

"Alas," Papa repeated, continuing to stroke my head with his hand, on which I could feel the hard circle of his wedding-ring. "Even if she were to open her eyes, it would only be for a very short time and she would still be dead."

"You mean she'll be dead forever?" I faltered with dread in my voice, beginning to understand the irreparability of what had happened to Mamma.

"Yes, I'm afraid so," Papa replied in a whisper. "Electricity's helpless against death."

He went on staring into the distance, his face twitching as though he were holding back his tears, but he was not able to cry, and this tore at my heart. What a relief for him if he could have broken down and sobbed. But he could only gaze into the unknown with red, unseeing eyes. . . .

I thought that if we could all remain like this in the silent apartment forever—Mamma in her bed beside the icon-lamp, Papa in the rocking-chair, Zhenia in his wet-nurse's arms, and I on Papa's knees —one might gradually become accustomed to it and resign oneself. . . .

But it was not to be. . . .

Very soon the apartment was filled with familiar and unfamiliar faces. Two seminarians in cassocks, friends or possibly relatives of Papa's, were seated in the sitting-room, their long hair hanging down over their faces, composing an announcement of Mamma's death for insertion in the Odessa *Post*. At first it was long and took up a lot of space, but then, for reasons of economy, they began to cut it down, as one usually cuts down a telegram, so that in the end only a tiny announcement appeared in the paper next day, framed in black beneath a thin, little cross. It was very short and almost unnoticeable among the verbose announcements of rich people, and Mamma was not even called by her full name, but simuly and somehow forlornly "E. I. Katayeva."

The samovar was kept constantly on the boil in the kitchen, the visitors drank tea and ate sausage sandwiches, the undertaker came to take measurements for the coffin, and suddenly Fanny Markovna appeared from nowhere in the middle of the turmoil and, there and then, bathed in tears, began tacking a dress together for Mamma—a white dress, as for a bride. I do not remember Mamma being put in

the coffin or when the coffin was brought to the house: I was probably already asleep. But when I woke up next morning, I noticed
that Mamma's bed was standing empty in the bedroom, covered with
a Marseilles blanket. The icon-lamp was no longer on the night-
table: all that remained on its marble top was an oily circle. This
relieved me. I thought everything was over. But passing through the
deserted bedroom, freshly scrubbed, dusted, and tidied-up, where
the ether smell of chlorethyl and that of other medicines still lingered
in the air, I reached the threshold of the sitting-room, and the first
thing I saw was the side of a coffin and a tall church candle-stick
with a thick candle burning in it.

The coffin rested on two card-tables diagonally across the corner
near the ficus in its green tub, where I had recently seen another
coffin, not white but brown, in which lay Uncle Misha.

Mamma's coffin was a wooden one, nicely decorated in silver with
paper lace round the edges, so that it vaguely resembled an open box
of chocolates. There was a church candle burning at each corner of
it. Mamma lay in the hastily tacked white dress, with her hands,
clasping a small icon I had not seen before, folded high up on her
chest.

The door onto the landing from the hall, where the mirror had
been covered with a sheet, was wide-open, and the floor was strewn
with pine-tree branches: the coffin-lid was propped up beside the
door. Faces I knew and some that were unfamiliar to me, those of
relatives, neighbours, and merely inquisitive residents on Basarnaia
Street, were constantly passing by, and I felt lost and lonely in all
that crowd and still not quite able to grasp that Mamma was dead
forever. I still half-believed that everyone would go away, the coffin
would be removed, and Mamma would emerge from the other end
of the apartment with Zhenka in her arms, smile at me—and life
would go on as before, full of love and happiness.

But then the burial rites began. . . .

Priests appeared in the hall, slipped their brocaded, mourning
chasubles over their heads, and put on their lilac velvet head-dresses.
The deep bass of the deacon rang out, the aromatic smoke of benjamin incense rose from the censer's silver lid, spreading almost
stiflingly into every room and every corner of our small apartment,
and, through the greyish-lilac clouds, I saw the flickering flames of
the wax candles, Mamma's golden forehead, looking as though it had
been anointed with holy oil, and the shadow of her long eyelashes

: 438 :

on her pathetically thin cheeks that seemed even whitier than the night before.

Other services took place in the apartment on that day and the next; then, on the third day, as I looked out the window, I saw a high, white hearse with black wheels draw up in front of the building. The undertaker's assistants came up, wearing tight black coats with large silver buttons and black three-cornered admirals' hats edged with gold braid. They lifted the coffin and carried it downstairs, accompanied by Papa and some of the closest relatives, who helped to support it with their shoulders and manoeuvre it round the awkward angles of the staircase. The choir, in long, dark-blue loose-fitting, tasselled robes, sang in their high-pitched voices.

In the street, other assistants were standing with flaming *flambeaux*, as the horses, decked with white netting, ostrich-plumes over their heads, and black blinkers by the sides of their eyes, making them look blindfolded, waited patiently for the coffin containing my mamma to be pushed into the hearse and covered with the wreaths of artificial or porcelain flowers, bearing white moiré ribbons with inscriptions in large capital letters, cut out of gold, silver, or black glossy paper.

A little way behind the hearse, stood three or four old carriages in case some of the crowd should feel tired on the way to the cemetery and welcome a ride.

The funeral procession moved off down Basarnaia Street, past the chemist's, where the huge glass vessels, filled with multi-coloured liquids, standing in the windows, shone in an eerie way; past the Dwarf's shop, outside which, following Mamma's coffin with frightened eyes, were Mrs. Dwarf in a wig and Mr. Dwarf, clasping his old bowler hat, with its white silk lining, tarnished with time, exposed to view.

Papa led me by the hand along the road behind the hearse and all I saw in front of me were two big black wheels rolling implacably on and on. . . .

The procession moved exhaustingly slowly; the priest, at regular intervals, swung the censer in which the coals seemed to be smouldering angrily, the clouds of incense became dissipated in the air, and the March weather was typically cold, overcast, and evil. I soon grew tired and was put with Sasha in one of the carriages, where we found the smell of its musty upholstery fascinating and rather pleasant.

At last, the hearse, jolting along the uneven roadway, passed beneath the cemetery arch, which had an icon decorated with pink paper roses in the centre of it. From there, Mamma was driven up a dismal, deserted side-avenue to the cemetery church, where the funeral service was to take place before she was carried out to the newly dug grave and buried. To be quite honest, everyone was exhausted and secretly longing for the final rites to be performed speedily, so that they could leave, heaving sighs of relief.

But just before the coffin was carried into the church, a telegraph-boy we all knew turned up with a telegram from Ekaterinoslav in the leather pouch attached to his belt; it informed Papa that two of Mamma's sisters, Aunt Natasha and Aunt Margarita, would be arriving in Odessa by train on the following day and begged him not to bury Zhenia before they got there. And, so, the burial had to be postponed for another long, painful day.

Mamma's coffin was taken out of the hearse and carried into the cemetery chapel—or, rather, mortuary—beside the cemetery gates, which had been built to deal with such unexpected postponements. Here, the lid was put on and Mamma remained, alone. Papa and I took a cab back to the apartment, which had already been tidied up, cleaned, and aired: the silence was only broken by little Zhenia's sucking noises as he was fed by his wet-nurse, who was seated in an arm-chair in the sitting-room beside the ficus, in the same spot as, a short while before, Mamma's coffin had rested on the card-tables.

I slept badly that night, constantly picturing Mamma in her closed coffin, lying alone in the chapel, except for an old nun, reading prayers by the light of a five-kopeck candle, mumbling her words, making the sign of the cross and wetting her wrinkled fingers to turn the ancient pages of the black, leather-bound, worm-eaten book. . . .

I was terribly sorry for Mamma and, at the same time, afraid to think of her: I had visions of her suddenly throwing off the coffin-lid, opening her eyes, and sitting up on the pillow, stuffed with shavings. These figments of my imagination, mingled with harassing dreams, so exhausted me that I had a struggle in the morning to get out of my bed, which had been rolled back to its permanent place between Papa's and Mamma's beds.

The last day of Mamma's bodily presence on this earth had begun. . . .

The train from Ekaterinoslav was late, but it was impossible to wait any longer. Papa and I went back to the cemetery, passing on our way a huge, sinister hill called Chumka, rising on the spot where, in an ill-fated year long ago, those who had died of plague had been disposed of: burning tar had first been poured over the bodies, then a layer of quick-lime added, and, finally, earth had been piled up over them. The high hill, so formed, now overgrown with grass, burdocks, and thistles, remained as a stern reminder of the terrible year, when carts rumbled along the streets, loaded with corpses, and there were fires on every corner, on which clothes, beds, and other possessions of the dead, which had been dragged from their houses by hooks, were being burned. Carbolic acid was then sprinkled through every room in the infected buildings in the hope of arresting the plague. There were dark rumours that fabulous treasures lay beneath the earth of Chumka—rings, bracelets, and precious stones that no-one in the terrible year had dared remove from the dead bodies, which had been buried with such valuables as they wore or carried still on them. Enterprising businessmen offered the local authorities large sums to be allowed to excavate, but their offers were always turned down, lest the Black Death should emerge again from under the earth and once more reap its toll of the town's inhabitants. Passing Chumka in the cab with Papa, I imagined what it would be like if the residents in Basarnaia Street were suddenly struck down, and closed my eyes to blot out the greening hill, while sending up a prayer to God to speed us quickly by and preserve us from catching the plague.

When we entered the cemetery chapel, which was already full of people, I saw the coffin, now open again, covered with pink and blue hyacinths and, beneath them, the white dress of my dead mamma. During the night, her closed eyes had sunk in, but there was the same frozen smile on her face, lying at a slight angle on the pillow, and I noticed a tiny drop of pus at the corner of her darkened lips. Someone had placed a white piece of paper with a prayer printed on it on her forehead. A student, having cranked up the camera-holder on his wooden tripod to the right level, was focusing the camera on Mamma's face. Then there was a sudden flash and a small cloud of white smoke from the magnesium powder in the metal container he was holding above his head and recorded forever on the plate were the coffin, the dead woman in her white dress, the wreaths, the priests' chasubles, Papa standing at the head of the coffin, and me, too, perhaps, beside him.

And Mamma's sisters still had not arrived. . . .

The funeral bells, which were driving me crazy with their monot-
onous repetitions, continued ringing from the steeple of the cemetery
church; my head whirled from their clappers, beating like a hammer
on my temples, and I almost fainted from the stuffiness and the sweet,
putrid smell of fading hyacinths.

Two or three seminarians had begun screwing down the lid of the
coffin, hiding Mamma's face from view, when her two sisters, Aunt
Natasha and Aunt Margarita, who had just arrived on the delayed
train from Ekaterinoslav, rushed into the chapel. They had come
straight from the station in their travelling-coats and mourning hats
with black crêpe veils and were still carrying their suitcases.

With frozen faces, they approached the coffin and the seminarians
raised the lid again.

"Zhenia!" Aunt Natasha cried out heart-brokenly on seeing Mamma's sunken, drawn face. Aunt Margarita, who looked like Mamma,
wearing pince-nez as Mamma did and having the same black eyebrows, though she was much younger, having only just left school,
bent down and kissed Mamma's forehead and hands.

But Aunt Natasha fell on her knees in front of the coffin and
bowed her head, tipping her hat sideways, while tears poured from
her kind eyes.

As the cemetery bells went on tolling, the lid was put on the
coffin again, this time forever; but I did not yet fully understand and
somehow imagined Mamma to be still alive, though motionless.
Before reality dawned on me, I had first to stand at the foot of the
deep grave, from which two gravediggers tossed up the last spade-
fuls of clay as Mamma's coffin was placed alongside it. The various
strata of soil they had removed lay in a heap in the reverse order
to nature's, a black layer of clay on top, then a brown one, and, at
the bottom, a damp, light-yellow layer of sand. As was the practice
at that time, the gravediggers and their assistants lowered the coffin
with ropes—not webbing slings—into the depths of the narrowing
grave, dislodging small lumps of clay in which severed roots were
embedded. As it came to rest at the bottom, the choir started to chant
and Papa threw in a handful of clay, which, by mischance, fell with
a hollow thump on the middle of the high coffin lid. The gravediggers picked up their spades again and began shovelling over the
coffin with incredible speed, so that in a matter of minutes a
rounded mould had risen over the site of the grave. And it was then
—only then—that I woke up from the strange dream in which my

mind had been wandering and I realised with piercing clarity that my mamma had just been buried deep in the earth, that I would never see her again. As hot, bitter, but blessed tears streamed uncontrollably from my eyes, Papa put his arm round my shoulders and murmured: "It's all over now. Our mamma has left us. Oh, if only I could cry like you! But I have no tears to shed. . . . God has punished me: I don't know how to cry. . . .

I looked up at him, saw him standing dry-eyed and understood what pain, what torment he must be enduring when he could not relieve his sorrow by weeping. . . .

A woman in a black shawl—I think it was Akilina Savvishna—untied a linen towel, in which she had wrapped a large plate of cold rice-pudding, thickly covered with powdered sugar and decorated with multi-coloured pieces of cheap marmalade, and began distributing it among the cemetery beggars, who held out their cupped hands or ragged prisoners' caps.

When we got home, I bounded eagerly up the stairs to our second floor and gave several tugs at the bell-handle. I was bursting with all my experiences of the last few days and in a tearing hurry to share them with Mamma.

"Mamma!" I cried excitedly, kicking at the bottom of the locked door in my impatience. "Mamma!"

The door opened and I saw the wet-nurse holding Zhenichka in her arms and breathed in the sickly smell of Easter hyacinths: then I suddenly remembered that Mamma was dead, that we had just buried her, and that I would never have a mamma again. And having suddenly grown a few years older in a matter of seconds, I walked slowly into our desolate apartment. . . .

Frozen Roads ✍

FOR SOME REASON, a special significance was attached to the fact that I was born when the ground was covered with a hard coating of ice. Actually, there was nothing extraordinary about it: during the winter—especially in January—the ground in our town was frequently crusted with ice. The fogs we called "sea-sirens" drifted in from the south, enveloping the town in a milky-grey, soft mist, and if they were followed by Epiphany winds from the north, everything around would become covered with ice.

In bright winter sunshine or beneath the stars at night, it presented a beautiful, magic picture, but walking on the slippery pavements was extremely hazardous. No doubt the midwife, hurrying to assist my entry into the world, carrying her professional bag, fell down several times, despite clutching at walls and the trunks of the acacia-trees, crusted with ice like everything else.

I once saw, in a bound volume of copies of *Niva* for the year before my birth, a photograph with the caption "Exceptional weather turns Odessa streets into ice-field," or something to that effect. It showed two tilting telegraph-poles with a cross-beam between them, so that they formed a capital *A*, half-buried in a great heap of ice.

The loosened wires drooped down towards the ground and, in front of them, up to their knees in a snow-drift, were a policeman in a warm hood and a yardsman, gripping a wooden spade, in a peasant's sheepskin coat and an apron, with a metal plaque bearing his number on his chest.

Blinking into the sun, they stood stiffly to attention, posing for an unknown amateur photographer, some student or school-boy hoping to sell the picture to *Niva*, who was focusing his clumsy camera on its wooden tripod with immense care. His head was covered by the black cloth attached to the back of the camera, giving him the appearance of a Cyclops with an eye in the middle of his forehead (his shadow appeared in the foreground of the photograph). Beyond the shadow, one could just make out the faint outlines of our Basarnaia Street, with its two-storied houses, and a sleigh plying for hire.

Perhaps, at that very moment, the birth-pangs were starting and Mamma was moaning with pain in her bed, while Akilina Savvishna held her hands and wiped the sweat from her tanned forehead. . . .

First Love

IT WAS LATE AUTUMN, and in the deserted Alexandrovsky Park the trees were already bare and black, but the weather was still warm and I came to our tryst without my overcoat.

She appeared at the end of the path, large as life, covered with small, yellow acacia-leaves. She was not wearing a coat, either, over her school-uniform, with the black alpaca apron tied with criss-cross tapes at the back.

I shall always remember her little-girl's buttoned shoes and her oil-cloth satchel, from which projected a pencil-case, with half-erased transfer-pictures on it. On the middle finger of her right hand there was a shallow indentation left by her pen and a small ink-stain.

She was fourteen—I was fifteen.

I had arranged the meeting, though there was no real necessity for it: we could see each other every day, either in her home or those of her friends. But it seemed terribly important to me that we should have a "secret assignment:" the phrase alone made my head swim and seemed to promise the joys of Paradise.

Oh, how afraid I was that she would not turn up! But she arrived punctually after school at three o'clock, the appointed time. Yet I sensed something hopeless in this exact punctuality, something that smacked of indifference.

She had thick, chestnut-coloured hair, a little, freckled nose, a small, stubborn chin, brown, limpid eyes, already those of a woman, with protruding eyelids, and a miniature, slender figure that looked adorable in her well-cut, dark-green school-dress with narrow sleeves, unadorned by lace cuffs. She had taken off her black-straw uniform-hat, with a salad-green ribbon and round crest, and held it by the elastic band, together with her satchel, in one hand, while she patted her hair with the other.

We stood facing each other, alone in the huge, frightening empti-ness of the autumn park; a thin school-boy and a small school-girl, scarcely more than a child. I can see those two little figures, so close to each other and yet so far apart, standing in the middle of that eerie path, which seemed to have no beginning and no end.

A delicious aroma came from the recently pruned trellis of ever-green myrtle, thuja, and southern pine. The roses in the rose-garden were already covered with protective straw, but the sky shone softly down on us—a sky so pure, tender, and somehow sad that I was almost moved to tears.

"I received your secret message," she said without any expression in her voice.

We walked side by side, silent for a long time, because I could not find words in which to explain to her why I had found it so

vital to make the assignation. She waited patiently, and I, feeling . . .
(*eighteen lines scratched out here*) . . . and such an infinite sadness
enveloped my soul, that . . . (*six more lines scratched out here*).

One can only love once and that love will be pure. . . . Like a blue
sky in spring, like dew on a leaf. . . . I knew that it was love eternal. . . .

The Eclipse of the Sun 🖋

I CLIMBED right up to the attic of the new four-storied House-owners
Society's building at number 3 Pirogov Street, into which we had recently moved, and then crawled through the skylight onto the roof,
lay down on the hot, pink tiles, and began to wait for the eclipse of
the sun. There was nothing around me except the tiles stretching to
the gutters, in which there was already a thin layer of grey, summer
dust, carried there by the wind from the French Boulevard, where
cars weaved their way among the cabs and carriages, leaving clouds
of blue benzine smoke behind them, and the electric trams, ringing
their bells, raced with a noisy clatter along the rails.

It was a short time after the general mobilisation at the beginning
of the First World War and everything in our town had returned to
normal. However, Grandmother, Mamma's mother, who had spent
the summer with us, playing selections from *Faust* on the piano,
suddenly decided to go back to Ekaterinoslav, fearing that the Turkish navy would begin bombarding Odessa. . . . A sweltering August
silence fell on the world, deep and sinister . . . and "fraught with
events." . . .

From where I was on the roof, I could see neither the boulevard
nor the sea, though I knew its blue water lay hidden somewhere
behind the gardens. I knew, too, that out of sight were valleys, the
white lighthouse, fields golden with sweet-corn cobs and green with
ripening cabbages—and, further away, beyond these, foreign lands,
where a war was going on, in the existence of which I did not quite
believe.

All I could see were the sloping, pale-pink tiles, the sky colourless
from the heat, and the midday sun, at which it was painful to gaze
with the naked eye. It was only when I looked at it through the

smoky, greyish-brown surface of a piece of glass thickly coated with soot that I was able to see its glaring white circle.

. . . How strange it was that the sun seemed so small. . . .

Yet this small circle was so clear, so precise, so eternal that any idea of its being eclipsed appeared impossible, particularly when the event had been foretold over a hundred years before. All the same, I was well aware that somewhere in space, the cold moon's black shadow was already on its way, had already touched a part of the globe as it raced towards me. And I knew that, down below in the yard, people were already standing motionless, holding strips of smoky glass in front of their eyes. The whole town, in fact, was full of people wearing dark glasses, as though they were blind.

But I was alone, confined within the limits of the tiled roof, with its perpendicular pink-brick chimneys.

The silence that usually precedes an eclipse of the sun descended all around me. But I still did not believe it would really happen. The circle of the sun, as white and glaring as if it had been made of magnesium, retained its usual perfect geometric shape, as it floated high above me, remote and unattainable.

I could not tear my eyes away from my dark, sooty square of glass, with the small brown stains on it. It was an old photographic plate that I had blackened over a candle and I could still just distinguish the outlines of people, trees, rocks, and boats imperfectly photo-graphed. The sharp, white circle of the sun seemed alien and out of place in that strange, dim, smoky world.

And then I suddenly noticed a slight roughness, blurring its edge, then a black spot that gradually became transformed into an oval, as though it had been squeezed with tongs, and finally the dazzlingly white disc of the sun turned into a half-moon. A whiff of ice-cold air from high up in the heavens seemed to ruffle my hair as the shadow of the moon raced across the battle-fields.

1969–1972
Peredelkino